TO A
HIGH
COURT

 FriesenPress

One Printers Way
Altona, MB R0G 0B0
Canada

www.friesenpress.com

ISBN
978-1-03-918049-9 (Hardcover)
978-1-03-918048-2 (Paperback)
978-1-03-918050-5 (eBook)

1. LAW, ENVIRONMENTAL

Distributed to the trade by The Ingram Book Company

Also by Neil Thomas Proto

To a High Court (2006 edition)

*The Rights of My People: Liliuokalani's Enduring Battle
with the United States, 1893–1917*

Fearless: A. Bartlett Giamatti and the Battle for Fairness in America

The Reckoning: Pecora for the Public (stage play)

TO A
HIGH
COURT

Five Bold Law Students
Challenge Corporate Greed
and Change the Law

NEIL THOMAS PROTO

Type set in Adobe Garamond Pro and Arboria.
Design and Typesetting: Ashley Young, Publications Professionals LLC

Map (Northwest D.C., GWU Campus, c. 1968): Neil Thomas Proto and Ashley Young

NORTHWEST D.C.
GWU CAMPUS, C. 1968

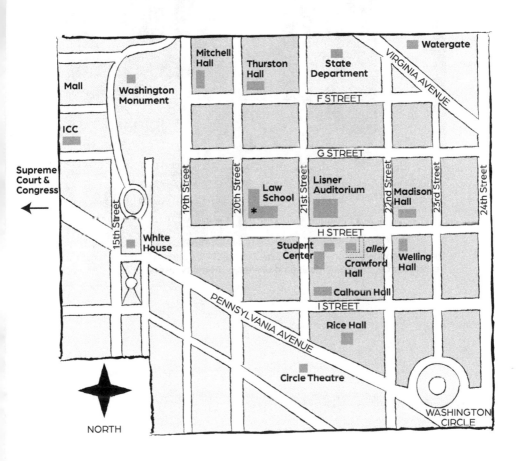

Watergate

Mitchell Hall

Thurston Hall

State Department

VIRGINIA AVENUE

Mall

Washington Monument

F STREET

ICC

G STREET

Supreme Court & Congress

19th Street

20th Street

Law School

*

Lisner Auditorium

21st Street

Madison Hall

22nd Street

23rd Street

24th Street

15th Street

White House

H STREET

Student Center

Crawford Hall

alley

Welling Hall

Calhoun Hall

PENNSYLVANIA AVENUE

I STREET

Rice Hall

Circle Theatre

WASHINGTON CIRCLE

NORTH

The George Washington University Law School, 1970. Courtesy of the Gelman Library, George Washington University. All rights reserved.

CONTENTS

AUTHOR'S NOTE ix

PROLOGUE. xv

1   No Sanctuary, Fall 1968 1

2   Banzhaf and the Placid Eggshell, Spring 1971 9

3   The Conversation, Spring 1971 17

4   Students Challenging Regulatory Agency Procedures (SCRAP),
        Fall 1971. 25

5   The Participants, Fall 1971 45

6   Standing, Fall 1971 65

7   Disciplined Calm, Fall 1971 81

8   The Midnight Surprise, Fall 1971 91

9   Managing the Deluge, Fall 1971 111

10   Finding Clarity, Winter 1971 127

11   Thinking Ahead, Winter 1972 141

12   In Preparation, Winter 1972. 147

13   The Social Forces, Winter 1972 159

14   The Lines Are Drawn, Winter 1972 167

15   Searching for Comfort, Spring 1972 179

16   Finding Our Own Rules, Spring 1972 187

17   In Court: A Colloquy in Law and Money, June 1972 195

18   In Court: The Forces Collide, June 1972. 215

19   Victory, June 1972 225

20   Into Hostile Territory, July 1972 233

21   Washington, D.C., Fall 1972 and Winter 1973. 239

22   The United States Supreme Court, February 28, 1973 245

EPILOGUE 263

ACKNOWLEDGMENTS AND REFLECTIONS 269

APPENDIX 273

ENDNOTES 289

INDEX 311

ABOUT THE AUTHOR 319

AUTHOR'S NOTE

On June 18, 1973—now 50 years ago—the United States Supreme Court decided *United States of America v. Students Challenging Regulatory Agency Procedures (SCRAP)*, reported at 412 U.S. 669 (1973). Five law students at the George Washington University were found to have constitutional "standing to sue" the United States of America. The decision evoked more than the judicial process and the recorded outcome.

*   *   *

Providing definition in facts and in crafting legal arguments for a controversy that leads to the Supreme Court of the United States is a special experience in law. It is uniquely so for a law student. Yet that is precisely what we did, in our own names, in an era of tumult, especially in the nation's capital.

Our imperative from the fall of 1971 was to discern corporate wrongdoing that harmed the public and to examine the failure of government in its public duty—as prescribed by laws enacted by Congress—to confront and correct it. For reasons described in *To a High Court*, the corporate wrongdoing was deeply embedded in the nation's Railroads and the failure of government pervasively embedded in the acquiescing culture of the nation's oldest regulatory agency, the Interstate Commerce Commission (ICC). Their conduct was occurring quietly in the nation's capital. Supported by the presumed skill of famed white shoe law firms and, as often, by the United States Department of Justice.

To penetrate and confront this wrongdoing and failure of duty, we needed to master more than freight rates, economics, corporate complexity, corruption, natural resource ownership, recyclable materials, and the Interstate Commerce Act of 1887. We also needed to master the newly enacted, largely judicially untested National Environmental Policy Act of 1969 and the related self-centered mischief and competition among ancient and newly formed national environmental groups. For me, as chair, and for my four student colleagues—each of us taking four additional courses and working part time—it took imagination, discipline, and a learned, responsible irreverence for the law as settled, mysterious, or the province of aged gentlemen, alumni, or faculty, many of whom were threatened by our skill and fearful of our judgment. In September 1971, at the George Washington University Law School, George Biondi, John Larouche, Kenneth Perlman, Peter Ressler, and I formed Student's Challenging Regulatory Agency Procedures. The acronym: SCRAP.

*   *   *

Publishing this new, photo-documented edition of *To a High Court*—out of print since 2013—had two imperatives. The decision in *United States of America v. SCRAP* was written by President Dwight D. Eisenhower appointee Justice Potter Stewart. He was considered a "strict constructionist." He was neither fearful that his decision would affect his duty as a Justice—though he was told to be—nor that the judiciary's proper place among the three branches of government under our Constitution would be overburdened, overextended, or lessened in dignity or purpose. Nor was he fearful—as he also was told to be—that executive branch conduct under Article II would be subject to challenge. *Justice Stewart believed that the Framers knew precisely what they were doing when they wrote Article III, created the Supreme Court, and defined its responsibility.* Justice Lewis Powell, who joined the Supreme Court with corporate interests and the freedom to exercise political judgments firmly in mind, and later Justice Antonin Scalia, with more stridency, and the current Chief Justice John Roberts Jr. added words and requirements to the Constitution (and thus impediments to standing) that Justice Stewart did not find. For Chief Justice Roberts, the lingering effect of *SCRAP* may be what *New York Times* legal commentator Adam Liptak described as Roberts's "personal precedents" ("The Problem of 'Personal Precedents' of Supreme Court Justices," April 4, 2022) that he cannot, culturally, get beyond.

In 2007, the Supreme Court ruled five to four that the United States Environmental Protection Agency had the duty to examine global warming in its decision-making process and that the Commonwealth of Massachusetts had "standing to sue" to invoke the court's duty to reach such a conclusion. Linda Greenhouse, *New York Times* commentator, wrote at the time that "[T]he case is likely to be remembered for two other reasons. One is how the 5-to-4 majority widened access to the federal courts, reinvigorating the doctrine of environmental standing …. The other is how vigorously Chief Justice John G. Roberts Jr. expressed his displeasure at that development" ("For the Chief Justice a Dissent and a Line in the Sand," April 8, 2007).

"It was his vehemence rather than his dissenting vote," Greenhouse continued, "that was the surprise. The chief justice was spending capital and speaking in his own voice." He homed in on *SCRAP*. "[A]ccording to Chief Justice Roberts, SCRAP is back. 'Today's decision is SCRAP for a new generation,' he said mournfully near the end of his dissent."

In his April 2022 review of Justice Roberts's personal precedents, Adam Liptak points to "a little noticed article on standing in 1993, more than a decade before he joined the Supreme Court in 2005. It was not cited in a Supreme Court brief until 2006. Since then, it has been cited more than 50 times." Roberts's vigorous dissent in 2007 served, in Liptak's framework, "as a declaration of his … highest priorities." His personal preference. Within that "preference" is more than Roberts's view of *SCRAP* as legal precedent. It's also his generational admonition to law students. Stay in your place. Wait your turn. Be deferential. The student, an informed sycophant or reverential apprentice.

The second imperative flows from the first. *To a High Court* was not written as a "lawyer's book." As a story, beginning with the group's formation in fall 1971 and with our "Midnight Surprise" before the ICC in December— long before there was any thought of the need for a lawsuit—and the eventual hearing before the Supreme Court in early 1973, it has what Broadway and television actor Dan Lauria once described this way: "Students fighting Goliaths. A timeless theme, engaging characters and plot twists. *A Civil Action* merged with *Paper Chase*. I can't wait to see the movie!" When you finish reading the book, you may still wonder, "*Who* were the Goliaths?" In our learned, responsible irreverence as to the law's purpose and meaning, perhaps, like David, it was not a question we dwelled on or ever asked. We recognized immediately the rough power of law exercised by the ICC and the comfort and skill of the corporate interests and law firms, which often seemed insepa-rable from the commission in defining the law's meaning and who benefited from it. There was no one between us and them.

The story has taken on new meaning today among those students with imperatives that matter to them, not their law school or its alumni or faculty. "Making Law by Making Trouble" was the title to lawyer Antoinette Stone's review of *To a High Court* published in the *Philadelphia Lawyer* in summer 2006. Her title captured more than our intention and its effect in the 1973 Supreme Court decision. It captured the story. June 18, 2023, is the 50th anniversary of the decision in *United States of America v. SCRAP* (1973). It is still taught in law schools throughout the nation. The decision. Not the story.

*   *   *

SCRAP still rankles. Fifty years later.

Neil Thomas Proto
Washington, D.C., and New Haven, Connecticut
January 2023

The author. Photo by Isabel Chenoweth/Southern Connecticut State University.

TO A
HIGH
COURT

Hope your exams get over soon. How are you making out with the R.R. suit? I hope it gets to a high court.

—*Celeste Proto*, letter to her son (July 9, 1972)

SCRAP involved "probably the most attenuated injury conferring Art. III standing" and "surely went to the very outer limit of the law"…. Today's decision is *SCRAP* for a new generation.

—*Chief Justice John G. Roberts Jr.*, in dissent, *Massachusetts v. EPA* (2007)

PROLOGUE

THE SUPREME COURT, FEBRUARY 28, 1973

The Quakers. Their placards are still resting against the White House fence. Some people are bundled in blankets, huddled together against the morning chill. Another—an older woman, her hands gloved—holds a thermos and a cache of white foam cups. All are moving, gently, unanimated, and more alone now. The taxi slows in the congestion. The rancor and passion and sadness do not feel distant in time. We angle to the right past Treasury and speed quickly along Pennsylvania Avenue.

The grayness of the sky offers little contrast to the Supreme Court's Corinthian colonnade or the marble steps that lead to it. Only the flag holds its own character, unfurled, the crimson and white in its stripes fully visible. The two massive, engraved bronze doors depict with solemnity Justinian publishing the Corpus Juris and King John sealing the Magna Carta. The moments show a principle now permanent in our own culture: the triumph of law. The duty to ensure that triumph is housed here. The Great Hall displays Charles Evans Hughes, John Marshall, and Harlan Fiske Stone—Chief Justices, their busts solid in composition, stern and vigilant in purpose, watching, protecting, still fulfilling a duty. People are walking or clustered in small groups, talking, waiting. A few stand apart with folded newspapers, reading. Others seem preoccupied by their own thoughts, as I am. William O. Douglas was afflicted with a debilitating paralysis as a child. Congressman Gerald Ford sought to have him impeached for stopping the execution of Julius and Ethel Rosenberg in 1953. Thurgood Marshall was tempered by the experience of America's worst flaws. Byron White worked for Robert Kennedy. William J. Brennan's father was in a labor union. Potter Stewart was a Yale graduate and a "strict constructionist." He wrote the opinion in *Sierra Club v. Morton* that helped guide us here.[1] In the marshall's office, a smartly dressed woman standing behind the rail asks my name, scans a typewritten list, finds "Proto, Neil," and directs one of the pages to escort me into the courtroom.

Before the Justices had stood Daniel Webster, Robert Jackson, Thurgood Marshall, and Louis Brandeis—men who had studied their mood, their precedents, their personality and who, with care and respect, gave meaning to the words that formed the briefs and petitions and oral arguments that were presented daily to the Court for consideration. In the end, however, it is here that each Justice stands alone, with his experience and knowledge and wisdom, with his ability to know whose life and what values are affected by what the Court is being asked to decide, by what is not written and what is not said. It is here that neither money nor power determines what is right under the law. It is the one thought I keep firmly in place all day.

The page leads the way through an opening in the thick, dark red draperies on the right side of the courtroom. The room is full. Standing next to one of the wooden benches inside are George Biondi and John Larouche. Only a few months ago, we were students together. We shake hands and take our seats.

"The Honorable, the Chief Justice and the Associate Justices of the Supreme Court of the United States," begins the marshall exactly at 10:00 a.m. We all rise. Eight Justices file through the draped backdrop behind the long, slightly concave bench. They seat themselves in noticeably dissimilar custom-made chairs: Marshall, Stewart, Douglas, Burger, Brennan, White, Blackmun, and Rehnquist.

"Where's Powell?" I whisper to George. He demurs.

The Chief Justice calls the first case: "The *Atchison, Topeka and Santa Fe Railroad Company versus the Wichita Board of Trade*, Number 72-214." The Court is being asked to review an order of the Interstate Commerce Commission. The order permits particular Railroads to increase their charge to grain shippers by 100 percent to stop the train in transit, inspect the grain, and determine its grade. The agrarians object.[2] They are the Railroads' captives. It was the rough and quixotic abuse of this dependence that spurred the Granger movement and the presidential efforts of William Jennings Bryan. It also moved literary realists like Theodore Dreiser and Frank Norris— abhorred, angry, seeking to further awaken the nation to the Railroads' intimi-

The Honorable Warren Burger.
Library of Congress.

dating grip on the land. Norris said it: "[T]he symbol of a vast power ... leaving blood and destruction in its path; the Leviathan, with tentacles of steel clutching into the soil, the soulless force, the iron-hearted power, the monster, the Colossus, the Octopus."[3] In 1887, Congress created a national institution to regulate the Railroads and to protect the public interest: the Interstate Commerce Commission. That attempt had not worked. Montana's Senator Mike Mansfield sought yearly to legislate the Commission's abolition. He could not do it.

The Chief Justice thanks the participants in a *pro forma* but polite way. He settles back into his chair. The attorneys representing the next set of adversaries move into place. George places his hand firmly around my forearm. "We got here," he whispers evenly. John looks at the two of us and smiles. It is one of his cunning grins. He sits back, prepared to listen. He will not miss a word. Neither will I.

"We will hear argument next in 72-535 and 562, United States and ICC against Students," says Warren Burger, "and Aberdeen and Rockfish Railroad against Students."[4] The Chief Justice pushes his hair back, seeming to bring recognition to its whiteness. He adjusts his posture—erect, framed, subtly moving his head downward so as to assure himself that the attorneys for each side are prepared to argue their case. He obviously has done this before.

Erwin Griswold,
Solicitor General of the United States.
Getty Images, printed with
authorization.

The solicitor general of the United States, Erwin Griswold, has taken his seat at the counsel table directly in front of the Chief Justice and slightly to his left. It is Griswold's responsibility to represent the United States and the Interstate Commerce Commission. He is the former dean of the Harvard Law School and is experienced in Supreme Court argument. He is wearing his morning coat. Seated next to him is Hugh B. Cox, senior partner at Covington & Burling, Washington's most prestigious law firm. He is representing the nation's Railroads. Cox also is part of the tradition. He is familiar to this setting and knowledgeable about its culture. He, too, is wearing a morning coat.

Seated at the other end of the table is the attorney for the appellee, Students Challenging Regulatory Agency Procedures (SCRAP). Peter Harwood Meyers is twenty-six years old and a 1971 graduate from the George Washington University School of Law. This is the third oral argument he has ever presented. The first two were in the SCRAP case in the court below.

Meyers is sitting erect, hands folded on the table, nodding slightly when the Chief Justice looks downward. Meyers has trimmed his hair to a fashionable length and is wearing a white shirt. While he has no morning coat, he looks comparatively better without the lavender shirt he wore in the court below. Also at the table, to Peter's left, is Professor John Banzhaf. "B as in Boy, A-N, Z as in Zebra, H-A-F." That is the way he spells it for the press, an institution he is acutely sensitive to and depends on for success. He, too, is without a morning coat. Despite the respectful appearance of the two, I know for a fact they have not done this before.

We had decided to file this lawsuit against the Interstate Commerce Commission in May 1972 because the Commission had failed to prepare a detailed statement on the environmental impact of a rate increase granted to all the nation's Railroads on all freight. This obligation, we contended repeatedly to the Commission since fall 1971, is imposed on the Commission by a new law, the National Environmental Policy Act (NEPA).[5] The increased rates are discriminatory. They encourage the extraction of natural resources, including iron ore and timber, and they discourage industrial use of recyclable materials such as scrap iron and steel and textile and paper waste. They also impede the ability of the nation's cities to move enormous amounts of solid waste. We urged the Commission to consider the environmental consequences nationwide, the same geographic reach of the Railroads' own rate increase.

The Commission and the Railroads disagreed. It is their custom to do so. The 1970 report by Ralph Nader's study group characterized the Commission as a place where "the men in ... upper staff ... share a protective attitude toward the transportation industry. They are afraid of change."[6] This custom of insulation has a legal counterpart. The Supreme Court has regularly deferred to the Commission's decisions. The Commissioners can do largely what they have always done: resist the public and protect the Railroads. They knew that fact going into our lawsuit. So did we.

SCRAP is holding its own. In an opinion written in July 1972, a specially impaneled three-judge district court agreed with SCRAP's position. "[SCRAP] alleges," Judge J. Skelly Wright wrote, "that this price increase will discourage the environmentally desirable use of recyclable goods and that ... under the terms of NEPA, cannot take effect before a 'detailed statement on the environmental impact of the proposed action' is prepared." The court stopped the rates from going into effect.[7] The Railroads and the Commission are uneasy; their relationship has been penetrated, restricted by law, pronounced by a court of law—at the request of five law students. Since the lower court's decision, the nation's Railroads have been stopped from collecting approximately $400,000 a month for one recyclable material alone: iron and steel scrap. We got their attention. The Railroads, along with the United States and the Commission, immediately appealed to the Supreme Court. It is the first time the full Court will interpret the meaning of NEPA. The Chief Justice already made his views known. He is for the Commission.

There is, however, a threshold legal question. It stems directly from the Constitution. In Article III, the framers created the Supreme Court and limited its jurisdiction to deciding only "cases ... and ... controversies." Any party that attempts to invoke the Court's jurisdiction has to show that it has, in fact, been injured by the government's action. A party able to make that showing is said to have "standing to sue." It is not done easily. The Constitution does not tell you what is required. The specific requirements are set by the Supreme Court speaking through its decisions. The requirement has changed over time. Without "standing to sue," the Court must dismiss the lawsuit.

In the district court, the United States and the Commission challenged SCRAP's "standing." In its brief, the government made its case directly: "The plaintiffs [SCRAP's] lack of standing to maintain this action was settled by the recent decision of the Supreme Court in *Sierra Club v. Morton*," rendered only a few weeks before our lawsuit was filed. According to the government, SCRAP has an even lesser claim: "The complainant in that case, Sierra Club, was a significant and respected organization, with a long-standing concern for the preservation of the environment.... S.C.R.A.P.'s purpose may be commendable, and the zeal of the five law students who comprise it perhaps should be encouraged. However, we respectfully submit that its concern for the public well-being does not give S.C.R.A.P. the requisite standing to maintain this action."[8]

The district court rejected the government's argument. It concluded that SCRAP had "standing to sue." But the question is not settled. The United States and the Commission, joined by the nation's Railroads, continue to raise it before the Supreme Court. If the members of SCRAP lack "standing to sue," then the Commission's failure to comply with NEPA cannot be reviewed by a court of law.

The solicitor general rises from the counsel table and steps with authoritative comfort to the podium directly in front of the Chief Justice. General Griswold's head moves slightly left to right, seeming to scan the bench as if acknowledging that everyone is present. Hugh Cox is seated to Griswold's right. Cox is prepared, formidable in skill, and potent in the history and industrial force that buttress his position.

"I am representing the United States and the Interstate Commerce Commission," the solicitor general states. "Mr. Cox is representing the appellant railroads in No. 72-562. We have filed separate briefs, but there is no divergence between our positions."[9]

Finally, it is beginning. The line is drawn clearly. Now we will see whether it makes a difference that they have been here before and we have not.

1

NO SANCTUARY,
FALL 1968

George Washington University's outer perimeter was Pennsylvania Avenue on the north, Virginia Avenue on the south, Nineteenth Street on the east, and Twenty-fourth Street on the west. In a north–south direction ran its inner streets—Twentieth, Twenty-first, Twenty-second, and Twenty-third—and in an east–west direction ran F, G, H, and I Streets. Each was a heavily traveled public thoroughfare owned and maintained by the District of Columbia government.[1]

Rush-hour traffic that affected the city affected the university's streets and alleyways. Self-centered and absorbed motorists gunned through the campus. It was not Ole Miss. A fire station was on G Street. It was quaint and solid in structure. It also may have been reassuring. But when an engine rushed to its task, the din of its sirens shuddered otherwise pensive students who were thinking, working, or listening to lectures. The Sino-Soviet Institute was a stately, refurbished townhouse, its brick facade imbued with the reds and browns of its original colors. It housed the faculty's "cold warriors." It seemed a world apart.

Rice Hall, the main administrative building, was seven stories high, with white masonry, glass exterior, and urban-renewal modern in form. The classroom buildings, detached and barren of refinements, were brick or masonry and were painted buff, one of the university's colors. The interior was painted

"Marvin Green," a putrid, uninviting color apparently adored by a former university president who bought enough paint to last a lifetime, albeit not his own.

The residence halls were largely converted hotels or apartment houses. Mitchell Hall was a comely building, seven stories tall, made of dark brick with white wooden trim. A veranda extended its full length. In an inviting fashion sat comfortable chairs, like memorabilia from a different time. It seemed "southern" to me. But none of the dorms had the character of Welling Hall on Twenty-second Street. It was a former "flop house" that still looked the part—four floors; a rough, cracked, stucco exterior; holes in the walls; and infested with cockroaches of legendary size. It had been occupied since its conversion by soccer and basketball players who took their sport inside, down the stairwells, and out the windows. Interspersed among these buildings, in no discernable pattern, were Quigley's Pharmacy; a dry cleaner that seemed to starch buttons, coats, and slacks; a couple of malodorous, indistinguishable fast-food takeouts, including the subterranean Galley; and Bassin's, a local joint on the corner of Twentieth and I Streets that had beer for forty cents a glass and was crowded with mostly undergraduates—boisterous, uneasy in manner, and unsettled in direction.

Amid the students, faculty, and administrators were pedestrians, muggers, panhandlers, con artists, drug dealers, vagrants, and alcoholics; people who lived in the apartments or townhouses scattered among university buildings; police officers walking, driving, or giving out parking tickets; and trash collectors, arriving early in the morning, necessary but untimely and, with the assuredness of royalty atop a golden carriage, blocking traffic as they performed their duty in step with their own cadence. They all walked about freely—day and night—near, around, and sometimes into university buildings as they talked, argued, carried groceries, or clanged garbage cans. Some moved quietly—sometimes fetid or silently deranged—drinking, selling, or looking for a warm place to sleep. This cacophony of sound and movement multiplied dramatically in the early fall and from the spring blossoming through the close of school. It came from the dormitories and fraternities that lined G Street. Windows were opened; students postured before them or gathered in groups outside while stereos quivered in undulating and dissonant tones in the rush for new members or the display of new amplifiers—deafening, irreverent to place or purpose, loud, harsh, and usually playing the Stones, or Neil Diamond, or Dylan, early Dylan.

There was, of course, the relative calm of the Circle Theatre on Pennsylvania, near Twenty-first. It was large—with uncomfortable seats and unkempt

President Richard Nixon.
Library of Congress; photograph
also authorized by Whittier Museum
(November 19, 2022).

Civil Disturbance Unit (CDU), Washington, D.C., Police,
G Street NW, GWU campus. Courtesy of Gelman Library,
George Washington University (GWU) and GWU *Hatchet
News*. All rights reserved.

floors that were sticky and aromatic—and cheap, with great, engaging movies that ran during the day. At the Circle, I saw the *Battle of Algiers* and its direct, rough portrayal of methodical, urban warfare and the ideological imperatives of those opposed to French colonialism; and *Point of Order*, with its documentary portrayal of the harshness of Senator Joseph McCarthy and those who tolerated him. But for all its calm, the Circle was rarely a respite from learning or familiar faces or from the deliberate use of time.

The university solicited graduate students' interest in "dorm jobs" with the fraudulent claim that the responsibilities were part time. In the fall of 1968, when I started working at Mitchell, changes emerged—residents had long hair; were reclusive and uneasy; and dressed differently, with old jeans, "granny glasses," and torn, oversized coats. Arguments took on a different form: the irrelevance of fraternities and disdain for parents, attending class, receiving grades, or learning anything other than religion or philosophy. When a resident disappeared for a few days, I had to visit his room. It might be painted wholly black, the furniture removed except for a mattress and wooden chair. Sitting on the chair would be a water pipe. In the corner, a pile of clothes.

In November 1968, the D.C. police quelled a confrontation and fisticuffs that "began when a Volkswagen bus was driven down G Street by five members of the National Socialist White People's Party who sprayed red paint on demonstrators filing from G Street into the quad behind Monroe Hall."[2] Police arrested the five provocateurs, but "G Street was full of students … Some began to chant 'the streets belong to the people.'" In the melee that followed, twenty students were arrested.[3] In the spring of 1969, the Sino-Soviet Institute was occupied one night by the Students for a Democratic Society. The Institute's

CDU, in formation near Watergate Hotel. Courtesy of Gelman Library, GWU, and GWU *Hatchet News*. All rights reserved.

Author, outside Welling Hall, GWU, Observing CDU break-in at Madison Hall. NTProto Collection

front doors were locked and its files examined. A sit-in at Rice Hall occurred. The university's president, Lloyd Elliot, was confronted by students, many of whom were participating in a demonstration for the first time. Their concern: that their planned rally against the Vietnam War "was being watched by the District police" sitting in squad cars on I Street. The police, they contended, must be kept "off the campus." Many of those students lived in the dorms.[4]

In late February 1970, following a demonstration in front of the Watergate—the home of Attorney General John Mitchell—over the conviction of the Chicago Seven, the police moved in with batons and tear gas. Demonstrators fled up Twenty-second Street toward the university. Welling (the dorm in which I lived and worked, now as a first-year law student) was in their path. I came outside in time to see demonstrators running frantically, pursued by the District's newly formed Civil Disturbance Unit (CDU). Between Welling and the fleeing demonstrators was Madison Hall, another dormitory on the corner of Twenty-second and H. My friend Pete Steenland was its director. As the demonstrators kept coming, the normal flow of automobile traffic up and down H acted as a barrier. A bottleneck occurred. Students who were unconnected with the demonstration mixed with those who were fleeing. A few turned to the right—anxious, unnerved, frantic, looking for alleyways to enter. They were caught by the CDU. But the students who turned left saw a shred of hope. Students inside Madison opened the front doors to let them in. The police hesitated. Some students on the second floor emptied large containers of hot water onto the police. The response was immediate. The police pushed through the door and into the lobby. Students involved with the provocation were grabbed at random—scared, nonplussed, immobilized by the fact that the CDU was inside a university building. Some students tried to escape up stairwells or down hallways. Residents were cornered; one was bloodied; others were pushed, beaten, and arrested. It was all over in a few minutes.[5] The need for a rule was clear, and one was agreed upon immediately among the directors. The doors were to be locked, and students were to stay away from the windows: "If you leave the dormitory to demonstrate and succeed in attracting the police to our front door, don't expect to be let back in. The residence halls are not a sanctuary."

There was no respite. The relative quiet of April barely survived the month. In early May, the United States invaded Cambodia. The Senate Foreign Relations Committee accused President Richard Nixon of engaging in an "unauthorized presidential war." The National Student Association called for a nationwide student strike. It spread quickly and pervasively. The White House was cordoned off. The killing of four students at Kent State on May 4 closed down the university.[6] The dormitories were bedlam. Few students slept. Most argued, prepared posters, and demonstrated in and around university buildings and near Dupont Circle. Some marched to the White House. Words, like thunder, emerged from the shootings at Jackson State. Law students monitored demonstrators and recorded the conduct of police. Some students cried. Few studied.

During the evening of May 8, I walked with friends to the New York Avenue Presbyterian Church to attend a memorial service for the slain Kent State students. It was laden with weariness. Former Chief Justice Earl Warren; Coretta Scott King, widower of Dr. Martin Luther King Jr.; Ethel Kennedy, widower of Senator Robert Kennedy; Senator Mark Hatfield; and Ambassador Averell Harriman filled the pews in front. A student from Kent State spoke.

I returned to Welling, tired. A demonstration was planned for the next day. We called the boys together and described the cautions, the rules, and the risks associated with demonstrating in an urban setting. They expressed apprehension about taking examinations, completing papers, and graduating. As dusk fell, the clouds and stench of tear gas and the sounds of sirens, faint at first, filled the night air. Within moments, they were coupled with discernible human sounds, a kind of guttural noise from deep inside. George Biondi called me. The clash was near Calhoun Hall and moving. He thought that some of my boys had been arrested. "It's very bad," he said. "Hanson is trying to get everyone inside. They're mostly on H Street."

I left Welling and walked with care up Twenty-second to I. Tear gas seeped into my nostrils. The street was littered with newspapers, discarded pamphlets, and wet rags. A few students ran past me, coughing. The human sounds were getting louder as I got closer to Calhoun. I saw one of my boys and yelled to him. He understood my motion to get off the street. Before us both were dozens of students breaking car windows, yelling, gasping for air, throwing rocks at oncoming police, running without guidance or direction. A street lamp was shattered. The sound was abrupt, frightening. The street fell dark. A Volkswagen, already pushed into the middle of the street, was set afire. Its glow cast moving shadows and disjointed flecks of light onto the faces of moving students.

When I returned to Welling, Pete Steenland was there. He had just returned from central lockup on Third and Indiana, where he had gotten some of his boys out. He thought a few of mine where there. We went back. It was late when we arrived—a time when people should be sleeping, the day ended. But the bright illumination and activity of police wagons, arrested students, and sweaty and embattled members of the CDU created a stark, harsh, eerie scene that was troubling, unnatural, not right. As Pete and I walked toward the front door, I found a policeman standing tall in my path—his face strained, his frame powerful, a baton and gas mask in his hands. Sweat mingled with dirt was streaking down his face. Pete took me inside. Two of my residents had been there. Both had paid their fines and left. As quickly and carefully as we could, we left too.

Within days, the university canceled examinations. The law school did not follow suit. I returned to my studies, between reassuring parents and collecting room keys. For reasons I did not understand fully, the law school gave us a choice: take the examination or take a "pass" for the course. It was my first year of law school. I took the pass.

With the university empty and within a few days of my departure for home, dorm directors Pete Steenland, John Hanson, Fred Spurlock, Cliff Brown, and I got into Pete's Volvo and drove south, unshaven and carefree, amid a blue sky and warm temperatures. We intended to climb Old Rag Mountain near Sperryville, Virginia. We laughed, joked, and told stories. We sped down Route 66 and stopped in Warrenton for breakfast—at a greasy spoon place with the smell and, eventually, the taste of bacon, eggs, sausage, and toast. We drove through town, bought some food and beer "for when we get to the top," and made our way deeper into Virginia.

When I returned to Old Rag's base, no one was there. No other cars, no friends—only heat, gravel, and mosquitoes. It took me only a moment. Just beyond Pete's car was a deep and wide ravine surrounded by trees and clumps of bushes. I was not sure whose idea it had been, or who had gone first. But there were my friends, splashing and laughing in the stream that widened nicely at the ravine's base, where it was pushed and channeled by rocks and boulders. Within moments, we were all down the mountain, our clothes off, skinny-dipping in the fresh pool of water, laughing at and with one another, pleased that—at least for now—it was over.

George Washington was—and still is—an urban university in the nation's capital proximate to the White House. Finding detachment or enduring quietude was hard. You could buy a cup of coffee on campus, sit alone, conjure up important thoughts, and outline research papers on fragile napkins. You could do it, but it required discipline—and an ability to absorb and understand, but not be distracted by, what is around you.

2

BANZHAF AND THE PLACID EGGSHELL, SPRING 1971

Stockton Hall. The law school's classroom building had solid stone front steps. Students were always moving in and out of its front door and along Twentieth Street, jutting between the traffic, pulsating, animated, and talking about the "facts" or the "case." Their appearance reflected their unease: ashen faces, lined, mawkish from late-night studying. Most were arguing. Some read while they walked, carrying coffee that was steaming and sometimes dripping. They almost always wore blue jeans. Many had long hair that covered their ears. Few were unkempt. All carried books—stuffed in knapsacks, under an arm, on the back of a bicycle, or in the new briefcase usually bought by proud parents. And standing amid those students, like newly painted totem poles, were those with part-time jobs who, compelled by custom, wore white shirts and dark ties.

Bacon Hall, on the corner of Twentieth and H, housed the law school faculty. All the buff and Marvin Green paint could not hide its decay. Windows were caked with scum and urban soot. Exterior and interior walls were cracked, bulbous in places, their texture and color uneven, weathered, and dreary. Midway through my first year, I visited two professors, one after the other. Their offices had no paintings, drawings, photographs, or posters. Old exam booklets and mimeographed sheets, dusty and discolored from age, were lying in makeshift, presumably once-orderly piles. The furniture was beyond disrepair: a chair for the professor and a chair for me. There was nothing memorable or grand or pretentious.

Few law students lived on campus. Many drove in from Arlington. I brought my own car down from New Haven during my first year. It was a 1958 Volkswagen, with a sunroof made of canvas, a great radio, a little heat, and a bleak-looking exterior. It was fun to drive. I also did not have to worry about parking. It was part of the deal: a free parking space alongside Welling.

In September 1969, the law school was not a mecca—not spiritually or geographically or in terms of some long tradition that made Stockton Hall a symbolic connection into a mythological past of scholars or jurists or great thinkers. The law school was not revered. It certainly was no presumptive meal ticket to the future. But more in life engulfed a student studying law in the nation's capital. It took the form of violence: the urban riots in 1967 and 1968; Resurrection City, constructed by civil rights demonstrators and volunteers on the Monument grounds and then roughly dismantled by government officials; the murders of Martin Luther King Jr. and Robert F. Kennedy; the university and college demonstrations and confrontations; the widely televised clashes at the 1968 Democratic and Republican National Conventions; the explosive conduct of radical groups like the Weathermen or the Black Panthers; and the Vietnam War—the vivid, televised killing and burning; the daily, increasing loss of life; and the pathos or anger of stricken parents. Presidential commissions also produced highly publicized reports: the *Report of the National Advisory Commission on Civil Disorders* (1968) and the reports prepared for the National Commission on the Causes and Prevention of Violence, such as *The History of Violence in America* (1969), *The Politics of Protest* (1969), and *Rights in Conflict* (1968).[1]

The violence was now largely dissent: a showdown by those feeling trapped, abused, alienated, or fearful of government, parents, business, law, or the university. The dissent invaded and formed the culture. The inequity in class and race, particularly, was parodied with disquieting unease in the words of Pete Seeger, Woody Guthrie, and especially Bob Dylan, as he described the lonesome death of Hattie Carroll or the enigmatic pawn who murdered Medgar Evers.[2] The full range of the debate pervaded George Washington University, particularly for those in law, where government, in the form of the judiciary, is an arbiter of conflict and, in the form of the executive, an enforcer of rules. Many students also worked part time for the government, law firms, or public interest groups. Some among the faculty did the same. Their experiences tempered what they wrote and talked about, whom they met, and what they brought into the classroom about the law and how it is practiced.

Still other students had views—strong ones—about the war or poverty or legal aid or consumer issues. They gave their time to ad hoc groups, community agencies, or fledgling newsletters that came and went and came again.

Two books were published within a short time of one another: Supreme Court Justice Abe Fortas's *Concerning Dissent and Civil Disobedience* (1969) and Supreme Court Justice William O. Douglas's *Points of Rebellion* (1970). Their approach was dramatically different. Justice Fortas, lawyer-like, called upon court decisions and established rules to describe rights and responsibilities and to urge self-restraint. Justice Douglas talked about "smaller relationships," such as landlords' mistreatment of tenants, consumers being denied credit to purchase homes, individual privacy being invaded by government action, and struggles to preserve diversity within neighborhoods.[3] He also spoke about how the duty of government is invoked and by whom. "Corporate interests," Justice Douglas stated, "as well as poor people—unemployed people as well as the average member of this affluent society are affected by these broad generalized grants of authority [by Congress] to administrative agencies. The corporate interests have been largely taken care of by highly qualified lawyers ... and by Bar Associations proposing procedural reforms that define, for example, the 'aggrieved' persons who have standing to object to agency orders or decisions. But the voices of the mass of people are not heard, and the administrative agencies largely have their own way."[4] Douglas's perspective resonated to many, with his reliance on experience in life and his efforts, however imperfect, to talk about values and the purpose of law.

Beneath the veneer of a decent faculty and case books—and all the traditional trappings of a law school—was a subtle but deliberate tumult, a sway of forces and ideas reflective of urban living in the nation's capital and of changing cultural values. There was no prospect of a volcanic eruption. It was more in the nature of a hatching where some stirring random body part breaks through the seemingly placid eggshell. As fortune would have it, Stockton Hall's tradition was no stronger.

BANZHAF: "SUE THE BASTARDS"

When I first viewed his photograph, John Banzhaf III reminded me of Sam Huff: big chest and shoulders, fair complexion, light hair cut short, with a round head. His biceps, displayed plainly beneath his rolled-up, short-sleeved shirt and reminiscent of the same early rock 'n' roll era, were quintessential Ted Kluszewski. Unlike Huff or Kluszewski, Banzhaf had features that were not hard or filled with character. On the contrary, he looked young, almost boyish,

Professor John Banzhaf III.
Courtesy of Gelman Library, GWU.

if not mischievous. His open-collared shirt added a feeling of irreverence. The students I met described Banzhaf in a remarkably similar manner: arrogant, aloof, conceited, and boastful. Most also respected the way he taught law. "He sensed the big picture." "He taught you what was at stake." "Tough on everyone." He had, they seemed to suggest, an unbounded, rough, but at times sly, boldness. John Banzhaf was an associate professor. He had two discernible sources for his notoriety. One preceded his arrival; the second developed and was nurtured intensely once he was there.

Banzhaf had initiated and, in effect, won a lawsuit of national significance about cigarette advertising on television. In December 1966, having graduated from Columbia Law School and engaged in private practice, "Citizen John F. Banzhaf III" (as the court of appeals described him) asked CBS "to provide free time in which anti-smokers might respond to the pro-smoking views he said were implicit in the cigarette commercials it broadcasts." Because the commercials raised only one side of a controversial issue, Banzhaf believed that CBS was under an obligation to make its "facilities available for the expression of contrasting viewpoints held by responsible elements."[5] CBS said no. Banzhaf filed a complaint with the Federal Communications Commission (FCC). He contended that the station violated the *Fairness Doctrine*. The FCC agreed, with one caveat. It required CBS to provide "a significant amount of time," not "an equal amount of time." Banzhaf sought judicial review of the decision in the United States Court of Appeals for the District of Columbia.

Here, for those—like myself—who were not yet versed in law, lay the first strategic move that tempered Banzhaf's reputation. He suspected that the tobacco industry would, as it was allowed to, seek judicial review in the Court of Appeals for the Fourth Circuit in Richmond, Virginia—which Banzhaf characterized as "Marlboro Country." To deter such a possibility, Banzhaf put together a simple petition for review, articulated a complaint about his "loss," and submitted it promptly in the District of Columbia. He now had the judicial forum he wanted. His second move was to support the same FCC decision he was challenging. "[U]biquitous," the court of appeals described Banzhaf's conduct.[6] In a November 1968 decision by Judge David Bazelon, the court upheld the FCC decision. Banzhaf had his first claim to fame, in the outcome of the controversy and in his seeming ability to outwit his adversaries.[7] Another matter also struck me, but in ways I did not yet understand fully. The parties opposing the FCC decision and Banzhaf were formidable: the National Association of Broadcasters, ABC, CBS, Liggett & Myers, Phillip Morris, R. J. Reynolds, and P. Lorillard. Banzhaf understood, experienced, and withstood their power.[8]

The second basis for Banzhaf's reputation began after he arrived at GW in 1967. He extended into an academic setting the experience of his FCC case. He had transformed his Unfair Trade Practices course into a quasi-clinical law program. Students could form a group and undertake a legal project intended to confront a serious, "real-life" consumer problem. It was a course that valued experience and the exercise of judgment. It also was no piece of cake. Banzhaf would provide guidance and advice. The group identified the problem and did the work. The course taught us that, in the real world, success or failure was up to us. "Sue the Bastards," Banzhaf called it.

One group was Students Opposing Unfair Practices (SOUP). In a petition to the Federal Trade Commission (FTC), SOUP charged that the Campbell Soup Company should be obligated to acknowledge publicly that it engaged in deceptive advertising. (Campbell had been detected placing marbles into soup bowls to support the vegetables poured in by a smiling mother.) The FTC refused. Campbell was allowed to stop the practice without admitting wrongdoing. The FTC did allow SOUP to participate in the proceeding. I was not certain fully why, but the reason was less important to me than two other facts. First, a product as pervasively used as soup was sold through suspect advertising that affected the profitability of a major industry. Second, in the absence of the government stopping the practice, no one else would.[9]

Banzhaf also was adding definition to something more: a social movement involving law, government reform, and an insistence on corporate responsibility. The movement's most visible advocate was Ralph Nader—the son of immigrants—who had a quiet, indemonstrable caring about fairness, public participation in government and corporate decision making, and the public disclosure of information. To make his point—first about the automobile industry and then about the congenital failure of various federal agencies—Nader relied on students to do research and draft documents. His reports seemed to sting the consciousness, not unlike the works of Upton Sinclair, Ida Tarbell, or Lincoln Steffens a generation earlier. The difference was that Nader was a lawyer. He understood the means of ensuring reform beyond the rhetoric of advocating it.[10]

In reading further about Banzhaf and the conduct of the groups formed in his course, questions emerged that engaged me and others. Who, specifically, was affected by the practices of industry? How are the interests of such people advocated in those regulatory settings and by whom? Who advocates the "public interest" in a setting where the people affected are likely to be unaware that questions will be decided with practical consequences for those about whom they care? And what is the duty of government when it makes those decisions? Now, as a law student, I found that this last question particularly took on a practical, if seemingly elementary, meaning. The "government" included the judiciary. Moreover, one principle already had emerged in my study. "It is emphatically the province and duty of the judicial department," Chief Justice John Marshall wrote in 1803, "to say what the law is." I read those words early on, in *Marbury v. Madison*, and revisited them regularly. In the end, I thought—and suspected that those more experienced in the law believed—that the judiciary had the final obligation to answer these questions: What is the duty of government? And who advocates and protects the public's interest?[11] At the right time, I wanted to take Banzhaf's course.

THE REPUTATION ON TRIAL

Spring semester, 1971. The law school faculty voted 18 to 13 to deny tenure to John Banzhaf. I was surprised by the decision when told by two third-year students. I should not have been. "Banzhaf is not a universally popular man," wrote Joseph Goulden in *The Superlawyers* (1972). "He is outspoken, and many of his colleagues think him a bit cocky, and they did not care for his implied criticisms of their teaching methods." Banzhaf's own *pro bono* and student group activities also displeased a number of well-known Washington lawyers who were GW graduates. He was intruding upon well-established and quiet relationships.[12]

The response among students was quick and severe. More than 800 students signed petitions protesting the decision. They presented the petitions to the law school's dean, Robert Kramer. Students demanded a full public airing and a formal reversal. It was not Banzhaf's personality that prevailed. It was his approach to the law.

I attended the only open meeting late one evening in Stockton Hall. Its largest lecture hall was packed with students—standing, sitting atop desks, or crouching uncomfortably on the floor—content just to listen. A few were animated, ready, their bodies taut, their arguments in place. Most were barely moving and deadpan in expression. All were visibly tired. I looked around, found a space against the wall, and moved over and around others to occupy it. Some faculty members, dressed in ties and jackets, were standing in small groups. Banzhaf was not among them. The dean presided over the meeting. He stood, in his characteristically ramrod fashion, front and center. I did not think this was his kind of meeting. He was no democrat and did not have to be. At stake now was something bigger than Banzhaf that gelled in and around the dean. He may have feared more serious consequences if he did not lead.

What ensued was a spectacle of the first magnitude. Teacher denounced teacher. Students denounced teachers. Fingers were pointed. Accusations abounded about who voted which way and who made the vote public and why. The dean could not control it. The most enthusiasm for Banzhaf came from Professor Monroe Freedman. His approach to legal education—I learned harshly in his course on contracts—was decidedly conventional in nature. It made no difference; he touched raw nerves that night. Some students clapped. Others remained quiet. Most were uneasy with what they saw, perhaps stunned by the faculty's performance or because they disliked Banzhaf's temperament.[13] What emerged for me, as I left to make my way to Crawford Hall, was that it appeared likely Banzhaf's approach could be accommodated into the law school's manner of education. Or, as good fortune would have it, the placid eggshell that enclosed Stockton Hall had been cracked once again. The tenure decision was reversed.

3

THE CONVERSATION, SPRING 1971

Pete Steenland, in his reliable Volvo, stopped at Crawford Hall at dawn on a Thursday. The street was still of life. We drove and talked as we made our way west along Route 66 and then southwest down Virginia's Route 81.

In fall 1969, I read Harry Caudill's *Night Comes to the Cumberlands*.[1] The images had been widely shared: children walking barefoot, bruised, scuffed, scarred by the emptiness of an elementary want that few adults experience; fathers, their faces stained indelibly with soot, hands swollen, breath shortened by blackened and acrid dust from deep below the earth's surface, sitting amid coal slag and puddles of putrid water; and—in between—mothers, protective, subtly powerful, yet aware that at any moment the insidious death of black lung could be displaced with irrevocable abruptness by fire, suffocation, or the failure of a wooden beam to support tons of indiscriminately falling rock, gravel, and coal.

Pete pulled into the Hotel Roanoke. It was old world—a Tudor mansion built through the brute force of extracted coal and a disregard for the human cost of the wealth that passed through its doors or that sat and supped within the grandeur of its dining room. The Norfolk and Western Railroad owned it. We saw what we needed to. We moved on. We drove deeper into Virginia and across the border into Tennessee. We pulled into a roadside motel in Kingsport—clean, basic, and cheap. We settled in.

Less obvious to me, until I read about it, was how the natural resources of this region moved. Caudill described it. "[T]he stage was set [by early in the twentieth century] for the most momentous single occurrence in the history of the Cumberlands—the building of the railroads." In a short time, "the vast, backward Cumberland Plateau was tied inseparably to the colossal industrial complex centering in Pittsburgh.... [But] in the remote and isolated valleys of the Kentucky mountains ... public scrutiny was often non-existent and always indifferent, [and] the disgrace [of the conditions in which the American railroads were built] was vastly compounded."[2] The most primitive forms of conservation and working conditions were trivialized and castigated as unmanly. Government was there, too—sometimes watching, passive, complacent as blood trickled and men were beaten, shot, or mangled—but usually not. Usually government was there to enforce the law; to put the workers in their place; and to support the timber, coal, and railroad interests. Caudill concluded, "The nation has paid no noticeable heed to its darkest area."[3]

At dawn, with coffee to go steaming against the morning chill and maps set out on the dashboard, Pete drove northeast on Route 23, back through Virginia, into the Cumberlands, onto Route 421, and into Harlan County, Kentucky.

As I had made my journeys between Washington and New Haven—whether by train or car or bus—the familiar had taken on a different meaning: the Dupont Chemical complex in Delaware, surrounded by water that was pea green, brackish, pungent, and dead; the Standard Oil refinery in northern New Jersey, fires burning, smelling noxious, defiling the air with their stink and residue; and there, paralleling the highways, the coal cars of the Norfolk and Western, moving quickly and with strength. Now I knew where the coal was from and what cost was paid to get it.

Harlan County was, as we suspected, gray, tinged with a wet and befouled soot, worn, unpainted, sullied, and hard. It was here, in the winter of 1931, that Theodore Dreiser, John Dos Passos, Sherwood Anderson, and others sought to focus national attention on the dismal, sickening plight of striking miners and on the mayhem—organized by coal operators and inflicted by law—that reached into the miners' homes and crushed their rights and lives with certain impunity.[4]

Pete pulled into a one-pump gas station. I got out of the car to stretch. The ground was soggy; the stench from burning rubber was pervasive; nearby, its source was visible and untamed.

It happened in November and December 1969. The United Mine Workers election. The *Washington Post* and the *Evening Star* had carried the insults, intimidation, and rough machinations of both candidates for president: Jock Yablonski, the insurgent, whose father had died in a mining accident, seeking to take control from Tony Boyle. Imposing, burly, with bushy eyebrows, Yablonski complained of Boyle's close relationship with the coal operators. Boyle seemed to have money, patronage, and an astringent tongue. Yablonski's lawyer, Joseph Rauh, asked Attorney General John Mitchell to provide Yablonski with personal protection. The attorney general refused. The election was held on December 9, 1969. Boyle won handily.[5] I heard the news first on the radio, as the alarm awakened me and as the announcer, in mid-sentence, described the event. On or about January 4, 1970, Yablonski, his wife, and his daughter had been shot to death; their "blood-caked bodies" had been found "pajama-clad" in the upstairs bedroom of their family home in Clarksville, Pennsylvania.[6] It was methodical, brutal slaughter.

Here Pete and I were, in a setting engulfed by poverty; by black lung; by pervasive unsafety in the region's most critical industry; by calculated, cold-blooded murder in the midst of a highly visible election; and by the quiet, plain death of plain people from malnutrition or from the learned absence of hope. There were, no doubt, differences between now and forty years earlier. Two realities, unequivocally, remained the same: saddened lives and degraded land.

> I woke up this morning with the worst blues I ever had in my life;
> Not a bite to cook for breakfast, a poor coal miner's wife....
> All the women in the coal camps are a-sitting with bowed-down heads;
> Ragged and bare footed, the children a-crying for bread....
> No food, no clothes for our children. I'm sure this ain't no lie,
> If we can't get more for our labor, we will starve to death and die....[7]

"It's like we thought, fellow," Pete said gently. We moved on to Hazard.

Largely in silence, we drove north through Hyden, past squalid streams that were gray-green in color, embedded in uneven gullies, strewn with tin cans and broken bottles, running parallel to the road and separating it from the shacks and outhouses and the animals that surrounded them, and the children who walked or were stooped nearby. After Hazard, we continued northeast, past hills that were torn and gouged into blacks and grays; past underground mines, boarded because they were unsafe or uneconomical, and rusted shovels or a rail spur, now unused; and then on to Pikeville. As the day came to an end, we drove southeast onto Route 460. As the sun set, we stopped near the Virginia border, within the Breaks Park, to view the rough splendor of the mountains and trees and fast-flowing streams that, it now was clear, still hid—shrouded in a deceptive beauty—the history and tormented culture that lay beyond.

We settled at Bluefield. The next day, as we drove north into Charleston, West Virginia, only the haunting power of the illuminated, large industrial and chemical complex that straddled the Kanawaha River intruded into the deep and subtle permanency of what I had seen and felt the day before. The connection: the interlocking and financial relationship between and among the Norfolk and Western and the region's other railroads, the Penn Central and the Baltimore and Ohio; their influence and the raw power that held sway over the Appalachians that Theodore Dreiser, as a political "outsider," and Harry Caudill, as a home-grown "insider," both described with documented knowledge and strong passion. They had brought me face-to-face with an indelible impression: the law and its institutions and values were not available here, not yet—and not to protect the land or the people.

APRIL 1971

It began on the Washington Monument grounds. The front doors at Crawford were locked. Word went out quickly: "If you leave the dormitory to demonstrate and succeed in attracting the police to our front door, don't expect to be let back in. The residence halls are not a sanctuary."

On H, between Twenty-first and Twenty-second, noxious fumes filled the air while the demonstrators ran, stumbling over broken bottles and knocking each other down. Cars were pushed into the middle of the street. The CDU just kept coming—methodically, determined, relentless. We stood behind the glass front door. We let some demonstrators in. They reeked with gas, their eyes tearing. Someone handed them a wet rag; their coats were thrown into an isolated room. Holding her books, a woman with short hair and probing eyes stood on the sidewalk five yards away—caught, it seemed, amid moving students. I motioned her in. "Thanks," she said. "I walked out of class trying to get to— "

"It's okay," I interrupted. With delicate fingers, she began opening her sweater—a dark crimson, fitted; she wore jeans that were fitted as well. "You were not out there to—?" I asked, watching and calculating the movement of police.

"No, not here," she said softly. Three things were plain: she was no undergraduate; a ring, dark blue in a gold setting, heavy, with a school emblem was on her finger; and she was Irish—Irish American, to be precise.

"Okay. That's it. Everybody back," I said loudly. Draperies and blinds were closed. "No provocation. Absolutely nothing must be done to provoke the police." We locked the door. A resident yelled that he heard on the radio that the police had encircled the university. The CDU regrouped in front of us, their faces intense, their fingers pointed in our direction. I saw Jerry Wilson, the city's chief of police, arrive and leave. One policeman took a bullhorn and announced a curfew. Anyone on the street would be arrested. Slowly, the boys returned to their rooms.

"Patience for a while," I said to the woman. "We'll get you to your car."

"Thanks. Can I use a phone?"

"Jeff'll get you to one. I've got to report in."

"Thanks, again."

"I'm Neil Proto. I'm sorry, I didn't—"

"Nice to meet you. I'm Kathleen McKeeley."

"Big fellow," Jeff said. "There's more going on. I'll get her settled."

A plan had emerged to stop traffic from Arlington and Alexandria before it crossed the Memorial Bridge: "STOP THE WAR MACHINE." Demonstrators were to meet at 6:00 a.m. Crawford was filled to twice its capacity. I walked through the hallways, as the entire staff did, and up and down its narrow stairs into the early morning hours, talking with organizers, cautioning them about the pretense of provocation, and then talking with others who were ensnared in the cause or simply in the cultural imperative of wanting to belong. We wanted to be certain they understood that, in the end, they did what they believed and not what others said they ought to.

At the night's end, I called Fred Spurlock, who was now responsible for Madison. He would have one of his staff members a few blocks from the demonstration. I took as hot a shower as I could stand. The tension was all in the neck. At 2:45 a.m., I sat on the edge of the bed and set the alarm for 6:00

a.m., remembered that I needed to set up an electric coffee pot so all I had to do was plug it in, got up, set it, and returned. "Sleep fast," my father would say the night before we were going on a long car trip. "We have to be out of here by six o'clock—before the traffic starts." I could not remember whether he ever used an alarm clock. He seemed somehow magically to be up before all of us, coffee and toast ready, bags in the car, change ready for the tolls, and always making certain we got there safely. *I should hire him for the dorm*, I thought.

The phone rang. I thought it was the alarm. It rang again.

"Wake up, partner!" It was Fred.

"What the heck time is it?"

"6:02."

"What?"

"6:02. There've been arrests down near the Lincoln Memorial. One of my boys just ran back to tell me. He saw it and high-tailed his bod out of there. I don't know if it's coming but you better get ready." I could picture him on the other end. Prepared. Solid. He had probably already plugged in his coffeepot. I put the phone down and put on blue jeans, a shirt, and sneakers. I ran down the hall to the front door. Students—bantering, boisterous, in groups of six or eight—were walking toward the rendezvous point. Within minutes, the entire staff met in the dorm office. I brought the coffee. The radio reported that arrests were occurring on the bridge. Some people had driven to work at 5:00 a.m.; others would not come in until 9:00. More arrests. Students were scattering. We waited. A car was burning. The fire was doused quickly, and the car was towed. At 7:15 a.m., it was over—officially.

I called Fred. "It all turned to mush," he said. "We're still on call."

"Us, too," I said.

I walked back to my room, shaved, poured another cup of coffee, and took out my corporation text to prepare for class. I sat quietly. Today, if I had read the correct assignment, we were going to be "piercing the corporate veil."

SEMESTER'S END, 1971

I stood outside the doorway to Crawford as the last of its residents departed for the summer. It was midday, perhaps 4:00 p.m. The street was quiet except for the dark blue MG that had just pulled behind my Volkswagen in the alleyway. I've seen her before, I thought.

I was clad in my usual fare—jeans, long-sleeved shirt, rolled-up sleeves— with hair getting longer, eyes feeling and looking puffy, and the pain in my neck solidly in place. I took a seat atop the stone bench in front of Crawford, sat back, closed my eyes, and tried to imagine lying prone on a beach. "Hey, big fella." It was George Biondi. The beach would have to wait.

"George. Sit down. How you doing?"

"Good, good," he said, with a big smile.

"What are you doing here?" I asked.

He took a seat on the bench. George was dressed neatly. He wore exactly what I did, and a tie. "I just came from Rice Hall. I had to pick up a summer schedule."

"You staying?" I asked.

"Yeah. So, if you come down, let me know."

"I'll probably be down in a few weeks."

"Great. Sounds great."

"Well. How did you like your first year?"

"Great. Sounds great." George laughed, then fell silent for a moment. "No, really, it was okay. I did okay."

"You worked hard," I said.

"What I liked were the rules. People have to—or should—abide by the rules."

"The harder question is who sets the rules or—"

"Who interprets them?" he asked.

"Yeah," I nodded, starting to understand what we meant. "You know, George. I'm thinking I want to take Banzhaf's course—where you get to do a project."

"How come?" he asked

Two motorcycles moved by with a rumbling, penetrating sound that forced us into silence. The woman in the MG emerged from the alleyway, carrying books. She smiled and started to walk across the street. "Excuse me," I said to her. I turned to George. "Hold on." He nodded.

She seemed confident in an incongruent way; she was about 5'8", I could see as I got closer, with fair, delicate features. "I'm only parking for a minute—"

"You can't—"

"And it's also a public alleyway." Her darkish blonde hair, long and straight, fell across her face.

"You could get a ticket."

"Are you the dorm police?" she asked, as she pulled her hair aside, gracefully.

"No, the director. You're parked illegally."

"A law student," she said. I nodded and smiled.

"Okay. You know, the District has the 'Denver Boot.'"

"I have no tickets," she said, unyielding.

"Hmm."

"That your car in front of mine?"

"Mmm-hmm."

"You have any tickets?" Of course I did. "I'll be back soon." There was an affected energy in her carriage as I watched her dodge traffic. I returned to George.

"You ready for marriage?" I asked.

"Pretty?" George asked, nodding in her direction.

"Yeah. Well. A little."

"Sassy?"

"She used to live here, I think, or maybe I met her here."

"What's her name?"

"Ah, I can't, ah … one of those American types."

"WASPy, huh?"

"Mmm-hmm."

"Salvageable?" We laughed.

"Well, anyhow. Marriage. You ready?"

"Yeah, this is it," George answered. "It'll be a little tight in Calhoun Hall, but we'll manage."

"Kathy can handle the boys?"

"Better than me."

I stood up, clasped my hands behind my back and, in a slow, deliberate manner, stretched hard. "George, this was a rough year."

He looked at me with a knowing smile and a few gentle nods of the head.

"I know," I said, smiling slightly and feeling relieved because of it. "They've all been that way." He nodded again.

It was June 1971. I was glad to be going home.

4

STUDENTS CHALLENGING REGULATORY AGENCY PROCEDURES (SCRAP), FALL 1971

n uneasy calm. The dormitory staff orientation program was conducted at Rice Hall. As I looked around the room, few of the old-timers were there. "I think the demonstrations are over, George," I said, speaking softly and leaning slightly to be closer to him.

"You mean you hope so," he said. He didn't move a muscle—only his lips—while seeming to listen to an explanation of damage reports.

"Yeah, that's exactly what I mean."

He adjusted his chair to be closer. "This summer. The Pentagon Papers case?"

"Good thing it happened then," I said, lifting a copy of the explanation. "Read the dissent in the Court of Appeals, J. Skelly Wright."

"Instructive?"

"There's passion and then there's being the best lawyer. He's both."

George nodded. "What do you think of this crowd?" he asked.

"Well, maybe we can just be dorm directors. You remember those days, George?"

"Nope. Do you?" George had inherited a cadre of basketball players. He would have his hands full.

"Just job possibilities and the bar exam."

"Connecticut?"

Judge J. Skelly Wright.
Library of Congress.

"Yeah."

During the next break, I dutifully greeted my new colleagues and then moved with George to a corner. "I'm going to register for Banzhaf's course. I have some thoughts about a project but nothing definite."

"He's hard on these groups," George explained. "You sure?"

I nodded.

"You know Jerry Barron?" he asked.

"No. Well, by reputation."

"Mass communications law. Excellent teacher," he said. "Engaged by the subject, First Amendment, Federal Communications Commission, and no exam. You can do a paper."

"My kind of course," I said.

THE IDEA

The classrooms in Stockton are large—windows on one side; a desk located in front that is elevated, judicial-like, with steps leading to it. Traversing the entire width of the classroom are long, permanently placed tables. Chairs are simple, metal, and hard. It was in such a classroom that students had assembled the year before to challenge Banzhaf's tenure denial. That night, no one on the faculty had walked the few steps necessary to dominate the room—no one, including the dean.

Banzhaf entered the classroom without a tie or jacket. He bounded up the steps with a rough strength, put his books down, stood straight up, and looked around. It was not in a manner reminiscent of a shepherd surveying his flock with care but rather of a surveyor looking to a point distant on the plain, as if everything in between did not matter. He immediately rolled up his shirt sleeves. He appeared self-possessed and conscious of his renown. We were not certain whether we were seeing bravado, cockiness, defensiveness, or simple sincerity. There was no mincing of words, no congenial opening statement, no anecdotes. The text will be Oppenheim's *Unfair Trade Practices* and a supplement.[1] If you haven't purchased them yet, you should have. A syllabus was distributed. Readings already were posted. Attendance is not optional. Class participation will affect your grade.

Banzhaf then began to explain the course option: doing a project. Each group could be a maximum of five students. Experience, he said, had shown that this size was sufficient to accomplish most objectives. Inevitably, some members would do more than others. Each student would be graded individually. Most groups ended in a semester. Only a few had gone beyond that. A description of the project must be submitted in one week.

In selecting a project, be conscious of whether it might take longer than a semester. Do not start something you know you can't finish or can't easily pass on for someone else to finish. Expect to be harassed and overwhelmed by paper from expensive lawyers. You will be taking on the Goliaths. Tactics and strategy are critical; they may be all you have. We are here to help you with that—and only that. If you cannot do the work, decide up front. There is too much at stake for you, for me, and for the public interest you are trying to serve. Don't waste time or effort. Don't cause disappointment.

I was not sure if he actually used the word, but he also said something about being cunning. All groups would meet regularly with his assistant, Peter Meyers. Peter, seated in front, waved his hand. Banzhaf did not look at him. Peter had been the chairman of SOUP. He graduated last year.

Talk to him if you have any questions. And, to make it clear, all the course requirements apply except the exam. Doing a project excuses you from nothing.

I looked around. I recognized two students I had known since my first year, Ken Perlman from New York City and Peter Ressler from New Haven. More than 400 students had entered the law school with me. We had been divided into sections. The criterion was the alphabet. I had gotten to know the Ms, Ns, Os, Ps, and the others, through the Zs. By my third year, the prospect of exposure to others increased—but not the likelihood that we'd be able to assess one another's skills. Nice guys, I thought, and a week is not much time. We exchanged glances, a few facial gestures, a horizontal flexing of the index finger. Then I pointed to George, and he nodded his head. We now had four.

Banzhaf continued—talking about corporate practices, private remedies against deceptive conduct, and the duty of the Federal Trade Commission. I turned my head slightly and saw Peter Meyers. The physical contrast between him and Banzhaf was stunning. Banzhaf was detached, bold in manner and temper, neat, solid, strong, and clean-cut, like the early Beach Boys. Meyers was reserved, seemingly reclusive but easily approachable, tall, angular in body and face, in need of a shave, straight but unkempt hair that was well below his ears, and neatly dressed but in the manner of Dylan, early Dylan.

The class ended. I motioned to Ken and Peter to stay seated. Students were moving about, trying to find others to work with. I noticed someone who looked familiar: reddish hair, glasses, medium build. He was standing alone. "Do you want to join our group? I think you know Perlman and Ressler." I was hoping he'd confirm that he was an M through Z. He did not.

"What are you going to do?" he asked.

"I don't know yet. We're going to talk about it. You have any ideas?" I sat on the table near him. George had walked over to Ken and Peter. They were all seated. George, I knew, had to return to Calhoun.

"I might. I took a course in environmental law last year. Arnold Reitze's course. We talked about railroad freight rates and recycling. There is some new law. The National Environmental Policy Act." He seemed uneasy, his eyes still roaming.

"Well, we'll see what the other guys want to do," I said.

"Excuse me a second, Neil," he said. "I'll be right back."

At least he knows me. "Sure." The room began to empty, except for four or five scattered groups discussing projects. I joined George, Kenny, and Peter.

Peter Ressler was prepared, articulate in class, polite, and always dressed neatly—usually in khakis, sport coat, nicely fitted sweater, or sometimes jacket and tie. He worked part time. He was one of the totem poles. Ken Perlman was direct in manner. He defined his time, commitment, and attitude with precision. He intended to graduate with excellent grades. His directness was natural and easy, predictable when you thought about it, and, at times, funny. Ken, too, was a neat dresser but not a totem pole. He never wore a tie except for job interviews. He was always in jeans (usually pressed) and an open-collared, long-sleeved shirt; he had long, almost shoulder-length hair that was noticeably thinning. Kenny and Peter had one characteristic in common. Both were here to be serious, highly skilled, conventional lawyers.

George reminded me that he was in a hurry. Peter was going to work. Kenny said I had five minutes; he had to study. I told everyone I thought I had a fifth person. "Anyone have any ideas?" I asked. A few moments into the conversation, my hoped-for addition called me. I said, "Keep talking," and walked quickly around the desks until, with the room almost empty, we two stood alone.

"Listen, Neil. I'm going to join another group. They want to complain about some detergent commercials on television. They've already done a lot."

"Sure," I said. "That's okay. This other idea about railroads and recycling? Do you care if we use it?"

"No, go ahead. I'm not sure I even understand it."

We began our meeting with only four members. From the middle of the classroom came a terse sound; a student was still sitting, blurting out something about "looking for a group." Kenny looked at me. We both shrugged.

"Do you guys need a fifth?" he asked.

"Yeah, we only have four." George, still seated, waved him over.

"Sure. It's all right," Peter said. "Five means more guys to share the work."

John Larouche introduced himself. He was in his second year. You noticed his smile right off; it was more of a broad grin. He carried an army knapsack loaded with books. Otherwise, he was typical: jeans, shirt, long hair (black, receding), and about George's height, 5'8" or so. He was from Milo, Maine. None of us had been in or near or had even heard of it before.

George and Kenny remained seated; John and Peter were standing; and I sat on one of the desks. No one else remained in the classroom. "Let's go," George said.

"Okay," I said. "Anyone have any ideas?"

"We can file petitions with the FTC or the FCC. That's the easiest."

"Petitions on what?"

"I don't know. Something provocative. Sexy. You know—Banzhaf."

"We need a corporation. Someone big, like General Motors."

"I've got another class," George said, looking at his watch.

"How about botulism?"

"Botulism?" Kenny said. "What the hell are you going to do on botulism?"

"You know. In the chain stores. They sell old canned goods, or bent cans, or old bread—stuff that has botulism."

"Who told you that?"

"It harms the poor, who buy the stuff. We can petition the Food and Drug Administration."

"The FDA? They take a decade to rule on anything."

"Forget that."

George looked at me and picked up his books. Students started entering for the next class. "All right," I said. "Let's meet tomorrow. Late in the afternoon." We agreed. I added, "In the meantime, think about what you want to do. I have some thoughts. We have to decide soon, elect a chairman, and divide the responsibility."

George and I walked down the steps and through the first floor of Stockton. We had a group. Its skills were relatively known but its commitment to work was uncertain, and its ability to work together was unpredictable. We had no project but did have ideas. I told him about railroad freight rates and recycling. He liked the idea. George was taking a course in transportation law. "The Interstate Commerce Commission is where rates are approved," he said. The railroads interested me. Neither of us had taken environmental law. Larouche could not have, George reminded me. He was just starting his second year. I doubted Perlman or Ressler had. I said I had worked on some water pollution issues one summer in New Haven. Maybe others in the group had similar experiences. Milo, Maine, we thought, must be in the wilderness.

The next day, we met again in an empty classroom on the first floor. It was about 4:00 p.m. We sat randomly near the front. Peter kept wandering; he had other things to do. A proposal was made to do a project on biodegradable detergents and call ourselves SOAP. We liked the name but not the idea. "This friend of mine mentioned an idea," I said. "It seems that the railroad rates for transporting recyclable materials like, I think, scrap iron and steel are higher than for raw materials, and because it costs more to transport them, they're not used. The raw materials are used instead."

"So what?"

"Well, it has an adverse environmental impact. Junkyards," I said, more authoritatively than warranted. "The stuff doesn't move."

George got into it. "We could file a petition with the Interstate Commerce Commission. The ICC. They approve rate increases. Or maybe we could propose some legislation," he said.

"Other groups have done that," added Peter.

"Do these freight rates violate any laws?"

"I don't know enough yet. There is something called the National Environmental Policy Act," I said. "Let's divide this up. We can pick a chairman later. Agreed?"

"Yeah. That's fine." John smiled and nodded plainly.

"Sounds all right. We don't have much time."

"Done," I said. We then discussed preliminary research. I would read the National Environmental Policy Act of 1969 (NEPA) and whatever related materials I could find. The other tasks included (1) reviewing the Interstate Commerce Act and determining how freight rate increases are granted (George); (2) determining which groups or corporate interests would support our position or supply us with information (Ken); (3) identifying what constitutes "recyclable materials" (all of us); (4) finding out which members of the local press are responsible for transportation, environmental matters, or both (Peter); and (5) learning which committees or individuals in Congress might be interested in what we are doing (Peter). John proposed to look at other environmental statutes. We also agreed that this division of labor would be temporary. Materials would be distributed. We all needed to be familiar with the laws involved and the amount of work each of us was doing. We exchanged phone numbers and agreed to reconvene in a few days. Without anyone saying it—and I was certain that everyone shared this sensation—the unease that arose inside was related not to what work had to be done but whether each one of us could rely on the others to actually do it.

UNDERSTANDING THE IDEA

The alarm rang at 6:00 a.m. Within moments, the coffee was plugged in. Reading materials sat neatly on my desk. With good fortune, it would be two or three hours before the phone would ring or someone would knock on the door. It was Sunday morning.

I began with NEPA. The act became effective on January 1, 1970. It declared a national policy "which will encourage productive and enjoyable harmony between man and his environment." I was taken by its easily readable language and compelling grasp of simple realities. The act identified the man-made influences affecting the environment such as "high-density urbanization" and, most relevant to our fledgling project, "resource exploitation."[2] Both were familiar to me. Cities—their history, culture, and harsh realities—had been in my experience. Resource exploitation had one direct and powerful meaning: Appalachia.

NEPA stated that "[i]t is the continuing responsibility of the Federal Government to use all practicable means" to "enhance the quality of renewable resources and approach the maximum attainable recycling of depletable resources."[3] At that moment, the coffee—steaming in the soup-sized mug to my right—felt and tasted familiar, comfortable. I thought about places I had walked and played as a kid—parks or settings for family outings with trees, pinecones, trails, and brooks that were now gone, sheared, paved, or covered.

In Section 102 of NEPA, Congress imposed on the executive a directive: "[A]ll agencies of the Federal Government shall" include in "major Federal actions significantly affecting the quality of the human environment" a detailed statement on "the environmental impact of the proposed action; and … any irreversible and irretrievable commitments of resources." Before making such an impact statement, the responsible agency was to "obtain the comments of any Federal agency which has jurisdiction by law or special expertise."[4] *Process*, I noted and began to outline it on my pad.

Each agency was directed to determine "whether there are any … inconsistencies … which prohibit full compliance." If any are found, the agency is required to "propose to the President not later than July 1, 1971, such measures as may be necessary to bring their authority … into conformity."[5] Finally, Congress established the Council on Environmental Quality (CEQ), whose members were to be appointed by President Nixon. It was obligated to promulgate "general guidelines" to assist federal agencies in devising regulations to implement NEPA. I had a copy. The guidelines had been promulgated on April 23, 1971. It was now September 1971. The ICC must have regulations in place, I thought. We needed to get them.[6]

As to the environmental impact statement (EIS), the CEQ stated that it was to be prepared "[a]s early as possible and in all cases prior to agency decision." To meet these requirements, a "draft EIS" would be made available to the public for at least thirty days, during which time "comments" could be made. Perhaps even public hearings were required. "This is us," I said aloud, adding to my outline. The agency then reviews the "comments"; revises the EIS; issues it in final form; and, along with "other considerations of national policy," decides whether to proceed with the action. The process sounded logical. The question it posed was simple: Did the ICC go through it?[7]

I had already sought the advice of a recent graduate, now an attorney representing the government when it was sued for failure to comply with NEPA. "History and cases," I said. "That's all I want, and please keep it simple." The Supreme Court had not yet reviewed NEPA. Only the United States Court of Appeals for the District of Columbia had explored it fully.

"*Calvert Cliffs Coordinating Committee v. the Atomic Energy Commission.* Read it," he had said.[8]

I stood, stretched hard, took the decision in hand, got another cup of coffee from the pantry, and placed the decision on the counter within range of the morning light now coming through the pantry's window.

The opinion was written by Judge J. Skelly Wright. During the previous summer, Judge Wright had supported the *Washington Post* Company in the Pentagon Papers case, dissenting vigorously over the decision that delayed publication. He was from Louisiana; his decisions as a district court judge ordering racial integration were not warmly accepted. President John F. Kennedy had elevated him to the U.S. Court of Appeals for the District of Columbia. History and passion were in Judge Wright's opinions and, simultaneously, a thoroughness and care in his legal reasoning. He was willing to hold government to a high standard of responsibility.[9]

The Calvert Cliffs are located on the western shore of the Chesapeake Bay. In January 1968, Baltimore Gas and Electric (BG&E) proposed a nuclear power plant in the cliffs' vicinity and sought a construction permit from the Atomic Energy Commission (AEC). It was granted. The Calvert Cliffs Coordinating Committee, a group of citizens, complained to the AEC that it had taken too long to publish its regulations implementing NEPA (eleven months) and that BG&E should be required to show cause as to why its permit should not be suspended pending the preparation of an EIS. The commission denied the committee's request. The committee then sought judicial review.

"These cases," Judge Wright began, "are only the beginning of what promises to become a flood of new litigation—litigation seeking judicial assistance in protecting our natural environment. Several recently enacted statutes attest to the commitment of the government to control, at long last, the destructive engine of material 'progress.'"[10] Larouche was right. Other statutes may be relevant to us. Judge Wright continued, "But it remains to be seen whether the promise of this legislation will become a reality. Therein lies the judicial role. In these cases, we must for the first time interpret the broadest and perhaps most important of the recent statutes: the National Environmental Policy Act of 1969.... Our duty, in short, is to see that important legislative purposes are not lost or misdirected in the vast hallways of the federal bureaucracy."[11]

The court found shocking the AEC's eleven-month delay in preparing final regulations, which would not apply until fourteen months after NEPA's passage. The opinion cited other decisions I would have to read, and legal terms of art and history and policy that I did not know. One passage struck me with clarity: "NEPA," Judge Wright stated, "establishes environmental protection as an integral part of the Atomic Energy Commission's basic mandate.... Its responsibility is not simply to sit back, like an empire, and resolve adversary contentions at the hearing stage. Rather, it must itself take the initiative of considering environmental values at every distinctive and comprehensive stage of the process." In making this statement, Judge Wright summarized again the judicial duty. "[T]he courts," he said, "have become ... increasingly impatient with agencies which attempt to avoid ... their statutorily imposed role as protectors of public interest values beyond the narrow concerns of the industries being regulated."[12]

Before finishing *Calvert Cliffs*, I noted who had filed briefs in support of the AEC: Duke Power, Consolidated Edison, Indiana and Michigan Electric, and Portland General Electric. The last two were represented by Covington & Burling.[13] This was Banzhaf's point. Douglas had made it in *Points of Rebellion* (1970). Nader had too. The challenge is, as Judge Wright put it, to control the "destructive engine of material 'progress.'" Compliance with environmental regulations would not be determined in the quiet gentlemen's agreement characteristic of certain agency–industry relationships. There is now a third party present, like the Calvert Cliffs Coordinating Committee or the United States Court of Appeals.

I called George to tell him what I had learned.

"The ICC is the oldest regulatory agency," he said. "Neil, there are hundreds of court opinions dealing with freight rates. This will not be simple." George had an identifiable cadence in his voice—slightly worried, like when you're full with more information than you need, but you're not sure yet what you don't need and when you need it. To decide, you must be challenged, questioned, put to the choice. This whole undertaking might be hard, but George was smart and so, I thought, this would be fun, too.

"What is clear," George continued, "is that there are some powerful interests involved."

"I see it in *Calvert Cliffs*."

"Railroads, labor unions, truckers, corporate shippers. All kinds. Neil?"

"George."

"The influences here are substantial. I'm not sure yet what or who they are, but they're substantial."

"George. Can we do this?"

"Why not?" he said. I knew he was smiling. "In terms of law, the ICC has a lot of power." He explained the court cases that deferred to the ICC's rate decisions. He tried to explain how it works—how new freight rates go into effect, how shippers protest increases, and how rates can be "suspended." "The rates," he said, "must be just and reasonable. That's the way they describe it—'just and reasonable.'"

"Recently," George said, "the ICC granted a freight rate increase to the Railroads. I was told it's 8 to 15 percent on all commodities. That's the way they do it. My source is reliable."

"You got a source?" I asked.

"Yeah. I got a source. He won't get involved openly. We both know him."

"What ... ah ... what do we call him?"

"Let's call him the ICC Practitioner."

"We need to find out about the increase," I added.

"He says we're pounding our heads against the proverbial wall. Neil?"

"Yeah?"

"One thing he said."

"Yeah?"

"The Railroads are strong."

UNDERSTANDING THE TASK

Early afternoon. First-floor classroom in Stockton. All five of us. We were back into it: law school. That uneasy, distracted feeling that you are wasting time if you are not sitting, reading, studying, underlining, and memorizing. You had to get to the point quickly. George started. "The ICC granted a freight rate increase that occurred after the enactment of NEPA. Because, I presume, that the increase is—hold it—quote, 'a major federal action significantly affecting the quality of the human environment,' we need to get over to the ICC to find out if an impact statement was prepared."

"We all need to go?"

"Yeah. We do," I said. "There's no choice. We've only got two days to report to Banzhaf." Nobody liked the prospect. It was raining, intermittently but hard. For some reason, the temperature had dropped. We drove in two cars. I took John and George with me. George had the address: Constitution Avenue, directly across from the Smithsonian's Science and Technology building.

The three of us hurried across Constitution. The rain was falling again—slowly, large drops, and then a torrent. The sky was solid gray. Headlights on passing cars were turned on. The hood of my parka, yellow and blue and a size too large, covered my head easily.

We greeted the guard. None of us had any idea what exactly a rate increase proceeding entailed or where within the Commission its documents were located. The guard let us examine a directory. As we stood there, others were walking by—employees, I thought—each moving through the corridor, quickly and deliberately. Most seemed plain in appearance, sullen, not talking; they were all carrying folders, papers, or thick books. The corridor seemed long, the ceilings were high, and the interior was stone, granite maybe, brown or gray, solid and permanent. "The oldest regulatory agency," George had told me. It showed.

We decided on the docket room. The guard gave us a floor plan and circled the docket room. I turned to George. "This is a big place. One mistake, and we won't be found for days." On our way, we stopped briefly to look at a display of large photographs of each commissioner.

"George," I said, "come here. These are some of the people Nader talked about."

"You think they know we're here?" he asked.

"You think they care?"

"Where've you guys been?" It was Kenny, chiding us from inside the docket room's doorway. Once settled into individual desks, I asked the clerk if we could look at the files in the most recent rate proceedings. "*Ex Parte 265/267*," he said, pointing to the wall behind us. There, sitting on a shelf, were a dozen bound volumes, each about ten inches in width.

"Goddamn," I said to George. "Somewhere in there is supposed to be an environmental impact statement." None of us had ever seen one before. I know we all shared the same thought. If it was there, the EIS was identified plainly in LARGE CAPITAL LETTERS. We each took a volume. We sat near each other, trying to be methodical. The pace was slow. It was now late afternoon. The day was growing dark. The rain had stopped falling, and a heavy mist was readily visible through the windows, accentuated by bright overhead lights.

The first volume contained a petition filed on March 3, 1970, by the Eastern and Western Railroads requesting the Commission to "institute an investigation into the adequacy of freight rates ... of all railroads in the United States ... and to authorize a 6 percent increase in all freight rates." The Railroads wanted to put these new rates into effect with only one day's notice to shippers.[14] "How could that be right?" I said out loud but not directed to anyone. "One day?" The Commission instituted an investigation on March 6 and designated it *Ex Parte 265, Increased Freight Rates, 1970.*

"Ex Parte?" I whispered to George.

"Yeah. Only one party. The Railroads."

On the same day, the ICC also authorized the Eastern and the Western Railroads to collect the 6 percent increase on not less than seventy-five days' notice with one condition: If the ICC determined that 6 percent was too much, then the Railroads would have to refund the difference with 4 percent interest.[15] "What assumptions," I said. "The Railroads get the increase before the ICC determines it's justified. Then the shipper gets the difference plus interest."

"Yeah. Some or all of the rate is going to be approved, even before it's examined," George replied.

"You mean," Peter asked George, "if the ICC does nothing, the Railroads get everything they want?" George nodded. He looked at me to confirm my unease.

On March 12, the Railroads in the southern territory sought a similar 6 percent increase. This request was accompanied, as was the earlier one, by "verified statements"—detailed economic compilations to support the increase on particular commodities. We saw dozens of them—some were simple, a few pages in length; others were longer, with graphs, charts, and terminology that was alien to us. Within the eastern territory, almost all the verified statements came from the Penn Central. The ICC combined the petitions into *Ex Parte 265* and immediately granted the Southern Railroads the same conditional authority to collect the increase.[16]

Not content with waiting, most of the Eastern and the Western Railroads filed a request on September 1, 1970, to have the Commission "authorize a 15 percent increase in all freight rates and charges as increased pursuant to the petitions in *Ex Parte 265*." On September 2, the Commission instituted such an investigation and designated it *Ex Parte 267, Increased Freight Rates, 1971.*[17]

"Neil," George said. He looked at me and then at the others as we all stood or kneeled near George's desk. "This is a 21 percent increase in all freight rates on all commodities transported by rail. And it's all requested within, wait, a little more than six months."

"I don't get it," I said. "How could the increase in the cost to transport every single commodity be uniformly the same and be the same for each Railroad in the nation?"

George nodded; his lips tightened. "You get it."

The "Railroads" are members of the Association of American Railroads (AAR). Its office is located at 1720 L Street, within walking distance of GW. The Commission also received "protests." Kenny accumulated the names and addresses of those associations or industries that transported or used recyclable materials. They were potential allies.

Answering this question was not as simple as we thought. Paper waste, scrap iron and steel, and aluminum cans were common "recyclable" materials. We were finding others, such as petroleum waste and fly ash, that small, independent businesses were recycling—or trying to—in at least a marginally profitable manner. Two associations had filed lengthy protests: the Institute of Scrap Iron and Steel, at 1729 H Street (a two-block walk from the university), and the National Association of Secondary Material Industries (NASMI), in New York.[18] City, county, and state governments, including New York City's, also submitted protests. Here was the solid waste problem: the accumulation of tons of discarded paper, cans, and other waste that governments—particularly in the northeast—wanted to move by rail. It was unclear, however, where they wanted to move it.

"If the freight rate on iron ore is substantially less … I think I got this … than on scrap … ah, it's discriminatory. Listen." We once again drew near George. "Discrimination means, it seems, that two commodities, one a raw material and the other a recyclable one, compete in a manufacturing process to create some product."

"Okay. So—?"

"And the cost to transport the raw material is less and so it is used," George continued. "The scrap material is not used."

"Maybe."

"No. It makes sense. It's the same for paper." I could feel George's confidence as he said it. "You can use either scrap paper or wood. I don't know about fly ash. We need to know what it's used for."

"What the hell is it?" Kenny asked.

"Like soot." I said.

"Maybe it's economics. Like, one is easier to transport. Or maybe it's ownership. Who owns the iron ore and the timber?"

"We've got to talk to someone." Kenny agreed to call the Institute of Scrap Iron and Steel next week.

Within a few minutes, Kenny's hand went up. "I just found a … whoa, look at this. In the 'Protests.'" It was dated October 9, 1970, from the Executive Office of the President, Chairman, Council on Environmental Quality, to the chairman of the ICC, George M. Stafford.[19] We gathered around Kenny's desk. He pointed to the second paragraph:

Also important is the pending rate increase [*Ex Parte 267*] before the ICC. In general, across the board percentage increases only widen existing price biases against secondary materials. Also, those increases raise the costs of doing business, which can hinder the salvage and reclamation industry.

In light of the President's concern with environmental quality, the growing problems of solid waste and the importance of recycling to alleviating them, I would like to express the Council's hope that the Interstate Commerce Commission's actions on the key issue of scrap material transportation rates will be consistent with the Nation's environmental quality goals.

Sincerely,
Russell E. Train
Chairman

"I think we've got a project," John said. Kenny was pleased.

"Yeah, but look," I said. "This is dated a year ago. We need to know whether it made a difference."

The hour grew late. The working day was about to end. We had not found an impact statement, at least not one identified in LARGE CAPITAL LETTERS. John had left to locate someone in the general counsel's office who could answer our questions. He returned as we were finishing. Kenny and Peter had to leave. Both had an evening class. George and I followed John up some steps, down a long corridor, partially darkened, and past small offices, brightly lit. Their doors were opened. The offices were filled with folders, large charts, and old furniture, with people inside who were working intently behind stacks of large bound volumes of paper not unlike what I had seen on the shelves in the docket room. John had found the attorney responsible for compliance with NEPA, James Tao. We entered his office. It was very small. One of us stood. I had an awkward feeling because we were not exactly sure how to ask, "Did you comply with the law?"

Tao's manner was unassuming. The ICC had proposed regulations to comply with NEPA, he said, in a proceeding titled *Implementation of NEPA, Ex Parte 55*.[20] Those regulations were not final. An EIS had not been prepared in *Ex Parte 265/267*. Yes, the entire proceeding had begun after NEPA's passage. *Calvert Cliffs* is the important case, he said authoritatively. Before that, the Commission did not know what to do. He handed John the final decision in *Ex Parte 265/267* and the proposed NEPA regulations under consideration in *Ex Parte 55*.

It was a brief meeting. The three of us were relieved. In reviewing the multivolume record in *Ex Parte 265/267*, no one had missed the EIS. "They didn't do it," John said with a grin.

George stopped, raised his finger, and said, with a disdainful confidence, "They didn't do it!"

We walked down the corridor, at moments gleeful because we had a project but then silent because, as we talked, unease took hold. It was not definable. Our new questions were more troublesome, more cultural and political. "Why did the Commission wait almost two years to even propose regulations?" I asked.

"The CEQ guidelines were published in April 1971, *Calvert Cliffs* was decided in July, and it's now September," John posited.

"Why are they still waiting?" I said, almost to myself.

"This is no bureaucratic delay," George said. "Twenty-one percent increases, and it's not a major federal action?"

We started to walk faster, wanting, I think, to move away, to be alone.

"What about the CEQ? They raised the problem," John said.

"The CEQ is the president," George said, almost plaintively.

"I don't think that made a difference," I said. I felt my mind moving elsewhere, deeper, backward in time.

The corridor before me now seemed longer, harder to walk through; the atmosphere seemed staid, suspect, as if something else were there, pervasive, awesome, and watching. It was as if we knew something we were not supposed to know. We reached the first floor, turned the corner, and walked past the glass-protected photographs of the commissioners—people from another era, brooding, disdainful, like Daedelus, the protector of the maze. We reached Constitution Avenue and waited. The night had grown colder. The mist had turned to a heavy rain, and the government had unleashed its hordes. Cars were moving, honking, struggling. We crossed Constitution. My hood was firmly over my head. I was thinking about what we had learned, absorbed, what we had tried to ask and to understand, and what my own reading and experience told me.

John and George continued onward, probably doing what I was doing. I stopped, still thinking about the questions, and then I turned and glanced, my head moving upward so that I could see the building fully in a way I had not before. The Commission: historic, the nation's oldest regulator of the Harrimans, the Stanfords, and the Vanderbilts. Inside, the Railroads moved with effectiveness, flexing their power with cunning—according to their own rules—from office to office, malignant, alive, active, still shrouded in the self-righteousness of a different era, concealed, away from the public. They were still orchestrating. Nothing had changed. The Commission, I now thought, was their place. The Railroads—the nation's Railroads—they owned it.

The rain intensified. John, George, and I settled into my Volkswagen, now illegally parked behind the Smithsonian. There was no ticket.

"What do you think?" I asked.

"I don't know. I'm not sure. How could the Commission not— "

"No, it's not the Commission." I said directly. "I know the law applies to them, but it's not the Commission. It's the Railroads."

"I'm cold back here. Where's the heat?" John complained.

"Look at all this traffic. It's on, John."

"Look," George said. "You're right. Sometimes they don't comply with the law because it's complicated or because there's a disagreement. But here, NEPA is not complicated. The Commission has no regulations and no impact statement. They haven't done anything."

"The Railroads don't want anything done," John added.

"This is going to be a pain in the wazoo," George said.

"Well," John said distinctly, "we sure got a project."

"How many people," I said, "—and I don't mean state governments or shippers—how many people really understand what the ICC does? Other than the letter from CEQ, did you see anything from a citizens' group?" I looked out the rearview mirror, saw an opening, and moved gingerly up Constitution. "How's the heat, John?"

"Better."

"Forget about the environmental stuff," I said. "The increases were on fruits and vegetables. Where are the consumers? I started reading Nader's book. This is where the decision is made. You think your parents know how this works? I mean, who would care?"

"Precisely the point," George said plainly, finger pointing, his eyes straight ahead. "The Railroads." We fell silent.

"This *is* going to be a pain in the wazoo. Take me home, will ya," John said, more with determination than anxiety. I dropped into second gear. The Beetle flew in and around other cars, through rain and puddles and, with a smooth feeling and the power of a Mercedes, off Constitution and onto Virginia.

SCRAP

George and I entered the classroom and sat near John, Kenny, and Peter. Banzhaf came in with Meyers. The groups were asked to identify themselves and to explain their projects. The week was up. "All right, gentlemen. What are you going to do?" Banzhaf asked.

Hesitation. John, who rarely minced words, said audibly for all, "Proto should be the chairman."

"Fine," said Kenny and laughed. "Proto is the chairman."

George smiled. There was no debate. Banzhaf wanted an answer. I stood.

"Our project will involve the Interstate Commerce Commission," I said. "Under the National Environmental Policy Act, the ICC was to have filed an environmental impact statement before it approved a freight rate increase."

"Did they file an impact statement under NEPA?" *NĔPĂ*, he pronounced it. We were not alone.

"No, we don't think so," I said.

"Don't you know?" Banzhaf asked.

"No, they didn't file one. We checked with the Commission's lawyers."

"Are you ready to file?" he pressed.

"File? No."

"Do you have a name?"

"No."

"Then get one—and submit it and a brief description to Peter."

We walked out talking casually about a "name," an acronym to be exact. You had to start backward. A good name would be helpful in dealing with the media. Banzhaf insisted on creativity.

"Let me say right off, you don't recycle rubbers. Well, maybe *you* do— "

"We're going to call ourselves what, exactly?"

"Do you mean galoshes ... or condoms?"

"We need rates in it. *R*."

"How about DUMP?"

"I'm not going to be called DUMP."

"How about TRASH?"

"What's it stand for?"

"I don't know. The second word can be 'rates.' Maybe 'Train Rates Are Something.'"

"What's the 'something'"?

"He actually asked if we were ready to file," I said to George.

"He's nuts. Well, maybe not so nuts," he answered.

"How about SCRAP?" John suggested. "Students Challenging Rate—"

"Forget the 'Rate.' Students Challenging Regulatory Administrative ... Agency Practices."

"'Procedures' is better. It's more legal," I said.

"Legal? You gonna be a lawyer?" Kenny questioned, his face dead-panned.

"We don't have 'rates' in it."

"That's all right. We might want to challenge something else later."

"When later?" Kenny asked. "This kid is crazy. Tell him."

"SCRAP. Students Challenging Regulatory Agency Procedures," I said, smiling.

"Great," Peter said.

"We all agree?" I asked. There were a few nods—and a smile from George.

Peter remained in Stockton to attend a class. Kenny went to the library. John, George, and I continued to walk toward the University Center, on the corner of H and Twenty-first. I proposed coffee. We were in good spirits. We had a project.

"We could have shirts with 'SCRAP' on the front," John said. There was that grin.

"Red, white, and blue?" George asked.

"You think I'm kidding?" John asked.

"Maybe a little green," George posited.

"That sounds like a flag."

"We need music." I laughed the moment I said it. George grabbed my arm.

"Neil."

"George. I'm telling you. A theme song. We've got to have a theme song."

"Hey. How about a clenched fist on the shirts?" John asked, his grin firmly in place.

"What are you? Some bourgeois, revolutionary type? But listen. You can see it—the picture, us on top of this old wreck."

"With the theme song," I insisted.

"They'd put our pictures up at the Commission. We'd be dart practice."

"You think it's only for practice?" John said but with a kind of serious restraint.

The next day, I located Peter Meyers. He had occupied a portion of a large storage room on the fourth floor of Bacon. He seemed unfettered as I introduced myself and handed him a 5" × 7" card with the information Banzhaf required:

Purpose of the Project: an investigation of the nature of the railroad freight rate structure as it affected materials capable of being recycled, with the

possibility of either administrative action
in front of the Interstate Commerce Commission or the preparation of legislative
materials to the Congress.

Chairman: Neil Proto
Members: George Biondi, John Larouche,
Ken Perlman, Peter Ressler
Name: SCRAP (Students Challenging
Regulatory Agency Procedures)

Meyers smiled, read it, and smiled
again.
"Anything else?" I asked.
"No, this is okay."
I turned and hurried over to Stockton.
I was late for Mass Communications Law.

John Eric Larouche.
John Eric Larouche Collection.

5

THE PARTICIPANTS, FALL 1971

A strategy. "We'll meet at least once a week in an empty classroom or at my place," I said. "Written minutes have to be taken." George and Kenny agreed to do it. "Okay. Let's talk about what to do and when to do it."

"This is going to last a semester, which ends in mid-January, and we've got other courses," Peter said without retort.

"So, file our petition in, say, the third week of December. That allows the Commission time to respond. Is that what you're—?"

"We don't know the rules yet," John said.

"I'm working on that," George said.

"So, let's start with what we're going to request, and we'll come back to when and how," I said.

"The easiest," Peter suggested, "if we got this right, is to request compliance with NEPA in all future freight rate increases. A straightforward—"

"It doesn't do anything," George said. "It's not related to how they operate. They do 'rate proceedings.'" George used his fingers to form quotation marks. "We need to affect them where it makes a difference."

"Do we wait for a new one?" Peter asked. "It may not come—"

"In the semester? We can't risk that," I explained.

"Then, how about we submit comments in *Ex Parte 55*, the separate proceeding. The NEPA regs?" Peter posited, wanting to explore all the possible avenues for action.

"Unwise," George said.

"It's there? This *Ex Parte 55*. And not finished yet."

"The Commission doesn't need enlightenment from us to do what it should have done long ago."

"You're getting testy already," Kenny said, calmly.

"*Ex Parte 55* is a sideshow. It'll go on forever," John added.

"We aren't doing that." George said, irritated.

"Not a question," I said softly. "Let's focus on *265/267*. The Commission didn't ignore NEPA. It provided what it characterized as 'hold-downs' on the rates on recyclable materials."[1]

George took over, speaking carefully, with notes and documents in hand. "Well into the decision," he said, "the Commission first examined waste sulfide. It's extracted from petroleum refinery waste by the Merichem Company of Houston. It's used in paper manufacturing. Because it's shipped in a diluted form—not less than 80 percent water—in tank cars, its cost in the marketplace is strongly affected by the rates. Merichem sells only the 'usable' waste, not the full tank car."

"The rest is water? I mean dirty water?" Peter asked, seeking clarity.

"Yep," George said. "Merichem argued," he explained (decision in hand and ready to access for relevant quotes), "that it had 'established a market for refinery wastes' that otherwise 'were released into watersheds causing pollution of water resources.' The paper industry has a choice. Use salt cake or caustic soda, which is shipped via rail but as 98 to 100 percent usable material, or use Merichem's 'recyclable' waste sulfide.[2] Merichem's problem?" George posited, "The same increase on each commodity has a much greater negative impact on waste sulfide."[3]

"Now. The Railroads," I said.

"This could not be better," George said assuringly. "The Railroads argued that Merichem wants to shift the burden. The Commission agreed. It did 'not believe that the transportation industry should be called upon to support the control of pollution created by another industry.'[4] George continued, "Nonferrous metal, wastepaper, rags, and textile waste. These were represented by NASMI. 'Their principal contention,' the Commission says"—George using his fingers again for the quote marks— "'is that the recovery and recycling of these materials serves a public and environmental function ... the collection of solid industrial scrap material.' The proposed rate increases, they say, 'will make the reprocessing operation uneconomical or shrink the area from which these materials may be obtained.'"[5]

"The Railroads?" Kenny asked.

"No merit in that," George answered.

"No surprise there," Peter interrupted. George nodded in agreement.

"Fly ash," George continued. "Produced by industrial and electric generating plants that burn coal. It's 'caught' in the stack and recovered 'in order to avoid air pollution.'"[6]

"We're not calling it soot anymore?" Kenny asked.

"No," I said, smiling, my chairman's finger raised. "From now on, 'fly ash.'"

"It's used in making concrete. For this use, it competes with shale and volcanic ash. The Chicago Fly Ash Company said that 'a 15 percent increase in rates will result in termination of its contracts.'"[7] George looked up; he nodded his head slightly. "Finally. Iron and steel scrap. The Institute of Scrap Iron and Steel. Quote: 'Iron and steel scrap is extremely sensitive to changes in freight rates.' The Commission and the Railroads. No sympathy. Quote: '[T]here is little, if any, correlation between rail freight rates and the market for iron and steel scrap. We are not persuaded that rail freight rates on scrap have any material impact on the decisions which result in removal of wrecked automobiles and other scrap metals pursuant to antipollution measures.'"[8]

"New York City and the CEQ disagree," Kenny said. "We got that."

"This will make us feel better. The Commission turns to an analysis of, quote, 'the National Environmental Policy Act of 1968.'"[9]

"They didn't get the date right. And Banzhaf couldn't even pronounce it."

"You think this law exists?" John asked.

"Well, Proto says so," Kenny added.

George raised a couple of fingers to gain attention. "Quote: 'Our attention has been called to the possibility that increases in freight rates … may tend to restrict the movement of scrap … and thus, indirectly, detract from efforts being made to gather and recycle such materials.' That argument was opposed by the Department of Transportation."[10]

"DOT," I said, matter-of-factly. "It's with the Railroads."

"The Commission made no reference to the CEQ," George added.

"Either the president carried no weight, or the CEQ's position carried no weight."

"Except with us," I said.

"Instead," George continued, "the Commission's 'NEPA' analysis gets us into these financial formulas premised on economic assumptions not in the decision." George looked directly at me as if there was no one else in the room. "It's the freight rates. We need to understand freight rates." His statement hung for a moment.

"Yeah," I nodded, with unease. "I see that."

"The Commission granted the Railroads the full 6 percent in *Ex Parte 265*, 15 percent in *Ex Parte 267*. Without explanation, it limited the increases on recyclable materials. 'Hold-downs.' On fly ash—not to exceed 11 percent. Iron and steel scrap—not to exceed 11 percent. Petroleum waste—not to exceed 8 percent. Nonferrous and alloy scrap, and textile and paper scrap—not to exceed 11 percent."[11]

"Did they make a difference? To the rate discrimination?" Peter asked.

"I don't know," George said. "We need to find out."

"From someone who really knows," I said.

"I'm doing that," Kenny said. "Next week."

"Well, we know this. Only two pages were devoted to NEPA."

"Not enough?"

"No, it can't be," I said.

"Well, I've got to get to class."

"Me too."

"Hold on," John said. "We still need to know the participants—who has an economic and political stake in freight rates and recycling."

"We're already getting some of that," Peter said.

"And," I added, "how they relate to us. Can they be helpful?" I brought the discussion to a close. "The most difficult problem will be getting the truth."

"Who's telling it?" Kenny asked.

"Yep. Who's telling it."

THE SCRAP DEALERS

Kenny Perlman was in line for the Order of the Coif. His academic priorities were unequivocal—an A in everything. I was never certain what really engaged him or if being "engaged," even by the prospect of drafting contracts or commercial paper, was at all relevant to his reason for being in law school. He wanted his assignments to be precise, manageable in effort, and definable in time. Nothing cosmic, fuzzy, or potentially uncertain in outcome. Such a role was essential. The mechanical tasks alone—gathering information, contacting interested parties, arranging meetings, locating cases—were fundamental to our purpose: to move responsibly into the real world of law, money, and other people's livelihoods and political agendas.

Kenny contacted the Institute of Scrap Iron and Steel and spoke to its transportation consultant, Dr. Herschel Cutler. Dr. Cutler was teaching at American University that day but was willing to return to his office between classes. George and I walked to the Institute together from Rice Hall. It was a mild day as we crossed Pennsylvania Avenue at the corner of Nineteeth Street. It was the beginning of fall 1971—the third week of September. A slight breeze, an occasional leaf showing some sign of color, and—albeit barely noticeable—a decline in the humidity. We reached H Street where it intersected with Pennsylvania and turned right. The street was dotted with small shops and stores, shabby, unkempt, uninviting, certainly not reflective of the fact that the president of the United States lived a few blocks away. When we reached H and Eighteenth Street, a transformation occurred. It was in the architecture and the ambience: more serious and urbane; a bookstore, intimate, sophisticated in its reputation; office buildings, finely built, with engraved designs, subtle colors, distinctive from one another; and people, mostly well-attired, walking, carrying bundles, and talking, probably about business, government, money, and power. For a moment, the setting reminded me of Boston—Boylston or Newberry Street— where the retail and commercial boutiques, architecture, and colors seemed to create their own life and definition of urban living. We arrived in time to meet John. He was leaning against the rose-hued, smoothly honed granite facade that surrounded the front doorway, itself distinctive but nicely so against the grayish stone that enclosed the entire building. We exchanged greetings, followed the directory, and took the elevator to the second floor. Kenny and Peter already were seated in a conference room with Dr. Cutler. Peter had a tie on. George, John, and I introduced ourselves.

I briefly explained the course, explained the name and purpose of the group, and ended with a plea to "tell us whatever you can about freight rates as they affect scrap iron and steel—and presume, with some degree of safety, that we know nothing at all about it." I did not tell him we intended to file a petition with the Commission.

Cutler appeared to be in his early forties. He wore black, horn-rimmed glasses; had dark hair, black or deep brown; and was slightly balding. He was dressed neatly, with a wide tie, in the fashion of the day. He was articulate and pedagogical in temperament, more so as he spoke. "The Institute of Scrap Iron and Steel is composed of approximately 1,300 member firms," he said. "Many operate the traditional junkyard. They collect discarded iron and steel scrap, cars, appliances, tools, and machinery; process it by removing its non-metal impurities, condensing or packing it; and then sell it. Many are located in the northeast and midwest, close to concentrated urban areas."

Cutler paused and reached for, but didn't open, a set of booklets nearby, as he explained that the steel industry is the primary user of the materials sold by the Institute's membership. He distributed the draft of a study prepared by Battelle Laboratories. He asked us to turn to the summary. He read or paraphrased it aloud, pronouncing each word with care, wanting to be certain we understood. Then he got to it: "In making steel, the producer requires the element iron. Iron is obtained both in virgin natural resources, iron ore, and recycled materials, or ferrous scrap. Steel production can be looked upon as a set of inputs into a 'black box' representing the steel-making processes." Cutler looked up at us. I looked around the room. We were still with him. He looked down and began to read: "'One, scrap markets are retarded because of transport rates which encourage the usage of iron ore; two, iron ore—a limited natural resource—is being exploited when it can be conserved; and three, scrap iron that should be recycled is unable to move, and unnecessarily accumulates as solid metallic waste.'"[12]

He put the draft study aside. The existing freight rate, he said, was approximately $4.12 per ton. It cost $1.64 per ton to move iron ore, more than two and a half times lower than scrap. A steel company would choose iron ore. "Discriminatory transportation," he said, and rested.[13] My thought was unequivocally clear. Here we were at the Institute that had spent who knows how much on this study just to examine one rate. And to understand it, we needed to understand at least four corporate interests: steel, railroads, scrap dealers, and iron ore companies. We also had to learn what happened inside that "black box." Cutler welcomed questions.

"The ICC granted the railroads 'hold-downs,'" George said. "The increase on scrap was 6 percent in *Ex Parte 265* and 11 percent in *Ex Parte 267*. This is less than the 21 percent increase on iron ore. Was that helpful?"

"No," Cutler said, smiling. A 17 percent increase on the $4.12 equals about 70 cents, he explained. A 20 percent increase on the $1.64 that it costs to transport iron ore equals only about 32 cents. Thus, the difference increased.

I moved in quickly. "Why isn't a different form of transportation used by scrap dealers, like trucks?" Cutler's tone remained direct. He seemed to enjoy this. Steel companies were constructed with rail lines into their plants, he explained. They receive the scrap in quantity and hold it until they're ready. The Railroads let the cars remain.

"Is iron ore easier to transport?" John asked. Cutler seemed uneasy. His lip curled, but the teacher in him took hold.

"Yes, in certain ways," he said. It's a dense material. It moves from a mining operation in large quantities. It can be loaded and unloaded with greater ease. Scrap yards are located in more places, and it's often difficult to project exactly how much will be available. And there's another problem. Cutler grew serious. Scrap moves in an all-purpose car called a gondola. It's like a boxcar without the roof. We compete with others for it, and the Railroads don't always have them.

"You mean they deliberately withhold them?" Kenny asked.

Cutler smiled, as if to himself. "Ask them."

"What sort of role do the steel companies play?" I asked. Cutler explained that the industry has old furnaces that burn iron ore. They also generate home scrap, which makes them a supplier of scrap.

"NASMI?" George asked, for clarification.

Our interests are not the same, he said.

I stuck with the same theme. "The ICC's decision said that a substantial amount of ore is transported from the Lake Superior area by the Duluth, Missabe, and Iron Range Railway. A wholly owned subsidiary of U.S. Steel?"[14]

Cutler looked at his watch. "That's a good question," he suggested. "You gentlemen are getting to the heart of this quicker than you might think." He had a class to teach and excused himself. We stood, shook his hand, and thanked him for his help.

We walked into the corridor. I pushed the button for the elevator. We waited alone. "I wonder how many other institutes there are in this building," I said. Silence.

Perlman started the dialogue. "It seems as if we want to take the same position these guys take."

"Bull," Larouche responded and grinned.

"It isn't bull," Perlman said. "If we complain that the rates discourage the movement of scrap and the ICC buys our argument, then the rates change. If that happens, the shippers of scrap benefit."

"Bull," Larouche repeated. I didn't detect a grin.

"Hey, John," Kenny said. "You know any other words?"

"Our concern is not with who profits. All we care about is that the environment is protected, that iron ore is not extracted and that scrap—"

"Swell. But somebody benefits. Financially. I don't care whether it's railroads or scrap shippers or steel companies."

"It's not important."

"It is important. We damn well better be aware of whose toes we're stepping on."

"The steel industry for sure."

"Where the hell is the elevator?" I said, pushing the button again. We were still alone but more spread out, moving into corners, not like prize fighters but like lawyers, who create distance to bring attention to their argument. "Look. Maybe you're both right," I argued. "We're not representing anyone's interest. We sure aren't shippers of scrap."

"No, we want to stay somewhere above everyone. The good guys."

"Careful of *that* bull."

"No. He's right. We can't find ourselves connected with anyone," I said.

"Well, we don't have to worry about, ah, you know, anyone claiming we represent the Railroads," George added, in a conciliatory tone.

"Maybe we'll get bribed," Peter postured, hand out.

"Great. We're worth about a dollar and a quarter. No. Two dollars. You've got a tie on."

"Screw you. Just because you guys always look like vagrants," Peter responded.

"Vagrants? You know what these blue jeans cost?" Kenny retorted.

The elevator arrived. We boarded, fell into silence, exited in the lobby, and made our way out the front door. It was about 6:30 p.m. The rush hour traffic was still active. The weather had remained mild.

"When do the clocks change?" someone asked.

Peter had a date ("That's why I wore the tie") and had brought his car. It was parked nearby. Kenny and John were headed for Stockton. The four of us walked toward the university.

"Well, how much do we have to understand?" George asked.

"Enough," I said.

"What's that mean?" John interjected quickly.

"Enough to explain it to the ICC," I added.

"You mean so we don't sound like dummies?"

"So we don't sound like raving good guys. We have to know what we're talking about. Otherwise, the Railroads will make us look like jerks." We crossed Pennsylvania.

"You know, we're only students," Kenny said.

"What does that mean?" John asked.

"It means we're not metallurgists or ecologists or whatever the heck— "

"And so?" John interrupted.

"We can't be expected to deal with this stuff in some super-sophisticated way," Kenny said evenly.

"Expected by who?"

"I don't know who. All I'm saying is that we can learn only so much."

"Look, he's right" I said. "We need to have a working knowledge of freight rates. We're going to create a forum for these people and get the Commission to look at it in light of the environmental problem."

"Just the environmental problem. The economics will drive us crazy."

"You can't avoid the economics," George said sternly.

"Damn. You're a pain in the wazoo with this ah—"

"I'm telling you, the bottom line for all these guys is money," said George.

"Look. We need to be smart about our time—"

"Not just smart. Banzhaf would say—"

"Cunning."

"We want the Commission to prepare an impact statement."

"That's what *you* want. *I* want a good grade."

We reached the campus. "Let's be sure we all read the stuff Cutler gave us. We'll talk." Kenny and John headed for Stockton while George and I walked to Calhoun. His wife, Kathy, had come home from work. She was sitting on the front steps.

"George, where have you been?" She said it with slight agitation in her tone, actually with a rough caring, the way Alice would say it to Ralph.

"Where have I been? Well, Neil. Tell her where I've been."

"We were at the Institute of Scrap Iron and Steel," I said.

"In this SCRAP again?" She was still looking at George.

"Ah, yeah," George said, in a somewhat diminutive tone, his head down slightly. I stood plaintively.

"Well," Kathy stated, "while you were off gallivanting, George old boy, three residents knocked on the door and wanted their rooms changed, and one of the basketball players got in a fight with somebody. And I have two phone messages here for you. Rice Hall called, and they want an updated roster. And there's another meeting tomorrow, something about co-ed dorms. The other call was from one of your old flames. But I don't think she'll call back."

"No, which one?" He smiled. Their greeting was over.

Kathy turned toward me. "Neil, do you want to stay for dinner?"

"No, thanks. I have work to do. I'm doing a paper on children and television violence, and—"

"Is this one you're taking with George?" she asked.

"Yeah."

"I'm sure you'll enjoy it more than this SCRAP stuff," George said in a somber tone. As he did, two boys came out the front door, one carrying books, the other in shorts carrying a basketball. Both said hello to George. He looked at me. His eyes rolled. We both laughed.

"See you tomorrow. Good night, Kathy."

"Good night," she said. "And come for dinner sometime—soon."

I began the two-block walk back to Crawford, down Twenty-first, toward H, past the University Center on my right. Students were standing in groups, most wearing jeans and short-sleeved shirts; the women, at least a few, were in miniskirts.

"Hi."

"Hi." I raised my index finger.

"The car next to the dorm?"

"Of course. I remember."

"I'm Caroline Bentley. I'm parked there again." There was a grace in her manner, like ballet lessons or etiquette class or a mother who instilled both. But it wasn't revered.

"It's okay. A public alleyway." She smiled, knowing, I thought, that one of us would engage the other. "You want to walk for a bit?" I asked.

"Sure. I have time."

Some students walked between and around us—quiet, carrying books. One had a radio (the Stones again, a remnant of "Satisfaction"), and two others walked beside bicycles with books held atop the seats.

"Undergraduate?"

"A senior."

"Where you from?"

"Here. For now, with my parents. In Georgetown."

"Hmm. Nice area. Originally from here?"

"I am."

"Not many of those."

"My father is from Louisiana. He's a lawyer."

"I see. Both parents from Louisiana?"

"No. My mother's from Boston. And you? Not the dorm, I hope?"

"No. Connecticut. New Haven."

"Yale?"

"No. I went to a state college and then here for grad school before law. I'm a law student. Okay. You got that." As we reached H, I saw Jeff Gocke—my administrative assistant—his face flushed, waving deliberately for me from the front door of Crawford Hall. "Goodbye," I said. "I need to get back." I knew, as fall approached, that SCRAP was going to consume time disproportionate to other courses. So, too, might other things.

ANOTHER SCRAP DEALER

Our first contact with the National Association of Secondary Material Industries (NASMI) was by telephone with its transportation director, John Vaccaro. He immediately forwarded to George books, pamphlets, position papers, testimony, and economic studies. NASMI, we learned, was composed of 700 corporations, including many of the nation's steel, textile, paper, rubber, and plastics companies. Its Washington legal counsel was Smathers and Merrigan, located at 888 Seventeenth Street, about two blocks from the university.[15] The firm was housed in a nondescript building—narrow and tall, its external facade largely glass and chrome. It could be anywhere. Smathers was the former Senator from Florida: George A. Smathers. The other partner, Edward Merrigan, represented NASMI. George arranged the meeting with Vaccaro and Merrigan. He and I walked over carrying and drinking coffee.

"The Washington power establishment," I posited.

"Only one thing to keep in mind. Caution."

I described our purpose but not our intention to file a petition. Both Merrigan and Vacarro could see where we were moving: into an adversarial relationship with the Railroads. They were not pleased. He understood our intention, Vaccaro said, as if preparing to withdraw candy from a child. We, too, felt some discomfort. I posed the first question, saying more than I intended: "Many steel companies are members of NASMI. They support recycling, certainly of internally generated scrap. Simultaneously, however, they oppose rate increases on the transportation of iron ore. Why is that?"

Vaccaro was direct and hard in response. NASMI intended to solve the freight rate problem through legislation—by going to Congress. The Commission, he said, was not the place to go. He was adamant about it. Any pretense at cordiality was gone.

We left the meeting, disquieted but not discouraged. George and I knew what we wanted to do. On the elevator down, he looked at me plaintively: "I don't know if we sounded like, ah, 'only students' in there." His smile broke through.

THE COMMISSION

The ICC was not familiar to any of us. We knew it regulated railroads, pipelines and motor carriers. We acquired the knowledge we needed in four ways: reading history, reading cases, reading Nader, and sharing personal experiences.

Our intuitive apprehension was confirmed immediately. "The main source of railroad abuses and difficulties in the late nineteenth century was their freight rates."[16] During the 1860s, agrarian interests forced the establishment of commissions to regulate rates in Illinois, Iowa, Michigan, and Wisconsin. Agitation came for another reason: the insidious practice of "rebates" between the Railroads and large industry. Most notorious was John D. Rockefeller.[17] But in 1886, the Supreme Court of the United States, in *Wabash, St. Louis & Pacific Railway Co. v. Illinois*, concluded that because the freight was transported beyond the borders of Illinois, the legislature was without power to regulate such "interstate commerce."[18] William Jennings Bryan and later Theodore Roosevelt elevated the dispute into the platform of the Populist Party and national politics.[19]

Within months of the decision in *Wabash*, Congress passed an "Act to Regulate Commerce" between the states. It established the Interstate Commerce Commission.[20] A freight rate set by the Railroads must be "reasonable and just." Optimism was high.[21] The Railroads challenged the act. They found a receptive forum in the Supreme Court, which held that the Commission could not determine whether freight rates were "reasonable and just." Only the Railroads could do that.[22] They had regained the power. Conditions got worse. Financial control of the Railroads tightened to only a few people. Those people siphoned money for other ventures. E. H. Harriman, George J. Gould, and James Stillman (heads of the National City Bank of New York) "were top men in a syndicate which financially ravished the Chicago and Alton [Railroad] between 1898 and 1905. The once well-run road was ruined." William H. Moore of Chicago "was just as ruthless when his syndicate looted the Rock Island [Railway] in the same years." I also learned more about my hometown. "[T]he financial ruin [that J. P. Morgan Sr.] brought to the New York, New Haven, and Hartford Railroad between 1903 and 1913 was worthy of a Gould or a Moore."[23]

I decided one afternoon, as I sat in the law school library, to locate a congressional hearing or floor debate on Morgan and the New Haven. I found a speech by Senator Robert M. LaFollette of Wisconsin given in 1910 and a reference to Louis Brandeis years before he was appointed to the Supreme Court.[24] I made my way to the university's main library. I had time for only a quick scan of the stacks, enough to get a feeling for what Brandeis thought about the New Haven.

"Oh, hi." Kathleen McKeeley was seated alone, books and punched cards on the table in orderly piles. "Neil?"

"Right. You staying out of trouble?"

"Trying. That was a hard day. I had been down near the Ellipse with friends and then, well— "

"This looks serious."

"Computer stuff. It's a grad course. Statistical analysis."

"Shhh!" said a librarian, albeit with a smile. I nodded compliance.

"I've got to get a book," I said.

"I had the impression you were a—"

"Shhh!" the librarian repeated.

"A law student?" I asked. She nodded and smiled. "Good to see you again," I whispered, feeling immediately as if I were more detached than I wanted to be.

I located *Brandeis: A Free Man's Life* by Alpheus Thomas Mason (1946). I turned to the chapter titled "The New Haven Railway: An Empire Crumbles." Brandeis commented in 1913: The "decline of the New Haven ... teaches a lesson of national importance.... There are thousands of men in America who could have performed for the New Haven stockholders ... better than did Mr. Morgan ... [and] Mr. Rockefeller[.]"[25] This admonition did not impede Morgan or his successors. The New Haven merged with other railroads to become the Penn Central. Its fate probably was preordained. It later went bankrupt.[26]

In 1910, Congress again amended the Interstate Commerce Act to give the rate approval authority back to the Commission.[27] Congress wanted the last word. Embedded in the language was the thorniest legal concept we had confronted: the "suspension stage." The Supreme Court of the United States defined it in 1963.

THE SUPREME COURT

While the Commission is investigating whether a proposed increase is reasonable and just, it retains "primary jurisdiction." During the investigation, those proposed rates are "suspended," although they can be collected by the Railroad. Here was the irony. A court could not question whether the rate increase—even if being collected—was unreasonable and unjust on the shipper who challenged it. The shipper's remedy: a refund at some later date. A court could neither examine the harm caused to the shipper by the new rate nor stop its effect. This expansive role for the Commission and diminished role for the judiciary was confirmed in 1963 by the Supreme Court in *Arrow Transportation Co. v. Southern Railway Co.* George read it first. "It's as important to us as *Calvert Cliffs*," he said.[28]

The Southern Railway had petitioned the ICC for "authority to *reduce* rates on the shipment of grain" but the reduction applied "only to multi-car shipments from certain Mississippi and Ohio River ports." Arrow Transportation, a barge line, was a competitor for shipping the same grain. Arrow complained that the reduced rates were intended to drive it out of business. This complaint was supported by Guntersville, Alabama, which was served by Arrow. The Commission suspended "the effectiveness of the rates" but did not reach a decision. Although the investigation continued, the rates went into effect.[29]

Arrow and Guntersville filed suit in the District Court for the Northern District of Alabama. They contended that "the proposed new rail rates ... threaten to force Arrow out of business." The district court agreed: "[T]here is grave danger that irreparable injury, loss, or damage may be inflicted on [Arrow and others]." Nonetheless, the court believed itself powerless. Congress "rested exclusive power in the Commission to suspend a change of rate for a limited time and thereby precluded District Court jurisdiction to grant injunctive relief."[30] The Court of Appeals for the Fifth Circuit in New Orleans affirmed the district court decision. The Supreme Court agreed.[31]

The decision was written by Justice William J. Brennan Jr. His reasoning: before Congress's grant to the Commission of the "suspension power" in 1910, a court's power to enjoin rates reached "diverse results," sometimes with respect to the same rates in different parts of the nation. There was a "disparity of treatment as between different shippers, carriers, and sections of the country, causing in turn 'discrimination and hardship to the general public.'" The harmful effect on other modes of transportation such as barges or on the municipality they served had not been explicitly addressed by Congress. The Southern Railway prevailed.[32]

Three Justices dissented: Chief Justice Earl Warren and Justices Thomas Clark and Hugo Black. "The Court," those dissenters stated, "by its action today sounds the death knell for barge transportation on the Tennessee River. The war of extermination between the railroads and the barge lines began years ago ... affected by [the railroads] cutting rates where the [barge] competition existed, to whatever extent was necessary to paralyze it, at the same time maintaining rates at a very high level elsewhere."[33]

Three additional facts struck me. None of the dissenting justices were still on the Court. Justice Brennan was still there. The attorney representing the Southern Railway was Dean Acheson, the former secretary of state under President Harry S. Truman. Acheson was a partner at Covington & Burling. And the Commissioners, we believed, knew, understood perfectly, and exercised unabashedly the full strength of their power and—as we were coming to recognize—the full strength of the power necessary to protect the Railroads.[34]

THE RAILROADS

Ralph Nader characterized the Association of American Railroads (AAR) as "incredibly powerful."[35] In 1971, its seventy members operated 99 percent of the trackage, employed 98 percent of the workers, and produced 98.5 percent of the revenues of all the nation's Railroads. The AAR's general counsel was Edward A. Kaier.[36] In September and October of 1971, four northeast Railroads—the Boston and Maine, the Central of New Jersey, the Lehigh Valley, and the Penn Central—were in reorganization. Kaier was everywhere.[37]

The *Washington Evening Star* and the *Washington Post* devoted considerable attention to the Penn Central. We all had ridden the Penn Central and, for me, it was the mover of freight and passengers in and out of Connecticut. I had seen the deterioration of railroad rights of way; bridges; a splendid, architecturally renowned railroad station; and passenger service. With the decline in the freight service came more trucks onto Connecticut's highways and into its municipalities and neighborhoods—accompanied by air pollution, decreased safety, unprecedented noise, and increased state expenditures for maintenance and repairs. The reason also was now plainly unveiled. The Penn Central's directors had siphoned millions in railroad revenue for investment in executive jets, amusement parks, and real estate ventures.

The Railroads also sponsored a highly publicized effort known as "America's Sound Transportation Review Organization." Its television commercials featured former astronaut Wally Schirra. "Who needs America's Railroads?" he asked, as a passenger train whizzed by, the precise service that the Penn Central had degraded deliberately.[38]

The AAR's statistical representation of the financial condition of the "nation's Railroads" always included the Penn Central's disastrous account ledger. The effect was a cloak over the fact that some Railroads did not need increases—or did not need them on particular commodities. It hid something else: the freedom of Railroad executives to manipulate shippers and to insist on government support. The Railroads also owned hundreds of millions of tons of iron ore and millions of square miles of virgin timber. Through 1970, the Union Pacific and the Northern Pacific were mining iron ore and harvesting timber on approximately 18 million acres of their own lands. A harder question was posed by the Duluth, Missabe, and Iron Range. We had raised the same question with Dr. Cutler. The Duluth possessed a virtual monopoly on the transportation of iron ore in the Great Lakes region. U.S. Steel was not going to permit a wholly owned subsidiary to implement a freight rate policy that was financially harmful to its ownership of iron ore mines on one end and steel mills on the other.[39]

Those facts contained complexities that brought us back to the same reality: not to get sidetracked while enchanted by questions not essential to our purpose. The purpose of SCRAP was to formulate the questions reasonably and to have the Commission provide the answer in an EIS. That, we now believed, was its obligation under NEPA. The threat to that discipline was often unexpected in origin.

It was October—the third week—in the evening. I took a shower and changed into corduroys and a long-sleeved cotton shirt. I gathered a yellow legal pad and pencil, plus copies of a few Supreme Court decisions, and sat—with comfort and warmth—in the corner of the sofa in my apartment. Jeff Gocke was on duty, probably in the office filling out a damage report. I had left him less than an hour ago. Because the main dormitory phone rang in my apartment too—it sat on an end table, along with a lamp, to my left—Jeff and I picked up the receiver within moments of one another.

"Crawford Hall," he said.

"Jeff?" George asked.

"Yeah, George. How are you?"

"Fine, fine. Things all right there?"

"Sure. You want to talk to the head cheese?"

"Yeah, is he in?"

"Hold on. I'll buzz him."

"The head cheese?" I said. "George, you see what I have to go through."

"You think you're alone?" George responded.

"Before I forget," Jeff said. "Everything is cleaned up. Buzz me when you want to check for damage."

I thanked Jeff and greeted George. "What's your story?"

"Well, you got a few minutes?"

"Sure," I said.

"I want you to listen to something."

"Yeah, go ahead."

"I'm talking to a friend of mine last week, telling him about Smathers, you know, that his firm represents NASMI. He said that he just read about

Smathers somewhere. Well, today I get a package from this guy with a whole copy of the October 12 *Newsday*, which I'm looking at right now. Are you sitting down?"[40]

"Yeah."

"There's a front-page article on George Smathers. There is this special report—five or six pages long. It says he is the attorney for ... are you ready for this? ... the Association of American Railroads."

"Read it to me." I sat back and moved downward, my body settling deeper into the couch, my neck resting firmly on the cushion behind me. I felt my eyes shut gently, and with the fingers of my left hand I began rubbing my forehead and temples and then my face—hard. There always seemed to be more, I thought—a veiled relationship or an unsuspected turn of events. It was only October.

George read, "'And when he left the Senate and opened his Washington law firm Smathers and Merrigan,' the article says, 'one of the first organizations to bring him its business was the Association of American Railroads. Among Smathers's activities for that group was the development of the current public relations campaign that features former astronaut Walter Schirra stumping for the railroads, in television spots.' Neil, you know what I'm telling you?"[41]

"Yeah, you're telling me, how can the same law firm represent two clients that are opposed to each other? The answer is, 'I don't know how.'"

"You mean, you don't know how they do it ethically. I've seen the Schirra commercials. Something about who needs America's Railroads."

"I don't know who needs them." Neither of us laughed. We both knew where this was going. "All right," I said. "So. What you're telling me is that the same law firm, in fact the two named partners, represent adversaries. At least, in front of the ICC they're adversaries."

"Yep, that's what I'm telling you," George said, with simple clarity and an uneasy tone.

"And you're saying that's unethical."

"Well, I'm saying it's wrong. It's wrong as—"

"Are you saying it's unethical?" I pressed.

"Yeah, I'm saying it's unethical. I don't have the American Bar Association's *Canons of Ethics* in front of me, but doesn't it sound bad?"

"George. It sounds bad. I don't know. You know, this is Washington. You've been here as long as I have. Does this stuff surprise you anymore? I don't mean does it make you angry, or do you think it's wrong. I know that. But does it really surprise you?"

"No, I guess not."

"What do you want to do?" I sat up. I could feel the anger. I knew we shared the thought that we'd have to make another choice.

"I don't know," he said.

"What else is in the article?" I asked.

"Stuff about land deals with Bebe Rebozo and meetings with Nixon." Silence.[42]

"So. George. What do you want to do?" We agreed to tell the members of the group. We were uncertain whether anyone else would care. "Look," I said. "There were questions we could have asked Cutler, about why his attorney never said anything about NEPA, or why didn't they bring a lawsuit? That kind of stuff. Maybe they don't want to offend anybody. Maybe the Railroads get vindictive. You know, 'We don't have any gondola cars for you just now—and while you wait, the price of scrap drops.'"

"Maybe they've got bad lawyers."

"Or maybe they've got real smart lawyers." I paused. "I know. We need the information, and so far they've been good, particularly Cutler. NASMI? That's different. We can get their stuff elsewhere."

"Maybe we—?"

"Tell somebody? You know what I'm going to say. Do you have time for some tangent, yelling and screaming about George Smathers?" We both knew the answer. "Time. George. Time," I said, my voice quickening, its tone elevated. "Just before you called, I was trying to work on this violence paper. One of my guys knocks on the door. He wants to talk. A freshman. Nice kid. His parents are getting a divorce, and he wants to drop out of school. I'm trying to convince him not to leave, and then the phone rings. It's Jeff. He's telling me that a toilet overflowed on the seventh floor. The water had already reached the second. So I grab this freshman and we go out into the hall. Well, the water is coming down the stairwell onto the first floor, and there are half a dozen guys trying to mop it up. What a mess. We finally cleaned it up and got someone from maintenance to come over."

"Sounds like my building. Where's this freshman?"

"He went to Bassin's with some of the guys. He said he'd come back later. Ya know, George Smathers is not going to write my violence paper."

"Yeah, we understand each other. And no Banzhaf."

"God, no. Who knows what he'd want us to do?"

"I agree."

I put the receiver down and sat there alone, quietly—knowing, slowly at first, that this discovery meant more caution, more of an effort to discern other people's motives. There was an even knock on the door. "Hold on," I said, getting up from the couch.

"It's time, big fella." It was Jeff. I needed to check the hallway, verify that campus maintenance had fixed the toilet, and assure myself that the stairwell was dry and passage in it safe. We did it together.

FRANK NORRIS

In his three-volume series *The Epic of the Wheat*, Frank Norris intended to write the story of "American wheat from the time of its sowing as seed in California to the time of its consumption as bread in a village of Western Europe." *The Octopus* was published in 1901 and *The Pit* in 1903.[43]

I read late in the evenings, during restless nights when I was awakened by noise in the alleyway or by a resident's need to talk. I read while walking to class or when I visited my brother in Laurel, Maryland. I read early in the mornings before anyone awoke. Norris's writing had a special cadence, its power hidden until it sprang suddenly—and then it captured you until it was finished, its power spent but its lore now imbedded and memorialized. He captured the cynicism and malevolence of the Railroads. He added life and character to their hidden intent, their scheme, and their cunning, particularly with the farmers and ranchers in California's Joaquin Valley.

"Yes, the Railroad had prevailed," Norris wrote at the end of the story. "The ranches had been seized in the tentacles of the octopus; the iniquitous burden of extortionate freight rates had been imposed like a yoke of iron. The monster had killed Harran, had killed Osterman, had killed Broderson, had killed Hooven. It had beggared Magnus and had driven him to a state of semi-insanity after it had wrecked his honor.... It had enticed Lyman into its toils to pluck from him his manhood and his honesty, corrupting him and poisoning him beyond redemption.... It had cast forth Mrs. Hooven to starve to death upon the City streets."[44]

I was moving backward in time but without recognizing conduct that was any different from what we had learned about the Penn Central and its deliberate degradation by those that controlled it—and about the commissioners, their suspect relationship to the Railroads, their approval of double-digit rate increases, and their acquiescence in bankruptcies and in the "judgment" of Railroad executives entrusted with the fate of lives and jobs and communities. They all acted with comfort and ease, with deference from a law that really intended something different. Like a pawn moved

Frank Norris (Alamany authorized). NTProto Collection.

by a larger force or, more sadly, because you could see the connection, the Commission's actions were moved through strings that reached deeply and pervasively. They were pulled at the right time, deftly, defiantly, and with almost mystical omnipotence.

Norris did not finish *The Epic of the Wheat*. He died. The Railroads, I knew, still had the power. At times I thought the story was still being written.

6

STANDING,
FALL 1971

A strategy solidified. "Should we file in *265/267*? And, if we do, what authority within the Interstate Commerce Act do we rely on?" I asked. George and I had spoken by phone the previous day and were now meeting with John in an empty classroom.

"First, *265/267* began after NEPA's enactment, and no EIS was written," George replied. "Second, the rate increases granted were geographically and financially enormous. All railroads and all commodities. So were the environmental effects. Or, in the terms of NEPA, it was a 'major federal action significantly affecting the quality of the human environment.'"

"I think we meet the law," John said.

"Who knows?" George said. "It's not like there are a lot of court cases out there. We probably know as much as anyone."

"That's a little overstated," I said, not certain I was right.

"The only question," he replied, "is whether we know more than the Commission."

"Okay. We have the CEQ letter. We don't know whether the CEQ will ever say that again."

"Let's assume it won't," John added quickly.

"Finally, the decision in *265/267* is a certainty. Final. Over. Its consequences are still being felt physically and financially."

"Whatever *Arrow Transportation* means, it's not involved here," George said, with a noticeable comfort.

"More?" I asked.

"Well? Yeah. I don't think another rate increase is going to be requested before the semester ends. Even if it is, there might not be time for us." It was John, reminding us we were only students.

"They already got two," I said. "There must be some limit."

"Do you believe that?" George asked. John grinned.

"We still need to discuss this with Kenny and Peter," I said.

"But we agree?"

"Right, we've got to select a course and stay with it."

"All right. Let's talk content," I said.

"More complicated. I spoke with my friend."

"The so-called ICC Practitioner," John posited.

"That's what we're calling him."

"Okay with me. John?"

"Yep."

"Now, although *265/267* is finished, we have to formally 'intervene' as a party, identifying who we are and how we're harmed. The rules require it, but, as my friend said, he didn't think the Commission heard regularly from groups like ours."

"There's an understatement," John said.

"We also have to ask the Commission to 'reconsider' its now-final decision," George continued. "There's a separate rule governing that."

"That's where our arguments about NEPA have to be set out in detail." John nodded in agreement as I said it.

"We're convincing the Commission it approved thousands of rate increases illegally."

"Well, that'll be easily done," John added.

"A couple of sentences."

"Okay. The third petition." George leaned back, smiled, and waited.

"You'll love this, John."

"Because rate increases are being collected, preparing an after-the-fact EIS is not enough. The rate increases, under our theory, were collected without legal authority. They have to be refunded."

"What a theory." There was the grin. It was plain that John relished the approach.

"It's not inconsistent with the way they operate. We're not shippers and can't request a refund. We have to request the refund of *all* increases on all commodities transported by all railroads."

"Petition for extraordinary relief?" I asked, liking the name.

"There's no rule that allows it."

"So?" John added, knowing the answer.

"We each take one petition," I said, "prepare a draft, circulate it, see if Meyers and Banzhaf want to review it. By late December, just before the holidays, we file all three. Kenny and Peter will agree."

"One more thing," George said, with a discernible affectation.

"Yeah?" John asked.

"There's another rule. We have to serve all the parties." He paused and raised a finger. "Probably hundreds."

"How the heck are we going to do that?" John asked, with a discernable unease.

"Banzhaf," I said. "When the time is ripe, Banzhaf will know what to do."

LEARNING THE RULES

Unfair Trade Practices met three times a week. Each class was fifty minutes in duration. Doing a project was the equivalent of taking another course. You were as obligated as everyone to read, recite, answer questions, and learn the law. Banzhaf marked your failure and, it seemed, your tentativeness, uncertainty, and mistakes. It did not endear him to any of us.

Today's class was to be taught by a guest lecturer; Banzhaf had access to some provocative personalities. George had not yet arrived. I saw Kenny in the distant corner engaged in an animated conversation. A female student sat next to me—a Vassar graduate who had good grades and was active on either the newspaper or law review. She yawned slightly, expressing uncertainty "that this will be fruitful." Students continued to enter and were sitting or standing randomly. I was looking for the other members of our group, intent on suggesting the time and place for our next meeting.

In walked Peter Meyers. He was alone, moving deliberately in and around students. He jumped the three steps ascending the elevated, wooden desk, placed a yellow legal pad and some other materials gently on it, and took a seat. He glanced downward, ruffled through his papers, and looked upward rather abruptly. His face reflected a sense of determination, almost defiance. He pushed his hair back with both hands, dropped them to his sides, and placed them in his trouser pockets. He turned his upper body around in the chair, looked up at the clock overhead, turned back to the pad, and lifted and glanced at each of its first four or five pages. No one was paying attention. All waited for the only event that would provoke silence: Banzhaf's arrival. A few moments passed. "Ah ... Professor Banzhaf has asked me"—Meyers began and everyone hurriedly took a seat—"to lecture on the law of 'standing to sue.'" There were rumblings.

"We can't leave" was the softly whispered retort.

"First, I have revisions in the reading assignments. B says, I mean, Professor Banzhaf," Meyers said.

"B?" The murmur, barely detectable around me but you knew it was deep and irrevocable in its effect, spread instantaneously. "B? I don't believe it," was the first whispered voice I heard.

"Pay attention."

"Okay. I'm fine."

Meyers began in earnest: "Article Three of the Constitution provides that the judicial power shall extend to all cases arising under this Constitution and the laws of the United States and to all controversies to which the United States shall be a party."[1] Early in its history, he continued, the Supreme Court concluded that the words "cases" and "controversies" meant a real, live disagreement between two parties. No advisory opinions. The reason, the Court has stated, "is to avoid any use of a, quote, 'federal court as a forum for the airing of generalized grievances about the conduct of government.'"[2]

Meyers had confronted the issue of "standing" as chairman of SOUP. John, George, and I had talked about the need to describe who we were and how we were affected by the ICC's action. We realized too that we might have to prove it. John, sitting nearby, nodded his head when I turned his way.

At the risk of simplification, Meyers said that "standing" is a legal concept that defines who can file a lawsuit. If you lack standing to sue, the court cannot consider your case. Standing is a prerequisite to federal jurisdiction. Here is an example, he added. If the Department of Agriculture issued a regulation that restricted the ability of farmers to grow soybeans, who could challenge that regulation? Could a farmer of soybeans? Could a farmer of peanuts? What if peanuts compete with soybeans? Could a consumer who purchased a soybean product challenge that regulation? Each may disagree with the regulation, but who among them may challenge it?

Meyers described the process; his words were precise, practiced. "The plaintiff must explain the government's action and which law it violated. That explanation is in the complaint. Additionally, the plaintiff must explain how he specifically has been, or will be, injured or harmed because of this action.

These, as you know, are 'allegations'—what the plaintiff believes to be true and intends later to prove at trial. It is these 'allegations' that a court looks at to determine whether the plaintiff has 'standing to sue.' We need to look at two recent Supreme Court decisions," Meyers said, paused, and looked straight at the class. "Disagreement lies among the justices."

"*Association of Data Processing Service Organizations v. Camp, Comptroller of the Currency*, decided in March 1970." Data Processing is an incorporated association of organizations located throughout the United States. The comptroller issued a ruling that permitted national banks to make data processing services available to bank customers. A particular bank was prepared to perform services for one of Data Processing's clients. Data Processing filed suit against the comptroller, claiming that his ruling caused economic harm to Data Processing's business resulting from what it alleged to be "illegal competition." The Supreme Court had to determine whether Data Processing had "standing to sue."[3]

The opinion was written by Justice William O. Douglas for himself and five justices. "'The first question,' Justice Douglas stated, 'is whether the plaintiff alleges that the challenged action has caused him injury in fact, economic or otherwise.' Data Processing satisfied this test.[4] The second is 'whether the interest sought to be protected by the complainant is arguable within the zone of interests to be protected or regulated by the statute or constitutional guarantee in question.' This test, Justice Douglas explained—and this is crucial," Meyers emphasized, "is apart from the 'case or controversy' test. It is not required by the Constitution." It is a "rule of self-restraint" that the Court imposed on itself.[5] The act of Congress that Data Processing claimed was violated provides that a bank cannot engage in services other than performing banking services. Data processing performs those other services, so it met the "zone of interest" test. It had standing to sue.

"The dissenting opinion," Meyers posited, as if it were a chapter heading. "Written by Justice William Brennan, joined by Justice Byron R. White. Both agreed that Data Processing had standing, but they disagreed with the reasons." Because their dissent applied to both *Data Processing* and the next decision, *Barlow v. Collins*—decided the same day—Meyers first discussed *Barlow*. It also was written by Justice Douglas on behalf of the same five colleagues: Chief Justice Warren Burger and Justices Hugo Black, John Harlan, Potter Stewart, and Thurgood Marshall.[6]

In *Barlow*, the Supreme Court found that tenant cotton farmers and sharecroppers, who were eligible for cash payments under the upland cotton program, had "standing" to challenge the validity of a regulation issued by the secretary of agriculture under the 1965 Food and Agriculture Act. "The two tests for standing," Meyers said distinctly, fingers raised. "The farmers and sharecroppers suffered economic injury in fact from the likely loss of profit that would result from the regulation. Because one of the purposes of the 1965 act is to protect tenant farmers, they also were within the law's zone of interest."

Meyers returned to the dissenting opinion. He stood, turned to the blackboard and, with a barely perceptible unease but with everyone's attention, wrote, "1. Injury in fact (Const.). 2. Zone of interest (non-Const.)."

"Justices Brennan and White concluded that, quote, 'The only inquiry needed to be made is whether the complainant alleges injury in fact,'" Meyers said, pointing to the board, text in hand. There was emphasis in the moment of silence that followed.

Meyers sat and, without skipping a beat, read: "[R]equiring a second, nonconstitutional step ... may 'deny justice' to certain parties. Justice Douglas's approach, the dissenters wrote, quote, 'does little to guard against the possibility that judges will use standing to slam the courthouse door against plaintiffs who are entitled to full consideration of their claims on the merits. As my Brother Douglas has said: "The judiciary is an indispensable part of the operation of our federal system.... With the growing complexities of government it is often the one and only place where effective relief can be obtained. Where wrongs to individuals are done ... it is abdication for courts to close their doors."'"[7]

Meyers then posed this question: "The injury suffered in *Data Processing* and *Barlow* was 'economic.' Are environmental or conservational interests also protected? Douglas stated that such interests may reflect 'aesthetic, conservational, and recreational as well as economic values.' Brennan and White agreed. 'Injury in fact has generally been economic in nature, but it need not be.'"[8]

Recently, Meyers said, the Supreme Court granted *certiorari* to determine what this means. "It's *Sierra Club v. Hickel*, the secretary of interior, decided by the United States Court of Appeals for the Ninth Circuit in San Francisco in September 1970. Here are the facts."[9]

In July 1969, the Sierra Club, a nationally prominent environmental organization of long standing, brought suit to stop Disney from constructing a large ski resort in and near Mineral King Valley within the federally owned Sequoia National Forest in California. The Sierra Club alleged that the project would cause the "permanent destruction of natural values" and "irreparable harm to the public interest." The district court agreed and enjoined the construction. The Department of the Interior appealed, claiming that the Sierra

Club lacked standing.[10] The court of appeals agreed: "[T]he Sierra Club in its complaint alleges that it is a nonprofit corporation.... It claims a membership of approximately 78,000 nationally, with approximately 27,000 members residing in the San Francisco Bay Area. It asserts that it has for many years taken a special interest in the conservation and sound management of the national parks and forests and particularly lands on the slopes of the Sierra Nevada Mountains. It states that 'its interests would be ... aggrieved by those acts of the defendants.'" Based on the decisions in *Data Processing* and *Barlow*, these allegations, the court of appeals concluded, were not sufficient.[11]

There was a directness in Meyers's manner as he emphasized this point made by the court of appeals: "The Sierra Club 'does not assert that any of its property will be damaged, that its organization or members will be endangered, or that its status will be threatened. Certainly ... the proposed course of action ... does not please its officers ... or a substantial number of its members.' The court of appeals concluded: 'We do not believe such a Club concern without a showing of more direct interest can constitute standing in the legal sense.'"[12]

The Supreme Court agreed to review the decision. Briefs had been filed. Oral argument was held on November 17. Meyers was reaching the end. "But it is important to keep in mind that the composition of the [Supreme] Court is changing. President Nixon has nominated Lewis Powell and William Rehnquist. Both share his view about 'judicial restraint' and 'strict constructionism.'"

Some students clapped. Meyers was pleased, you could tell.

I waited outside. George and Peter arrived first. "I know, Proto, you want another meeting," Peter stated, in good nature.

"Hey, don't give me a hard time. When Banzhaf gives you an A, you'll be—"

"He better give me an A," Peter said, laughing. The others joined us.

"Oh! Did you hear that?" Kenny said. "B. Hey, B, how are you?"

"Careful," Peter said, looking around.

"The Sierra Club doesn't have standing?" I said almost quizzically to George. His eyes widened; his look was uneasy.

"Yep, I got that too," he said.

We moved over to the side of the hallway. "We need to have a meeting," I said. "We have to decide, finally, what we're going to say, who's going to write what, and when we're going to file. How about Friday?"

"When Friday?"

"What's the hurry? It's only November."

"And soon it will be December," I emphasized, "and the holidays—"

"I want to get this done and out of the way for exams."

"When Friday?"

"How about two at my place?" I asked. It took a few more moments. It did not help that Meyers did all the talking during class. "George?"

"I think so. I'm meeting with one of my guys at 1:30. It might run over."

"What are you, the house mother?" Kenny chided. George stared and exhaled, then laughed.

"Coffee included?" Peter asked.

"I'll do coffee," I said.

"And donuts. Got to have cinnamon," Peter said.

"Just come."

"My woman is coming in," Kenny said.

"You got a woman?" Peter chimed in.

"Yeah, I got a woman."

"She must be blind."

"She's smart and beautiful and rich. Eat your heart out."

We all started to separate. The crowd within the hallway was thinning. Two students walked by me, quick time. "Don't worry," I said. "We'll keep it short. Half an hour, forty minutes."

George had to return to Calhoun. I had to walk to Rice Hall. "Demonstrations?" George asked, with a slight resignation in his voice. He was a few feet in front of me, as I struggled to get my jacket on—a heavy corduroy sport coat, old, solid, warm, and brown.

"No. It doesn't look like it," I told him.

"It's too cold," he said. "The season's over." We kept walking down the steps. I put my gloves on. George needed a shave. He looked tired.

"Seasons? George. That's true for the students. But the president? He doesn't know for seasons."

"Should we talk to him?"

"You think he's home?"

WHO WE ARE

I returned to Crawford from my noon class. It was approximately 1:10 in the afternoon on Friday. I recalled walking into Crawford four years earlier when it was occupied by women. There had been a piano in the large foyer—grand, aged, its ivory keys glistening from use and from the light of the overhead chandelier. The piano was surrounded by leather-bound furniture, neatly placed and resting comfortably on subtly colored, attractive rugs. The silver tea set was out on a mahogany table near the piano. When I approached the friend I had come to visit, the silverware was noticeably tarnished, and regardless of purpose it may have served in the 1940s, 1950s, or early 1960s, the set seemed (even four years ago) to be somewhat misplaced. Most of the women were coiffed properly and wore dresses about knee length or shorter, complemented by white, sheer stockings that stopped about knee level. Here and there were blue jeans and long hair, and a sitting posture that was not exactly appropriate for a school that believed itself imbued with a "southern" tradition.

"I'd like you to meet Caroline Bentley," my friend said. "She's living here just for a semester." Her posture was impeccable. Her dress: blue jeans. Her attitude: detached.

Since then, rough cultural change had transformed the foyer into its present state. The rug was tattered and stained, the furniture was vinyl, and the tea set was in a locked closet, partially enshrouded in a soft, velvety sack next to a torn, corrugated box filled with sheared rags prepared for protection against tear gas.

I began my trek down the hallway. Tacked onto the bulletin board, which usually contained little more than the roster of residents, was an 8" × 10" sheet of white paper, with three stanzas typed in red ink:

THE GREAT FLOOD

Steph ... took a piss one night
and saw the toilet didn't flush right.
So he decided to flush it harder,
and put seven floors under water.
From door to door the water gushed,
that toilet, Steph wished he'd never flushed.
By the time the water had finally stopped,
poor Victor's ceiling had sagged and dropped.
As the water tumbled toward the first,
it seemed as though a dam had burst.
With dripping feet, sighed Jeff Gocke,
"How could those f... do this to me?"
The sponges.[13]

What a mess. I unlocked the office door and pushed a rubber stop under its base. A few minutes after 2:00, Jeff returned, accompanied by George Biondi. Both were layered in heavy shirts, coats, and scarves. George and I walked back to my apartment. He declined my offer of an apple. "Did you talk to your friend?" I asked.

"You mean, the so-called ICC Practitioner. Yeah. Yeah, I talked to him." I walked into the living room, munching on the apple. I rearranged the room's one chair and then got another from the bedroom.

"Hey, George," I said. "When you leave, stop at the bulletin board and see this poem some of the guys wrote."

"Poem?"

"Yeah. The night the toilet overflowed," I answered.

"They wrote a poem?"

"Well, sort of."

"You mean a little dormitus literatus."

"So to speak."

Kenny and Peter arrived at about 2:10 p.m. "Did you see Larouche?" I asked, as I took the coats and tossed them on the bed.

"I saw him out front. He's trying to lock his bike to a tree."

"Yeah? Look's like he didn't have much success."

John was lifting his English racer up the three steps at the end of the hall. His army jacket and knapsack were tight around him, a scarf circled his neck, gloves secured over his hands, and a hat (black wool, knitted) over his head—not a fashion statement but warm. John walked the bike into my apartment. "You gonna lock it in here?" Kenny said.

"Well," John replied, smiling broadly, "I trust Proto but—"

"All right, gentlemen," I said. "Let's all, ah, take a seat." George sat in the only chair, which normally was in the room—contoured, yellow toned, metal legged. Kenny took a seat on the couch alongside Peter and directly opposite the chair I was sitting in. John sat on the floor to my right, his back against the wall. I began, "There're a number of things we have to decide. Time's getting short. I've prepared a list we can begin with. We can add stuff as we go along. The first question is what are we going to file?"

George described what was required by the Commission's rules and concluded that "We're going to have to file three separate petitions."

"Three?" Kenny responded immediately. "I thought we were going to do one."

"It's not complicated," I said. "It's just that we're late. We want to file in *265/267*, and the thing is over. We have to explain why we didn't get in when everyone else did." Kenny's unease seemed to diminish. "It isn't more work," I insisted. Then I added, "Look. Three petitions will make it cleaner, simpler."

George continued. "My friend thinks the Commission might be more willing to look at our stuff if we file a separate request to become parties. It'll also look like we did a lot more work." I knew this was a persuasive argument. John and I explained the reconsideration petition. Consensus was essential. George especially, worked at getting it.

"I agree," Peter said. "I think we all do."

"The third petition," George explained, "is a petition for extraordinary relief." John grinned. So did I.

"Yeah. We want them to pay our tuition," Kenny said.

"Is there really such a thing as a petition for extraordinary relief?" Peter asked.

"Well, yes and no," George said. "When a shipper thinks he got screwed, he applies to get a refund. Our problem is we aren't shippers."

"Did anybody ever ship anything by rail?" I asked.

"Yeah, they got lost."

"You didn't know it," Kenny said. "but they got recycled."

"Look," I said, "the environmental part of our theory is that we want the iron ore to stay in the ground and the trees not cut. The money doesn't help us."

"So. Well, ah," George said, "it's extraordinary because I can't find anything that permits it, but nothing that precludes it either. And besides, it has pizzazz."

"Pizzazz?" John asked, not expecting an answer. The room fell silent for a moment. I could see the look on Kenny's face, that "let's get on with it, what's the assignment, who exactly is doing what, why isn't it easier to take an exam" look. He was no different from the rest of us; we all sought definition. The semester was beyond midpoint.

"Anyone want coffee?" I asked. I walked into the pantry and plugged in the pot. I reached for some mugs—heavy, deep brown—located in a cabinet over the sink. "Well. What do you guys think? Kenny?"

"Sounds all right." Peter liked it. George and John seemed relieved. I knew they both had started writing, as I had. I came back in but remained standing. "The petitions don't have to be long. We can't all draft them. Too many writing styles. John, George, and I will each draft one. We can circulate them, make revisions, and then file. George will draft the last one, the petition for, ah—", and I looked at George, as if on cue.

"*Extraordinary* relief," he added.

"I'll do the one for intervention. John will do the reconsideration— that'll be the longest. What little case law there is will be there. We can explain all we've learned about the environmental impact, the discrimination, and the stuff about cities. But it's something we should all talk about first," I added, as I walked back into the pantry. "Banzhaf may ask any one of us about it."

The coffee was still perking. I took out milk and sugar. "It's all right with me," Peter said. "We'll do whatever is necessary to help."

"It's easier that way," I said, standing in the doorway. "Don't worry; your time'll come. Besides," I added, "writing this stuff might be the easiest thing." I returned to the pantry for a few spoons. "We have to decide next about timing," I said. "When, exactly, are we going to file?"

"The end of the semester?" Peter asked, seeming to set an outer limit.

"Too late. The third week in December. Draft done by about the middle of December. Finalize everything just before the holidays. We need a typist," I said. "George?"

"I'll do it. But I need a good machine."

"We'll find one. Peter, you can get your list of people ready, and we can all type envelopes."

"Where are we getting envelopes?" Kenny asked.

"Well, I'm sorry to say, that's a good question. We've got a slight problem."

George explained, "Under the Commission's rules, when you file a petition asking for a change in the rates, you have to serve all the parties."

"There were hundreds of them," Kenny said.

"We don't know exactly how many," George said. "I called the Commission. They don't keep a service list."

"Who's paying for this?"

"Maybe we can file *in forma pauperis*," George said. "Just tell them we're broke."

"I doubt the ICC gets many requests from indigents," Peter posited.

"Once we have something in workable form, we can approach Banzhaf," I said.

"You mean, B?" Kenny quipped.

"And see what he says. But not before then. I don't want to get involved with him before we're ready. When he asks me again, ah, 'Are you ready to file?' I've got to be able to say, 'yes.'" I walked back into the pantry and found the coffee ready. The boys continued talking. I could hear a sudden burst of laughter. I distributed the coffee, including one for myself, turned the chair around, and straddled it.

"All right, gentlemen," I said. "There is this other matter. Standing. We all heard Meyers. When John and George and I do these petitions, we'll write some stuff about our interests and who we are. We'll say something about how we've been harmed. I'm not certain what difference it will make to the Commission. They're not going to like our attitude. Now, I want us just to talk about it. And it doesn't have to be only environmental harm. Think about economics too."

"You want to just talk?" Kenny asked.

"Yeah. We can write things later. I'll take notes. George, you too. Do you have paper?"

"Yeah."

"The question is," I said, "how does it affect us, all of us, as a group and individually? You know, every day. Remember, the important legal test is whether we've been injured in fact by the action we're complaining about."

"Do we have to do it for the ICC?" Peter asked. "The standing argument?"

"Maybe not," George said. "But if we don't, they'll jump all over us."

"All right," I said. "Let's put the environmental stuff aside and concentrate on economics. How it affects us economically. And keep in mind that we may have to prove this. We don't know." Most of us had transported large trunks and books by railroad, mostly by the Penn Central.

"It's not the same kind of freight, like, ah, widgets or something." Peter said.

"That's all right," I said. "Anybody else?" Railroads, we knew, delivered goods and commodities to where we lived. More so, trucks did it now, but a few of us, including me, had seen trains unload in or near our hometown. We all had ridden on a railroad, mostly the Penn Central. "All right. What other economic relationships?"

"Remember that stuff about the cost in New York?" Kenny said, referring to what we had read during our first visit to the Commission. "Well, it's the same in other towns. The cost of keeping junkyards. We all pay taxes."

"Kenny is from New York," I said. "New Haven has junkyards—and at least one where waste is burned."

"They certainly look ugly. And stink."

"I still pay car taxes in New Haven," I added. We all had part-time jobs here. George and I were paying taxes in the District.

"We can allege it, the aesthetic harm and the economic harm, and if we have to, we'll try to prove it," George said.

"What else?" I said.

"Well. This is a little obscure. It's the cost to repair highways. Railroad rates are high, and so shippers turn to trucks," Kenny said.

"That's obscure," Peter added.

"It's a possibility," I said, wanting not to exclude anything. "Trucks get the business, and that's one reason we build highways. That's federal. It also means increased air pollution. I don't know. Put it down."

"In that Sierra Club case," John said, "there is a specific project."

"Well, we're doing this as a group, too," I said, "and on behalf of the public. So, we say to the ICC we're a group called SCRAP and we're interested in freight rates. Then we say each member of SCRAP—Neil Proto, Kenny Perlman, et cetera—has a particular interest that is affected apart from the group. Then we say SCRAP is representing the public generally, which includes the impact of the general rate increase. I mean, we have to separate them all, and show interest and harm in different ways."

"Well, we're harmed, but you guys are going to write it," Kenny said.

"We'll see how it looks. All right, back to the economics. And look, if you think of anything, call George, John, or me," I said.

"Yeah, in the middle of the night, jump up and call Larouche," Kenny said.

"If you call, it'd better be goddamned good."

"I'm calling anyhow."

"Talk about economics," I said, raising my index finger.

"It's our grade that I'm talking about," Kenny said.

"There were some articles," George said, obviously interceding, "about products that could be made cheaper in the marketplace with recyclable material."

"I've used paper like that," I added.

"The marketplace. Very economic," Peter said.

"Now, let's go on to the environmental stuff," I said. "Does anyone want more coffee?"

"Yeah," George said. "I'll get it." Silence prevailed. The mood had gotten decidedly serious. I sat down on the floor near John. George returned and took his seat. He started, "It would be easier to describe the harm if we had a situation like a dam being constructed that we could say, 'We use the area, and the trees being cut harms us—our use, our enjoyment, what we see or are precluded from doing.' Disney. We have the whole country, all the railroads."

"Maybe it doesn't make a difference," I said. "If we're going to show how it affects us specifically, then maybe we can say that we use such and such a park, or we drive by a particular dump site, that one of us does, individually, that trees are destroyed, or it scares the wildlife."

"Do we have to be specific? I mean, do we say, 'Ressler fishes in Jones Park, located on Route 49 in Topeka, Kansas, and he saw a tree being cut'?" asked Peter.

"No, we … write a paragraph that says we camp and fish and hike in different geographic areas, and the destruction of the trees and the mining affect our ability to do those things," George said.

"Oh, yeah. You been fishing?" Kenny asked.

"I've fished. And I've been hiking. A couple of places in western Virginia. Some of them were on state land, and there was logging going on."

"I climbed up Old Rag Mountain. In central Virginia," I said.

"I heard about that," George said, smiling.

"I've been on the Potomac, canoeing."

"You mean down here?"

"No. In Maryland. Once for a weekend, and then a few other times."

"I've been canoeing in Wisconsin," I said. "The Flambeau River. With Pete Steenland and John Hanson. Guys who used to work in the dorms. It was wilderness all right. They thought I was an Indian. I've also climbed a mountain in New Hampshire. Fortunately, it was snowing out of control so we stopped."

"The Presidential Mountains," John said. "I've been there too."

"Did you say an Indian?" Peter asked.

"Yeah. It's a long story." I turned to John. "I've got some pictures too. I could prove it."

Silence. "All right," I said, "as long as we can prove we use the forest and parks. Okay. What else?"

"There are the junkyards. I see them every time I drive home," Kenny said.

"Yeah, me too. We probably all do," George added.

"All right, anything else?" I asked.

"What time is it?" John asked.

"Ten after four," Kenny answered.

"Anything else?" I asked again.

"No," George said. "At least not now."

"There's more coffee," I said.

"No, none for me."

I looked around the room. The reality of a fast-approaching weekend was making headway. "We accomplished all we wanted." Everyone got up except George.

"You're doing a heck of a job, Proto," Kenny said. "B will give you an A."

"He better give all of us As," I said.

"I'll be happy with a high B. Just as long as I graduate with honors," Kenny said.

"With the average you've got, Perlman, you'll be summa cum summa summa," I said.

"Right, cumma gamma summa lambda."

"No, no. That's a fraternity."

"You were in a fraternity?" John asked, nodding toward Kenny.

"Are you kidding? What do I look like, a jock?"

"All right, gentlemen," I said. "That's it. I'll be in touch. If you think of anything else, call." John pulled his bike from against the wall, said goodbye, and left. Peter and Kenny followed.

"That was good," George said. "I mean, we accomplished a lot." I nodded with satisfaction. "What are you doing tonight?" he asked.

"I have a meeting now. Well, at four-thirty. With the dorm council."

"About what?"

"Security. Incredible, George. Students stealing from students."

"You free for dinner at my place?"

"Dinner?"

"Yeah, some pasta. You know, a little cheese, bread, a little wine."

"You make the sauce?"

"No, Kathy did. I've been teaching her."

"Like your mother's?"

"Hey, nothing is like my mother's. What a question! Your sauce like your mother's?"

"You're right. Nobody makes sauce like my mother."

"You coming?"

"Sure," I said. "I'll bring the wine."

"Great. Come early so we can talk. Kathy hasn't seen you in a while."

"All right."

"Six-thirty?" George asked.

"Six-thirty? What are you, bourgeois? Five-thirty."

"Yeah, all right. Keep me in line. See you later," he said.

I walked back into the pantry, unplugged the coffee, and washed the mugs. We were making progress—with a workable game plan, time frame, and legal theory. And, at least for now, we were all getting along fine. No surprises—some hard questions and some delicate moments, but no surprises.

7

DISCIPLINED CALM, FALL 1971

Moving forward. It was the middle of the afternoon when I left Crawford to walk next door to the University Center to get coffee. The weather was bland, the sky light gray, the temperature cold but not biting. There was no wind. I entered the Center through the doorway on H Street. The overhead lights were not on. Here, too, it was gray and still.

The coffee felt as hot as it looked. I began my walk back to Crawford. "Oooh. Neil," someone called. I turned and walked toward the dining area and stopped. "Neil. Hey. Here." George stood. As I walked toward him, I could see that fewer than half a dozen people were in the room, scattered randomly in groups of two. George was talking with John. Their cups were steaming.

"Gentlemen," I said.

"How are you, fella?" George asked. John grinned and nodded.

"Nothing a week in Miami Beach wouldn't cure. What are you doing here?"

"We were at the library," George said. "Decided to have some coffee. Sit down."

"Did either of you guys read the Nader book?" I asked.

"I did," John said. "Well, parts of it."

"Hard," I said. "The stuff on freight rates. How are we going to deal with it?"

"Well," John caught himself, "we'll say something."

"Yeah. What?" George asked. He understood freight rates better than any of us. The challenge, we all knew, was to determine what was relevant and how to describe it. John leaned back and gently placed his feet on the chair nearby. "I don't know. We'll say the rates are discriminatory, as Cutler says, but in language we understand."

"Yeah, I know that," I said. "But what else? Look, to figure out how much it costs to transport something, you go back to the last time the Railroads published a list of how much it actually costs in dollars. Then you have to find out what increases were granted, and then you add those on. The shippers know. We could say the public doesn't know, and the Commission has to stop this percentage crap and has to say it now costs $0.29 to ship a pound of, ah, I don't know, law books."

"Law books?" John asked.

"Right. We'd probably get an opinion on it," I added, in mock seriousness.

George sat back, balancing himself precariously. He smiled broadly.

"Well," I added, smiling and looking at George, "what was I going to say? Widgets?"

I nodded knowingly in shared disbelief of what we still needed to learn. I took a sip of coffee and glanced momentarily away from the table. Plainly in my sight, closer to the windows, was Kathleen McKeeley, seated with another woman. She smiled and nodded. I did the same. Irish, I thought.

George ended my musing. "Actually, the Railroads are obligated to publish a tariff that shows the exact cost of transporting each commodity. But they don't. The ICC lets them get away with not doing the addition. So you never know what something costs."

"Until you—"

"—do what Cutler did," George said.

"Yeah," John said. "I'll put that in." He smiled, stretched his arms outward, and placed both hands behind his head.

"How's your petition coming?" I asked.

"Slowly," he said.

"Well, we got time. I've done some on mine," I said as I looked at George, "but I want to get this paper for Jerry Barron out of the way first." George nodded. "Well, gentlemen, that's enough. I'm off," I added. At that moment, I could see that Kathleen was now sitting alone. I got up and began walking toward her table.

"Where you going?" George asked. "Sit down." He grabbed my arm. "I've got to tell you something. Sit down."

"Then let me get more coffee," I said. "You want anything?" I started to stand up again.

"Hey, I'll get it," John said. "George, you want coffee?" He did. John stood, yawned slowly, and made his way to the coffee dispenser and, for himself, to the hot water dispenser and tea bags nearby.

"George. Give me just a moment," I said.

I walked to Kathleen's table. "Hi. Thought I'd just say hello." I pulled a chair close to her and sat. "Between classes?" She wore a navy blue suit and heels.

"I am."

"You said you're a graduate student?"

"Part-time. Social welfare. But I'm doing a clinical project now."

"What is it?"

"In D.C., working with unwed mothers who do—and some who don't— want to be pregnant. We counsel women who make both decisions to be comfortable with their choice."

"Not easy."

"No."

"Can I ask you a question?" She nodded, with a soft, barely audible sound. "The ring? On your finger?"

"My husband. It's from the Academy. He was killed in Vietnam."

"Hmm. I see. I'm sorry. When did, ah—?"

"Last year. Right after we were married."

"I see."

"You with your friends?"

"Yeah. We're ... well, I'd better get back. It's good to see you again." I stood.

"Still running your dorm?"

"Yeah. You staying out of demonstrations?"

"No, actually, I'm not."

"Hmm." I smiled and nodded goodbye.

"Bye."

"Let me tell you," George said, as I sat down. "One of my guys is a member of some national fraternity, and you'll never guess who's an alum? George Smathers."

"You're kidding." I sat back.

"Listen. The kid's going to get a picture of Smathers. You know, a glossy."

"No? That is wild. From what we know, tell the kid to be careful." We both had a very low estimate of Smathers's ethics. I swallowed the last remnant of coffee, still warm, and felt unable to let the moment pass. "George, is this the law? Smathers? How he practices it?"

John returned with coffee and tea on a tray along with some napkins and a few containers of cream. "You mean what we do? Or are trying to do?" George asked, seeking carefully to force clarity.

"What he does, and how he does it," I said softly, posing—in reality—a question probably to be answered over time.

"It's crap," John said with disdain. "Nobody at the Commission is going to listen to us. I don't care what we say. There's no in between. They've cut themselves off from anybody except the Railroads." His words settled.

"Maybe we might represent something unknown," I said. "Without the same rules. If they're smart, if they can figure out what's going on—not just with us, but outside—we may have an effect." George smiled; John grinned. "Okay," I said. "The chance is remote. We agree. It's remote."

"Look, we do a good job, we get good grades, and then we leave," George said, but without conviction.

"I don't know. Maybe." I shared his uncertainty. For now, we agreed that we needed to keep our eyes open. "Understanding the law is hard enough without these characters running around."

"Who needs America's Railroads?" George asked mockingly.

"Wally needs them," John laughed.

"You mean George Smathers needs them," I said. We each chuckled slightly and without animation. Apprehension had taken hold—we didn't know what new event or relationship might arise beyond our capability, or if we had the time to handle it. I stood, stretched my arms behind my back, and clasped my hands. "All right, gentlemen. I'm off."

"Yeah, me too," John said.

"George, you going back to the library?" I asked.

He was, but only to get his books. He had a 4:30 meeting at Calhoun and, as he explained, "This is my night to prepare dinner."

"Listen. Let me ask you guys. Do we agree we're not doing legislation?" I asked.

"Forget the legislation," George said.

"I'll talk with Kenny and Peter. Take it easy," I said.

"Yeah," John exhaled, in resignation.

"George, I'll talk to you." I said.

"Yep. See ya. Neil?" George said. He grasped my arm gently and got close. "She looks Irish to me," he said. "Don't buy the cop thing or let the church stuff get in the way."

I laughed at his insight and then said somberly, "That's the least of the problems."

"What do you mean?"

"Serious."

"What?"

"No. She is."

"About you?"

"No. About life."

I walked toward the same doorway I had entered earlier, my mind moving among Railroads, the textbook awaiting me, and the cold outside. I did not see her coming. Caroline held tightly to her books. "Excuse me," I said.

"Well, hello. Where you going? Come. Have coffee," Caroline suggested.

"No, I can't. I got to get back to studying." We moved away from the doorway and the sting of the cold whenever it opened. "But how would you feel about a movie? Saturday."

"Sure."

"I'll come up to Georgetown and pick you up."

"Okay," she answered, but with a lingering disquiet. "Well, let me call you."

"I don't mind."

"I'll call you," she repeated, gently. I nodded and backed away with a slight smile and modest wave.

"How about *Z*?" I proposed. Her mind seemed elsewhere. "The movie?"

"Sure," she answered. I put my hands in the back pockets of my blue jeans, turned, and walked out of the Center.

THE VISIT

I could tell, as he opened the car door, that my dad was in a good mood. It was in his smile. "No traffic, and your mother crocheted all the way and listened to the news," he said. My parents emerged weary but, as usual, full of life and ready—as they were every year—to see what I was doing and to meet the boys in the dorm.

My mother had stayed with me and my friends in late March 1968 when I lived on N Street during graduate school. She unabashedly humiliated a few cockroaches; engaged us in evening discussions about politics and foreign affairs; met and befriended young, sociable, and streetwise Jerome, the grandson

Matthew and Celeste Proto. NTProto Collection.

of our neighbor, a retired policewomen who lived across the alley; and, before she left, helped me perfect my ability to sew on buttons. Within days of her departure, the Johnson Administration sought to quell the city's riot following the assassination of Martin Luther King Jr. National Guard troops occupied the neighborhood. A curfew was imposed. The University shut down. My room-mate, also from New Haven, and I packed and made our way through silent streets toward the Trailways Bus Station. The National Guard troops we passed were our age. When we arrived in New Haven, my father was there to meet us. My mother also visited me at Welling Hall in 1970, where I left her alone one evening only to find, on my return, my apartment filled with residents in a free exchange with her about the merits of the war and the need, as she put it, "to fight for what you want, but," as she placed her hand gently aside my face, "don't give my son Neil a hard time."

During the next few days, we visited my brother, Richard, and his family, and talked about the health and activities of aunts, uncles, and cousins and about Richard's work at the National Security Agency. I described SCRAP.

"Methodical mischief" Richard declared with an informed smile. "You were always good at it."

"Reasoned mischief. And so were you," I said.

"Look where it got you both," my mother subtly noted, looking at my brother.

On their last evening, joined by my friend Tom Bolle from Wisconsin and two former residents, Morton Branzburg of Philadelphia and John Tomsky of New Haven, we had a home-cooked meal (my father's pasta fagioli with chicken and parmesan) amid conversation about the war.

"My nephews fought in Europe," my father said quietly, as he removed dishes into the pantry kitchen. "Celeste's brothers, in Africa. Our parents worried," he said, seeming to recall a moment. "We celebrated when they joined and then when they returned."

For the rest of the evening, we entertained a few of the residents, engaged by my mother's inquiries and my father's ease of manner. The next morning they left. I would not see them again until Christmas. In the meantime, course reading, Crawford Hall and its residents, and SCRAP, planned carefully and on track, required my attention.

THE GAME

December 4. Intramural basketball. I moved to my left, ball in hand. My favorite move: the jump shot moving left. I got it off easily, quickly, with a fine arch—high, neat, and smooth. Cliff Brown moved into the lane from the far corner—his solid frame strong, tall, pushing and then leaning toward the basket and waiting; his head turning upward, watching the ball; his body poised; his knees bending; his arms moving upward, ready to tap the ball in or to grab it off the board for another shot. It was all timing and power. I saw Mort Branzburg to my left, in the corner. He had been free. He had wanted the shot; I could tell now.

The ball reached its midpoint, falling quickly, nicely; it looked good. I moved instinctively—as my brother and, before him, my father had shown me—toward the basket, to the left of the key, watching, my eye on the ball, my peripheral vision looking and sensing who was around me, in front of me. I got closer to the basket. Now I couldn't tell. By moving, I had lost my feel for the ball. It was in front of me but detached, the last touch distant. I saw Branzburg—just a glimpse, momentary, fast. He was moving backward, up court as he was supposed to do to cover for the fast break and because this late in the game none of us old-timers could get back quickly enough to stop the fast break. The rebound was our job.

The ball ricocheted. It hit the far side of the rim, then the near side—its speed fast, strong; the outcome was resolved in an instant. I missed the shot. The ball flew to the right, away from me and away from Cliff. We were still behind by four.

Cliff moved toward the ball. One of our opponents—small, uneasy on the defensive end of the court—grabbed and held the ball. Cliff engulfed him like a cloak, like Batman—arms flapping, following the ball, up and down and then reaching, inward, incisively, touching it, causing confusion but not for himself. He did it again. This time he got off a solid hit. The ball crashed hard on the floor. It bounced, once, twice, away from both players but closer to Cliff. He grabbed the ball and with one dribble moved in toward the basket. Another adversary, taller than Cliff—good at this, real good at this— stood between Cliff and the basket. Cliff could not get by him. The smaller opponent, now recovered from his loss, came up in front of Cliff with his back to me. He reached for the ball. Only the four of us were near the basket. Everyone else had moved down court.

Cliff flipped the ball to me. I was near the foul line, closer to the top of the key. The ball came in an arch but not on target. It was high. In that second or moment or instant so, too, was the small guy's hand. He had turned abruptly, his eyes looking up for the ball; his hand was reaching for it and for me. As if by training (more my father's than brother's), I jumped up and reached out for the ball, my right hand tapping it away from my oncoming opponent—to his right, my left. It was just enough. I landed solidly, took the ball and—to protect it—turned around, my back now to the basket. There in front of me, perhaps ten feet away—running hard and toward my right, toward the basket—was Branzburg. This time, I knew, I would get it to him.

I dribbled the ball to my left, only once, and made as strong and convincing a head move as I could. My adversary moved left to block me. I turned my body right, just enough, and with relative accuracy bounce-passed the ball to Branzburg, still moving and now with comfort—like Elgin Baylor, like Oscar Robertson—ball in hand, one bounce, two, slick, smooth, into the air, toward the basket, everyone else still moving in the other direction. The fake took others with it too, and Branzburg moved from their right with both hands now on the ball, his whole body moving—like George Petit, like Jerry West—laid it up, off the backboard, in, swish, two points. We were down by two. I heard Jeff Gocke yell from the other end of the court, "Morton. Two big ones."

The clock was moving. 15–14–13. It had been a rough year. We kept losing, always close—three, four points; hard games … 12–11–10. I could hear the other team, or someone from the sidelines, counting—loud, poignantly, with menace. Cliff and Morton encircled the small guy, now off sides, holding the ball—hoping, as I did, that he would try to throw it in, which, we all knew, he would not … 9–8.

Matthew Proto, circa early 1930s.
NTProto Collection.

We were wrong. He tried to toss it to Cliff's right, beneath Cliff's arms, which were still moving, flailing but with determination, knowledge, precision. Cliff knocked the ball down. It happened quickly and with stunning certainty. Cliff realized he was trapped, cornered, surrounded by two opponents who wanted him to languish … 7–6–5 …. His last hope was me. I had moved from guarding my man, who was still standing at half court, to standing a few feet beyond the circle—a good twenty feet from the basket. I was alone. Cliff leaped—straight up, high … 4–3—with the ball in both hands and tossed it hard, direct, straight toward me. I saw it coming. I knew the move I wanted to make. It was my dad's. The two-handed set shot … 2 …. I got the ball. My left foot moved gingerly; my right foot followed. Both hands moved firmly on either side of the ball, ready. I had the feeling; the seams fit perfectly … 1…. I let it fly—high, real high, like Adolph Shayes's, only better; like my dad's. "Over," someone intoned, loud, crude. "It doesn't count," someone else yelled, louder and rougher in tone. The ball seemed to glide—beautiful, carried, destined—and it was in! The net snapped hard; you could hear it. My dad—all I could think about was my dad. What a story I would have. I made it. The two-handed set shot, like my dad's—just as he taught me. Then a chorus began from the sideline—angry, dissonant—and we all stopped, tired, sweaty, adrenaline still running but clearly taking us nowhere.

I sat on the floor, looking at the ball bouncing to the side of the court and listening to the sound of the net. The feeling of the move was still there, nice, deep. "Too late," the ref said. "It was too late."

The chorus intensified. "Protest," someone said.

Protest, I thought. "What is this, the NBA?" There were only about eight people on the sidelines watching. This was intramurals in the "Tin Tabernacle"—GW's ancient gymnasium. But as I sat and listened, I started to love it—the chorus, the boys on my team not giving an inch even though they knew what I did. The protest would add to the story but would not change the outcome.

I walked over to Morton and shook his hand. "It was a nice move," I told him.

"We'll get 'em next time," he said. I knew for certain that we would try. But I knew, too, that it would not make a difference. What would make a difference was the story: the shared experience, telling friends. For me, it would be something more; telling my dad—seeing him smile, happy, pleased that I had learned the move from him.

"Neil? Hey. Here." I turned to see George on the sideline. A newspaper was in his hand, and unease was on his face.

8

THE MIDNIGHT SURPRISE, FALL 1971

Challenged. John saw it first. The *Wall Street Journal*, December 2, 1971: "Roads to Ask ICC for 2.5% Surcharge on Freight Rates." It was now Wednesday, December 8.[1]

John had telephoned George. Then I called Kenny while John contacted Peter. We met at my apartment, late in the morning. I read the article aloud: "'The nation's railroads have decided to ask the Interstate Commerce Commission for permission to assess an "emergency surcharge" of 2.5% on all freight charges.' Damn. How did we miss this? 'The roads said a petition would be filed with the ICC "as soon as practicable" for authority to assess the increase.'"

I moved forward, scanning, looking for more on timing. "What do they mean, 'as soon as practicable'? Talk about a distinction without a difference," I said, not looking up. "Listen to this: 'An official said the railroads probably would apply later for a general rate increase that would supplant the surcharge.'[2] Well, what do you think?" I looked around. "John?"

"We know they'll get it," he said.

George, looking through the *Evening Star* and *Chicago Tribune* articles he got from the library, was troubled. "There's really only one question. Timing. What do you think?" he asked me.

"We should file now before the Railroads do. File in *265/267* before they start another proceeding."

"We aren't ready," Peter said, positing a central fact.

"We don't even know when they're going to file," George added. "The article says soon, maybe Monday. How are we going to file before that? Damn. They might have filed today."

The coffee was made. I asked if anyone wanted a cup. I boiled water for Larouche's tea. "Lipton will have to do," I said.

Peter was leery about filing quickly. "We're supposed to serve a copy on all the parties," he reminded us. "There're probably hundreds of them."

"Talk about a harsh reality," George said.

"So," Peter continued, "we have to get everything printed and stapled, then get envelopes and address each one. And how much have we written? I mean, Neil, you're crazy."

"Should we tell B?" George asked, mostly directed to me.

"We could ask him what he thinks," Peter interjected. "I mean, does it really make a difference when we file?"

"We'll look silly if we wait. Besides, think about the reaction," I said.

"What?" George asked as if he suspected what the answer would be.

"I don't know. Maybe if the Railroads have all their attorneys there during the weekend, we go in, hand them these petitions already filed with the Commission. They'll go bananas."

"I like that," John said.

"B will love it." I proposed that we go see Banzhaf, tell him about the article but be affirmative. "We'll tell B that we are almost ready to file, and see what he says."

"Why don't we just wait to see what the Railroads do? If they request another increase, we can protest that one," Peter argued. There were no takers.

"First, let's find out for certain when they're going to file," Kenny said.

"How?" John asked.

"Call and ask," George said in a matter-of-fact tone.

"Huh? How the frig are you going to do that?"

"Why not call?"

"Look, it's not a corporate secret we're after," I said, "or something about the attorney–client privilege. All we're looking for is a clarification of what's already public." The unease continued. "We're not adversaries yet. We haven't even filed these lousy petitions yet."

"They have the power. Have you read that Interstate Commerce Act?" George asked generally. "It's incredible," he added. "They have plenty of time and plenty of lawyers—and for them this is a matter of bucks, millions of bucks."

"All I'm saying is I don't know. Maybe we're making this bigger than it is," Peter added, with a slight gleam in his eye.

"You're right. Let's call," John added, nodding toward Peter and then me.

"I agree," I said, certain of my own views.

George said he would do it.

"Tell them you're a law student and you're taking a course in transportation law," John told him. He reminded us that both of those things were true. "Your professor talked about the rate increase, and you want to know if their request will be available soon. Be a student. Everybody talks to students," Peter said.

George then made the call. He was good. "I see. Monday," he said. That was all we needed to hear.

"We're not out of this yet," John said softly to everyone. My mind was moving quickly. We had to do this.

"Yes," George said, firmly, knowingly, after he placed the phone down. "The director or whatever his title is said, 'Yes, we are working the entire weekend; all of our attorneys will be here. We're shooting for Monday, if we can get to the printers soon enough.' He was very cooperative."

"George! What kind of lawyer you going to be?" I said, smiling. My index finger jutted upward. He smiled and nodded his head.

"Listen, this is the public interest we're talking about," said John, with a knowing irony.

"Yeah. Right," Kenny added, evenly.

John, Kenny, and I walked to Bacon Hall to locate Banzhaf. It was after 1:00 p.m. While we did that, George contacted the ICC Practitioner. George and Peter were responsible for getting the names and addresses of the parties to *265/267*. We hoped George's friend could help. If not, we would try the Commission again. After that, well, we were not sure.

We located Peter Meyers in the large room on the fourth floor of Bacon. He was sitting beside an old wooden desk. It was big; had varying shades of brown; and was scarred by age, rough handling, and ink blotches that were embedded and permanent. The desk was at the far end of the room, to our left as we walked in. Meyers was smoking. In front of his desk and extending away from it was a wooden table perhaps ten feet long. The table was surrounded by five or six chairs, in different sizes; a few had arms. Each was gouged and worn but somehow serious and inviting—like witnesses to consequence. At the end of the long table was a smaller one, equally weathered and forming—along with Peter's desk—a sort of H-shape. On the far side of the long table were a few stained and yellowed windows that looked out to H Street.

I took a seat near Meyers. Kenny and John sat on the table's far side. I began to explain who we were, what had happened, and what we were thinking about doing. A few moments into the presentation a woman walked in, proceeded directly to a stack of eight or ten cardboard boxes that covered almost the entire wall beyond the small wooden table, extracted some documents, and left. "Go on," Meyers said to me in a polite, deliberate tone. "She's with the admissions office. We, ah, share this office. Go on." He took a very casual but deep puff of his cigarette. We continued our presentation. Meyers telephoned Banzhaf, whose office was on the third floor, then crushed his cigarette in an ashtray and placed it in his desk drawer. John and I exchanged glances. Banzhaf arrived momentarily. He took a chair from near the wall behind Meyers's desk and sat down a few feet from the table and us. "Well?" he said.

We repeated our presentation. Banzhaf became increasingly attentive. Once, a faint smile creased his lips but disappeared immediately. At first, he interrupted only sparingly to ask an occasional question but in a manner that suggested a great deal of calculation was going on in his head. The questions then came quickly: What have you written so far? Do you have the right forms for the petitions? Do you have a service list? Is everyone free for the weekend? Must it be printed? Must you submit three petitions? When we finished, Banzhaf summarized what he thought our options were in light of what we had told him and what some of the consequences might be. He and Meyers were available this weekend, and the room was too. The choice was ours. He left.

I called George and Peter at Crawford. They agreed that we should file now. We discussed the matter with Meyers until Banzhaf returned. We told him our decision. He was visibly elated. But his mood quickly changed. He seemed to retreat. It was not a radical change—more like a withdrawal. He looked intense, calculating, and quiet. Yet you could sense his enthusiasm—a feeling that he knew where this was going, that, again, another one of his groups was getting ready to act. He may have been egotistical, but when you were ready, he was ready.

Our undertaking also would be delicate. None of us knew Banzhaf personally. We had only his reputation and our impressions from his classroom. But my own uncertainty was diminished by two factors. First, Banzhaf—I knew—entered these legal frays well-tempered by the rigors of public interest law. Shortly after his appointment to the faculty, he created an organization titled Action for Smoking and Health (ASH). Its office—cramped, cluttered, and filled with antismoking posters, signs, curios, news clippings, and medical charts—was now located adjacent to Banzhaf's. Second was Banzhaf's response to us and the way he sought to define his role. It would be as mentor, not instructor. He would be supportive, not lead us. He would review, guide, and suggest. In his own way, he began to redefine the relationship quickly and deliberately. The major interaction with Banzhaf would be by me as chairman. The group members expected me to handle that interaction properly. Our grades were on the line. The amount of time we had and now would commit to ensure the project's hoped-for success was substantial.

John, Kenny, and I left. We huddled long enough to agree to talk by telephone that evening and to arrange our schedules for the weekend. Kenny and I walked to class. John went off to work; he had taken a part-time law clerk position.

Most of the daylight had passed when I returned to Crawford. George had left a message tacked to my apartment door. The now-infamous ICC Practitioner could get us the most complete list available. It was from the AAR. He proposed to devise a legitimate-sounding story to "borrow" the list, and he promised its prompt return. As he later told George, he had assured his contact, "Yes, you'll have it back on Monday. I know you need it to file for another rate increase."

The list would be waiting for us at the front desk of the AAR. "Just mention my name," he had said to George. We acquired the list early the next morning Thursday, December 9. George and I walked down to 1920 L Street.

"George. A woman I'm ah.... Well, you met her."

"The Irish—?"

"No. Before that. In front of Crawford?"

"The WASP? I'm sorry. Yep. I remember."

"I had to cancel a movie date with her because of this. Instead, she showed up at the dorm last night."

"So? What ah—?"

"Well, she didn't want me to go to her house to get her."

"She said that?" he said evenly.

"Yeah. Pretty much. It came out."

"Is it her? Or her—?"

"No. I'm certain it's not her."

"Is it her parents?" We reached L and Nineteenth. I paused before entering the front door.

"You know, George, it's like— "

"You mean you don't want to save the WASP?"

"There're limits."

"Neil. Patience."

"George, she brought over a paper she wrote."

"On?"

"Appalachia."

We entered the Railroad building and told the receptionist why we were there. No questions were asked. She handed us the list, arranged alphabetically on index cards. "Perhaps we look like law firm messengers," I said to George as we walked out.

"A little shaggy for the 'better' firms," he replied.

On the elevator, as it moved downward, we looked at the list. Many of the cards had more than one name on it. We looked at one another. It was an approximate calculation. Almost 500 parties had participated in *265/267*. Each would have to be served with our three petitions.

THE PLAN UNFOLDS

December 10. It began on Friday afternoon in the large room on the fourth floor of Bacon. We sat along both sides of the long table. John would redraft the petitions prepared by George and me—as well as redrafting his own—to ensure consistency of content and prose. His work would be reviewed by George, Peter Meyers, and me only for egregious errors. Kenny would make arrangements for printing approximately 500 copies of each petition at a shop less than a block from Bacon. The shop was quick, reliable, and cheap. Kenny also would acquire envelopes from the same source. He had one other responsibility. Along with whoever had a free moment, Kenny would type gummed labels with the names and addresses of each party to be served. There was only one typewriter, circa 1950. The task would be tedious.

Peter Ressler and I would prepare an additional list of individuals and organizations we wanted served, including members of Congress who were involved with transportation or environmental matters. We identified all the radio, television, and print media sources that would receive hand-delivered copies and a press release. The press release was our final assignment, which would come later.

Banzhaf arranged for two ASH volunteers, Freda Winnings and Faith Randall, to come in on Friday night and begin typing. Freda also was prepared to work all day Saturday. And Banzhaf—well, Banzhaf would be around, he said, in his office or in the ASH office, to advise on strategy or to review materials for proper form or to interject a thought or two when he found it appropriate.

So it began. No classes, no friends, no weekend. Only coffee, writing, thinking, whispers, disagreements, more coffee, typing, Meyers's cigarettes, Kenny's one-liners, yelling, gentle asides, more writing, laughter, advice, anticipation, expectations, a lot of "what ifs." There also were walks for more coffee but only one of us at a time, instructions, veiled commands, watching and sometimes diffusing disagreements, and periodic introductions of sumptuous and aromatic steak and cheese subs from the Galley. ("With mayo and onions. You want the red hots?" "No, hold the red hots.") Nothing but SCRAP.

We moved quickly to our assigned tasks. I monitored everyone's flow. Idle hands were not permitted nor were idle minds. Each movement of the pen from John or George or me raised a question of law or tactics: "If we say it this way, is that enough?" "Where does that leave us?" "How will it be viewed?"

As we progressed, new tasks suggested themselves—tasks that could not be left to chance: "Can we get in and out of Bacon Hall without campus security stopping us?" "At two o'clock in the morning?" "Will there be someone at the ICC to accept our petitions during the weekend? Is a guard sufficient? Does he have to sign a certificate of service?" "If we don't finish until late Saturday or early Sunday, will we be able to serve everyone on the same day?" "Is that required?" "Will the post office stamp all of these for us? Do we need to find a postage meter? Are we doing stamps?"

Each problem was considered and resolved as it arose. The dilemma persisted. There always seemed to be more. "Proto, have you thought about this?" "What else is there?" "I don't know." "Well. Think. What else is there?"

The writing moved at a steady pace. At the outset, Banzhaf appeared and addressed us. "First, tell them what you're going to tell them; then tell them; then tell them what you've told them." The request for action must be obvious and plain. No ambivalence. "Additionally," he said, "keep it concise. You don't have much time, and you have even less money." B said he had contacted someone at the Sierra Club and asked for "seed" money. We were uncertain how much that was—perhaps a few hundred dollars. The Sierra Club had said no. There were other possibilities, Banzhaf told us. He would pursue them. For now, B was responsible for financing. The bill for printing would go to him.

John labored away at the short table surrounded by copies of the Interstate Commerce Act, NEPA, petitions borrowed from the ICC Practitioner, the decision in *265/267*, yellow legal pads, and extra pencils. His silence was broken by an occasional obscenity or a question to George or me. But John's concentration had to compete with the click-click-click of Kenny at the typewriter or with the discussions between Peter and me concerning the identification of groups and organizations. He eventually gathered his paraphernalia and documents and relocated himself on the stairwell between the fourth and fifth floors, just outside the large room. It was Friday evening and few people remained in the building. It would be quiet. He distributed his statutes and pads and pencils on succeeding steps in an order logical only to himself. He sat down on a lower step with his back against the wall side of the stairwell. His "desk" was the vacant step between his "seat" and his "shelves."

John entered the large room periodically to ask George or me a question. At times, I would walk out to get John's views on strategy. The dialogue was always purposeful and direct. John finished his redraft of the petition to intervene. Minor changes were made. We liked it. It began to define us—to put on paper who we were and what we claimed. It included reference to a rule that separated us, that distinguished SCRAP from those who (we believed more so now than before) had violated a public trust. We took the draft downstairs to Freda. She had nestled into the ASH office. She, we were relieved to see, had an electric typewriter.

Freda began typing while George and I took turns answering her questions about word spellings, acronyms, or sentence structure. Meanwhile, John began his redraft of the next petition, the one for reconsideration. Peter Ressler contacted the printer. The petition to intervene would be in the printer's hands by late evening. He would work through the night. Kenny needed to rest his fingers and his back. He offered to walk to the Galley to get coffee, tea, or Coke for everyone. George immediately took Kenny's place at the typewriter.

It was 9:00 when Banzhaf made another appearance. Our world was now narrowly defined. His appearance emphasized it. The rush-hour traffic had ended. There were no classes on Friday evenings. Bacon Hall was vacant and dark except for us. The overhead light shown brightly from the fourth floor windows and into the interior hallways. The light was singular in its origin and effect, peculiar in its time and place. Inside the room, the click-click-click of Kenny's typewriter maintained its pace—methodical, determined. Each gummed label was finished, and each envelope was affixed with it. Each of us moved in tandem, purposefully, our movement rhythmically juxtaposed against the more accelerated click-click-click of Freda's machine from the floor below, its sound subtle and discernible throughout the stairwell, shattered only by the occasional "thump" when one of us inadvertently stepped onto a warped floorboard.

Peter Ressler and I had prepared a draft press release for Banzhaf to examine. Our concern was how to tell the *New York Times* we were saying something important *and* how to get it in the Sunday paper. Our draft was too long, B said. We saved the best part till the middle. No good. The opening paragraph should be "punchy." It should "grab them by the—." He was graphic when he expressed it.

It was not just the words or gesture that endured. It was the unsaid feeling—the sense I had had, and now the others had, that our adversaries were suspect in their motives, evil, disrespectful of the public interest, unaccountable, and unassailable in their own domain. Banzhaf understood that feeling and knew how to convey it to us that night, not in order to be part of what we were doing but to tell us something more. We were stepping over a line, were crossing into another realm, that was serious in purpose and harsh in consequence. He had been there before.

There should be a headline, he said. No, he explained, it probably would not be used—certainly not by the big papers—but it would provide a suggestion. Next, he said, the nuts-and-bolts information should go at the end, along with your names, something about SCRAP, and then phone numbers to provide more information. Put my number and a member of the group: Proto. One last thing, he said. Find out how much the Railroads will have to return if the Commission grants the request. Call somebody or figure it out. An estimate is fine enough. And remember, the press release has to be good. It's important. Important. Very Important. He was gone.

It was an essential part of our strategy to get prompt press coverage. We understood that need fully. The Railroads were trying to preempt us, however unwittingly. It was a race, not to the courthouse but to the public. We could not change the rules at the Commission, certainly not in the short run. Within the public forum, where the rules were less predictable, we could affect the Commission and the Railroads in a way that left them without recourse to stifle debate or deny accountability.

If the scenario went the way we now hoped, the petitions would be filed very early Sunday morning. They would not be hand-delivered to the Railroads until much later in the day. In the interim, we wanted a news article, knowing that even the most obscure article—however brief or hidden in the traditionally large Sunday paper—would draw attention. The Railroads covered the nation, and our petitions covered all freight rates on all commodities, moved over all Railroads: the Penn Central, the Burlington Northern, the Southern, and the Norfolk and Western. The Railroads would understand the meaning of what we were saying. They were on the verge of requesting yet another rate increase by using a mechanism essential to their livelihood in a forum that was familiar, comfortable, and without surprises. What they would read was not about students writing a scathing report that someone could dismiss with no comment. No, this was more troublesome, more intrusive. Those students want our money. They actually want to participate in one of our rate proceedings. They want to change the rules.

Our glee mounted with each new speculation. They would wake up on Sunday morning and see it as they were having breakfast. Bam! Zing! Bananas! And no one would have an actual copy of what was submitted except the guard at the ICC. Bingo! "Hey," I said to Kenny. "Keep typing." I did not need to tell him. He never stopped. At times, "keep typing" brought all of us to laughter.

We realized that we would never know the reaction, but the speculation had a strong effect. It made us conscious of our advantage. We had a means available to bring attention to our arguments: With a few words—the right words—distributed and printed in a timely manner, we could establish our challenge as advocates, and as adversaries.

By 11:00 p.m., Freda had finished typing the petition to intervene. We reviewed it for typographical errors and rechecked the citations. She made the corrections. We had her add Banzhaf's name as our attorney. Kenny and I walked it over to the printer. His presses were ready to go. We could have the copies in the morning. They would be collated but not stapled, which would make the print job cheaper. "We have to staple all of these?" Kenny asked. "We need a stapler."

"The dorm," I said. "We have two. George'll have one."

On our return from the printer, it was apparent that fatigue was not having an effect. John was on the steps talking with George about the petition for reconsideration. Their conversation focused on the words of a statute that John was holding. I could hear Peter Ressler pecking away on the typewriter, click-click-click, the pace steady and committed. I walked out to see George and John. Instead of waiting for John to redraft a whole petition, we would examine his work at some logical division and give it to Freda. This plan worked effectively until at about 1:30 Saturday morning; she left, promising to return by 9:30 or 10:00. John had redrafted; George, Peter Meyers, and I had reviewed; and she had typed slightly more than half of the petition for reconsideration.

Winding down took a while. Peter Meyers left right away. Banzhaf had not returned after his review of our press release. The five of us sat randomly and talked briefly and precisely about what remained to be done. Kenny and Peter left moments later. Both had a long drive across the Potomac into Virginia. At 2:15 a.m., John, George, and I gave out—tired, eyes red, John rubbing his wrist and hand, me massaging my neck. Yet, it seemed, we were strangely tense, not ready to draw a sharp line between what remained to be done and the need to regain some strength in order to stay ahead of the Railroads. So we prepared to leave too, flicked off the lights, and walked out.

I met George at 8:15 Saturday morning in the University Center. It was still December 11. We each purchased a large coffee and fresh donuts and walked briskly to Bacon. It was cold. George stopped at a machine and bought the morning paper, a *Washington Post*. "It's going to get colder," he said.

"Did the Railroads file?"

"We have the mailing list."

One at a time, the group's members made their appearance—uniformly unshaven, eyes swollen, coffee in hand, and ready and looking for me to say, "Go." Kenny and I left to pick up the petition to intervene from the print shop. John began his writing. His stairwell desk arrangement was still in place. George and Peter Ressler continued typing. They were almost finished. The printer had thrown in a stamp with "S.C.R.A.P." on it. The return address was Banzhaf's office. We liked it. Cohesion came to our effort in peculiar, sometimes small, ways.

Peter Meyers arrived, took a seat, silently drank a cup of coffee, and had a cigarette. He announced that he was ready. He walked out into the stairwell to see if John needed help. Freda arrived and began typing immediately. The process had started again. Our methodology was well oiled, our actions were meshed with precision, and our motivation was stirred by the possibility that this entire scheme might work. The gummed labels were finished, and the envelopes would be ready by noon. The petition for reconsideration had been typed and taken to the printer. The petition for intervention was stapled and counted into groups of 100. Banzhaf had arrived midmorning to put the final touches on our press release. He was pleased when he saw our estimate of the monies the railroads would have to return.

Railroad Freight Rate Structure Challenged on Environmental Grounds: Billion Dollars in Refunds Demanded

Railroad freight rates set by the ICC, which allegedly discourage recycling of waste materials, were challenged Saturday on grounds that the environmental impact was not considered in their authorization, as required by law. In a midnight filing, a group of law students charged the ICC with violating the National Environmental Policy Act, and asked the Commission to invalidate the rates and return an estimated one billion dollars to shippers throughout the country.[3]

Now it was in print—a fact before the fact, not yet truth but a prophecy of sorts, portentous, the first connection, tentative, fragile, like a web—one of many between our decidedly determined, still contained, stealth-like rumblings in the large room and the comfort, contentment, and publicly disclosed contempt being played out down at 1920 L Street among the nation's Railroads.

The remainder of the day and part of the evening were devoted to reviewing typed pages, including the petition for extraordinary relief; walking back and forth to the printer; stapling the petitions and arranging them in order; and stuffing the three of them into each gum-labeled, properly addressed envelope. The more we saw and touched a finished project—a petition stapled, an envelope labeled, a pile getting larger—the more energy we seemed to get and the more speculation grew. We were brought back to reality only by the questions we asked over and over again: What else is there? Did we miss anything? Think. The details. What else is there?

After Freda finished the petitions, she typed the press release. The printer agreed to fifty copies. By 11:30 p.m., we were finished. Three petitions, 500 each, had been typed, printed, collated, stapled, and stuffed. The originals were signed and dated; had a certificate of service to be signed by the ICC guard; were neatly arranged, clipped, in conformance with the rules; and were ready to go. Press releases were attached to copies of the petitions, stuffed into envelopes, labeled, and prepared for hand delivery. Sunday afternoon, we would mail the petitions—all of them—to shippers, railroads, the CEQ, and members of Congress. Tonight—momentarily after midnight—would be the filing and the delivery of the press release to the *New York Times*, *Washington Post*, *Washington Evening Star*, UPI, AP, and local radio and television stations. We would make the delivery, hoping that someone would print it, say it, sense its importance, help us.

Nothing was left to do. It was an interlude—waiting in the large room until midnight. I took the seat behind Peter Meyers's desk, pulled out the bottom drawer, sat back, and placed my feet on it. Banzhaf had gone down to his office. Meyers had gone home. Everyone else seemed quietly absorbed; a few sipped coffee.

Scattered on Meyers's desk were copies of the petitions, along with unused napkins, empty cola bottles, and a few foam cups filled partially with stale, cold coffee. One had been used hastily by Meyers to dispose of half-smoked cigarettes. I leaned over and picked up a set of petitions, intent on reviewing the product of our weekend labor.

"Petition under Rule 72 to Intervene for the Purpose of Petitioning for Reconsideration Pursuant to Rule 101, and for Extraordinary Relief Pursuant to Rule 102."[4] Not exactly a provocative title. I doubted it would sell in Peoria. Fortunately, someone at the ICC was required to read it.

Nine pages. The Introduction: SCRAP be allowed to intervene in order to request the Commission to reconsider its decision and "declare unlawful the rate increases granted[,] and to refund to all shippers monies paid in the amount of the rates thus far charged ... in excess of prior existing rates." That was provocative.

"Identity and Interest." Our "standing." We identified ourselves as "an unincorporated association entitled Students Challenging Regulatory Agency Procedures (S.C.R.A.P.), formed for the primary purposes of investigating the transportation freight rate structure of the railroads of the United States and its impact on the nation's environment, and enhancing, for its members and for all citizens, the quality of the environment through a change in said freight rate structure."[5] We also identified ourselves individually: "[F]ive law students of the National Law Center, The George Washington University, whose names and addresses are as follows: Neil Proto, ... New Haven, Connecticut; John Larouche, ... Milo, Maine; George Biondi, ... Atlanta, Georgia; Kenneth Perlman, ... New York, New York; and Peter Ressler, ... New Haven, Connecticut."[6]

I read the names again. The feeling was unexpected. I was reading my name in a formal government document, along with four other guys, uncertain where we were going, but I felt right about having my name used in this way and for this purpose. "Each member of S.C.R.A.P."—this was the critical part, the harm put into words—"(1) has utilized and will continue to utilize the nation's railroads for personal and/or freight transportation purposes and has an economic interest in said railroads' ability to efficiently ... serve the interests of each petitioner and the public generally; (2) is a taxpayer in the United States and the State in which he is a legal resident, and said tax funds have been and will continue to be utilized ... to abate the kinds of substantial adverse environmental effects herein alleged to be a consequence of the ... discriminatory railroad freight rate structure as applied to recyclable materials; (3) has paid more for products purchased in the marketplace made more expensive by the nonuse of recycled materials in their manufacture; and (4) has traveled throughout various portions of the United States, and has utilized its rivers, streams, forests, and mountains for camping, hiking, fishing, and other recreational purposes, and has an interest in the continued preservation of these natural resources for recreational and aesthetic purposes."[7] It was close to what we had talked about. We could prove it.

Our lateness. It had to be reasonable. The ICC had failed to "provide the public, including Petitioner S.C.R.A.P., with … information [concerning] the environmental impact of the proposed rate increases [and] to notify the public, including … S.C.R.A.P.[,] of a public hearing at which said information … would be considered." This failure, we stated, violated NEPA. The consequence: "S.C.R.A.P. was unable to … make its views known." Elementary but definitely reasonable.[8]

I flipped the petition back onto Meyers's desk. It landed safely between two cups. In withdrawing my hand, I bumped a third cup. It tottered on the brink of disaster for a moment, its equilibrium disrupted by the stale coffee now swishing about and holding aloft three thoroughly soaked cigarette butts. Did B ever catch Meyers smoking? I sat back again and focused on the "Petition for Reconsideration." Here was our legal argument. It needed to be credible.[9]

Seventeen pages. The Introductory Statement: The "record in *Ex Parte 265/267* is procedurally and substantively incomplete and inadequate, and the conclusions derived therefrom are necessarily unreasonable and unlawful, and must be reconsidered." The Commission "had not met its legal obligations under NEPA" and, in light of the "possible irreparable effects on the nation's environment … particularly, but not exclusively, as they apply to scrap iron and steel, textile and paper scrap, glass, fly ash and petroleum waste," the Commission also violated "the letter and the spirit of"—what a list—eight statutes dealing with solid waste disposal, resource recovery, clean air, water quality, fish and wildlife protection, and the Ninth and Fourteenth Amendments. Yes. The Ninth and Fourteenth Amendments. Who knows what consternation they will cause.[10]

The procedural violations of NEPA. Easy. Failure to prepare an EIS and to provide or solicit environmental information. "On the contrary," we wrote, "there appears to be evidence that the Commission disregarded what gratuitous comments it received on the environmental question," specifically the October 9, 1970, letter submitted by Russell E. Train, chairman of the CEQ. Let the Commission deal with the president.

We also identified three "illustrations of foreseeable environmental hazards." First, the availability of scrap iron and steel as well as paper waste would "decrease the need for excessive extraction of the raw materials now used and simultaneously decrease the incidence of particularly destructive methods of extraction, such as strip mining." Appalachia.[11] Second was the harm to "the ability of the nation's larger cities to ... move the enormous amounts of urban solid waste[,]... the cost ... of waste disposal, and losses of revenue from being forced to destroy recyclable materials ..." as well as other harmful effects on human health and water quality. Third was "The Actual Dollar Cost. The Commission has traditionally utilized a method for granting rate increases by percentage without indicating what in fact the percentage increase means in terms of the actual dollar cost." It was the so-called hold-downs. A charade.

Aha. The finale. "The Commission's failure," we concluded, "constituted a blind and irresponsible action of the agency in contravention of its legal obligations to the American people."[12]

"Well," I said softly but to no one. "That's a little strong."

"Who you talking to?" Kenny asked.

"No one. It's nothing. What time is it?"

"Who has a watch?" Kenny asked, looking around the table.

"It's eleven-fifty on the nose," George said. "We'll wait a few more minutes."

I turned to the "petition for Extraordinary Relief."[13] "Extraordinary" was provocative. They would understand *that* in Peoria. Seven pages. SCRAP, "being without other procedural rules under which to make known its requests for relief to this Commission,"—God, what an understatement—"requests the Commission to ... declare invalid and unlawful the proceedings entitled *Ex Parte 265* and *Ex Parte 267*[,] ... immediately suspend the further implementation of the rate increases ... because of the possible irreparable harm being done to the nation's environment[,] ... order the nation's railroads to refund to all shippers monies paid ..."—that's what we want—and, quoting from the Interstate Commerce Act, "to give due regard to the natural and proper development of the country as a whole."[14] That's it. Close enough. I was persuaded.

"Proto." It was John. "How can you keep looking at that stuff? Huh?"

"Let's go," George said.

"We ready?" Peter asked.

"Yeah, it's just after twelve," George said, looking at his watch.

"We all going?" I asked.

"Yeah," George said. "B says to come to his office. We're taking his car."

"B's Volvo?" I asked.

"Yeah." We all started to get up. George put on his scarf and coat.

"Isn't he suing Volvo?" I asked. "One of the groups from our class: CAR or TIRE or something?"

"Who knows?" George answered. "Let's go."

"You have the petitions?" John asked. "And the certificate?"

"Yeah, twenty-five copies," George said. "Let's go before I fall asleep."

"You tired?" Kenny asked. "What did you do? Huh? You been working?" George smiled. I grabbed his arm. We both laughed, the way friends do. We all walked down the stairwell, putting on our coats to confront the cold night air. It felt good to be moving again. We had a long night ahead of us.

George broke off from the pack to get B. The rest of us continued across H to the faculty parking lot. No one was in sight. The streetlights provided the only illumination. In the emptiness, our words sounded hoarse, echoed, distorted. Somehow, without comment, we started to talk softer and then, at once, not to talk at all. George and B followed close behind. Within moments, we pulled out of the lot. I sat in the back seat between Peter and Kenny. It was cold—felt below freezing. There was no wind. It was now Sunday, December 12, 1971.

Washington was quiet and abandoned. We passed a few cars, some moving, others parked in front of randomly placed restaurants along the way. Young people were coming and going, animated, wrapped warmly, and laughing. "That's what normal people do on Saturday nights," George said. "SCRAP. Who ever heard of such a thing?"

We drove down Pennsylvania Avenue past the White House. The car took on a warmth. Our conversation was sporadic, not directed at anything. Banzhaf's presence made talk awkward. We also were uneasy. None of us had done this before. When we reached the White House, bright exterior lights illuminated its white columns and gave the grass a certain richness, despite the effects of the weather. Someone commented about the small peace vigil in front. Quakers.

We turned right onto Fifteenth Street and drove south toward Constitution Avenue. The federal buildings were empty, the workers gone. The Department of Commerce was on our left, the Ellipse on our right. The demonstrations. Maybe it had been May Day when I had seen it. Someone was wearing a tattered light blue shirt—without the commonplace, stenciled, clenched red fist on the back. Instead, there was "Boycott Coke." Wasn't there a migrant labor camp in Florida owned by Minute Maid who owned Coke? Economic pressure. Very practical. But as I looked around that day in May, *everyone* seemed to be drinking Coke, even the kid with the light blue shirt.

Maybe his father owned stock in Coke and the kid was conflicted. Maybe the *kid* owned stock in Coke.

We turned left onto Constitution. The lower portion of the Washington Monument was visible on our right, brightly lit. I had been to the top by the elevator back when my parents came to D.C. with Uncle Al and Aunt Gertrude. "Another two weeks and I'll be home," I thought. Christmas— Mom, Dad, gifts, good food, aunts, uncles, my sister Diana, snow, good food, sleep (no, not sleep—don't think sleep). Within moments, B pulled to a halt just beyond the Smithsonian's History and Technology Museum. No other cars were parked on Constitution. The Commission was on our left. It was dark, quiet, asleep, cocky, overconfident, and bloated.

"We ready?" Banzhaf asked. We walked across the street. Banzhaf led the way.

"I hope the guard will take these," George said to me.

"Who knows? B will know," I responded.

"What the heck are we doing here?" It was Kenny. I understood the question.

The glass front door was locked. The guard noticed us immediately. "We want to file these documents," Banzhaf said. It was late and our number exceeded whatever could possibly be necessary to deliver one envelope, but the guard let us in and took our request under advisement. It was warm inside. Sleep would come easily when it was finally permitted. Not now.

The guard indicated some uncertainty about the procedure. He finally agreed to note the time of our filing and to sign our certificate of service. We each greeted him good night and left. We walked down the few steps in front of the entrance. There was silence. What exactly had we done? Was that all there was to it? "Do you feel uncertain?" I asked George. Before he could answer, I added, "Patience. 'Patience' is what my mother would say now." We dropped back a few yards from the others.

"You mean *pazienza, pazienza.*"

"No," I said. "My mother is a good American. 'Patience,' she would say. 'Patience is a virtue.'"

"Ah," George said. "Patience. Virtue. America. Now we understand each other." We got back into B's car and returned to Bacon. Kenny, Banzhaf, and I each had cars available. The press release packets were divided among us. George came with me. He and I served the *Evening Star* and each of the major local television and radio stations.

I returned to the dorm at 2:40 a.m. The anticipated restful slumber did not come. I knew another day of this remained. I woke early, very early.

It was barely 7:30. And it was still December 12. The closest outlet for acquiring Sunday papers did not open until 10:00. I showered and shaved. It was a long shower. Two days of black stubble, interspersed with a few white hairs, came off easily. I decided on tea, resolving in the process that I would not drink coffee for a month. I placed some eggs in a frying pan, set the burner on low, and walked back into the bedroom to change. I found a clean cotton shirt to go with the blue jeans. It was obvious I needed to wash some clothes.

At 10:00, I left Crawford; walked to the drugstore; and purchased a *Post*, *Star*, and *New York Times*. They were expensive and heavy. As I walked back carrying an enormous bundle of newsprint, I began to sense again how important it was to have an ally in what otherwise was a tough, inequitable confrontation. I could not wait. I leaned against a tree, selected the *Times*, and put the other papers under my arm. I could not hold them in place. I squatted down and sat on the *Post* and *Star*. I opened the *Times*, page after page, scanning, stopping, scanning again, confident I would not miss it.

There it was! Buried, deep in the first section, but there nonetheless. Wow. The *New York Times*. I said it quietly and in awe. "Law Students See Ecology Peril in I.C.C. Rail Freight Increases." It had worked. Bam! Zing! Some Railroad executive was reading this at the same time I was. Bam! Bam! Zingooo! All right, Proto. Now relax. Just relax. There is no one here. Just relax and read this article.

"Law Students See Ecology Peril in I.C.C. Rail Freight Increases, by Juan M. Vasquez, Special to the *New York Times*. Washington. December 11." How did he get this date? He must have been as tired as we were. He did not write it until this morning. No. That's right—we put "Saturday" on the press release. Not important. I will never forget Juan Vasquez. Back to the article.[15]

"A group of law students charged today that the Interstate Commerce Commission violated the provisions of the National Environmental Policy Act in granting freight rate increases this year." Great start. "The group of law students known as Students Challenging Regulatory Agency Procedures—SCRAP—" He did it; SCRAP. That was us. "—was formed to investigate the effects of railroad rate policies on the environment. The students say that the increased freight rate schedule discourages the recycling of waste materials because of higher rates for recycled materials than for raw materials." What a relief, I thought. We did it. Zing! Bam!

"The most immediate impact of the complaint," Vasquez wrote, "will probably be on a proposal for new, higher rates, which the railroads are expected to file, possibly as early as Monday." Fabulous! We did it.

And then I read it, the quote. "'This gives our proceeding priority,' a law student asserted." Wild. It must have been Larouche. I could see him. He must have cornered old Juan and given him the clincher. Incredible. No! The *Times* woke up a "spokesman for the Commission"? "A spokesman for the Commission, Warner L. Baylor, said, however, that the agency did not necessarily have to dispose of the complaint before acting on new rate increase proposals." Baylor might be right, but who cares? It made no difference. Reporters from the *Times* woke this guy up. They had to. We did not deliver the press release until 2:00 in the morning. Incredible. Thank you, Juan Vasquez.

December 12. John, George, and I arrived at the AAR. We emerged from the elevator, probably looking tired and ragged and certainly feeling it. A receptionist was seated behind the desk. A few neatly dressed people—the men with ties but unbuttoned shirts, sleeves rolled up—were walking casually back and forth carrying papers. One man was reading to himself. To my left, I could see into a large conference room. It was filled with long tables and numerous chairs; the tables were cluttered with papers, pads, booklets, and foam cups. I could faintly hear Muzak playing.

John said hello and told the receptionist that we wanted to serve the association with petitions. He asked, "Would you please sign the service copy to show we delivered them?"

She inquired of one of the men standing near her. She then turned to John and declined to accept the petitions. We said politely this delivery was formal service. We could have mailed the petitions. Ah, I thought, we *could* have, but we wanted to ruin your weekend. She made a phone call, and her original decision was reversed. She signed the certificate of service. We left.

Serving the Railroads was largely anticlimactic. Perhaps we were too tired to be truly attentive to the nuances of the recipients' facial expressions, or perhaps the reality of what we had done was sufficiently imbedded in our minds by the article in the *New York Times*. We walked back to Bacon. All that remained was to mail the remaining petitions. Our concern was not necessary. Banzhaf had already taken care of it.

On Monday morning slightly before 9:00, George and I went back to the AAR. "Did you ever think this would be a familiar walk?" I asked, more in the manner of declaring a fact rather than asking a question. He was carrying the list of parties in *265/267*. We got off the elevator and walked to the receptionist's desk. It was unoccupied. We heard sounds of books closing and papers shuffling from the next room, but no voices. I took the list from George and quietly placed it in a conspicuous location on the desk. We left. This time we felt certain no one would mistake us for law firm messengers.

"You know," George said, "we are now notorious."

"You mean 'Wanted' posters in every train station in America?"

"Yep," he said, "but not of the whole group. Only you. THE CHAIRMAN."

Later that day, the nation's Railroads filed their request for a 2.5 percent "emergency surcharge" on all freight moved by all railroads. They had done what they said they would. So, too, had we.

9

MANAGING THE DELUGE, FALL 1971

Environmental Defense Fund. There was no respite. Monday afternoon, December 13. I received a phone call from John Dienelt, an attorney at the Environmental Defense Fund's (EDF) Washington, D.C., office. He had read the *Times*. After a brief digression into EDF's monitoring of the ICC, he asked if I would send him copies of our petitions.

EDF, he said, would be interested in joining us and providing support, including legal representation. His proposition made me uneasy. Beyond a few paragraphs in the *Times*, Dienelt did not know me or the other members of SCRAP or what our purpose was. I expressed my gratitude and told him I would talk to the others. The Sierra Club's refusal to provide any seed money, the skepticism generated by the "Smathers Affair," and the fledgling nature of public interest law in the 1970s—other than in civil rights—formed my discomfort. Dienelt told me that he had been with the firm of Covington & Burling. It was familiar to me. Skilled, powerful lawyers. Dean Acheson. The Railroads. *Arrow Transportation Co. v. Southern Railroad*.

I discussed my conversation with George and John. We met after our Monday class in B's Unfair Trade Practices. Our conversation was more like a debate; each of us moved from one position to another, wanting to identify and explore all the ramifications, not necessarily to be fair but so as not to be wrong. "I don't think we're deluding ourselves." I said. "We're at least an irritant."

"Our most vulnerable legal position is 'standing,'" George posited, with equivocation.

"The Sierra Club was unable to convince the Ninth Circuit," I said.

We were not certain how well we had explained our standing before the Commission and, as George reminded me, "There are only five of us."

"Maybe EDF would scare the Commission?" John posited, without conviction.

"I don't think the Commission knows who EDF is, let alone cares," I replied.

"The Supreme Court's decision to review the *Sierra Club* case makes this decision harder," George said.

"Our response to Dienelt shouldn't be premised on standing," John added, with conviction. "It's too soon."

"The legal representation? Do we need it?" I asked. Kenny and Peter had had it. The "midnight surprise" and all the other obligations of Unfair Trade Practices were enough time to devote to any one course.

"The question, then, is what else is there to do between now and the end of the semester?" George asked. None of us had seen the Railroads' new petition for a rate increase. We would have to file a response in order to remain credible with the Commission.

"And with Banzhaf," George added quickly. Getting a good grade, now easily within reach, should not be jeopardized.

"Now, to the hard question," I said. "Next semester."

"Banzhaf has to get us credit. It'll consume too much time," John said.

"I agree," George said. "And," he added, raising his finger, "we'll learn a lot."

I nodded and raised my own finger. "They're gonna tell us to get lost. You know what that means?"

"Yeah. Court," George said.

"It will require good lawyers," I said.

"Banzhaf." John posited quickly.

"He has the law school and ASH." I said, still trying to lay out facts. "EDF could."

"If we decide not to do it, we're responsible for transferring this—"

"—to other students," George reminded us.

"If they want it," John added. "An environmental organization like EDF might."

"Tell Dienelt we're taking a course and need to stay involved. Let him do the talking," George said. "We really don't have to decide now." John and I agreed. John also thought we might hear from others.

"You're right," I said. "Who knows who'll come out of the woodwork?"

EX PARTE NO. 281

John brought the Railroads' new petition to Stockton Hall. George and I met him on the first floor. We located a corner away from the front entrance so we would not feel the bursts of cold air. We stood alone, John's knapsack sitting upright between us. John read from the petition. "A 2.5 percent 'emergency surcharge' on all existing freight rates. *Ex Parte 281, Increased Freight Rates and Charges, 1972*," he told us, rubbing and blowing into his hands. "It's comparable to a tax. Another rate increase. The rates for scrap iron and steel increase like they did in *265/267*. But," he said with that grin, "the surcharge is on an 'interim basis' until the Railroads file another petition requesting a larger 'permanent' increase."[1]

"Another increase?" George exclaimed, shaking his head.

"Surprise, surprise. 'Interim' and 'permanent' are the same. The effect on the environment is the same," I said.

"Hold on, boys. The Railroads want the surcharge to be effective on January 1, upon five days' notice to the public," John said.

"January 1? That's two weeks, three weeks?" George asked, his face perplexed, searching mine. "Neil. What the heck are we going to do?"

"I'm not sure, George," I said, rubbing my face and eyes hard.

"They could get it before the damn semester's over," George said.

John looked nonplussed. "You haven't seen anything yet," he said. He reached down and with some labor opened and stretched wide his knapsack. In one grand movement, his arms encircled and extracted about eight inches of solid paper. "The verified statements."

"Damn," I said angrily.

"How many?"

"Maybe thirty-five, forty," John replied.

"They make the damn things up." I said, trying to calculate how we would handle them. "I know, I know, we've got to know what they say. But damn it."

Students walked near and around us, most bundled in sweaters and scarves, looking strained, taut, and uneasy. I sighed heavily. It was a deep exhale; I could feel it. We all agreed— we had to respond. I proposed to talk with Banzhaf, Kenny, and Peter. John added a fact that was not obvious until he said it. "An EIS cannot be prepared in less than three weeks and provide the basis for a decision."

"The Railroads don't give a damn," George said. We all looked at one another with a kind of simultaneously exercised telepathy and recognized another fact. Neither did the Commission. The failure to comply with NEPA was stark, obvious, and unequivocal. It simply could not be done. And the Railroads and the Commission knew it.

"Our comments should be succinct," I said firmly. "We summarize what we said before, remind the Commission we asked it not to act until they decided our petitions in *265/267*, and complain that compliance with NEPA precludes Commission approval by January 1."

George bought this approach but not fully. "The Commission and the Railroads already have worked this out. They're not waiting. Well, the problem for us is that if they grant it, with this five days' notice, we're stuck."

"The lawsuit," I said with resignation.

"Yep. That's what he's saying," John added with no less comfort. No one wanted a lawsuit, not between now and the semester's end. We stood there in silence, uncertain. I could feel the cold air on my fingers. "We can't play by their rules," I said. "We don't know what they think of us. They've got to think we're crazy. For all we know, they don't expect us to do anything. But they don't know for sure. It's all so damn quick. I think they figure we're students and we can't do it. For now, let's just stick with a response in *281*, get it in fast, and hope we throw them off, screw them up—like we know what we're doing, like, ah, ... we're not missing anything, like we live there."

George said plaintively, "We almost do."

John agreed to start writing. I walked over to Bacon and told Banzhaf to expect our response. He agreed to review and sign it. He also proposed that we hand-deliver it to each commissioner to enhance its effect. He mentioned the possibility of a lawsuit. He thought we should prepare for it.

NPCA

A representative of the National Parks and Conservation Association (NPCA) contacted Banzhaf. He proposed a meeting. I called George and John. "I knew it," John said. "If they get involved, it will have two effects. Increase our credibility with the Commission and our leverage with EDF."

Banzhaf, we were certain, would love it. "Guaranteed he'll want a press release," George said, as we walked over to Eighteenth Street and Massachusetts Avenue.

NPCA's headquarters building was solid stone with wrought-iron and glass doors that were elegant and heavy; in front was a circular driveway with trees, plants, and other greenery near and around it. NPCA's name was solidly engraved in a bronze plate that was slightly tarnished and displayed out front. The building was old world to me, like the headquarters for the Allied High Command in London then later in Paris, and later still in Berlin. The inside confirmed it. The wood was dark, distinguished, and imbedded with memories; the main room was big with high ceilings and with rugs—oriental, tattered, ancient, and Anglo-Saxon from somewhere in an empire that had now withered. Everything around me seemed shadowed as if any light that was not provided by a lamp or a fireplace or strained through colored glass was suspect, became intrusive, or lacked civility. "Who are these guys?" I thought.

It was a brief meeting. The executive director had reviewed our petitions. He had communicated with the association's lawyer, Sandy Weissbard, who worked with Fried, Frank, Harris, Shriver & Kampelman. The firm was located in the Watergate. He asked what NPCA could do. We suggested that it join in *265/267*. He agreed. We offered to prepare the joinder. "You also might find support from the Izaak Walton League," he said. "I'll call the executive director." We thanked him and left.

"Patricia Harris and Sargent Shriver?" exclaimed George. We were hardly out the front door. I had not seen him smile with such gusto in a long time.

"Not bad for a couple of law student types," I said. The walk back to campus was easy at first, filled with thoughts and words of triumph. George volunteered to determine how to join NPCA.

John introduced another subject: "Do you think NPCA and EDF and the other environmental groups talk to each other?" Or, as it was rephrased after a few moments, "Do you think they all get along with each other?"

"It's best to assume they do," I said, knowing that their contact would be mostly with me. "It's difficult enough figuring out our opponents."

That night, Caroline came by Crawford, unexpectedly. She proposed a walk and we headed toward Georgetown. "What kind of law does your father practice?" I asked as we stepped inside Clyde's. Caroline was still holding her trench coat over her head from the rain shower that drove us inside for coffee.

"Transportation. It's a small, old firm."

"What kind of transportation?"

"Airlines and, actually, sometimes trains. It's very established."

"I see."

"I mean corporate. Daddy's very respected."

"Did you know your grandparents?"

"No, not on my father's side. Only Sarah, the nanny who raised—"

"—in Louisiana?"

"Yes."

IZAAK WALTON

"He was a fisherman," George said to me. "Big time, I think."

John called the League's office, in Rosslyn, Virginia, directly across Key Bridge. He arranged a meeting with Ted Pankowski, the director. Pankowski was sympathetic but tough in his questions. Will you work on this beyond the first semester? he asked. If you stop, who'll do the work? The fact that we had been approached by EDF and had a commitment from the NPCA seemed to give him comfort. He agreed to talk to both organizations, but he declined to join SCRAP in *265/267*.

Pankowski raised the "standing" question directly. He was closely monitoring the *Sierra Club* case. He gave us a copy of the brief filed by the League as *amicus curiae*. The obvious question was whether the League and others were uneasy with the Sierra Club's position. To ask that question, we all thought and agreed beforehand, would get us into precisely the intrigue among the environmental groups that we vowed to avoid. Perhaps, we suggested to Pankowski, if the League joined SCRAP before the ICC, it would be helpful in the event of a lawsuit. He was uncertain. So were we.

George prepared a "Notice of Joinder of the National Parks and Conservation Association With Students Challenging Regulatory Agency Procedures (S.C.R.A.P.)." It was a three-page document: "Comes now the National Parks and Conservation Association and respectfully declares ... it has a substantial interest in the matters to be named herein, and that it desires earnestly to become a formal party to, and hereby adopts..."[2]

"Nobody writes this way anymore, George," I said after my first review.

"Wrong," he responded. "The ICC does. Well, we know they think that way."

George also identified NPCA and its interests. It was founded in 1919 and is "an independent private, non-profit service corporation ... composed of a membership of more than 50,000 persons located throughout the nation and dedicated to the ... improvement of the national park system and to the ... conservation of natural resources" (p. 2). This interest brought considerable credence to the "natural resource" harm we said resulted from the failure to recycle. Banzhaf, on our behalf, certified that the "Petitioner

S.C.R.A.P. fully accepts the National Parks and Conservation Association as co-petitioner."[3]

"What a hard argument that was," George said.

I called Sandy Weissbard. He was expecting us. We walked to the Watergate office building. Weissbard read our joinder notice and gave it his approval. We left it with him and, with expressions of gratitude, said goodbye. The notice was filed with the Commission within a few weeks. We were no longer alone.

TO THE HILL

Vic Reinemer called Banzhaf's office while George, John, and I were there. He was staff director to Senator Lee Metcalf of Montana. Reinemer requested copies of the petitions. I suggested that we hand-deliver them. We left Bacon Hall and hurried over to Crawford. John was carrying his knapsack filled with books and now four more sets of petitions.

The *Times* article had been followed by one in the *Star* on Tuesday, December 14. It, plus the petitions we mailed to key members of Congress, had generated calls from Senators Warren G. Magnuson of Washington,[4] Robert A. Taft of Ohio, and Edmund S. Muskie of Maine,[5] as well as from Congressmen John D. Dingell of Michigan and Charles A. Vanik of Ohio.

My Volkswagen was parked behind Crawford. We piled in, with John in the back seat. I headed through the alleyway, turned left onto H Street, drove past the Center, went past Bacon in the next block, and drove straight ahead. It was late morning, 11:17 according to the large clock in the 1700 block of Pennsylvania Avenue. In front of the White House, the Quakers continued to hold their vigil. Others did too and were drinking hot coffee or tea or perhaps soup to deal with the cold. One woman—not wearing a hat, a poster tucked under her arm—was talking to a White House guard. I took a right on Fifteenth Street (just past Treasury), shifted into second, and turned left back onto Pennsylvania. There it was in the distance. The Capitol Building—its flag waving briskly; its gold dome shining brilliant in the sunlight; and its portico white, clear, and sturdy. The postcard view. "I like going up here," George said quietly, turning toward me and then looking straight ahead. We continued past Justice, the Archives, the Federal Trade Commission on the right, and the United States Courthouse on the left.

"They going to stop me with this knapsack?" John asked.

"The guard will," George said, turning slightly, "but just be cool. Students looking like us are not universally in favor."

"You mean looking like you."

"Me? I look like a Senator compared to you," George said. I moved the car into the slight curve to the left where Pennsylvania merges into Constitution Avenue, downshifted, zipped up Capitol Hill, and took a right into the parking area located in front of the Capitol.

"I think we should get uniforms," I said.

"You mean with 'SCRAP' on the jacket?" George asked.

"Yeah. Red with white stripes."

"I told you we should have gotten shirts. You laughed."

"You laughed at theme music," I said.

"We could dance to the theme music. You know, like *West Side Story*."

I parked the car. We got out and walked quickly across the lawn toward the Old Senate Office Building. The Supreme Court was to our right. "You've been there?" George asked me, his head moving in that direction.

"Only once for about ten minutes." The Court did not seem distant or detached from my life now—just unknown, its process uncertain.

"You going to stay in Washington, Proto?" John asked, moving abreast of George and me, knapsack in tow.

"I registered to take the Connecticut bar. You decided what you're going to do?"

"Back to Maine." He sounded convinced.

We crossed Constitution, walked up the stairs and through the revolving doors. While the guard looked through John's knapsack, I asked which office Senator Metcalf occupied. "Room 427."

The Old Senate Office Building is a somber, stately looking structure, classical in tone with a grayish-white marble, granite, and limestone exterior highlighted by an open veranda running the length of Constitution. Inside, the double doors offer the fascination: ten feet in height, larger than life, implanted into walls that reach much higher. The doors are dark—mahogany perhaps—solid and strong, as if they protect power and so need to be impressive. They serve as entranceways to each Senator's office.

We located room 427. One of the doors was opened. "Yes, can I help you?" asked the receptionist in a soft, gentle voice that I instinctively felt had its origins back home in Montana.

"We're here to see Mr. Reinemer," I said.

"Do you have an appointment?"

"I just talked to him on the phone. He's expecting us."

"I see." She smiled, as if she was genuinely glad we were there. "May I have your name?"

"Certainly. It's Neil Proto."

"P-R-O-T-O?" she asked me.

"Yes. That's correct."

She picked up the phone, pressed a buzzer, and announced our presence—or at least mine. She smiled and gracefully pointed to the chairs on both sides of the room. "Please have a seat," she said. "He'll be right out."

The room was not large. Unlike others I had been in, its walls were not covered with photographs, enlarged news articles, or memorabilia. There were no portraits of Senator Metcalf or a glass-enshrined pen from LBJ. There was a plaque from a local farmers' group; a painting of a landscape—mountains and a waterfall—done in oils and primary colors; another painting of Indians, moving on horseback but not animated—gentle and soft in color and recent in its depiction. The room was simple and warm.

Lee Metcalf was the junior Senator from Montana. He was not "flashy," not a George Smathers. He was described in one news article as persistent and knowledgeable, a "populist" who was critical of the utility industry and large banking institutions and was supportive of agrarian interests. I did know that Montana's senior Senator, Mike Mansfield, had been trying to abolish the ICC.[6]

In a few moments, Vic Reinemer appeared. He was middle-aged, perhaps fifty years old, a little stocky but bouncy, smiling in a youthful way, confident and reflecting a kind of optimism. He welcomed us. He was gentle in tone, low-keyed—but there was an enthusiasm in his words as if he thrived on his work, was engaged by it, and believed it made a difference. He motioned us into a large interior room shared by three or four others. "These are the SCRAP fellows," he said.

They each smiled fully and nodded. One wished us well. Another said, "Great job."[7]

We sat down. I told him about the support from EDF, the Izaak Walton League, and NPCA. He expressed abrupt satisfaction. It was not a status report he wanted. He wanted more copies of the petitions: one set for the staff director of the Senate Committee on Commerce, Mike Pertschuk, and another for Dan O'Neal, chief counsel of the Subcommittee on Surface Transportation. The point had now penetrated: the nature of his interest and the depth of his feeling. It was the Railroads—the populist disdain for their manipulation, abuse, cockiness, and power. It was why we were here.

He reached to a shelf above his desk and pulled down a copy of a congressional hearing, *Failing Railroads*, that had been held before the Senate Committee on Commerce. He turned to an already marked interior page. It had my name on the upper right-hand corner. It's important to know who you're dealing with, Reinemer said. How the ICC and DOT permitted the destruction of the Penn Central and now want millions of dollars to bail it out. "Read it."[8]

A bell rang. Then it rang again. One of the people working—a woman, my age, who appeared worn and puffy-eyed, like a law student, like me—got up and walked briskly out of the room. She stopped momentarily to wish us luck. Reinemer's telephone buzzed. He seemed to acknowledge it but reached instead under a pile of papers. The telephone buzzed again. With one hand under the pile—still searching, touching, like tentacles—he grabbed the phone with the other.

I looked around the room. Books shelved, unshelved, and piled. Papers, some in neat arrangements but mostly not—mostly in piles, uneven, some in colors, some stapled, most piles topped with paperweights, rocks, or books. I saw piles of printed materials, pamphlets, and booklets stacked in odd places, in corners, on chairs, on the floor. I saw telephones, perhaps four of them, and thick reports bound in green or brown. Tables of different sizes were old, worn, and wooden. Desks—four, perhaps five—were laid out without an obvious pattern but with a definite rhythm, feeling, purpose, and commitment. There also was no clear wall space. Everything was being used.

George gently took out of my hand the hearing that Reinemer had given me. He flipped through it, concentrated on a particular page, stopped, and handed it back. It was a colloquy between Senator Vance Hartke, chairman of the Senate Committee on Commerce, and Secretary of Transportation John Volpe.[9]

SENATOR VANCE HARTKE. Now what is the source of your information today on the present condition of the railroad industry?

SECRETARY VOLPE. Well, our view of the railroad industry is even accelerated beyond the—

SENATOR HARTKE. I asked what is the source, not your view.

SECRETARY VOLPE. The information that we have come[s] from the railroad industry itself, the Interstate Commerce Commission—

I smiled and shook my head.

Reinemer got off the phone and turned toward us. John immediately handed him two sets of petitions and asked who else should get copies. Reinemer reached again to the shelf above his desk for the congressional directory.

He wrote down names and room numbers. He insisted that we remain in close touch. He was ready to do what he could. He was firm about it. He thanked us for coming. His manner was serious but warm, collegial, almost fatherly. We each shook his hand and left.

"That was great," John said, closing the door behind him. "He knew exactly what was going on. He was ready for us."

"He sure was. They all knew who we were," I said, almost inwardly.

"You mean, SCRAP," George said, his tone crisp, mischievous.

"Hey. What the hell did we do?" I said.

"I don't know. But damn," John said, with a bouncy enthusiasm. "There's a lot here. I mean we've got a lot to learn."

"Listen," I said and then stopped walking. "While we're here, should we see anyone else? John. You got more copies of the petitions?"

"One."

"Where do you want to go?" George asked, engaged by the adventure.

"How about the guy Banzhaf knows who works for Ted Kennedy? Susman. Tom Susman," I suggested.

Kennedy's subcommittee was in the basement. When we entered, George leading, it seemed more like an oversized broom closet packed with desks, tables, room dividers, typewriters, and bookshelves. It made Reinemer's office look systematic and palatial. George asked the first person we encountered—a woman, seated, newspaper clippings all around her, twentyish, and frantically manipulating a pair of scissors and tape—where Susman was located. She loosened her fingers and pointed to the back of the room. Numerous conversations emanated from behind bookshelves along with the rhythmic clattering of at least three typewriters. Her pointed finger directed us toward the back of a high bookshelf, obscured partially by another room divider. It looked like the entrance to a maze. We slithered through the opening, hoping to find Susman. We did, and George introduced himself. In an area that was perhaps five by seven feet was a desk, a typewriter, three bookshelves, a wastebasket, and one extra chair. George occupied the chair. In fact, he was forced into it.

We got right to the point. We explained that we were Banzhaf's students. In ten seconds, we explained the project. Fine. Yeah, I'll take a copy, he said. Did you go to the Commerce Committee? Don't expect much but keep me informed. Did you see Surface Transportation? Good. Keep it up. It's good. You gotta keep doing it. His phone rang. The typewriters marched in unison and then in combat. The conversations around us intensified in sound and fury. We nodded to one another. We thanked him and said goodbye.

Once out of the building, we crossed Constitution and walked directly toward the car. Our excitement had subsided. The cold weather, the new rate increase, our other course requirements, the arrival of the holidays, and, shortly thereafter, final exams—those realities did it every time, neatly, decisively, and without humor. But the moments of excitement were coming more frequently now, their effect evident in one way particularly: they highlighted and exposed our indecision about whether to continue. Everyone we talked to assumed we would continue to challenge the Commission. We were getting closer to the semester's end. "This is just the beginning," George said. He stated it with care and only to me. I kept walking, forcing myself back into the choice and how to think about it.

"I think you're right, George," I said, almost in a whisper.

We got into the car. I started the engine, slipped the gears into first, and headed toward the south side of the Capitol, onto Independence Avenue, and back down the Hill. We drove past the Longworth and Rayburn Buildings on the left, up Independence, past the DOT, L'Enfant Plaza, and the Department of Agriculture. The heat in the Volkswagen had taken hold. George opened the discussion. "Well. Are we going to do this next semester?"

"I don't think Kenny or Peter wants to," I said.

"Continuing would be easier if we could get credit for it," George said. "I'm not sure I can do it otherwise." None of us were. We also were uneasy about Banzhaf. We would have to work with him more, and there would be only three of us to share the contact. He had been supportive, helpful, insightful in definable, practical ways—but he also could be brusque and aloof, with a stinging disposition. We had seen it, not yet with us but in class.

"I can hardly handle just you guys," I said, gesturing with my right thumb toward both of them. Then, in a somber tone, "We also don't know for certain how Banzhaf views this. The telling signal will be the grade."

"We can't wait," John said. "Grades wouldn't be posted until the beginning of next semester."

"So, we need to talk with Banzhaf soon."

"Yeah, I guess," I added. To our left was the Tidal Basin and, beside it, the Jefferson Memorial. I took a right toward the traffic circle that surrounded the Lincoln Memorial. "Things look okay," I said.

"What do you mean?" George asked, after a moment of silence and recognizing that I wanted a response.

"Well, we filed our petitions and made the newspaper. The *Times* and the *Star*. We have, maybe, three national environmental groups supporting us and some congressional people interested. Banzhaf is happy. If we just keep up a little flurry through the end of the semester, we've got a good grade."

"You're right, but we've got to keep up the flurry," John agreed.

In fact, as George then put it, "There's flurry all around us. Our problem is keeping up with it."

I drove up Twenty-third Street, past the State Department and the World Health Organization on our right and onto the campus. I turned right at H. There were students all around us. It was like a parade. I stopped at the stop sign on H and Twenty-second Street. Madison Hall was on the right. With spunk—I liked this car—I drove through the intersection. I turned into the alleyway beside Crawford and, with care, eased into my parking space. "All right, gentlemen," I said. We got out of the car and began our walk back toward H. "Look," I said, "there's maybe a month left."

"Less, with the holidays," George reminded me.

We separated and, remembering one more thing, I called to both of them. "We have to meet with EDF next week." They each turned to acknowledge it with a nod and a look of resignation. Another uncertainty. I felt it too.

I waited a few moments. Students were walking by in groups of twos and threes, talking. It was the "parade" I was interested in. Jeff Gocke was coming from across the street, walking with one of the residents. We greeted one another, and I asked him if he knew about any demonstration. He had seen it. "It was about wage controls," he said, "the president's freeze—and that it was unfair." If I had seen thirty people, that number was more than he had seen.

THE ARGUMENT

I took the *New York Times Magazine* into the pantry and stood, reading, while I listened to the coffeepot perk. The December 12 edition had a front-page photograph and an article on strip mining.[10] "Like flaying the back of a man," it read. The photo was of this gigantic auger, screwing and gouging into the side of a mountain. It was surreal in power and size, not comprehensible in its effect on a person's sense of place. It was like punishment without justice, like the imposition of an indignity that is enduring, permanent, and crippling. It was what motivated Harry Caudill, what I liked about Reinemer. It was the Railroads and their effect on people that Reinemer disdained.

With coffee in hand, I sat down on the couch. Before me were a few neglected textbooks. I reached instead for *Failing Railroads*. The Nixon administration wanted $175 million to support the Penn Central. Senator Hartke wanted no part of it. "It was not enough for the old Penn Central management ... to get into real estate developments, golf clubs, beauty parlors, amusement parks, pipelines, and even the air carrier business.... But the pipeline sprung leaks; the real estate development company has run out of money; and the airplane venture has resulted in violations of federal law, the second highest penalty in CAB [Civil Aeronautics Board] history and millions of dollars down the drain.... It was the railroad that provided the cash for the subsidiaries, not the other way around."[11] Okay, Vance. Good job. The first witness was Willard Wirtz, a Penn Central trustee. He wanted to avoid "some sort of nationalization" and to ensure "a successful free enterprise reorganization." Public money was to be used as a reward for schemes usually associated with hucksters and hacks.

The phone rang. It was Jeff. An argument had gotten out of hand. It was over the Vietnam War. Three residents eligible for the draft had engaged in it. It had ended in yelling, personal insults, and the demise of a roommate relationship. It was a small moment in a large dormitory. Jeff had it under control by the time I arrived.

By the winter of 1971, the War had been displaced visibly by other stories: the border fighting between India and Pakistan over Bangladesh; the still-civilized jockeying within the Democratic Party over the 1972 presidential election—George S. McGovern, Edmond S. Muskie, Hubert H. Humphrey, George C. Wallace, and John Lindsay; and the fairness of the president's selective allowance of wage and price increases. The "forces of peace," as the president characterized them, had begun to occupy the federal courthouses, city halls, and police departments. Those factors were reflective of a more self-absorbed populace—those who simply wanted quietude, safe streets, and predictable, even-handed morality. The larger dissonance was being channeled. Congress was doing it with the Twenty-sixth Amendment that allowed eighteen-year-olds to vote. The *Washington Post* was running articles on the "New Nixon"—his confidence in winning reelection and his apparent reemergence as credible, moral, and mainstream.[12]

Cultural changes continued. Hair got shorter, and the mythology and storytelling about the days of withdrawal and demonstrations were all that remained for many. Some residents had no larger "movement" with which to connect, no broader culture of which they were part. I was uncertain where those cultural changes would lead, not for the nation, but for those eighteen-, nineteen-, and twenty-year-olds whom I counseled and with whom I shared a dormitory. I worried not for all of them but for those reduced to rough argument or withdrawal, for those getting "stoned" with their earphones on and the stereo blasting inside, with Joplin or Guthrie or Hendrix singing fiercely, at Woodstock, in yesteryear, and this was the only way to keep those moments alive.

ARCHER-DANIELS-MIDLAND

December 17. John had prepared a letter to the ICC protesting the 2.5 percent emergency surcharge. I revised it. George reviewed it. Kenny and Peter concurred that we needed to file it. I gave it to Banzhaf. He asked some questions and handed it to Freda for typing. I walked next door to meet George. He followed me back to Banzhaf's office. The letter was finished. It was directed to Commission Chairman George M. Stafford. It was on SCRAP letterhead: "S.C.R.A.P. is making its views known to you through this letter," it read, "instead of a formal protest because *Ex Parte 281* has not been formally opened for comments."

We took three legal positions. First, the Railroads had failed to demonstrate the existence of an emergency that warranted an increase in rates before January 1, 1972. Second, the 2.5 percent surcharge had the same immediate and discriminatory effect on recyclable materials that we described in *265/267*. Third, the Commission's review of the surcharge constituted "'a major federal action significantly affecting the quality of the human environment' and, as such, the Commission must prepare an adequate 'environmental impact statement' prior to any decision on the railroads' Petition." We also advised Commissioner Stafford that the "refund provision" available to an individual shipper "would not protect against the possibility of irreparable harm being done to the environment." Banzhaf signed it. It was a simple act. In performing it, I realized that our relationship with Banzhaf had taken on a new dimension. He was now our lawyer. Time and the interactions among us would further define the meaning of our relationship. We made copies of the letter and prepared to leave. John came with us. Within the hour, we had hand-delivered the letter to each commissioner.[13]

Our confidence also received a boost that day from an unexpected source: the Archer-Daniels-Midland Company of Decatur, Illinois. The company was among the parties we served with petitions in *265/267*. Its director of corporate transportation sent them back. Such extra copies always were welcomed; interest in them remained high. The unexpected boost was in the cover letter:[14]

Sir:

I return herewith three (3) petitions received this date.... These petitions were allegedly filed with the ICC by the Students Challenging Regulatory Agency Procedures (S.C.R.A.P.). On its face, and having given the petitions a cursory review, I would suggest the name of this organization be changed to LOBBY OF THE STUDENTS AS CHALLENGING REGULATORY AGENCY PROCEDURES (L.O.T.S.A.C.R.A.P.).... To be candid, I object to having my company, a party to those proceedings, being burdened with such an obvious academic exercise. As a professional traffic man, I object to having to be subjected to such inane protestations. As a sometime friend of the Commission, I object to such absurd and reveling accusations. As a private citizen, I object to your effrontery wherein you hold yourselves out to speak for me. But as a Christian, I wish you a Merry Christmas.

None of us were certain what business Archer-Daniels-Midland was in or why its director of corporate transportation chose to say what he did. Banzhaf posted it outside his office. We were relieved. The Railroads had at least one loyal supporter prepared to rescue them from the inane, beguiling, and torturous "Lobby of the Students." Besides that, L.O.T.S.A.C.R.A.P. was not dissimilar to some of our original ideas. George proposed we adopt it, maybe with a ceremony. "Hey. If Esso can change to Exxon—?"

"No. Better idea," I said. "We could form a new chapter called 'Friends of SCRAP.'"

"You mean FOSCRAP?" John added, making plain the acronym didn't work.

"People could submit names," George suggested.

"Who would chair it?" I asked. The answer was obvious even before I ended the question. George, posed in mock seriousness, raised his finger and said plainly, "George Smathers." And on that note, more dissonant and ironic and disconcerting than expected, we brought our parody to an end. SCRAP, we decided, was here to stay.

10

FINDING CLARITY, WINTER 1971

The haunted past. "Demonstrations," I was told. "Early the second semester." The Housing Office requested a meeting the following day at 2:00 p.m. Two new directors had gleaned the possibility of demonstrations through friends in a national student organization.

"Wishful thinking," George said. "It's over." I shared his skepticism and said so.

"Begin to plan and to orient your staff," we were told. George and I looked at one another with a perceptible shudder. I was asked to explain briefly what we did last year. George and another colleague, Gail Short—a skilled veteran—interjected. On the meeting dragged: questions, answers, ideas, experiences, and, finally, at 4:30 p.m. it ended.

I said goodbye to George and turned right to walk up I Street toward Twenty-second Street. It was the third week in December. The wind was brisk but mostly at tree level, as if a different world were being formed and changed and disrupted just a few feet above my head. As I thought about the demonstrations, walking while snapping the buttons on my parka, it was my resentment that really bothered me. I wanted to devote my energy elsewhere—to studying, enjoying friendships, learning, and living life.

I reached Twenty-second, turned left, crossed I, and headed toward H Street. The wind was stronger here, blowing in gusts and stinging when it hit my face, each gust taking the few remaining leaves from atop the small trees that lined the street. The sky was growing dark. Rain seemed inevitable; I knew it would be torrential and cold when it came.

On the far corner of Twenty-second and H was Madison Hall. My eyes moved quickly back to Welling Hall. It was now vacant. Its doors and windows were boarded, its paint chipped and cracked badly. Its memories and ghosts and goblins and stories had moved elsewhere, repeated elsewhere but not there—not any longer. Its fate was sealed and determined by the university's "Program for Greatness." Welling was scheduled for demolition.

I pulled up the hood of my parka to protect my eyes from the dirt and leaves being pushed and shoved by the wind. My pace slowed. I thought back to the demonstrations: watching students being beaten by police, stealing from one another, and destroying property; trying to counsel many in groups, alone, amid tear gas; working with others and with forced teams trying to cope, help students, and avoid pain; learning all the time about war, culture, disappointment, intrusion, responsibility (a lot of it), and discipline that was imposed but mostly instinctive, and more than I expected; sharing life, in quick ways, perplexing and harsh and, at times, laughing at it and then with one another; and forming friendships that were important, reliable, and still there.

My mind moved further backward: Robert Kennedy's campaign; the announcement published in the *New Haven Register*; "Young Citizens for Kennedy," statewide membership, I was chair. Exams remained. Reverend Ralph Abernathy called for volunteers to help construct Resurrection City on the Monument grounds. My classmate Steve Vossmeyer from Missouri was direct: "Let's go do this." We joined the men nailing plywood sheets together. As we were leaving, fires being lit, a man, tall and lean, some ten yards away, was moving between lean-tos, alone. An elderly woman stood next to me. She did not move her eyes from his movement. "Stokely Carmichael," she said in a respectful way. "He has come to visit." Government tore it down. The people vacated. The assassination of Robert Kennedy had made me acutely attentive. I'd walked past his coffin in St. Patrick's, as if the tumult and related unpredictability of other people's agendas wouldn't end.

I pulled the parka's hood tightly over my head as if in battle with the wind. You needed to know who you were and what you believed in; what it was, in the end, you thought valuable. I needed to hold tight to where I was from and disciplined about the values that got me here.

The wind now came in intense, cyclonic swirls, engulfing leaves and debris close to the ground. I turned the corner at Twenty-second and H, glanced up long enough to ensure my path was clear, and then walked on. We would handle demonstrations if we had to.

The rain finally came. It fell in enormous drops, darkening the sidewalk quickly and causing everyone within earshot to groan, cover their heads, and run. As I opened the door to Crawford, a few of the boys came in right behind me, sopping wet. They were with John Tomsky, George Biondi's administrative assistant. They asked me if I wanted to see a flick, *Midnight Cowboy*, at the University Center. I deferred. Time, I knew, was in short supply.

EDF: THE BOMBSHELL

John Dienelt called a few days before our scheduled meeting. There was a condition to his offer of support. If a lawsuit was filed, it must be in EDF's name, not SCRAP's. The press would mention only the lead group. I deferred judgment, thinking about what to say and what I understood he had said: You're going to do the work and we're going to get the credit. "I have to talk with the members of the group," I said evenly. He said he understood.

I found George in the law school library. We both found John coming out of class. We stood on the steps leading into Stockton. It was cold, in the upper thirties. I told them about my conversation with Dienelt. It was not told with detachment. John and George were angry, stunned, beyond consolation if someone had dared at that moment to offer it. I did not. The three of us were animated, walking up and then down the stairs, changing posture and position, calming and then provoking one another. Then we started, with more care, talking to each other as a group. The problem was "standing."

"We might need EDF to get it," John said. "Without them, we might lose the other groups. They know it."

"EDF is for EDF," George said sternly.

"I didn't realize the competition among environmental groups was so strong," I said.

"So, whom do we trust?" George asked, probably knowing the answer.

"Not EDF, for sure. They think because we're students they can play with us," I said. "We know we have Banzhaf and Meyers."

"Right," John concurred. "Whatever ego thing old B has, we trust both of them."

"SCRAP," George said in principled triumph, "has to be for SCRAP."

"It may mean more work for us, but—"

"You're kidding, Proto," John said. "It will mean more work for us. But we need to be smart. We can't anger anyone yet. And the publicity we're getting—we've got to use it more. EDF is not the attraction. We are."

"You thought the newspaper was for dealing with the Railroads."

"Yeah. Look. From now on, every time we file something, we do a press release, and we keep up our contacts on the Hill."

"What happened to the good guys?" John asked.

"Yeah. Merry Christmas," George weighed in.

"Merry Christmas? You think *this* is bad? Wait until the Commission sticks it to us," I said.

"Screw them too," George said, the hardness of his tone still intact.

"George. Patience," I said. He grew silent and looked at me directly. "You're right. Patience."

I called Dienelt later that day. I told him we would consider his proposition but the other members of the group wanted to discuss it with him first. He agreed.

THE SEEMING MIRACLE

December 22. I called the public information office at the Commission to ask about the release of a decision in *281*. The timing was impeccable. The answer was disconcerting. A public statement would be forthcoming by the close of business. The actual written decision might be delayed because of some printing problem. I was angered. "Damn. Banzhaf was right. We might have to sue. It might be Christmas Eve before we know the details."

"You know it's deliberate, Neil," George said, his eyes rolling, his mind on Christmas, plans, and family. We all wanted to go home. I had planned to leave that afternoon for my brother's house in Laurel and then early the morning of the twenty-third for New Haven. I walked back to Crawford, got my car, and drove over to Bacon. John and George met me out front, bundled heavily with scarves, gloves, and hats. They welcomed the warmth, relative as it was, of the Volkswagen. The thermometer outside registered near freezing. Snow was predicted. The prediction alone would cause incomprehensible traffic jams. Such prospects did little to soothe our disgruntled temperament as we drove down Pennsylvania Avenue, past the White House—the Quakers still there, huddled tightly together, enclosed by heavy blankets, unyielding while the War continued and men died— to Fifteenth Street, and toward Constitution Avenue. It was the familiar route.

"It's getting late," George said. "They'll be towing cars soon. Go behind the Smithsonian."

I downshifted and took a left onto Constitution. I looked briefly at George seated next to me. "What are your plans," I said, "assuming nothing happens today?"

He looked at me with gloom, anger, and determination. His answer was sharp, distinct, and rapid. "I'm going to New Jersey with my wife, and I'm going to see my in-laws, and I'm going to have a quiet and relaxing Christmas. And I don't give a damn what the ICC does or doesn't do."

At Fourteenth Street, I took a right, drove up a block, and took a left into the Mall area. "There's a space," John said, thrusting his arm in front of George and pointing toward the right. We parked, got out, and headed toward the back entrance to the Science and Technology Museum. A few tourists were walking in and out, clothed heavily and moving slowly. We entered and hurried toward the front entrance. I brushed and bumped some people and began to think about how little Christmas shopping I had done. We rushed past exhibits and displays that normally I would view in wonderment, eager to learn, and appreciative of their creation and form. Not today. Not now. At this moment, they were blurs, objects, impediments to our purpose and timing.

I had not been home in months. Now, well, regardless of what the Commission did today there would be no prolonged stay. The Commission would never deny the increase outright. Luck, Mom. Now is the time.

I looked at John, walking hurriedly in front of me like a second lieutenant leading the charge. He was quiet and seemed as pensive as we all did, not wanting to acknowledge how little control we had over being able to go home for Christmas. How critical such a choice now seemed, as it was being tugged away from us by our commitment, the obligation—felt even more now—to carry through on the effort we had started. If the Commission decided to allow the surcharge to go into effect by January 1 without permitting an opportunity for protest and without preparing an impact statement, what could we do? Prepare a complaint, a motion for a preliminary injunction, and a supporting legal memorandum in eight or nine days? With Christmas and New Year's in between? What a thought. And then I had another. The commissioners issued the order on December 22 and then went home—cozy, by a fireplace, sugarplums dancing—and here we were, left in the wake of their action, unhappy, discontented, and shivering.

We walked out the museum's revolving doors and down its circular driveway toward Constitution. It was frigid and windy; the sky was dull, gray, and ominous; the darkness settled all around us. We came alongside each other at the curb. The cars were moving quickly past us. We looked at each other, hands in our pockets, scarves over our noses, faces (what little was visible) red, stiff, and worried. George said it, plaintively, from beneath his scarf. "Do you think the occupants of these vehicles are appreciative of the fact we might forgo our Christmas holidays in order to perform a task 'in the public interest'?" The light changed.

We crossed Constitution amid a barrage of honking cars and frenzied pedestrians moving in a direction exactly opposite us. We ran up the steps in front of the Commission. My glasses fogged as we reached the interior. I took them and my gloves off immediately. John moved ahead of us in order to ask the guard for the room number. "Neil, what are you going to do?" George asked.

"George, I want to go home even for a few days. But what the heck are we supposed to do? If the Commission lets the increase go into effect by January 1, then we have to try and stop it. How stupid we'd look if we did nothing. I mean, we started this damn thing."

I knew I said what he felt. John got the room number. We walked quickly down the hall and around the corner to the public information office. It was there—not the decision but the "press release," a pile of them, being taken by people we did not know, people whose faces were not familiar to us. They had done it—well, not the Commission, but providence, luck, God, Mom. The caption read: "Quick Publication and Institution of 2.5% Surcharge by Nation's Railroads Denied by ICC Today." Home. I could not describe the feeling. We were going home.[1]

We returned to the car and began to read. There would be no prolonged holiday. The Commission had authorized a 2.5 percent interim surcharge, but the increase would be applied no sooner than February 5, 1972. If the Railroads wanted the rates to go into effect on that date—and they did—public notice would have to be published by January 5.[2] I turned the car and the heat on. I considered the denial a "victory."

"But they got the increase," John said.

"Hey, but not yet. Okay. A *kind* of victory," I suggested.

"They know how to manipulate the rules," George said with resignation and a tinge of respect. "They did it here."

The public could submit comments protesting the rate increase before January 20, which was less than a month away. In between was going home for Christmas, the New Year's holiday, completing papers, doing a final report on SCRAP, and preparing for and taking exams. We could not wait until mid-January. I would come back and write our formal protest before New Year's.

"Well," George said, contemplatively, "you can see it straight out. Public comment after the increase is approved."

"Yep. I know. It's in the law. They're now an ally of the Railroads. I mean, legally," I said.

"It's worse. Look at this. The 'interim period.' After it reviews the written protests, the Commission can decide whether the increase it already approved can go into effect on February 5 or be 'suspended.' And still go into effect."

"*Arrow Transportation*," George said. "The 'suspension stage.' No judicial review." His words caused vacant stares and simple awe. "I'm trying to understand it," he said with determination but unease. "How these two mesh. *If* they mesh. The Commission's power and its duty under NEPA. Come on. Let's go."

"No. Let's finish this now," I said. "We're into it." I read aloud: "Finally, the carriers' evidentiary case submitted with their petition does not include a statement regarding the environmental impact of the proposal.... In view thereof, we shall expect the petitioners to file and serve, within 10 days from the date of service of the orders herein, such a statement."[3]

"Another victory?" George asked, but in a way that suggested the Commission's vulnerability.

"A pyrrhic victory," I said, already thinking about what I had to write.

"Their understanding is primitive," George said.

"Dishonest, you mean," John declared with certainty.

"Let's agree to these. NEPA imposed the EIS obligation directly on the ICC, not on the Railroads. The Commission still has no final regulations implementing NEPA. It's now late December 1971, two years since NEPA's passage. And who're they kidding? How could it take only ten days, to January 2, to do an EIS on a freight rate increase for all commodities transported by all the lousy railroads throughout the entire nation? George, this is a good thing," I said.

"Exactly," John added. "I mean, they're making the violation clear."

George looked at me directly. "*Arrow Transportation*."

We returned to campus and described the Commission's decision to Banzhaf. I told him I would be back to prepare a formal protest. He dictated a press release concerning our "victory." The press and the Railroads must know we are involved closely. Banzhaf also told us one of the Railroads' attorneys had called him. Their response to our petitions in *265/267* was due on January 3, 1972. The Railroads wanted a 14-day extension.

Banzhaf had said no. He believed the Railroads wanted to disconnect *281* from *265/267*.

We sat and talked about the Railroads' request. Banzhaf listened and asked questions. He spoke as a teacher and mentor—instructive and thorough, helping to place it all in context. Now, too, as our lawyer, he was advocating our cause and not giving an inch. He said that the Railroads' machinations and the Commission's decision had one good meaning. We were being taken seriously. He also said he would do whatever was necessary while we were gone. We agreed; we thanked him; and, with visible, unequivocal, and deeply grateful relief, we left. That night, later than planned and through light snow mixed with sleet, I drove out to my brother's house. I was going home.

CHRISTMAS EVE

New Haven. We all were in the kitchen—my mother; father; sister, Diana; her husband, Eugene; and me. The tomato sauce was on the stove with crabs—cleaned, succulent, and large—cooking in it all day, with dashes and smidgens and pinches of olive oil and basil and garlic. I did not know the precise measurements. Unlike meat sauce, this sauce, I knew, was more difficult to make, more of an art—fine, done with care and rarely the same way each time. We always ate it on Christmas Eve. The expectation of its taste and the ritual of its preparation added stories and mythology to all the Christmas Eves that had preceded.

The kitchen was warm, the aroma comforting, and, for each of us, there was a task to be done in preparation for dinner—interspersed with conversations, not one but three, four, and five at a time, as well as directions given, questions asked, and moments filled fully with touching, feeling, and learning.

Dinner began with a prayer. We did it only at holidays. It was said by my dad in simple thoughts and sometimes the words changed, but you knew he meant it when he thanked God for all of us being there and he remembered those who were not there—like his parents and sister and my mother's mother, whom we all loved and missed—and all the others, as the prayer required, who were "faithfully departed." Dinner included fried calamari, clams made like my grandmother used to make when we had Christmas Eve at her house, and then the spaghetti—vermicelli, the "thin spaghetti" my dad would call it—covered in sauce, sprinkled with pepper, delicate, filling, and always accompanied by a second helping. We took turns serving, moving between courses, talking, and cleaning dishes. And then the crabs were placed on the table, still hot and juicy from the sauce, soft, meaty, tasteful, and messy—remarkably so. The tenor was fun, robust, historic, and generational and we knew it, as if, at times, those whom we remembered at the beginning were there for the whole meal, laughing, talking, and sharing it with us.

I talked about SCRAP during dinner. My mother wanted to be certain that I left the newspaper articles and the petitions we had filed so she could look at them. My dad talked about recycling—about the war years (World War II and the Korean War), and about how they separated out paper and bottles, about how everyone did it. I knew how deeply recycling was ingrained in him because he still did it. Now, as he said it aloud, I understood what he meant when he added that no one seemed to care, not the grocer nor the garbage collectors.

"We did it all the time. It was easy," my mother said with a matter-of-fact certainty. What I glimpsed here, over dinner, was something simply about culture—about how easily my parents had done what they were asked to do by Roosevelt and by Truman—the simple act of separating papers, done individually, done by families, all trying to help, to be "good Americans" as my mother would say.

We cleaned off the table and set it for dessert and coffee. The conversations took on a different hue, more personal and direct with subjects examined in more depth, with plans made and family matters settled. Before dessert started, however, at least on this night, we decided to open our gifts first. Doing so on Christmas Eve was customary. Its origins were no doubt deep and cultural if not religious, but to me it all began at my grandmother's house when my aunts and uncles and cousins, two dozen at times, would gather on Houston Street and celebrate Christmas. The oldest person in the family went first. The order had something to do with patience—learning it—and also with sharing, certain that your aunts and uncles and cousins would watch you, laugh with you, and clap when you got something good or weird or what you always wanted.

A lot was said and gifts were shared. Their wrappings—the paper and ribbons and bows—were folded and saved by my mother as in the old days when the beauty of such things was savored, handled gently, and used again when a special need required. When it was my turn, I got some money from my dad and also from my sister and her husband; it was always welcomed, and they knew it. Then I opened a box, wrapped neatly and with care, from my mother. It was a beige wool scarf, soft, pretty against the white sheet paper, gentle when I touched it to my face, and warm when I put it around my neck. We all clapped. I was not certain why. Maybe it was the look on my face or the smile I had when I looked at my mother, but they all knew and I did, too, that at *that* Christmas, at *that* time, this scarf was exactly what I wanted.

Dessert, too, was part of the ritual. Coffee—Italian, with small cups and small spoons and a bottle of anisette close by just for the taste. Just a small drop into the coffee while it was still hot made the aroma spread throughout the room. There were cookies (almond flavored with pignola nuts), and pies (pumpkin, apple, and cream), and nuts that were cracked and picked out and lined up and spun around. Here, too, there was an art. My dad had it down pat. He moved those nuts around in his hand until they felt right, solid against each other, ready, positioned. Then, with a timed force, he broke them two at a time in one hand. Even now, when we could do it ourselves, it never seemed to work just right—not the way he did it, not yet. Finally, there were chestnuts: big, warm, already cut slightly for cooking, remaining in the oven until ready and then tossed onto the table to be shelled here, with care, as my father did it; the pile of broken shells reflected our contentment.

Before midnight, arrangements were made for church the next day and for another meal—substantial and important but not the same as what we just had experienced. My sister and Eugene left. I changed into pajamas and a bathrobe and looked forward to sleep—good, long, and restful. When I walked into the living room to talk to my parents, I found my mother alone, her small frame curled up on the couch, seated close to the lamp nearby, her housecoat already on, reading intently the *New York Times* article of December 13, 1971—the article about SCRAP.

THE RULES OF ENGAGEMENT

I returned to Washington, D.C., and began drafting our formal protest. We emphasized that *281* had to be viewed cumulatively. The rate increase authorized by it came atop 21 percent increases that had been granted less than a year earlier. Our new argument: The public had been allowed to protest the Commission's approval only *after* it had been granted. "Constitutional due process requires," we said, "that parties having a demonstrated interest at stake ... must be afforded an opportunity to be heard ... before any irrevocable disposition of their interest is effected.... A refund provision ... does nothing to protect S.C.R.A.P.'s interest."[4]

While we were away, Banzhaf had been busy. So, too, had others. On December 23, the Institute of Scrap Iron and Steel filed a petition in support of SCRAP's petition to intervene in *265/267*. "They have their own interests,"

George said to me, "but they did it. It can't please the Railroads, and we can't be dismissed as radical bomb throwers."

"Don't be so certain," I said with a smile.

On December 22, as Banzhaf had described to us, the Railroads requested a 14-day extension. Banzhaf had heard from Louis A. Harris, an attorney representing a "Committee of Counsel for Railroads in *265/267*." The title alone did it. "They got a 'Committee of Counsel'?" George asked. "What does that cost? I mean, there's only us."

"George," I said, "you missed the point. They may have a 'committee' but we've got a 'group.'"

"You both missed the point," John said, grinning and hardly able to contain himself. "We may have a 'group' but they got an 'association.'"

"Aaah, an association," George lamented. "Well. That's it. We're done."

When Banzhaf said he would not agree to the extension, the odyssey started. Harris hand-delivered a letter on December 22 to the commissioner's secretary, Robert Oswald, requesting the extension. Banzhaf was served with the letter on the same day. Harris had not informed the Commission of Banzhaf's objection. Banzhaf called the Commission the next morning, as he later described it, "to ascertain how much time he would have to respond to this request." He was advised that the request had already been granted. Further, although he spoke at length with Chief Hearing Examiner Robert C. Bamford, a Mr. Taggert in Commissioner Laurence Walrath's office, and two gentlemen in the Office of Proceedings, no one was able to advise him when such an extension had been granted, who had granted it, and, most important, why no opportunity had been given to him to reply."[5]

"Neil, it's a great story," George said.

"George, even while we were gone, the 'Lobby of the Students' was sticking it to 'em."

I left George at the library and made my way up H toward Crawford. Coming toward me, books buried within her arms and gloves, was Kathleen. "Hi," I said. "This can't be your vacation."

"Hardly. And what are *you* doing here?" she said, with a warm, embracing smile.

"Well, if you have a few minutes, I'll tell you."

"I had to park down on Eighteenth. If you want to walk?" she asked. I offered to carry her books. She accepted with a familiar ease. As I talked, we walked deliberately and then slower, stopping at moments, at times looking directly at each other. Her eyes were experienced, listening—seeing more, I thought, than my words and gestures. I described SCRAP and my feelings about it. She probed carefully and with seamlessness spoke about her own decision to work at a women's clinic. She asked about law school and my decision to go and then described the small town in Rhode Island where she was raised and went to college. We reached her car, and she took the books. "Thanks," she said, putting them on the hood and removing her gloves before reaching for her keys. "I was in college when I met my husband. A Saturday night mixer." She paused, contemplative. "After he was killed, I decided to go back to school," she said.

I nodded and, looking inward as much as out, said somberly, "I see." A moment passed. I touched and held her elbow. "It was good to see you again." She took the books and opened the door. I stepped back and put my hands in my pocket, turned, and walked away. Within only a few yards, I turned slightly to see her still standing at the car door, her head moving upward, her eyes catching mine, her hand waving gently.

THE EDF MEETING

N Street. Weathered townhouses were three or four stories high, touched up nicely with shrubs, vines, wrought-iron fences, and wooden doors. An inn was close by, tucked away and quiet. EDF was in 1720, on the second floor. The secretary announced us. We entered Dienelt's office.

Dienelt was about my height, with blondish hair, full and fashionably cut. He wore glasses, steel rimmed or maybe tortoise shell. The office was not noticeably decorated. Everyone smiled, shook hands, and, throughout the meeting, acted cordially. The "agreement" he had proposed was discussed. Without seeming ungrateful, we introduced other factors: Who would handle public relations? How much work would we do? Whose name would go first in a second lawsuit? Whose name would appear first if we filed jointly before the Commission? Can Banzhaf's name continue to be on all the documents? These questions, we told Dienelt, had to be resolved with care. The cordiality wore thin—not in the words said or the facial expressions made but rather in the absence of ease, the obvious unwillingness on our part to welcome his support with a handshake and a warm, grateful smile.

Dienelt suggested he translate EDF's proposal and our concerns into a memorandum of understanding (MOU). We agreed. In the interim, he proposed that we file jointly a formal protest in *281*. We told him we were drafting such a protest now, our second. SCRAP's name would go first, he said. EDF's attorneys would review the draft, supply the secretarial support and the copying. With a cunning that, as I later characterized it to George, Banzhaf would have graded highly, we agreed "in principle."

The rules of engagement had been set early by EDF for reasons and in a manner we never understood fully nor accepted. What we had learned was to be suspect of "rules." We were not as good at this as others. In the absence of an agreement, we filed our second protest in *281* without having it reviewed by EDF. We explained that this protest did not preclude the filing of yet another protest. For now, until we resolved finally the question concerning the second semester, we could neither acquiesce to nor antagonize EDF. I thought they chose to take the same approach with us.

SCRAP LIVES

Bacon Hall. The large room. If it had a folklore, we now were part of it. The semester was nearly over. Examinations would start shortly. My report as chairman also was due to Banzhaf. Today's meeting with him was to review what we had done and to resolve what—for George, John, and me—was the most important question we needed to answer: Do we continue? Kenny and Peter already had decided one semester was enough.

In addition to the intractable problem of time—how much would it take and could we get credit for it—we each examined the special law enacted by Congress that governed judicial appeal of Commission decisions. We had no long-range strategy and definitely no time frame for suing the ICC. If we proceeded, there would be rules and deadlines that would govern our actions in a manner far more serious than what we had experienced thus far. We also had no illusions about the Commission. Seeking judicial review was likely. Part of our assessment required us to know what that meant. George started. "In 28 USC Section 1253, Congress believed the Commission's rate decisions were of national consequence. The process, as I understand it, is that a single district court judge reviews the complaint and request for an injunction and holds a hearing. It's his obligation to determine the merit of the complaint to an extent not yet clear."[6]

"He has limited authority to say no," I added.

"If some 'threshold' of merit is reached," George continued, "he forwards the request for the special three-judge court directly to the chief judge of the court of appeals. The chief judge, in turn, establishes a panel. If an injunction is issued by the three-judge court, the next level of review is the Supreme Court."

"There's no one in between?" Banzhaf asked.

"We break the 'threshold,' and we could be in the Supreme Court of the United States," I said, like a chairman.

I asked about getting credit. B said he was certain he could do it but not for a grade and only for two credits. "Well, what do you want to do?" Banzhaf asked.

"The Commission's actions are not right," I said. "I flat out dislike the Railroads."

"None of us like EDF. It's trying to move us to the side," George said.

"Forget transfer to EDF," I affirmed, without equivocation. "They've done nothing to force the Commission to comply with the law."

Banzhaf listened intently, especially to our concerns about EDF. He liked it—not just the decision to proceed but, I thought, the fact that we had no "true" allies. In important ways, we were still alone, at first five and now three of us. This reality was reflected in his tone and manner. It was still our project, he said, and we were responsible for the work. That we understood.

George, John, and I looked at each other. We smiled and nodded gently, with confidence. "All right," George summed it up. "SCRAP is moving into the second semester."

11

THINKING AHEAD,
WINTER 1972

The indictments. January 2. The *Washington Post* disclosed it: "Pennsy Directors Ignored Warning of Ruin, Hill Study Says." My morning coffee—eight ounces—was harsh and still steaming, even with the addition of milk. The sounds around me, normally piercing because of the Center's acoustics, seemed immediately to withdraw, wither, and then shut down. I pulled flush to the table. "Nearly nine months before its bankruptcy," the *Post* wrote, "the railroads received an urgent warning of the impending financial crisis from one of its own directors. But the warning was largely ignored, and—out of disgust—the dissenting director stopped attending meetings of the Penn Central's Board."[1]

"Where are the names?" I said aloud, moving methodically through the article. "The merger proposal ..." —that is, the New York Central and the Pennsylvania; I knew this story too—was "approved by the Interstate Commerce Commission in 1968." No Louis Brandeis to say no, don't do it, because the bigness will not work. I came to what I was looking for. "The staff leveled most of its criticism at Stuart Saunders, the Penn Central's chairman, and David Bevan, its chief financial officer, who were both board members." I hurried through the remainder of the article and read that "$215.7 million worth of dividends" were approved by the board "when the railroad needed funds to invest in new locomotives, freight cars and other improvements." But the names—who got the dividends? Who made the choices?

When I returned to Crawford, books and notes readied for study, I looked instead for *Failing Railroads* and the lawsuit reproduced in it: "In the court of common pleas of Franklin County, Ohio. JOHN H. KUNKEL, JR., 137 MILL STREET, GAHANNA, OHIO, PLAINTIFF v. EXECUTIVE JET AVIATION, INC., ... PENN CENTRAL CO., ... O. F. LASSITER ... AND DAVID C. BEVAN...."[2] There were allegations of stock manipulations, fast money transfers, and deception. Bevan also was alleged to have "entered into an illegal conspiracy to enable the Penn Central Railroad to dominate the world air transportation market."[3]

January 3. I called the House Committee on Banking and Currency. I wanted a copy of the report discussed in the *Post*. Someone would mail it. I called Vic Reinemer. "It'll be waiting for you," he said.

"*The Penn Central Failure and the Role of Financial Institutions.*"[4] The report's title alone said more than the *Post* had. I read it coming back in the cab and walking back to the law school and again later that evening before going to bed. The real story was in the charts: large pullouts, folded and tucked neatly into the report.

"Corporate Structure of Penn Central Transportation Company." There were at least forty real estate companies within the Penn Central's corporate purview and then others with innocuous-sounding names such as "Penndiana Impt. Co.," which was described only as a "non-carrier."[5] Next was the chart titled "Sources of Funds, Interlocks and Penphil Investments." Stark in depiction, and critical to the decisions made and the money moved were the "Individuals Controlling Investments." There were only two: Charles Hodge and David Bevan.[6] I turned to the next chart: "Penn Central Figures Involved with CBK." There was Bevan again, situated on top, his tentacles everywhere, reaching for and holding shares in companies and corporations interlocked by similar directors and by money from the Railroad and its employee pension funds.[7]

I had seen charts like this before. It was when I read about those who formed streetlight, intercity train, and electric supply companies in the nineteenth century and about how those individuals interconnected with banks and investment companies and sought, through the complexity, to insulate their financial interests from public scrutiny and regulation and paying taxes. I thought of Dreiser's Frank Algernon Cowperwood: the financier, the titan, "perfectly calm, deadly cold," selling stock he did not own. As the banker, he was entrusted with the money of others. "[L]ike a spider in a spangled net, every thread of which he knew, had laid, had tested, he had surrounded and entangled himself in a splendid, glittering network of connections, and he was watching the details."[8]

Then I came to the last section of the report: "Trading in Penn Central Stock: Financial Institutions and Privileged Information." Only days before the Penn Central's first public acknowledgment that it was in serious financial trouble, "a select few knew—and had known for some time—that the railroad was in dire straits."[9] They knew before the public, and before those investors and employees who now held the worthless stock of a dried, withered, bankrupt company. The chart was titled, "Daily Sales of Penn Central Common Stock by Three Banking Institutions." Morgan Guaranty Trust, Chase Manhattan, and the Continental Illinois National Banks waited; met with Bevan, Saunders, and others; and then quietly sold their stock in a sequence intended, it seemed, not to arouse public scrutiny and alarm until the sales were completed and the banks were protected.[10]

Here was David Rockefeller, chairman of Chase Manhattan, trying to explain to Committee Chairman Wright Patman that the fortuitously timed sale of hundreds of thousands of shares was unrelated to the fact that Saunders sat on its board and that Bevan met regularly with the bank's officers. It may have been only John D. Rockefeller's ghost that I imagined—spanning time, omnipotent still, alive, persistent, resting but never really gone, still tempering his grandson David, still manipulating and exploiting the Railroads and the people who worked and lived and cared about them.[11]

January 5. The *Washington Post*, Wednesday morning: "3 Charged in Pennsy Bankruptcy." District Attorney Arlen Specter indicted David C. Bevan for conspiring with Wall Street broker Charles J. Hodge and retired Air Force General Olbert F. Lassiter for illegally diverting more than $21 million from America's largest Railroad and contributing to its bankruptcy. Bevan denied such a role.[12]

VERIFIED STATEMENT NO. 37

Crafting the final report for the project was my task alone. The success we had achieved was collectively accomplished and warranted an A for each of us. I hoped to accomplish that goal. The range of such a grade (numerically, between 85 and 94 percent) was for Banzhaf to decide.

Examinations did not take an easy course. My SCRAP colleagues looked taut, haggard, disheveled, and puffy-eyed whenever we passed one another in the hallways or shared coffee or whenever I stopped long enough to describe the latest developments and get their thoughts. We also traded off the responsibility of calling the Commission and inquiring about the impact statement it had ordered the Railroads to prepare in *281*. It had been due January 2.

On January 4 the Railroads submitted "Verified Statement No. 37 by Mr. Charles L. Smith."[13] John waited in front of Stockton—bicycle in tow, dressed like Sir Edmund Hillary after the climb—waving an envelope. He had the grin. "This is the ah, quote, 'statement of the environmental impact required by the Commission,'" he said.

"I think our first response should be hot tea," I said. We met at the Center, huddled near each other, reading. Verified Statement No. 37, as explained by the Railroads, was "neither an environmental impact statement filed under NEPA and the CEQ Guidelines, nor an initial statement filed pursuant to the rules proposed by the Commission [to implement NEPA]."[14]

"What do you think this document is?" I asked, wanting, as always, to be certain that we identified all the possibilities.

"Well," John replied, "it's premised on, quote, 'personal experience, the statements submitted by other Railroad executives and the record made in previous *Ex Parte* proceedings.'"[15]

"And, so, what do you think this document is?" I asked again.

"The Railroads refused to carry the Commission's water. Listen to this," John said. "The only major environmental effect of the rate increase would be 'the deterioration in railroad service due to lack of funds'[16] and that 'the proposed surcharge will have no environmental impact whatsoever.'"[17]

"So, there's no hundred-page addendum? You didn't miss it or something?" George asked mockingly. John gently smiled. His eyes gleamed and his smile grew. It was contagious.

A FULL DAY

January 17. The Railroads replied to our petitions in *265/267*. Nine attorneys were listed on the front page. "Taken together, S.C.R.A.P.'s petitions constitute a wholesale attack on the Interstate Commerce Commission for alleged failures to comply with the procedural provisions of the National Environmental Policy Act of 1969 … and the 'letter and spirit' of at least seven other statutes, two constitutional provisions and various allegedly applicable regulations or guidelines. On the basis of the Commission's alleged failures, S.C.R.A.P. turns on the Nation's Railroads and insists the Commission declare the *Ex Parte 265/267* proceedings invalid and order the refund of freight revenues approximating $2.3 billion. All this it demands from an essential industry which is clinging to solvency by its collective eyelids."[18]

"Approximating $2.3 billion?" George asked, unable to contain his joy.

"It was the red hots on the steak and cheese," I said to George. "They distracted us. I told Kenny to hold the red hots."

George, barely able to get it out, said, "We should have called the Railroads."

The Railroads asked the Commission to dismiss our petitions and to declare that the increases authorized in *265/267* "have no discernable effect on the environment." The legal issue had been joined.[19] By January 17, however, our focus was changing. *Ex Parte 265/267* now reflected only the opening salvo, the place where we drew a line. The Commission was likely to make the same mistake again. They already had done it by relying on the Railroads to comply with NEPA.

We learned through EDF that the United States Court of Appeals for the Second Circuit in New York had decided *Green County Planning Board v. Federal Power Commission.*[20] We were told it would be helpful to our position. In *Green County*, the Public Authority of the State of New York (PASNY) wanted to construct a transmission line through Green County that required approval from the Federal Power Commission (FPC). The FPC directed PASNY to prepare an EIS. The Green County Planning Board wanted the EIS prepared by the FPC. The court of appeals agreed: "We view [NEPA] as did the District of Columbia Circuit [in *Calvert Cliffs Coordinating Committee*].... The primary and nondelegable responsibility for filling that function was with the Commission."[21] The court of appeals continued: "The [FPC] has abdicated a significant part of its responsibility.... [T]he applicant's statement will be based on self-serving assumptions."[22]

The EIS prepared in *Green County* began: "Neither the construction nor the operation of the Gilboa-Leeds transmission line will have any significant adverse impact on the environment." It was thirty-five miles long and 150 feet wide.

"They're talking about Verified Statement No. 37."

"The Second Circuit," George mused, "must have decided that SCRAP needed a little help."

"Yeah. The law."

The CEQ wrote a letter to the ICC's chairman, George Stafford. It was signed by the general counsel, Timothy Atkeson. It concluded that Verified Statement No. 37 contained significant deficiencies and did not reflect ICC compliance with NEPA. "We're gaining allies," George said. The CEQ letter

had one other effect. It told us that we had touched and tempered and unleashed motives and forces and customs we did not know about and could
not control.

EDF also had filed a joinder in *281* that included the Izaak Walton League
and the NPCA. They were now parties, and EDF was their lead attorney.[23] A
line was being drawn here too. Our discussions on the MOU for joint action
continued. We did agree informally to file a "joint protest"—our third submission—prior to the January 20 deadline. The protest emphasized particularly
the decision in *Green County* and our position that the Commission could not
delegate its NEPA responsibility to the Railroads. The first name on the front
cover was "John F. Banzhaf III, Attorney" for SCRAP. It was a small victory.
We were getting better at this.[24]

THE GRADES

Grades were posted one course at a time. Only your student ID number
appeared. Your eyesight needed to be good. I had seen it happen. A student
looks quickly, standing with friends nearby, hoping or thinking he did fine,
wrote a solid paper, or scored high on the exam—and in the excitement of the
moment he draws the horizontal line wrong. The effect could be devastating.
You needed to be careful.

My grades were coming in slowly. They were decent: a B in Domestic Relations; a high B in Mass Communications Law. I was satisfied. George called
to tell me Banzhaf's grades were up. We met at Stockton. He already had seen
his: a solid A, an 88. John had done the same. Kenny and Peter each received
an 85, also an A. I walked to the board where the grades were posted. George
was with me, smiling as if he knew. I looked carefully. Students were peering
and moving all around. Some just looked in disbelief. A few were coming
back for the second time, wanting to be sure they had it right, no mistakes.
And then I saw it and looked at George and then looked back again. It was a
94. The highest grade in the class! A big, fat, solid A. It was the highest grade
I had, would, or ever imagined getting. "B did it. We did it!"

"You deserved it," George said. I smiled and thought about how tired I
was. I left Stockton and walked immediately back to Crawford. I made one
phone call: to my mother and father.

12

IN PREPARATION,
WINTER 1972

EDF's move. January 24. I received EDF's proposed memorandum of understanding.[1] I called George immediately. "George, if you're not sitting down, you'd better do it."

"So? What's it say?"

"George," I said, with a slight detachment.

"Neil?"

"It's bad. Let me explain this. Four parties have to agree: EDF, SCRAP 'and its advisor John Banzhaf,' the National Parks and Conservation Association, and the Izaak Walton League."[2]

"Those boys have been talking," George inserted.

"Public relations will be dominated by EDF. Quote: 'When a joint lawsuit is announced, the public relations will be handled, in the first instance, from this office.' After the announcement, EDF 'will continue to act as coordinator.' SCRAP then would be free to engage in public relations efforts only if 'consistent with the general purpose.'"[3]

"Neil."

"George, forget the press. Next. 'Legal coordination.' No surprise. I'll read it slowly. You still sitting?"

"I thought that was the bad part."

"Quote. 'John Dienelt of the EDF ... will be primarily responsible for the coordination of the legal effort. The student members of SCRAP, however, will continue to carry on a significant amount of the actual work.' George?"[4]

"Got it. We do the work; he leads the effort."

"But listen. Two words. 'Student members.' That's it. Under the MOU, Sandy Weissbard of NPCA would be counsel of record in court matters. Banzhaf serves only as an 'advisor' and as counsel of record in, quote, 'administrative proceedings.'"[5]

"B is out in a court suit? SCRAP has no lawyer. I don't believe it."

"George, believe it. Wait till Larouche hears it."

"Wait till B hears it."

"Finally, 'court action.' SCRAP is out."

"What do you mean?" George asked.

"The MOU states, 'In the court action involving *Ex Parte 281* or any other action which is filed jointly prior to the filing of *281*, EDF would be the first listed plaintiff.'"[6]

"That's in *265/267*."

"Dienelt is covering all the contingencies," I added.

"Son of a—"

"George, those are the good parts. Listen. 'The relative listing of different groups in any subsequent joint suits (for example, *Ex Parte 265* and *267*) would be open to discussion.'"

"You're kidding?"

"George, I mean, correct me. We're not certain of being listed even second. Just 'open to discussion.' We're the only ones who have done anything in *265/267*. Are you listening?"[7]

"No, I'm hanging up."

"Here. The ultimate screw job. If there's a dispute over the listing, it's, quote, 'with the understanding that SCRAP will have a strong claim to first billing on a second suit in which its members have done the major portion of the work.' George, the only other lawsuit within our realm of possibility is *265/267*. And all we get is 'a strong claim'? This is a joke, George. It's a joke."[8]

"Neil, we're not signing this."

"George. Now, after all I read to you, this is surreal," I said, laughing. "I've got to read this next part to you."

"Neil, now I'm lying down," George groaned.

"Quote. 'It is understood that this agreement does not commit any organization at this time to participate in any court action.' Keep your eye on those SCRAP boys," I said, parodying the agreement. "They just may go off and do something radical without telling us."[9]

"Yeah, like sue the Interstate Commerce Commission."

In response, we proposed counterterms to EDF. We never initialed the MOU. We drove over periodically to Rosslyn to see Ted Pankowski and had little further contact with NPCA.

THE COMMISSION'S MOVE

February 1. The Commission issued an order that concluded the 2.5 percent rate increase was "just and reasonable" and "will have no significant adverse effect on … the quality of the human environment." The increase would go into effect without "suspension" or any further investigation on February 5. The Commission imposed one condition. The emergency increase would expire not later than June 5. In the interim, the Commission expected the Railroads to file for a permanent rate increase.[10]

The Commission's decision was plain in its challenge. The increase would go into effect in only four days. No decision had been issued yet in *265/267*. The Commission separated the two. The Railroads got what they wanted. We met in Banzhaf's office. The reality, as we saw it, required a strategic choice. The Commission had two advantages that protected it from a lawsuit. First, the environmental organizations "supporting" us were unequivocal in their view. If the Sierra Club does not have standing and they, as nationally organized groups, do not have standing, then SCRAP certainly does not have standing. Second, the second semester had just begun. We did not have the time to prepare and file a lawsuit in four days. The Commission also had three vulnerabilities. First, there was no impact statement, not from it or the Railroads. Second, as I put it, "We're unpredictable. We have no rules." We had gotten press coverage in the *Times*, the *Star* and, most recently, the specialized trade journals. Commissioners were being asked about SCRAP and NEPA. Third, we had Banzhaf. He had sued the FCC and won.[11]

The strategy emerged. We decided to threaten to sue the Commission to stop *281* from going into effect and to try, in exchange for not doing it, to get a binding acknowledgment that the Commission, not the Railroads, would prepare an EIS. One serious problem existed. EDF had to go along with the threat. If it did not, the Commission would not likely agree.

THE COMMISSION'S NEXT MOVE

February 2. Banzhaf got a phone call from the Commission. It had issued a decision in *265/267*.[12] We drove over to get it. I turned immediately to the last paragraph: "*It is ordered*, that the petitions for reconsideration and for extraordinary relief be, and they are hereby, denied. *And it is further ordered*, that the proceedings be, and they are hereby, closed."

"No surprise," John said, as he moved quickly to the opening paragraph:

> Upon consideration of the record …; petitions to intervene, reconsider and extraordinary relief, filed December 13, 1971, by Neil Proto, John Larouche, George Biondi, Kenneth Perlman and Peter Ressler, comprising the entire membership of … Students Challenging Regulatory Agency Procedures, seeking leave to intervene, reopening and reconsideration of the proceedings herein, a declaration that said … rate increases therein authorized are unlawful, … [and] an order requiring … refund of all amounts charged.

"Neil," George said. "That's us."

"George. We said all this?"

"Heah!" said John. "Look. They let us in. We are engraved forever in the annals of ICC history."

The Commission also had concluded "that the issues raised by the petitioners may warrant consideration in the light of the record and the statutory requirements applicable thereto" and that "the proceedings … are hereby reopened solely for the purpose of permitting the petitioners to become parties thereto, effective as of the date of this order, and to permit consideration of the matters set forth in their petitions."[13]

"The decision in *281* now makes sense," George said. "We're having an effect."

"Yeah. But on what?" I asked.

"I'm not sure. But we're having an effect."

"If you're right, we need two things." In silence, I turned toward George. "Keep moving ahead and—"

"Patience," George said.

"Yep. Patience is a virtue."

From these findings, the Commission reached its most important legal conclusion in precisely the manner the Railroads wanted: "[T]hat the record in these proceedings showed that the transportation pricing in issue did not have a significant impact on the quality of the human environment."[14]

"No surprise here, either," John said. "Except—"

"They're making moves," I said, with some introspection. "We just have to figure out what they are."

OUR GAMBIT

February 3. Early afternoon. We had informed Dienelt of our intention to encourage the Commission to believe we would file suit and to extract, if we could, an agreement that an EIS would be prepared. He opposed it. EDF had no intention of suing the Commission. He thought it was a bad idea that would not work. We asked him to meet with us and Banzhaf in the early afternoon. He agreed. In the interim, we drafted a proposed memorandum of understanding to be signed by EDF, SCRAP, and the Commission. Banzhaf simplified it and had it typed. We waited. Banzhaf went to class.

At this time of the year, the large room was subject to two temperature extremes: hot and the complete absence of heat. The old radiators and decayed nature of the building did it. The problem was in the weather. If your shoes were wet, the large room was nowhere to be. On February 3, the snow had converted to sleet and now was becoming mush. My shoes were wet. Dienelt arrived as planned. He, I noticed, was wearing galoshes but had on a suit and tie. We began our discussion. He reiterated his opposition. Banzhaf arrived a few minutes late. He kept his sweater on. Banzhaf had been in and out of here for years. He had adjusted.

Banzhaf apologized for being late. There was a detachment about the way he said it, not insincere but with a kind of *pro forma* tone to it. Banzhaf got right down to it. The group has decided to do this. Here is the MOU we prepared. It's in your interest to be part of it. Why are you not? No bombast; no hyperbole; no overt enticement. You are either with the good guys or, well, goodbye.

It took a while. John, George, and I interjected legal arguments, sometimes in a tone reflective of a harsh, "get lost" attitude rather than Banzhaf's more subtle, "Well, goodbye." Peter Meyers came in carrying a Coke and a large sub sandwich wrapped in foil. The meal was for Banzhaf. He opened the foil and started eating. The sandwich was not a dainty petit four. The aroma—meatballs, I thought—permeated the room. The effect was plain. We were not in the conference room at Covington & Burling.

Dienelt had his own arguments. What would we do if our bluff was called? Our answer: "The midnight filing." We could do it again. The thought of it, I was certain, caused pangs, pains, and headaches for all three of us. Dienelt eventually acquiesced, but he was not pleased. Banzhaf called the general counsel of the ICC, Fritz Kahn. He left the room to do it. When he returned, he said only that the meeting was arranged for about one hour later. Dienelt left. He would meet us there.

February 3. Late afternoon. The general counsel's office was different from any other office I had seen at the Commission. Old world—late nineteenth century; oak or mahogany wood paneling, carpets; lamps that were shaded, ornate, and fashionably tarnished; and books, ICC reports, and decisions nicely arranged. The general counsel, I believed, was important.

We were greeted pleasantly in the outer office by a secretary. She buzzed Fritz Kahn, told him of our arrival, and escorted us into his office. Banzhaf led the way, now serving as protector as much as lawyer. This role was new to us.

Kahn was decidedly pleasant. He was slender and about George's height. He wore a bow tie and glasses. He had been at the Commission for much of his career. My first reaction was that he was a deeply ingrained part of its culture and its relationship with the Railroads. He was the lawyer for our adversaries—all of them. None of us smiled when we said hello. It was not a tactic. He was the bad guy.

He invited us to move to a large table at one end of the room. As we did, I was struck by the neatness and quiet splendor of his office. It was a larger version of what I had seen in the outer office. In the table's center was a miniature railroad engine in bronze or copper. Banzhaf sat at one end of the table. I sat to his left. Dienelt sat to his right. John and George sat near me. Fritz Kahn sat at the other end. He called in two of his deputy counsels, Art Cerra and Betty Jo Christian. They took a seat to Kahn's right.

The incongruity around the table was too noticeable to avoid. The difference in cultures and era was vast. John, George, and I were pale except for the dark (for me almost black) circles around our eyes. It was late afternoon. The beard stubble was obvious on our chins. Our hair was long— below ear length; John's and George's was longer still in back and was over their collars. We all had on blue jeans and weathered, wet shoes. John was wearing his army jacket, dark and big on him, and I had on an old, tattered but favorite dark brown, heavy corduroy sport coat, a brown sweater, and the beige scarf I had gotten for Christmas. There was not a tie to be seen in our corner of the table. Banzhaf was neat and clean shaven, with his hair cut short. His own style: the 1950s. There was no tie on him either. Dienelt looked like a lawyer. Fashionable wool suit—nice cut, maybe Britches, not J. Press—tie wide and in style; hair combed, neat, and fashionably long. Mod Squad.

Kahn, too, was the 1950s, but with a bow tie—small, narrow, like the one worn by Dave Garroway or Ozzie Nelson. Betty Jo Christian was quiet, neatly dressed, seemingly subtle in her manner and presence. Art Cerra—well, he, too, had on a white shirt, plain necktie, and a dark suit with his coat jacket off. But Art Cerra struck me in a different way. His features were familiar—like those of a cousin. Perhaps—and as I thought about it just for a moment—if I could have, I would have asked him where he was from.

The meeting began but not formally. Kahn started by telling us—and he looked at John, George, and me—that he was a George Washington law graduate. He seemed to be sincere. He smiled, but we were like stone—no response; nothing. Again, it was not a tactic. We just wanted to get to the reason we were there: the MOU.

Banzhaf took the lead. He explained our proposed agreement. He said we would sue otherwise. Kahn listened closely and quietly. An exchange with Banzhaf occurred and then some questions. In his response, Kahn was equivocal about NEPA's application to the Commission. He contended that the Railroads were required to do an impact statement. I did not like it. My unease was with his tone, the way he brushed aside the law and tried to shift the responsibility. I told him so—direct, hard, and to the point. The Railroads had done nothing. The duty was on the Commission. It was expressed in a moment. I felt myself getting anxious, growing uneasy from being stern and direct and, no doubt, from looking intense and serious. ("With those Trotsky glasses," my brother said later, "you must have looked like a radical, revolutionary type.") There was silence after I finished—just for a moment, maybe longer—with Kahn and the other members of his team looking, staring, and clearly feeling uneasy. The tone of the meeting had changed.

Banzhaf and Dienelt rejoined the discussion but not to make an argument. We were not there to persuade the Commission, and Banzhaf did not particularly try. His approach was simple. Here is the proposition and our position on the law. Either accept it or, well, goodbye.

It was not a long meeting. Kahn agreed with the arrangement. Banzhaf told him we had reduced it to writing. He slid an original of the MOU across the table. Kahn looked at it and showed it to Cerra and Christian. Kahn said it was acceptable with the addition of "in *Ex Parte 281*" at the end of one clause so that it was clear the MOU applied only to that proceeding. Banzhaf promptly wrote it in on all three originals.

The deal was cut. Dienelt signed for EDF and Fritz Kahn signed for the Commission. I signed for SCRAP. I took our original and reread it. I was certain this MOU was the equivalent of the Magna Carta.[15]

> WHEREAS the Commission has issued its order in *Ex Parte 281*, Increased Freight Rates, 1972, on February 1, 1972, and

> WHEREAS, Students Challenging Regulatory Agency Procedures (SCRAP) and The Environmental Defense Fund (E.D.F.) are parties in *Ex Parte 281*, and were preparing to file suit and to seek a preliminary injunction restraining the rate increase from becoming effective on the ground that the Commission has not complied with the requirements of the National Environmental Policy Act of 1969, 42 U.S.C. 4321 (NEPA), with respect to that increase, and,

> WHEREAS the Commission, by its General Counsel, has agreed that it will shortly issue a draft environmental statement in accordance with the requirements of N.E.P.A., and will otherwise comply with the requirements of that Act, in *Ex Parte 281*.

> THEREFORE, in reliance thereupon SCRAP and E.D.F. agree not to seek a preliminary injunction enjoining the rate increases from becoming effective on February 5, 1972. SCRAP and E.D.F., however, expressly reserve all other rights they may have with respect to these proceedings and the right to take any other legal action necessary to protect those rights.

> For the Environmental Defense Fund
> *John F. Dienelt*

> For Students Challenging Regulatory Agency Procedures
> *Neil T. Proto*

> For the Interstate Commerce Commission
> *Fritz R. Kahn*

We returned to Bacon and made copies of the MOU. It was after 5:00 p.m. George and I said goodbye to the others. He wanted to talk. He said it in a way that captured my own feelings. We had accomplished what we sought but were uncertain precisely what it meant.

"I don't know, Neil," he said. "It was like we were in different worlds."

"Like Kahn and Cerra and Christian had no idea what we were talking about."

"Like it was not in their experience?" George asked.

"Yep."

"Do you think they'll comply with it?" I asked him, uncertain of the answer.

He waited for a moment. We continued walking, past the corner of H and Twenty-first where we normally would part. He looked at me and—in a way that friends know, from experience, is considered and deliberate—said, "They signed it. We have to make certain they comply."

"The rates will go into effect on the fifth. Do you think it's over? I mean, for us? If they do an EIS, what else can we ask for?"

"You mean," George asked, still somber, "we can declare victory?"

"Yeah, sort of," I said. When we reached Calhoun, we both seemed visibly—and I knew I was—tired.

"I don't think so, Neil." His tone was uneasy.

I shook my head, gently and slightly. "Neither do I." Inside, I felt a disappointment, a resignation that, in the end, the Railroads held sway. They would not let the Commission comply with the law.

THE AMBUSH

February in Washington had begun in a cold and uneasy silence. The wind was bitter against your flesh. It seeped in and through everything and brought with it—without recompense in this urban setting—a harsh, sullen challenge to simple and essential movement. By the first week's end, life was confined largely to the university. We were pushed inward, in and around GW's disparate buildings, barren trees, muddied and ice-crusted walkways, and soiled frost that enshrouded and made treacherous everything you touched and every place you walked. No manner of clothing was sufficient to temper the chill and the languishing shiver that followed.

Within a few days of our seeming triumph—already diminished by the fact that on February 5 the Railroad's 2.5 percent surcharge went into effect—the Commission issued its final regulations in *Ex Parte 55*, the proceeding initiated in May 1971 for the purpose of complying with NEPA.[16]

"There's no warm, cozy feeling here," George said after our first, hurried reading. "Fritz Kahn was aware of these regulations when he signed the MOU." We were in the University Center. George was on his way to class. I was returning to Crawford after my last one. We both wore partially unzipped coats. Neither of us had coffee. The warmth inside the building gave me the momentary feel of having arrived in heaven, except for the numbness in my hands and the sting that remained in my face.

"It's like we were Napoleon entering Russia," George continued. "He forgot the Russians had the winter." The content of the regulations and the Commission's power to issue them at this moment lent credence to the analogy. They were waiting for us. The harder problem, we agreed, was the judiciary. "The Supreme Court just defers."

"The Commission knows it, and they're telling us they know it," I said. I unzipped my parka completely only to feel the heat from my body dissipate and the chill return. I looked squarely at George. At that moment, our world was singularly defined by SCRAP.

I continued. "The MOU requires the Commission to comply with NEPA. It says the Commission would issue an environmental impact statement in *281*. Under these new regulations, the Railroads are still responsible for preparing the EIS."

"The Railroads already did that. That stupid, piece of crap, Verified Statement Thirty-seven. This," George continued, pointing to the regulations, "just codifies what they already did. Like the agreement we reached doesn't exist. Neil, it's only a few days old." George, I had come to learn, responded to the Commission's mores and utterances more evenly than I did. It was in his reading of the law. He believed the law's words had a plain meaning, one that should bind everyone who read them. He believed Kahn was bound by the MOU and that a court would agree.

"And that damn NASMI," George said. "We saw through those guys." Accompanying the new regulations was the Commission report that sought to explain the reasons for their issuance. According to the report, NASMI "support[s] our proposed Regulations in their present form."[17]

"George Smathers wrote NASMI's comments," I said. George pointed to John Vaccaro's name as the source. "Damn," I added, largely in disgust; "the Railroads might as well have written them."

"Shall we take comfort in the dissenting opinions?" George said with a sting. "Commissioner Murphy, joined by, ah, Commissioner Hardin?"[18] I exhaled noticeably, with a closed fist over my mouth. "No," I said. "The regulations, quote, 'will not only create an additional and, in my opinion, unnecessary workload on the Commission with its already overburdened staff but, more importantly, will add unduly to the economic burdens of the carriers.' That's a dissent?"[19] George looked at me and said firmly, "Not a single ally."

"Your Napoleon analogy," I said to George, "is correct in at least one way. We're at war." Our experience also had taught us something else. "It's not yet certain we're the French." We both knew that, in its action, the Commission had challenged us to reach deeper for more discipline and time and, most important, to reach for experience and knowledge we were not certain we had. "Their winter," I told George, "is the judiciary."

George was silent at first, his eyes puffy, their whites reddened around the edges. His hand was very angular—frail almost—as he reached forward with it, a simple finger jutting straight out from an otherwise closed fist, itself raw from the cold or too much writing as he said softly, his eyes fixed on mine, "Or, it is *our* Waterloo."

13

THE SOCIAL FORCES,
WINTER 1972

Finding a place. I sat alone in the Circle Theatre. The beige scarf hung loosely around my neck, still providing its warmth. Snow seemed imminent. Being inside was comforting. Under the dim yellow light and with the concentration necessary to exclude the subtle chatter and muted coughing around me but not the aroma of aged butter, I read the *Post* article titled "Nixon Off to China Today Amid Bipartisan Cheers." The President's meeting with Chou En-lai—the intellectual, the revolutionary, the stoic mandarin with an unalterable conviction that he was right. He had large ideas that moved or compelled peasants and warlords and that defied history, Karl Marx, Vladimir Lenin, Joseph Stalin, Chiang Kai-shek, Nikita Khrushchev, and Harry Truman. I could see the setting as I read: Nixon beside Chou in those overstuffed chairs that the Chinese seem to revere in diplomatic settings. Two antagonists of power and conviction talking.[1] I had only a few moments before the movie started. *Doctor Zhivago.*

It was in the movie's opening moments that the familiar theme struck. It was night. The Red Star, large, bright, and haunting, was emplaced solidly on the gray, monumental wall. The star was hard and bold in its size and omnipotence. It dominated and directed the movement of workers, who seemed to find birth and meaning as they emerged in line from the tunnel beneath the star's power and terror and its illusion of victory over souls and thought and an authoritarian past. The work shift at the power plant was over. Others, different only because they were less soiled, would take their place. Even the love story that would emerge only moments later was dwarfed and challenged by the vast, cold reaches of the Urals. Their permanence and swirling wind and snow and strength characterized the smallness of everyone passing through, including a young Zhivago, bundled against the cold and tempered already by death.

It was typical of my time. Few portrayals of the Russian Revolution—its origins, intention, zealotry, and the struggle of people's lives for or against it—failed to capture its largeness in symbols, effects, words, and ideas. Throughout my academic career and, for that matter, my time on earth, the intrinsic power of Marxism—its idea and view of history—had engaged people's imaginations and worst fears. Marxism defined wars, official investigations, and prurient conduct. It sullied and destroyed lives and determined who got college tenure, who wrote for which newspapers, and who immigrated freely into the United States. Marxism also provided the basis for defining curricula in most American universities. You had to learn it in order to understand America in the twentieth century. It was still affecting us. We were fighting in Vietnam against the "Communist domino." Nixon was on his way to China. The House Un-American Activities Committee was still operating. Massachusetts still had a loyalty oath.[2]

I watched, too, as Zhivago grew and learned, buffeted by historical forces and large ideas and small personalities and by the love he sought to define with those around him. Yet even in those "personal" and "family" matters scorned by the party as bourgeois values of a discredited past, Zhivago came finally—in the artificial tranquility of Varykino—to write his Lara poems. You knew that in the smallness and beauty of this singular warm room there was, too, the emergence of a large idea that would endure and be more than the link that connected Zhivago to his child born in the Urals—the child born without his knowledge and amid the uncertainty and terror of murder, intrigue, and a radical change in the social forces.

It was after 11:00 p.m. when the movie ended. I reached the corner of Twenty-first and Pennsylvania and waited for the light to change. Snow, in gentle, small flakes that caught on my dark blue parka, had begun to fall. I looked upward to see the flakes swirling about, falling fast in amounts and in closeness and without challenge. Then I looked down Pennsylvania and, with an arch to the right, looked toward and over the university's buildings in the direction I was headed. I wanted to see the Urals in the distance or hear the jingle of the horse-drawn sleigh or watch the moon casting its light over the fields and trees and snow, illuminating the mystery and beauty below. No such luck. I pulled the parka's hood over my head and put on my gloves. Two cars came barreling by. Their wipers seemed to thud and clash in unison, forcing all of us and certainly me to awaken to urban living in 1972.

I fought to keep the movie alive. I imagined I was in Moscow, on Nevsky Prospect, in the winter of 1917. The cold and falling snow, the decaying townhouses, and the dullness and shadows of the university's buildings enhanced my illusion. I saw to my left that the Galley was open despite the late hour. It stood in stillness, tucked quietly on the far corner of Twenty-first and I Street, its doorway a few steps below grade. Its lights within shown brightly amid the darkness on both sides and against the snow that was still falling light and steady. I had had no dinner and only an apple for lunch. A cup of hot soup would work. As I entered, the aroma of fried beef and grease permeated the small Galley. The red hots, shown bright in their fullness, were contained in a massive, clear jar atop the counter. I took off the hood of my parka and waited in line. I reached instinctively into my pocket for the folded *Post.* "Anti-Semitism in Florida May Help Lindsay Drive." The *Post* said it: "The 'interesting twist,' however, is that he is not being perceived outside Miami so much as a fighting liberal … as he is a white Anglo-Saxon Protestant who is fighting against unruly—non-WASP—ethnic groups."[3]

I took the soup, a kind of tomato-and-onion ensemble, and stood near the Galley's window, slightly below ground, looking out at the cold and falling snow through the frosted window panes. The steam from the soup rose quickly at first. I spooned and then sipped it and could taste, within moments, its heat dissipating as the wind and frigid air seeped in and around the doorway and window.

I recalled the evening in May 1970, when, only a few yards from where I stood, the streets were strewn with papers and pamphlets, rags and tear-gas canisters. Students were running, walking, and coughing from the pain of inhaling. Some shouted epithets at the police or each other with fists raised in defiance while someone's car—vandalized and dragged into the center of the street—was burning intensely and dangerously. As I thought about that evening and tried to recall my impressions and feelings, I could feel the ache in my neck, and my eyes, and my hands from the sapping cold, and the demands of learning, and the diversity of urban living. I was not certain what had emerged from that violence in May 1970 in the lives of the individuals who were there, or in historical terms, or in ideas. It was unclear whether the tumultuous force felt that night and expressed elsewhere had direction and purpose that would endure or whether the ideas that affected America would come from the reformers—those who reached back into a deeper American tradition. People such as Ralph Nader or Harry Caudill or others I did not know, who were trying now to fashion an equal rights amendment, or those such as Saul Alinsky, who were organizing their neighbors in urban settings that they refused to leave to fight small fights, block to block, for cleaner streets or safer homes or fairness and dignity.

I finished the soup and could feel already, as I had with greater frequency, that neither it nor the coffee that had started my day could ever be hot enough, or its warmth penetratingly deep enough, or its comfort long lasting enough. I walked outside.

The Russians, I knew, had twisted and perverted the intentions of Marxism. Stalin—with his methodical, vindictive purges—had displaced it all together. The authoritarian idea that was the czar had never been extinguished. I thought of the gallantry and courage of the Hungarian workers' uprising in 1956 and its brutal suppression and the disillusion it caused in the West. In 1968, slightly more than a decade later and in a time of seeming civility except in Southeast Asia, the Russians invaded again, crushing the gentle blossoming of democracy in Prague. The social forces did not lie still with ease. But the fate of the Zhivago idea remained uncertain.

I crossed Twenty-first and thought for a moment about the comfort of sleep and the warmth of extra blankets. In that moment, the buildings to my right stopped serving as a shield and the wind, as if gushing through a funnel, hit me sideways and pushed and whipped the cold and light snow in and around and through me as if I were wearing pajamas.

SCRAP, we knew, was coming closer to its moment of truth. The imbedded forces, if not the ideological imperatives, were too great for further delay. We waited only for the Supreme Court to decide *Sierra Club v. Morton*.

As I turned from Twenty-first and walked up H Street toward Crawford, I felt connected, not to my contemporaries on that May night in 1970, but to an older tradition with roots largely American in its populist and progressive thinking and in the actions of reformers and muckrakers and the writing of literary realists. I was feeling not the call of Henry David Thoreau but of Theodore Dreiser and Ida Tarbell. Perhaps, too, the call was in my immigrant roots, in the insistence by those who had arrived with my mother from Italy or those who had come earlier and who strove to retain their culture or religion, people such as Louis Brandeis or Thurgood Marshall, who acted to change the rules with cunning and determination and a smartness borne of experience.

The long hallway was empty when I opened the front doorway to Crawford. I unzipped my parka and shook the snow off its hood. I could see a note tacked to my door. It was from Jeff Gocke. Plans had been laid for our trip to Miami Beach. We would leave immediately following the very last midterm examination taken by me or him or John Tomsky. John would take his car. His grandparents' house was available. We would drive straight through. A chaise lounge existed with my name on it. George had invited us to stop in Atlanta on the way back. A piña colada was being prepared especially for me. I liked Jeff. He had what I believed at that moment was a large, enduring, and warmly felt idea.

THE UNPLANNED VISIT

I needed a shave and shower. The Volkswagen was responsive and in need of a wash. I was packed: a pile of dirty laundry. Staff schedules had been revised, and if I was driving, I was not studying. I had done my readings in advance, earlier in the morning and late into the evening. The nation cooperated, too. No demonstrations were planned. I was going home for one night. My mother was not well.

Before noon, I zipped into the driveway alongside our home. My dad and sister were in the backyard raking leaves. I hugged them both and noticed the tiredness in my father's eyes. He was fifty-nine years old and had been working two jobs.

"Mom's in bed," Diana said. "Her back is bothering her, and she has an infection. You know, woman problems. She's very tired."

Inside, the house was calm. Familiar cups were on the kitchen table; the aroma was freshly brewed coffee. I walked up to the second floor. My mother was looking through magazines to find ideas for crocheting, drawing, or sewing. *The Journal Courier* lay there, read.

"I heard you come in," she said. I sat on the edge of the bed and held her hand. "Don't worry," she said. "I'll be fine. I just need a few days. It's hard, too, with your father working nights."

It was in this room that I had once lain, at age 16, with a plaster cast from my hips to just below my armpits, essential until, as we all hoped, the disc and infectious material that had destroyed it would be replaced by the natural fusion of bone tissue so that I might walk again. My mother and I talked about that time now, how we waited almost six months, through tutors provided by the city, daily visits from friends and relatives, and wonderful gestures—free haircuts, drawing supplies, and the bed that cranked up in the back so that I could eat, write, and read.

"I read all the books you had," I said, "like *The Wayward Bus* and Mailer's book, *The Naked and the Dead*. *The Good Earth* and *The Caine Mutiny*. And the Hemingway book, the one they made into a movie?"

"*For Whom the Bell Tolls*," she said, gently, sharing my cadence. She nodded confidentially. "We did good," she said.

"Hi, Dee," my mother said, as my sister entered, carrying a tray of coffee cups; a pot filled with hot coffee; and a plate of sliced ham, Swiss cheese, a large, ripe tomato, olive oil, pepper, and a huge loaf of Italian bread, along with dishes, napkins, and a knife. My dad followed with a bowl of steaming chicken noodle soup atop a tray accompanied by saltines. "Lunch time," Diana announced.

My sister helped my mother sit up, and my father placed the soup-laden tray on her lap. She was hungry. I was too. I explained that I might take the bar exam in Washington, D.C.

"Just do what you need to do," my mother said.

"Don't worry about anything else," my dad added. "You'll always have a bedroom."

"Thanks, Dad," I said softly.

"I found some letters," my mother said, pointing to the end of the bed. "We were fixing the windows in your room. From Steve DiBiase. You were such good friends until he left." I opened the letter from Vietnam.

"July 26, 1969," I read aloud. "From the balmy shores of that South East Asian Paradise—the People's Democratic Republic of South Vietnam, comes a long procrastinated letter." I exhaled. Steve was back now in Connecticut, finishing college.

"It weighs on him, doesn't it?" my mother said, yet not as a question. "It did on my brother Tommy."

My dad cut the loaf down the center and, with the professionalism that comes only with practice, he created a culinary masterpiece that, once sliced, was devoured with fulfilling ease amid conversation, sips of coffee, and the renewal of family memory that, the next day, would stay with me through the long drive back to Washington. So, too, did the certainty that yet more confrontation with the ICC and EDF was forming. It would require yet more preparation on our part and, most important, the agreed-upon imperative among the three of us to seek the resolution in law that we sought from the outset.

FINDING THE REASON

From my pantry window, I could see the cracked pavement of the alleyways and truck routes and the back entrance to a sliver of the university. The view provided no aesthetic repose. Even my Volkswagen was streaked in black and gray from melted snow falling atop the soot that seemed to accumulate with ease and certainty. The anticipated warmth of coffee percolated a few steps away.

The *Washington Post* lay neatly on the counter. February 27, 1972. I had pulled from the closet a box of documents, pamphlets, speeches, and written papers, including my master's thesis and the United States Senate hearings on *The Prevention and Punishment of the Crime of Genocide*. It had never been ratified by Congress. My paper on the Genocide Convention was my next order of business. With seeming contentedness, I poured a cup of coffee. I also slid the *Post* close enough to look at an article on its front page.

"90 Feared Dead in W. Va. Flooding." The article read, "Logan, W. Va., Feb. 26. At least 37 persons died today when water, backed up in a slag dump cofferdam, broke through and swept over remote coal camps in Logan County." People were dead "in this Appalachia valley"—whole towns and families had been quickly destroyed with filthy, toxic, putrid water. Government had allowed it.[4] I thought about another connection made only through reading. Harry Caudill was in Whitesburg, Kentucky. I could write him, tell him about SCRAP and the Railroads and the extraction of natural resources. I could connect it to what he was doing. I started jotting notes and ideas for a letter that I hoped would say something useful.

With coffee in hand, I sat in a momentary stillness on the sofa. Among the documents I had gathered was an article by Colman McCarthy called "Destroy a Mountain and It's Destroyed Forever." Stinking Creek, Tennessee: Students from Vanderbilt University had determined the coal companies were being assessed property taxes based on the land's value without the coal. The assessment was undertaken by the coal companies and accepted by tax officials. Government had allowed it. Four hundred local residents filed a "citizen's complaint." They had turned to a court of law. Ralph Nader had joined the fray.[5] Individual rights. One's place within its meaning. The forum for their vindication—for those whose rights were at risk and who in the brevity of life had only a "short run" to experience life's meaning—was a court of law. There was nowhere else. And vindication was only there if, as Justice Douglas had stated in *Flast v. Cohen* and Justice Brennan had reiterated in *Barlow v. Collins*, the judiciary believed that "where wrongs to individuals are done ... it is abdication for courts to close their doors."[6]

14

THE LINES ARE DRAWN, WINTER 1972

The Commission defies NEPA. March 6. It had been raining intermittently all day, a light mist that was falling without sound or fury or notice until about noon. In its seeming transparency and gentle touch, the mist settled and slowly permeated your skin and your clothes and your books. It brought, at unsuspected moments, a chill and discomfort and disappointment. It was not a clear adversary.

My coffee was soothing. John and George sat on each side of me at the table. We were in the Center. It was almost 4:00 p.m. They sat in silence, waiting for me to finish. George had gotten the draft EIS from the Commission that morning. He and John had read it. "The Railroads' unwillingness to do more than Verified Statement Thirty-seven forced the ICC into it," I said when George handed it to me, poker-faced.[1]

"Chicken," George said to me. "And the Commission flinched."

"And the new NEPA regs?" I asked.

"About the Railroads' role? Unimportant," he told me.

"God. What are they doing over there?" I sat, legs crossed tightly, body flush against the table, with my hands over my ears to mute the sound around me. I reread it then looked at George. John, I could see, already had his grin firmly in place. "In Washington, D.C.?" I asked emphatically. "They wrote an EIS, an official government document that is only six pages long."

"Neil," George said, in a mock seriousness, "did you pay your taxes?" I sat back and looked straight at him.

"George, this has got to be only the appendix," I said.

"It's fabulous," John said, his eyes rolling, his grin seemingly permanent. He moved his chair closer to the table. "All we need to do," he said, "is wave the EIS in front of the court."

"Neil," George said, "maybe I got the wrong document."

"George, this is just the summary. I'm telling you. It can't be only six pages."

"Well," John said, sitting back, balanced precariously on the rear two legs of a decidedly fragile chair, hesitating just a moment to ensure our attention. "It is. It sure as hell is."

"There was enough information available to prepare a draft ten times longer—just from our material. And," I said, sifting through it, "it has a full-page summary at the beginning and a half-page summary at the end."

"They must have had Banzhaf for a teacher," George said, bringing us all to laughter.

"The summary also states that the draft EIS intends to examine, quote, 'the possible approval or disapproval by the Interstate Commerce Commission of selected increase proposals for commodity groupings to replace the 2.5 percent surcharge.'"[2]

"The Railroads haven't proposed anything yet."

"In our MOU, the general counsel agreed to examine the 2.5 percent surcharge."

"The MOU's been violated," George said, pleased our intuition was confirmed.

"Look. They make two points," I said earnestly. "Although titled 'Draft EIS,' it says it is not a draft EIS. Let's see. 'The service of this statement in no way concedes the applicability of NEPA requirements at the suspension stage,' and, second, every study submitted thus far that suggested harm has been disputed by the 'environmental statement (V.S. No. 37) submitted by the railroad[s].'"[3]

I stopped my reading and without removing my hands from my ears, looked up at John. "They said we have made no case on the merits, they have no responsibility to do an impact statement, they are not going to tell us what rate increase they're examining, and, in any event, 'take a hike, because we're going to win anyway.'" I went back to my reading, then looked up again. "The draft EIS states, 'no irreversible and irretrievable commitments of resource appear to be involved.' Here, in the previous paragraph, let me get this right, 'for example, one ton of reprocessed waste paper conserves seventeen trees.'"[4] I looked up. "Huh?"

"Before you say anything else, read this," George said. He slid it across the table. I read the first three paragraphs.

"Damn," I said.

"Yep," George affirmed, smiling. The Commission order was seven pages. It was longer than the draft EIS.[5]

"I'm not sure I understand exactly what they did here."

"Yep," he said again. The Commission's order authorized the Railroads to submit new rate increases that would be effective on April 1, 1972. These "new" rates would replace the 2.5 percent surcharge in effect since February 5. A hearing would be held on March 23, which was less than three weeks away.

"What do you think the hearing is supposed to examine?" George asked me.

I read the order again. The new rate increases, I knew, had not been submitted yet. I looked at George and John. "I think it's the new increase that replaces the 2.5 percent surcharge. It says that 'any person opposing the proposed increase in rates....' Well, I'm not sure. Up here, it says the Commission authorized, quote, 'the filing of tariff schedules reflecting the said general increase on a selective basis'—what the heck does that mean?—'to become effective not earlier than May 1, 1972, upon not less than forty-five days notice.' So, the public must be notified of the new rates, which are not yet submitted, by the middle of March, to make the forty-five days, but that's only a week or so before the hearing? Well. And here's the magic language. They're going to make them effective, quote, 'subject to possible suspension by the Commission.' I thought we already were in the 'suspension stage.'"[6]

"See?" George said knowingly. I rubbed my face. As I moved the chair back to stretch my legs, I could feel the rainy dampness in my blue jeans. I took a sip of coffee.

"I don't know what the hell they did," I said, still trying to parse the order's meaning. "They set a hearing for March 23.[7] They say here we're supposed to file these 'verified statements.' You know, the ones where everybody lies. Then they're going to consider them at the hearing, along with everything else. Damn. The 2.5 percent is still in effect at least until May 1 but maybe longer. Or this new 'general increase' that either is in effect already, or has been since February 5, or won't go into effect until April 1 or May 1—and all of it, or one of them, is or possibly will be under suspension."

"Yep," George added crisply. "And now, come back to this. Tell me which increase, effective on which date, the draft EIS examines."

John shrugged. "We're getting screwed," he said in a flat, direct, authoritative tone.

I offered to get more coffee. John wanted tea. "I'll come with you," George said quickly. Once we were near the coffee machine, he asked "What's going on with your WASPy friend? You meet the parents?"

"No. It's not going to happen. But I figured it out."

"Yeah?"

"It isn't the father. At least not for that reason."

"So?"

"The mother."

"Hmm," George moaned subtly, introspectively. "But it's not Caroline?"

"No."

"So it's still possible the two of you—?"

"There's more."

"Yeah?"

"It's not right, George. I won't go along with that stuff."

"Yeah. I understand," he looked me straight in the eye, "Neil, you shouldn't."

When we returned, our discussion started again. "Look," I said, "the draft EIS is crap. When you combine it with this other order, it has only one effect. They're drawing this process out to accomplish nothing under NEPA. No impact statement, and by the time the process is over, when they're out of this darn 'suspension stage,' then it's over. The increase is granted and it's too late. That's what the Railroads will say. So sue me and screw you. We win."

"They'll wait 'til summer," John said.

"Yeah," I said. "First, they'll call my mother and ask, hey, Mrs. Proto, is Neil home? And then zingooo!"

"It's the 'how long can these kids keep this up' strategy," George said, laughing.

George offered to call the ICC Practitioner to be sure we understood what the Commission had done. I proposed we ask EDF to represent us at the March 23 hearing. "It'll give them something to do," I said. "I'll offer to have us do an analysis of some of the so-called verified statements."

"Good," John agreed.

"And we should advance forward what we're doing in other courses."

"We already did that," George said firmly.

The early dinner crowd had started to arrive. The movement and chatter and clang of chairs and tables reminded me I needed to leave. I was on duty, which meant being in my apartment until the following morning. I reached for my parka. Kathleen was standing only a few yards away, a dripping umbrella in tow, her face red from the chill outside. She had been watching me. I smiled, awkwardly. It was a moment, a pause of uncertainty that warranted certainty.

John stood. "This sucks," he said.

Two women, one carrying a coffee to go, joined Kathleen, took her arm, and left. George, weary and unshaven, said, as if in utter futility, "I want to get home, take a shower, and have dinner. I want to see my wife. I want to lock all the boys in their rooms."

"No such luck," I replied.

THE EDF CONFRONTATION, MUTED

I called John Dienelt. EDF, he said, would participate in the hearing scheduled for March 23. He would represent SCRAP. As required by the March 6 order, he would submit a letter stating whom he wanted to cross-examine. Dienelt also accepted my offer to have George and me analyze the verified statements. I brought the analysis to his office.[8]

I sat down in a plain wooden chair directly opposite Dienelt's desk. I unbuttoned my corduroy jacket but did not remove it. There was no casual banter. I wanted it to be a simple, purposeful meeting. I described what George and I had found, citing one recyclable material after the other as examples. Dienelt seemed unmoved by what I said, distracted by other papers on his desk. I described how malicious I thought the Railroads had been in the "deceptive manner these verified statements were drafted"—how harmful the rate increase would be and how the Commission did not act as if it cared, given the mediocrity of the draft EIS, which I thought was "deliberately prepared that way."

The Commission, I said, was "a captive of the corporate structure." The Railroads' arrogance proved it. Dienelt looked up at me. He began a lecture, a monologue, direct and then forceful, almost angry in tone. It was not spontaneous. It was about me and my attitude. My problem was that I was "antiestablishment." It had skewed my attitude and our work. He was not that way, he said. I knew that, I thought. He insisted with an unequivocal firmness that I needed to change SCRAP's approach, so we could be more constructive.

My thoughts were clear. I sat still. I could feel the muscles in my lips and jaw tighten and my bite harden. I could not tell him to "get lost." That was a collective decision that we already had made but not explicitly—not yet— and that certainly should not be conveyed or implied now. I also had never been called "antiestablishment" before and thought immediately that Dienelt's frame of reference must be very limited. At that moment, I thought he was a banker and a direct descendant of Morgan. I was not sure whether I was Nicola Sacco, Bartolomeo Vanzetti, Leon Trotsky, or Louis Brandeis. I opted at first for Vanzetti. That would make Dienelt A. Lawrence Lowell, the president of Harvard. I then thought about Brandeis. I knew the least about him except he had investigated the Railroad industry and its abuse of public responsibility. I was not sure whom that made Dienelt. At that moment, I was gratified for the model he had made me grasp and hold. I did not respond. I would come by on March 23 for a portion of the hearing. He seemed nonplussed by my restraint. John and George had classes all that day, I told him, and could not attend. I gently placed the analysis on his desk and said goodbye.

THE COMMISSION DEFIES NEPA, AGAIN

The Commission had become a familiar place to me but only in its geography, in the ghosts that roamed its halls, and in the disdain I felt for its actions. I had never been there alone. Today, as I inquired about the location of the hearing room and walked the hallways to find it, I believed I could be perceived only by why I was there at all. I was SCRAP.

I walked with caution to the outer doorways of the hearing room. The proceeding already was under way. Its sounds echoed. I expected a large room built for a different era, when the entire nation believed that what was at stake tempered the nation's well-being and its future. I knew they all would be there: the Railroads' lawyers, whose names until now I had only read. They had written and acted and affected our lives, as I knew we had theirs. Inside was a sanctuary of a kind I now understood; protective, warm, exclusive, and private despite its aura of public purpose and creation in law. It was yesteryear. The power of size and tradition was solidly ensconced, unaffected by time, and unadorned by the commonweal. Here was where the Railroads had the maximum influence, where perversion of the public trust was most easily exercised, was made official by the Commission, and was crafted into law. I walked inside. I was an intruder. I stood motionless for a moment to get my bearings. As I looked around the room, I could see amid the tweeds and watch fobs and handkerchiefs in the breast pockets and large leather briefcases that I looked like an intruder. I thought of my brother. "With those glasses," he had said, "you look like Trotsky."

I sat in the back of the room. There was a considerable distance between me and the lawyers, witnesses, staff members of the Railroads, shippers, and others who were there to observe. The blue jeans, parka, and long hair certified it. Before me was a long, high bench made of dark wood. It was aged and had been witness to power and mischief and harm. It was long enough for six or eight people to sit behind and peer and listen. Behind it today was seated only the hearing examiner. I did not know his name and took no special note of his appearance. A number of individuals, presumably clerks, were mulling near him. Occasionally, one would thrust a piece of paper before him or ensure that the glass of water to his right was full. To his left and proximate to the long, high bench was a chair situated on a platform where, at the moment I entered, a witness—white haired, dark suit, a Railroad man I guessed—sat explaining some arcane concept of rate making. I believed I understood what he was saying.

With their backs to me, seated along a table that paralleled the examiner's bench, were the Railroads' lawyers. There may have been six or seven. They included, no doubt, those whose names were on the petitions and briefs I had seen. For me, there was only one who counted: the AAR's general counsel, Edward A. Kaier. My expectation of whom he would be in appearance and demeanor was met quickly in two ways.

First, I watched as the seated lawyers moved papers and notes toward— or stood and walked over to speak with—the lawyer in the center. He was diminutive, small featured, and solid in stature with steel-gray hair slicked back direct and hard, and with glasses. He wore a three-piece suit and dark tie, and he focused intently on the witness and the examiner before him. His eyes remained fixed except at moments that did not seem random. He nodded his head, got others to act with only a modest gesture, and orchestrated what I believed deeply was a total charade, directing the players to adhere to a script intended only to justify publicly a predetermined outcome already resolved in private.

Second, at the precise conclusion of the witness's remarks, the hearing examiner moved his head mechanically from the witness to this person seated directly in front of him. The drama now emerged plainly as the play unfolded, surrounded by those looking reverently toward him as if those others, including the lawyer who had been questioning the witness, were and had acknowledged themselves irrelevant. The hearing examiner asked, "Any further questions, Mr. Kaier?" Kaier responded. I could not hear it. It made no difference. I was convinced Kaier was really the hearing examiner.

Dienelt was in the room, near the front. At what apparently was the right time, he stood and requested permission to examine a Railroad witness. He was told he was out of order. The pretense was gone. NEPA had no real meaning to the Commission. The longer we waited, the more the Railroads and the Commission were surrounding and smothering us. It was their forum and their rules. Sides, perhaps three of them, had been chosen irrevocably. We were alone. I left.

I returned to Stockton Hall, then walked a bit farther on to Bacon. Banzhaf was not there. I located Peter Meyers and described what had occurred. He sat quietly, somber almost, and listened intently. He did not smoke. He asked a few questions. "I see," he said and then said it again. The choice to file a lawsuit was ours. Peter would be supportive. For him, however, the outcome of the Supreme Court's review of *Sierra Club v. Morton* was, as he had characterized it repeatedly, "crucial to our success." He advised prudence but not, as I read it, by waiting for the ICC to finish its decision-making process. With a look of empathy and with a shared knowledge he said, "*Arrow Transportation.*" I felt an anger and determination moving into my eyes and lips and cheeks and jaw and into my hands and fingers. "You know," he said, "I will do everything I can. You guys must decide."

I could not, at first, locate John or George. I called George's dorm and then left a message with John Tomsky. He reminded me of our planned trip to Miami Beach. A chaise lounge popped in and out of my head. Not now, I thought. I walked back to Crawford convinced we needed to make the decision to sue the Commission. The only question was timing. When I reached Crawford, I felt tired, mentally drained, and uneasy. I picked up a half dozen pieces of mail in the office, walked back to my apartment, and undressed. I looked in the mirror. The area around my eyes was almost solid dark gray and black. My hair was matted down from the hood of my parka and unruly around the edges. Strands of gray were appearing. My sinuses felt swelled. I headed for the shower.

I dressed again, just slacks and my pajama top. The soft cotton felt comfortable. On the way into the pantry to make some tea, I picked up the mail from the table. The first few pieces were from the housing office. The fourth was personal. The back of the envelope read, "Harry M. Caudill, Attorney and Counselor at Law, Daniel Boone Hotel Building, Post Office Box 727, Whitesburg, Kentucky 41858." It was addressed to "Mr. Neil Thomas Proto." I placed it on the counter, face up, and looked at it.

I took the letter into the living room, sat down on the couch, and felt the softness of its cushions around my back and legs. I took a sip of hot tea and placed the cup and its saucer carefully on the couch to my right. I opened the letter.

Dear Mr. Proto:

Thank you very much for your letter of March 12.

I read, with much interest, your enclosures from the proceedings before the Interstate Commerce Commission. I can glimpse a relationship between ICC policies and environmental decline, and I am grateful to you for calling it to my attention.

It is certain that Congressman Hechler will find them of interest also.

Very truly yours,
Harry M. Caudill [9]

I read the letter again and let it rest, opened, in my lap. I took another sip of tea, gently returned the cup, and laid my head backward. My eyes closed. I had connected to Harry Caudill.

It was a long evening, devoted largely to telephone conversations with John and George. I described my experience at the Commission and my discussion with Peter Meyers. We each would intensify our effort to dispose of other course assignments. "Neil," George said, "you keep saying that. How the hell more 'intense' can we get?"

"We're going to need time, George. I'm telling you." George would update all cases related to *Arrow Transportation* and the "suspension stage." John would do the same on standing.

"I don't know about *Sierra Club*. Waiting, I mean. I'll gather all the complaints I can from anywhere I can. Once we begin, no excuses. You know, George," I said, "it's not as if we can get notes from our mothers."

"Your mother wouldn't give you one."

"We're alone, you know. Just us."

"Neil. It's gotten us this far."

THE FINAL RESPITE

I was packed and waiting in the hallway thirty minutes before it was necessary. I had already started reading *Bury My Heart at Wounded Knee* by Dee

Brown, looking at its photographs and feeling the texture of its paper. It was near 9:00 p.m. when John Tomsky arrived. Jeff Gocke, who had packed earlier and was with him, came in to get me. He needed to. I had become fully engrossed in the book. "Since the exploratory journey of Lewis and Clark to the Pacific Coast early in the nineteenth century," Dee Brown began—and I was there or, at least, certainly not here—"[t]he greatest concentration of recorded experience and observation came out of the thirty-year span between 1860 and 1890…. During that time the culture and civilization of the American Indian was destroyed, and out of that time came virtually all the great myths of the American West."[10]

"Hey, big fella. Let's go," Jeff said.

John drove. He was taut, his face drawn and angular, his hair uncombed, and his diminutive frame held erect by the solid grasp of his hands on the wheel. Jeff sacked out in the back, with his coat over him like a blanket, his head against a pillow from the dorm, his eyes covered with a tattered, moldy baseball cap. "I haven't slept in two days," he murmured. I rode shotgun. The university was history in moments.

We drove straight to Miami Beach except for three stops. We stopped once at an all-night gas station across the North Carolina border. Jeff took over the driving. John moved to the rear. The tautness succumbed finally to exhaustion. We stopped again in Savannah to eat breakfast. The waitress looked at us as if we were northern hippie freaks. We ordered grits with our eggs. "They come with it," she snapped. Jeff thanked her and called her "ma'am." It did not temper her attitude. Once back in the parking lot, Jeff laid backward against the car door, his hands clasped behind his head. He was ready for the beach. I took the helm. About midway through Florida, John took over again. I tried to sleep and perhaps did. I kept looking at the billboards, stuck in swamps and barren land, announcing new construction (Buy now!) and great land deals. I thought about consumers and scandals and old people losing their savings. John took us home.

I liked Miami Beach. It was like a movie. Its first half was the 1950s, its second the 1930s. It was *Surfside Six*—the houseboat docked alongside the inland waterway near Collins Avenue. The story always took place in glorious sun and white surf, amid balmy evenings and swaying palms, with large hotels providing the backdrop. The cars were a sleek Corvette convertible or a souped-up Ford with tailfins and mud flaps and suicide knobs and with Bobby Darin blasting on the radio. The windows were down with the driver's arm hanging outside the door. The driver had his collar up and was bee-bopping through life.

Miami also was where honeymoons were experienced. Where older cousins and the sons and daughters of family friends seemed to go, staying in the Fountainbleau or the Doral, to consummate marriages in an era when people waited for such moments and when they came back tanned, filled with soft-spoken stories, and ready for life. And only a few miles north was Fort Lauderdale: Annette Funicello, Frankie Avalon, *Where the Boys Are*, Connie Francis, growing up, the twist, and beer everywhere.

It was here, too, in the architecture now chipped and faded, in the remnants of the Art Deco style that was visible as we drove south on Route A1 and backward in time and that adorned the smaller hotels (now condominiums and cooperatives), that I felt a different era. It was locked in a time not known to me, except by imagination and in the old movies I recalled that had captured it, of a Miami Beach that was mysterious and detached from America.

We settled easily into the simple, white clapboard bungalow with glass-slatted windows and a grapefruit tree in the backyard. The house was located in a quiet neighborhood with tree-lined streets and gently sloped, manicured lawns. Grapefruit and hot coffee started our day. My coveted chaise lounge was there. Each day, we would arrive, greet John's parents and neighbors, lie in the sun, read, talk, walk along the beach, swim in the pool, and meet and watch all varieties of people. Within a few days, the pain in my shoulders and neck subsided, withered, and seemed cured. What an illusion.

Mr. Tomsky was in the scrap iron and steel business. He described the metallurgical content of what his company bought and sold, how it was stored, where the markets were, and what the importance was of transportation costs in meeting demand.

We left Miami Beach feeling relaxed and almost ready for school. We drove north and then veered west, past the orange groves and Disney World, onto Interstate 75 and into Georgia. We arrived at the Biondi home in time for dinner. What would you expect from students, George's mother said, as she piled pasta and vegetables and meats and breads and desserts onto the table with a gentle manner and tone that made you eat with comfort. George's father was with the Internal Revenue Service. We talked about school and family and SCRAP and the nation's politics and the dorms.

That evening, George and I left the others in the living room, engaged by food and laughter. Mrs. Biondi had taken out some old family photographs. We sat in the bedroom that George and Kathy occupied during their visit. "You look tanned and rested," I said.

"Only in comparative terms," he said.

"Compared to whom?" I asked.

"No. Compared to time. A few weeks in the upper reaches of Bacon Hall, and it'll be gone."

"George," I said, "it won't take that long." I explained to him, with all the logic and passion I possessed, why we should sue the Commission now, without the Supreme Court's decision in *Sierra Club*.

He raised all the requisite questions. He added his own thoughts about the law and Peter Meyers's role in such a lawsuit and Banzhaf's personality and the Commission's attitude. "Let's do it," he said, with a seriousness and conviction that conveyed prudence and a knowledge of what we were about to start. I admired and welcomed inwardly our friendship and our decision, now eight months old, to undertake this venture.

We left early the next morning. We drove northeast and then north, past small towns and swamps and dense undergrowth. I thought about the power of the Civil War—the lynchings, the burnings, the dogs, and the snipers. I reflected on the way the Civil War's remnants still haunted America, still defined its politics and law, and still provided the images that affected all of us—especially me that day as I looked across the landscapes of rural Georgia into its hidden places that were wet and mysterious and tempered by death.

On April 19, the Supreme Court decided *Sierra Club v. Morton*.

15

SEARCHING FOR COMFORT, SPRING 1972

S *ierra Club v. Morton.* "Not so simple that it should give us comfort," I said after my first reading. But John reminded me the decision addressed only one of our concerns.

"Comfort is not something we have to worry about," he said. Justice Potter Stewart wrote the opinion. The Sierra Club did not have standing. Chief Justice Warren Burger and Justices Byron White and Thurgood Marshall agreed. Justices William Douglas, William Brennan, and Harry Blackmun dissented. Justices Lewis Powell and William Rehnquist did not vote. Less than a majority of the Court set this precedent. It was disquieting.[1]

"There's a lot between us and the Supreme Court." John continued. "Try the district court, a special three-judge court, the ICC, the nation's Railroads, Covington & Burling, the United States of America, and the Department of Justice."

"Now this," George said. "How's that for comfort?"

Justice Stewart set forth the two-tier test: first, whether the government's action caused the complaining party injury in fact, and, second, whether the alleged injury "was to an interest 'arguably within the zone of interests to be protected or regulated' by the statutes.... [N]either *Data Processing* nor *Barlow* addressed itself to the question," Justice Stewart continued, "as to what

must be alleged by persons who claim injury of a non-economic nature....
That question is presented in this case."[2]

The Disney project, Justice Stewart reasoned, would harm the scenery, natural and historic objects, and wildlife, and would impair the enjoyment of the park: "Aesthetic and environmental well-being, like economic well-being, are important ingredients of the quality of life in our society, and the fact that particular environmental interests are shared by the many rather than the few does not make them less deserving of legal protection through the judicial process."[3]

"So? What does it mean that we have no single project?" George said.

"I don't know, George. They had it. It made no difference," I responded.

John turned a page in his copy of the decision and looked up at us. "He says here 'the injury in fact test requires the party seeking review be himself among the injured.... The Sierra Club failed to allege that it or its members would be affected ... by the Disney development.' This was the dispute."[4]

"With the League and EDF and the others?" George asked, but in the tone of a declaration.

"Yeah," I said.

"The Sierra Club," John continued, "quote, 'regarded any allegations of individualized injury as superfluous, on the theory that this was a public action,' and that the, quote, 'Club's long-standing concern with and expertise in such matters were sufficient to give it standing as a 'representative of the public.'"[5]

"Well, that theory's out," George said.

"So is the Sierra Club," John declared.

"And so is EDF," I said, recognizing it would affect further how we dealt with them. There was an uneasy, momentary silence.

"You can see why they wanted to control us," George said.

"Fear," I added.

There were three dissenting opinions: by Justices Douglas, Blackmun, and Brennan.[6] Douglas's opinion drove deepest. Congress, he said, "is too remote to give meaningful direction and its machinery is too ponderous to us very often." To illustrate the executive's failure he cited the Nader reports, including the *Interstate Commerce Ommission* and the studies by Senator Lee Metcalf on corporate influence. He went right to the lawsuit we intended to file, with an extract from M. Josephson's *The Politicos*, written in 1938: "The [Interstate Commerce] Commission ... satisfies the popular clamor for a government supervision of Railroads, at the same time that the supervision is almost entirely nominal."[7] Josephson and Nader had said the same thing thirty years apart. Brandeis said it at the turn of the century. We witnessed it in 1972.

Douglas also focused on the oral argument made by the Solicitor General Erwin Griswold. "He considers the problem," Douglas wrote, "in terms of 'government by the Judiciary' and doesn't like it. How, and who[,] assures that an executive agency is oriented toward the public interest it is designed to protect."[8] For Douglas, the answer was plain: the judiciary. Without "standing to sue," it had no role.

"You got comfort now, Proto?" John asked.

"Blackmun would find it." George said. "He would, quote, 'be quite content' to join if 'this were an ordinary case.' It's extraordinary, he says, because of environmental degradation."

"Maybe what he's really saying is that *only* the Sierra Club can do it," I said, trying to understand how Blackmun's approach related to the need to demonstrate actual harm.

"The Justice Department will be hostile," John added. "The solicitor general made that plain." Disquiet remained.

"In the end," George said, "there're still only three of us."

"It may not work," John said with unease. "The Court told us what *not* to do, not what *to* do. I don't know if we can do it."

"So," I said, "that's for a court to decide. So?"

"Yeah?" George asked as he provoked me to say the obvious.

"Let's let 'em do it," I said.

THE STRATEGY

"We think there should be two lawsuits," George began. "Keep this in mind, Neil. We started with *265/267*. It's a big deal. Twenty-one percent, across the board, all the Railroads. We kept raising it when we started in *281*."

"What do you propose?" I asked, sounding like the chairman.

"That we file in 265/267. A declaratory judgment. We don't do anything with it. Just file it. No injunctions or anything like that," George said.

"We just let it sit?" I asked.

"Yeah."

"Well, let's assume we can. We still have timing," I said. "Do we want to file this, the *265/267* complaint, before the ICC decides *281*, which has got to be soon?"

"Ideally? Yes," George said.

"It would be unexpected," John was quick to add.

"We'd have to explain why we waited so long to file," I said, trying—in a now commonplace way—to ensure clarity. John reminded me the Commission had "reopened" the proceeding in order to accept our petitions, even though they rejected our arguments. That was in December 1971. "Not so long ago," he said. "This complaint would be an appeal from that decision."

"Plausible," I said, still sounding like the chairman but visibly agreeing.

We raised this approach with Peter Meyers. He agreed it would be helpful to get the history of *265/267* into the litigation. George believed the Commission would decide *281* soon or, as he put it, "they'll do something. You never know what—or even what it means when they do it. We sue them now and, then later; afterward, we consolidate the cases into one."

BACK TO THE LARGE ROOM

"B-52s Again Strike Deep Inside North."[9] The morning *Post* confirmed what the radio commentator had announced at 7:00 a.m. John, George, and I were meeting in the large room atop Bacon. Peter Meyers would be there later. Our goal was to file the complaint in *265/267* by Monday, April 24, or no later than Tuesday, April 25. The president was not helping.

The Vietnam War had reemerged with startling vengeance. The president took it north, deep, and with technology. Ho Chi Minh had taken it south. The Viet Cong and North Vietnamese regulars were occupying more and more ground. Retreat was evident. Saigon was in jeopardy. "What timing," I muttered. It was spring. The weather was warm and the boys in the dorm were restless. George called at 7:30 a.m. "So far as I can tell, only Jane Fonda cares," he said. We both knew it went deeper and broader. Members of Congress were maneuvering to cut off funds for the War. Lawsuits would be filed. Constitutional powers were being discussed. Our concern now was singular and simple: no demonstrations. We could not be distracted. Our boys were the only participants we cared about.

"George. There's nothing we can do. Meet me at Bacon at eight. I'll bring the coffee. In the meantime, talk softly and don't slam the front door when you leave. With luck, everyone will sleep 'til noon."

The three of us sat alone. The room had a chill. Rain was expected. John began to examine the legal issues we wanted to raise in our second complaint challenging *281*. George examined the local rules governing the federal district court. I agreed to draft the complaint in *265/267*.

By late morning, with the rain and wind striking and rattling the windowpanes, Peter walked in, said hello, sipped coffee for a moment, and announced he would be sitting in Banzhaf's office working. We should call if we needed him.

I brought with me old complaints I had collected. I studied their form, their logic, and their seeming objectivity. Certain characteristics were shared: the description of the jurisdiction and venue of the court, the certificate of service, and the formalism of the terminology. What emerged was the complaint's real purpose: tell a story that concluded with only one outcome. We were right; the other side was wrong. The art was in the storytelling. The "suspension stage" and the meaning of *Arrow Transportation* were not present. "Unequivocally final," George said.

I sat at one end of the long table, solitary in thought, trying to force my words into a simple, elementary story. I drew heavily on our original petitions and, with an agile cut-and-paste job, described who we were. Then I turned to "each member of SCRAP," with the court decisions firmly in mind:

> "(i) has been caused to pay more for finished products purchased in the marketplace" [from *Data Processing*]; "(ii) uses the nation's forests, rivers, streams, mountains, and other natural resources for camping, hiking, fishing, sightseeing, and other recreational and aesthetic purposes. These uses have been, and will continue to be, adversely affected to the extent the freight rate structure, as modified in ... *265/267*, encourages the destruction of virgin timber, the unnecessary extraction of raw minerals, and the discharge and accumulation of otherwise recyclable waste materials" [from *Sierra Club*]; and "(iii) lives in or near a large municipal center, uses its water resources, park areas, conducts many of his daily activities and is constantly exposed to the quality of air within or near that center. *265/267*, to the extent it encourages the discharge and accumulation of large quantities of solid waste in such municipalities, forces said municipalities to expend large sums of tax money to store, burn or dump such waste, and fosters the diversion of freight traffic from rail to motor carrier, increases the likelihood of an unnecessary threat to human health" [from *Data Processing*, *Barlow*, and *Sierra Club*].[10]

We skipped lunch. In mid-afternoon, George volunteered to get us more coffee and tea for John, donned his jacket, and pulled out a hat that defied description. "Protection from the rain," he said, with a deadpan look.

"That may serve some purpose but not protection from the rain," I said. I grabbed my year-round parka with the hood and handed it to George.

"And get out of here. I'll fall asleep if I don't get some coffee."

"Yes, sir, Mister Chairman, sir." George smiled and put the parka over his jacket. "I'll use the hat for the coffee." He left.

My longhand draft of the complaint had been typed. John and George began their review. Peter agreed to work with George on ensuring that all the procedural requirements were met. It was almost 10:30 p.m. when George announced he had to return to a dorm council meeting scheduled for 11:00. Neither of us had heard anything all day about demonstrations. "Neil," George said thankfully, "I'm going to offer to sing them lullabies."

NO STOPPING US

April 24. George called me. The Commission had issued an order in *281.*[11] He was not certain exactly what they had done. "I used to think at least *they* knew," I said. "Now I don't even know that."

"It appears," he said, "the Commission denied the selective increase that was supposed to replace the 2.5 percent emergency surcharge. The surcharge is still in effect." But, he also thought, the surcharge now was permanent.

"Not temporary?" I asked.

"No. But it's so hard to tell. They seem to 'suspend' everything so that you don't know what exactly is 'final' and what's in the so-called suspension stage."

George and John then walked over to Crawford. John did not believe the denial was final. "They never say no," George said.

The Commission had kept the 2.5 percent "temporary" surcharge. It had been "modified to eliminate the expiration date of June 5, 1972." It also approved—we thought, but with increasing uncertainty as we read it— having the June 5 expiration date actually "suspended to and including November 30, 1972."[12]

"That means," George said to me, "the so-called temporary surcharge has now been permanent since February 1. Really. It lasts at least until November 30 and then, if they want, they extend it again and they call it temporary."

"How the hell do you challenge that?" John asked. "Nothing is permanent or final. What the—?"

"No," I said, wanting to stay on track. "We argue that the June 5 date is the effective date for a *permanent* 2.5 percent surcharge. This April 24 order authorizing it was a major federal action. No EIS had been prepared. The 2.5 percent surcharge is no longer in the 'suspension stage.'"

"You certain?" George asked me. He, too, was forcing clarity to our action.

"Okay. No. But, you know, we're not waiting. These guys do temporary, permanent, temporary, suspend. They'll go on forever."

"You can't suspend the harm," John said. I felt angrier than I expected over what now should have been commonplace.

"Who the hell *are* these people?" I asked, my voice rising, my index finger pointing and jutting. "I mean, who the hell do they talk to?"

George said calmly and directly, "Soon it will be someone they don't expect." We agreed to sue the Commission in *281* before the June 5 deadline.

We returned that afternoon to the large room atop Bacon. Revisions to the complaint in *265/267* were made. Peter and George had prepared the forms for the district court. A draft press release was prepared. We knew it was important, yet while in preparing it, we felt that the press's role seemed less an object of our attention. Banzhaf walked in. He read and approved the press release. He had reviewed the complaint. He had no proposed revisions but did have one idea. He felt strongly about it and said so. No one in his right mind would oppose B. We waited attentively.

Banzhaf wanted to add the CEQ as an "involuntary plaintiff." His theory was that the CEQ had a duty under NEPA. It had submitted comments to the ICC. It should be enforcing this law, he said. The CEQ—in either Banzhaf's words or the rules' words, we did not know which—has expressed an official interest relating to the subject of this action, and its absence as a party may, as a practical matter, impair or impede its ability to protect that interest. I wrote the words down as he said them. I knew this change was going in. Banzhaf left to call the CEQ's general counsel, Timothy Atkeson. Atkeson had not been pleased, Banzhaf reported when he returned. "Put CEQ in," he said. In an afterthought, he added, "Any objections?"

He must be kidding, I thought.

On April 25, the complaint was filed in the United States District Court for the District of Columbia and was served on all the parties: "Students Challenging Regulatory Agency Procedures (S.C.R.A.P.), Plaintiff, and Council on Environmental Quality, Involuntary Plaintiff, v. The United States of America and The Interstate Commerce Commission, Defendants."[13] We were docketed as Civil No. 806-72. At the end of the complaint—which I read through in as much quietude as I could find, alone in the farthest reaches of the Center, sipping my coffee—was the formal closing. It is a fundamental mainstay and *pro forma* ending of every complaint ever submitted. In it was the simple gratification from the culmination of a long effort and the reflection of a new chapter:

Respectfully submitted,

STUDENTS CHALLENGING REGULATORY
AGENCY PROCEDURES

Neil Thomas Proto

George Vincent Biondi

John Eric Larouche

16

FINDING OUR OWN RULES, SPRING 1972

The second lawsuit. May 6. Bacon Hall. "Can you imagine coming here every day to work?" George asked as we climbed the stairs to the fourth floor.

"No," I answered.

"Then why are we coming here every day?"

"You giving me a hard time?"

"Me?" George asked, in mock innocence.

"The real question is why do we keep coming here on Saturdays?" I groaned.

"Why? You got a life to lead?"

When we entered the room, John and Peter Meyers already were settled and ready. Our agenda: the complaint in *Ex Parte 281*. Our purpose was three-fold: to make a list of every document we needed to prepare, to decide who would prepare it, and to set a time limit. Within moments, it was obvious that the first task required a discussion of strategy more thorough than any of its predecessors. Our talk centered on one subject: the temporary restraining order (TRO) and the preliminary injunction—their need, timing, and content.

"Our legal theory," Peter said, "is that harm to the environment is oc-curring now because of the effect of the discrimination. It's irreparable, certainly with respect to the extraction of raw materials."

John added, "The harm is being caused in urban areas by dump sites and in recreation areas by cutting timber and mining natural resources."

"Essential," Peter said.

"We also have a meritorious case under NEPA," I said, matter-of-factly.

"I should hope so," George added. "They didn't comply. I mean, they said NEPA does not apply."

"You should have no illusions," Peter said directly. "We'd be trying to stop the collection of all rates on all Railroads in the United States. Hundreds of millions of dollars."

"Wrong. Probably billions," George said, looking directly at Peter.

"The difficult part, of course," Meyers continued, in a professorial manner, "is that—and you must decide this—you have to convince the court, without much evidence, that you should win, that you are right on the law and on the facts —"

"Particularly on the fact that the harm is irreparable," I added. "But what George said is important, isn't it? There's no compliance with NEPA. In other words, we're okay as long as we can show that the Commission violated the law. We say, this is a major federal action, et cetera, and there is no EIS or compliance with NEPA. We're so strong on the merits."

"It helps," Meyers said. "You just have to write the complaint that way."

George then added, with a tone of inevitability, "What about *Arrow Transportation?*"

"Three responses," John said. "First, in the April 24 order, the Commission made the 'temporary' 2.5 percent surcharge 'permanent.' No longer in the 'suspension stage.' *Arrow Transportation* does not apply. Second, NEPA changed the rules. Courts of law can enjoin a rate increase no matter what stage. Environmental harm can't be remedied by refunding money. That's our fallback position. Third, we could argue that the Supreme Court did such an inane, stupid thing in *Arrow Transportation* that it should be ignored."

"You mean, *stupidium dumbilium*," George added, breaking up the crowd.

"We'll stick with one and two," I responded, with seeming authority.

I stood and stretched my arms as high over my head as I could. The sunlight was now slipping in and around the windows' gray streaks and soot from the winter and spring. It would be in the 70s today. "Okay, gentlemen. What's next?"

"*Port of New York Authority v. United States,*" George said.

"What do you have, a thing today?" I asked, knowing *Port of New York Authority* was unhelpful to us.

"Well, fella? We've got to talk about *all* the cases?" George asked, goading me.

"I know. I know."

"No," John said. "I think *Port of New York Authority* has stuff we can use."

"You mean distinguish?" I asked.

"No. Well. Both," John said. *Port of New York Authority* had been decided by the United States Court of Appeals for the Second Circuit in New York on November 9, 1971.[1] We had only recently become aware of it. It involved a new form of the "suspension stage," at least new to us.

"I'm not sure why we missed it," I said.

"Pavlovian," George insisted. "Every time we see the words 'suspension stage,' we recoil in terror and then into amnesia."

"I think we should break for coffee," I said.

"I told you. Pavlov's dogs."

The New York Port Authority had objected to an order of the ICC that permitted the Penn Central to increase rates for lighterage services (that is, the loading and unloading of freight). The Penn Central was authorized to publish a 50 percent increase in those rates while an ICC investigation continued. The Port Authority appealed to the full Commission. Without a formal hearing and protests, the Commission denied the appeal, letting the 50 percent increase go into effect and letting the investigation go forward. As far as the court of appeals was concerned, the Commission was in the "suspension stage" as defined in *Arrow Transportation*. The Commission's decision was not reviewable by a court of law.

It got worse. The Port Authority argued that the Commission had not complied with NEPA. The court of appeals disagreed: "The detailed evaluation of benefits and costs required by NEPA is not possible at this stage of the review."[2]

"Okay," I said. "Let's distinguish this."

"I got it," John said, acknowledging that "it certainly doesn't help us." He was right. "First," he said. "In our case, the full Commission held formal hearings and took protests. Not in *Port of New York Authority*. Second, the court of appeals stated that *Arrow Transportation* means a district court has no authority to enjoin a rate increase from going into effect. We're going to disagree with that."

"The 2.5 percent increase is now final. Or, well, we'll argue it's permanent, and we're no longer in the suspension stage," I said.

"Who the hell knows what 'stage' we're in," George said.

"We need to sound as if we know," I said quietly.

"We also have two positive discussions," John continued, looking down at the decision in *Port of New York Authority*. "In the NEPA analysis. Here. The court said, 'The City contends that the increased lighterage tariffs will cause the diversion of a substantial amount of traffic … to trucks, and that the increased use of trucks will substantially worsen the already poor quality of New York's air.' This is our argument. So we use this. The second thing is here, later in the decision. The court said—this is in November 1971—the Commission, quote, 'assured us during oral argument that it will carefully consider the environmental impact of Penn Central's proposed tariffs in the investigation now proceeding.' We know this is bull. The Commission has never prepared an EIS, and look at the timing. If the Commission won't do one for us in 1972 on a nationwide increase, you know it'll never do one. And we know it didn't for something called 'lighterage charges' in one city."[3]

"It's our strongest argument," George said. "The Commission hasn't complied with NEPA."

We assigned responsibility and a time frame for each document. "The complaint should be filed soon," I said. "The same with the preliminary injunction. The TRO. For the TRO, we wait 'til we get closer to June. In between, gentlemen, there are exams. So? Anything else?"

"Anything else?" George asked. "You see what it looks like outside. The sun's gone, it's Saturday, and I'm freaking starving."

"George," I said, standing and stretching my arms tightly and firmly behind my back. "We haven't even freaking begun."

DRAFTING

We wrote separately at first—at home, during the day, and into the evenings. John was still working part time. George and I both traded dorm responsibility with others in exchange for time later. The War hung on. The bombing continued in North Vietnam. Soviet planes and ships were damaged. Students were not engaged by the bombing. "The meaning is certain," George proffered. "Somebody wants us to do SCRAP."

Thoughts were exchanged freely among us. We had developed a sense of each other's literary cadence and temperament. Meyers was available for ideas and words. We argued one paragraph at a time, each argument preceded and followed by discussions of our adversaries. What are they doing? What will they argue? What do they expect we will do next?

We knew from our experience—and Peter emphasized it repeatedly—that once we filed the complaint and the motion for a preliminary injunction (and later the motion for a TRO), "all hell would break loose." It will be "crucial," Peter added, "that you be prepared, mentally and physically. Expect this response. Within a week, Justice, the Railroads, and the Commission will engage us in a powerful, frenetic display of legal skills and mounds of paper. The court. The single judge. He'll convene, the sooner the better for us."

"If we stick by our schedule," I said, "we can file the TRO in late May, just before the June 5 date."

"Yeah," John added. "After exams."

The complaint was an improvement over the previous one. The Commission had provided a good story. These were the facts: The Railroads' original petition for a 2.5 percent surcharge was filed on December 13, 1971. It was followed by the Commission's order of December 21 that delayed the surcharge from going into effect until February 5, 1972, and ordered the Railroads to submit "a statement regarding the environmental impact of the proposal before any actual rate increases were allowed to go into effect." The Railroads said in the now-notorious Verified Statement Thirty-seven that there was no environmental impact.

We protested. So did the CEQ. The Commission reacted in two ways. First, it ordered the 2.5 percent surcharge into effect on February 5 without an EIS. "Later in the afternoon of February 3, 1972," we wrote in the complaint, "Mr. Fritz Kahn, General Counsel to the Commission, entered into a 'Memorandum of Understanding' with plaintiff S.C.R.A.P. and the Environmental Defense Fund, whereby the Commission ... agreed that it would 'shortly issue a draft environmental impact statement in accordance with the requirements of NEPA.'" It did not. "Since February," we continued, "defendant Interstate Commerce Commission has apparently decided not to comply fully with the ... requirements of NEPA; has disavowed its earlier manifest intentions to [S.C.R.A.P.]; ... and has largely ignored its own rules."

Second, the March 6 draft EIS issued by the Commission did not comply with NEPA. On April 24, the Commission extended the 2.5 percent surcharge to at least November 30. This order was final and constituted a major federal action undertaken without examining its effect under NEPA. It had, we alleged, "an immediate and significant effect on the quality of the human environment." The judicial relief we wanted was straightforward. Set aside the ICC's orders, declare the Commission in violation of NEPA, and preliminarily enjoin the Commission from implementing—and the Railroads from collecting—the increased freight rates until there was compliance with NEPA.[4]

In our memorandum of points and authorities in support of motion for preliminary injunction, we addressed our standing to sue drawing from the facts set forth in the complaint. We began where we believed the Supreme Court would, with *Data Processing* and *Barlow*. We set out the two-part test. We easily met the second part: our purpose as a group, our actions since December 1971, and the kind of harm that we alleged placed us in the "zone of interest" covered by NEPA. The first part of the test presented the challenge: injury in fact. We reiterated what we had said in the complaint filed in 265/267 about our "economic interests." We focused special care on our aesthetic, conservational, and recreational injury and on *Sierra Club*:[5]

> [E]ach member of SCRAP uses the nation's forests, rivers, streams, mountains and other natural resources for camping, hiking, fishing, sightseeing and other recreational and aesthetic purposes. These uses have been, and will continue to be, adversely affected to the extent that the railroad freight rate structure, as modified in *Ex Parte 281*, encourages the destruction of virgin timber, the unnecessary extraction of raw materials, and the discharge and accumulation of otherwise recyclable waste materials. In addition, each member of SCRAP utilizes the nation's roads and highways for aesthetic and recreational enjoyment, and to the extent that the rail freight rate structure, as modified in *Ex Parte 281*, encourages the utilization of areas adjacent to and visible from these roads and highways as repositories of solid waste materials otherwise capable of being recycled, these interests are adversely affected.

Finally, we alleged injury to our procedural rights. The Commission's failure "effectively precluded the members of SCRAP from being able to review and comment upon the environmental impact of the railroad freight rate ... increases ... early enough to permit meaningful consideration of the environmental issues ... [which] constituted a denial of the Plaintiff's [right under NEPA and its] First Amendment right to meaningful participation."[6]

The documents—all of them except the TRO—were drafted, revised, typed, revised again, collated, and stapled, and were ready for filing by the evening of May 11. They were power. We knew it. As the documents lay before us, neatly arranged, we looked at them in silence. Then, with a contentment that we sought after each intensive work effort since the outset, we congratulated each other and tried to absorb—once again—what we had accomplished and where it had brought us.

The following day, the documents were filed in the United States District Court for the District of Columbia by George Biondi and Peter Meyers and were served on all the parties: "Students Challenging Regulatory Agency

Procedures (S.C.R.A.P.), Plaintiff and The Council on Environmental Quality, Involuntary Plaintiff v. The United States of America and the Interstate Commerce Commission, Defendants." The complaint was stamped: "Filed, May 12, 1972, James F. Davey, Clerk. CA No. 971-72."[7] I was in the law school library when George returned. "We did it," he said. He took a seat, opened a textbook, and began to read. We could think of no circumstance that warranted any further acknowledgment of what we had started. Before "all hell broke loose," we needed to finish school.

17

IN COURT: A COLLOQUY IN LAW AND MONEY, JUNE 1972

Judge Charles Richey. "He's newly appointed," Peter Meyers explained. "From Maryland. By Nixon. As I understand it, Richey's thoughtful and fair." I was not certain precisely what that meant. At stake now was my own case.[1]

"Could we win?" I asked, realizing the notion of chance—how, under the precise facts we had, the fortune of having one judge or another might yield a dramatically different outcome.

Peter looked at George and me and in a kind of brotherly way said, "Sure. You could win."

"Okay. I got it," I said. "You have no better idea than we do."

We moved for a temporary restraining order on June 1.[2] Our motion for a preliminary injunction already was pending. Judge Richey would consider both at the same time. The TRO was intended to stop the 2.5 percent surcharge from going beyond June 5, when it was originally scheduled to expire. Its prospects were slim. Our intention was to demonstrate our seriousness and, we hoped, to expedite the date on which the court would convene a three-judge district court. Peter, with Banzhaf there if necessary, would present the oral argument.

It was an uneasy evening. Grades were coming in. Graduation was scheduled for Sunday, June 4, at Lisner Auditorium. "Of course, we'll be there," my dad had said months earlier. "You've got to stop long enough to enjoy it. This is important."

"Just when I should be celebrating," I told my sister the night before they were to leave, "look what happens. SCRAP. Diana, I need a rest."

"Neil, as you know, you chose to do this. So, just have everything ready for us—clean sheets, nice dinner, a few nice walks—be sure the air conditioning works and be sure there is a parking space for us. We won't be a bother." I envisioned her, hair in curlers with housecoat on, suitcases nearby, packed and ready for travel. "And, Neil, if you need any help, Mom will go with you. She'll talk to that judge."

THE HEARING

June 2. George was uneasy from the moment he got into the car. Neither of us was sure how to think about the case. It seemed largely in someone else's hands, in accordance with rules and a culture we had invoked but could not control. We said little to each other. We arrived at the courthouse at 8:30 a.m.

The federal courthouse was bounded by Constitution Avenue on the south and John Marshall Place on the west. It housed both the district court and the court of appeals. We entered on John Marshall Place. I slowed and then stopped at the glass-enclosed board that listed the judges. Some were familiar to me: David Bazelon, J. Skelly Wright, and Harold Leventhal on the court of appeals. "I hope we get there," I said. George shrugged, raised his eyebrows but said nothing. We walked to the clerk's office.

"One of the smaller courtrooms," the clerk said and gave us directions. We decided, instead, to get coffee. While George located the cafeteria, I located the men's room.

I walked in and heard loud coughing from behind one of the stalls. It was Peter. He emerged dressed neatly but not like any other attorney walking the corridor that morning. He had on a light lavender shirt with a print tie and a sport jacket. His hair, still shoulder length, was matted down and combed. His eyes were puffy; his face was more drawn and angular than usual. I was not sure how difficult this was for him. It would be his first oral argument. He said he was prepared.

The courtroom was awkwardly designed, as if it were stuffed into a former storage room and hallway. George and I sat four or five rows from the front. A few people, including a clerk in uniform and tie, walked in and out with authority and placed papers on the judge's bench. John arrived and sat next to George. He had to leave early for work. He was going back to Maine for the summer and was under a tight schedule. "Grades okay?" I asked. He nodded. Banzhaf arrived. He said hello and walked over to talk with Peter, who was seated closer to the front. Banzhaf also was dressed in a sport coat and tie.

In walked our adversaries. I recognized Fritz Kahn immediately; I did not know the others. They all were talking. Each carried a briefcase and wore a dark suit and tie. This was a team. They gathered on the far side of the courtroom. Kahn was in the center, pointing, arguing, and seeming to give directions. The government's interests were certain and predictable. In walked John Dienelt and his colleague, Scott Lang. I was not sure whose interest they were here to serve. It was not ours.

Dienelt and Lang walked over to Banzhaf and Meyers. Banzhaf gave Dienelt a disdainful look, B's "you are irrelevant and untrustworthy" look. I liked B for that. Dienelt handed B some papers. They exchanged a few words and separated. There were now three groups in the courtroom.

Peter motioned to us to come over. EDF had moved to intervene.[3] It had filed its own complaint that morning. George and I quickly read through it and handed it to John. EDF had challenged the adequacy of the ICC's NEPA regulations promulgated in *Ex Parte 55*, which occurred months before the violations set out in our complaint and, as a practical matter, had been abandoned by the Commission. George and I were angered. We thought the "differences" would confuse the case and diffuse the focus on the real

wrongdoing: the freight rates. We described the differences to Banzhaf. He listened, his eyes looking directly at ours. "Yep," "yep," "good," "yep," and then silence.

Another lawyer entered the courtroom; fiftyish, gray hair, with a dark suit that was decidedly Brooks Brothers. He was more perfunctory, subdued, and businesslike in manner than those representing EDF or the government. He handed Peter some documents. A moment later, Fritz Kahn handed Peter some documents. In this stack of papers was a motion to intervene from the nation's Railroads that was signed by Charles Horsky from Covington & Burling, motions from the ICC and the United States to dismiss our case, and some lengthy memoranda of law to support each motion.[4]

Charles Horsky,
Covington & Burling.
Historical Society of the
District of Columbia Circuit.

Judge Charles Richey.
Library of Congress.

I examined quickly the memorandum submitted by the United States. There were two arguments: SCRAP had no standing, and the court had no jurisdiction to issue an injunction. "Suspension stage" was written repeatedly. So were the decisions in *Sierra Club* and *Arrow Transportation* and the Second Circuit's decision in *Port of New York Authority*. No surprises. The only unpredictability in the courtroom came from the third party: EDF.

The clerk announced Judge Richey. We stood. I was still uneasy—a feeling of watching something new and consequential with nothing in my experience to understand it. Then the understanding took hold. Our adversaries—the Commission, the Railroads, the United States, Kahn—had revealed themselves with clarity, and revealed our commitment that we were right in our purpose and our determination to advocate it. We were the plaintiffs; they were the defendants. We were combatants. With studied care, we had claimed they had wronged the public. In that realization, more plain and obvious than I thought at first, I felt my unease diminish and an intensity and sharpness of mind take hold. The lines were drawn. I liked it. I looked over at Peter. He smiled and nodded. We had gotten here. We were ready.

Judge Richey was slender and diminutive. The draped effect of the black robe made his facial features, at least from a distance, easy to see. His hair was graying. His face seemed weathered, experienced, lined from seeing or feeling some part of life deeply. "Thoughtful and fair," Peter had said, and I could see, within the moment he turned toward the clerk standing to his right and smiled gently, a politeness that confirmed part of Peter's characterization.

Peter stood and motioned to the three of us to follow him. There was considerable and audible movement of chairs and people as the lawyers—now five or six from the Commission, the Railroads, the United States, and EDF—sought to place themselves properly. They could not. Peter and Banzhaf had unabashedly situated themselves at the table where the plaintiffs normally sit. We helped solve their dilemma by placing two additional chairs on the left side of the table. Banzhaf then moved me between himself and Peter. "Follow closely," Banzhaf said. I recognized immediately that I was now a participant, responsible not only as the plaintiff but also as a craftsman of thoughts and strategy. I found the transition easy to make.

"All right," Judge Richey began. "We will proceed with Civil Action No. 971-72, which is known as SCRAP versus the United States and the ICC."[5] Charles Horsky stood immediately and moved gently toward the judge. He seemed to be gliding. "Good morning, Mr. Horsky," Judge Richey said. He knows him? What does that mean?

Horsky got right to his purpose. "On behalf of what I believe are substantially all the railroads in the United States, I would like to file a motion for leave to intervene in this proceeding." Judge Richey granted it.

Scott Lang stood in place. He wanted to intervene. Banzhaf leaped to his feet. "Your honor, John Banzhaf, speaking for SCRAP." He was not giving an inch. "We are somewhat surprised and chagrined that the Railroads have waited until, not the Eleventh Hour, but the Twelfth Hour, and have walked in here this very morning and handed us a very large document. The EDF," he said, "filed their motion only yesterday, although this matter has been pending for quite a while." Banzhaf succeeded in drawing the line. EDF and SCRAP were not on the same side.[6]

Judge Richey listened patiently and granted EDF's motion to intervene. They were in. Fritz Kahn, the Commission's general counsel, stood and introduced himself. Because the ICC was an independent regulatory agency, it had the authority to represent itself. The Justice Department represented the United States.

Kahn agreed that EDF could intervene. He objected strongly, however, to its newly filed complaint. "They seek to enlarge the issues and would seek review ... of orders entered in another proceeding." Lang stood and objected. Judge Richey disagreed. He was sticking with our complaint.[7]

"Let EDF file its own lawsuit," George whispered.

"To that extent," Judge Richey said, "I will rule, if a ruling is necessary, that [*Ex Parte 281*] will be involved, and we will consider that if we reach that point."[8] The only reason we would not was if SCRAP had no standing to sue.

Judge Richey rearranged some papers on the bench. "We only have three matters," he began and then smiled. "I don't mean to say that means that it is easy." The first was the motion to dismiss SCRAP's complaint because of lack of standing and because the court had no jurisdiction. All the lawyers said they wanted to be heard except Charles Horsky. The Railroads, for now, would remain silent.[9]

Kahn walked to the podium. He described the history of the case. It seemed to me that every other sentence contained the words "suspension stage"; every action the Commission took was still in the "suspension stage." Then he proceeded to the familiar refrain. The nation's Railroads "have been," he said, "plagued the last few years by ever-escalating costs at the same time they find their share of the transportation market is diminishing."[10]

Kahn turned to SCRAP. We had been a party in *281*, he said, "and had commented on the draft EIS issued on March 6, 1972." He continued, "Their comments will be considered by the Commission. And," as if an afterthought, "the Commission does, indeed, intend to file an environmental impact statement." He said it in such a *pro forma* manner, in the manner of the Commission: Trust us; trust me. We are the ICC, the nation's oldest regulator, and we will take care of it. SCRAP, he said, had no standing. And the court had no jurisdiction. "[R]efusal of the Commission to suspend the rates is not judicially reviewable—period." He minced no words: "*Arrow Transportation.*"[11]

Kahn then got to the Second Circuit's decision in *Port of New York Authority*. It helped him, he said.

Judge Richey had a different idea. "May I interrupt you just a moment?" Then the following dialogue occurred:

KAHN: Yes.

JUDGE RICHEY: In the *Port of New York Authority* case that you just quoted from ... let me read part of the second paragraph, and then ask you a question.... 'In the instant case this would mean staying Penn Central's proposed tariffs. But such a solution is too simple. It overlooks the fact that preserving the status quo can be as detrimental to the environment as permitting changes in the status quo.' Now, what did the court mean by saying that?

KAHN: I think it meant simply this.... [T]here will be diversion of traffic necessarily to other modes, which may impair the environment more substantially than does the continued operation of the Penn Central....

JUDGE RICHEY: You are apparently saying that the court agreed with some of the plaintiff's contentions.... That, by virtue of the increased rates which you awarded here, or, in effect, allowed to go into effect, it will divert traffic to other forms of transportation, and, thus, allow those other forms which are more detrimental to the environment to possibly damage the environment.... [I]s that correct? ...

KAHN: That is the argument that SCRAP would make.

JUDGE RICHEY: I understand. That is all I am saying.[12]

Kahn argued that SCRAP should not have sued. It has an "adequate remedy available," he said.

"Well, tell me what the adequate remedy is," Judge Richey asked.

Kahn's answer was simple and predictable: "[T]hey can bring a complaint … before the Commission, … that the rates on scrap iron and steel, the rates on waste paper, the rates on other recyclable materials, are too darn high … discriminatory against shippers … of those commodities. That is precisely the kind of issue that the Interstate Commerce Commission was created to consider."[13]

"Like two ships passing in the night," I whispered to George, who was slightly behind Peter and me. He shook his head.

Kahn returned to his argument that SCRAP lacked standing. He thought our position "is fairly weak," and sought to compare SCRAP to the Supreme Court's admonitions about the Sierra Club's lack of standing. "That case makes clear that the old law that a party, to maintain an action[,] must be aggrieved or legally injured, simply has not been changed…. [A]n association gains nothing from the fact that it is an association…. [T]he individual members must have standing[,]and their interest has to be something more than simply a citizen's common concern. And here, on the face of their complaint, SCRAP makes no allegations of injury, economic or ecological, except those that would be appropriate to any member of the public."[14]

Judge Richey remained silent. He thanked Kahn, who returned to his seat. William Cohen, representing the United States, walked to the podium. He seemed simultaneously serious and approachable.[15] "The question here," Cohen said, "… is not whether NEPA applies … but whether a final environmental impact statement is required at this stage in the proceedings, your honor, … an intermediate stage, a stage in which the Commission has set a temporary 2.5 percent, across-the-board surcharge…. And, also, the Commission has ordered that the railroads keep the accounts in such a way that they can make a full refund…. Our contention is no, your honor." The refund. This time, Judge Richey did not allow the point to pass:

JUDGE RICHEY: What happens to the environment in the meantime, if their contention is true: namely, that traffic is diverted to other forms of common carriers which burn gas and fuel and, thus, pollute the air…?

COHEN: This is just a temporary rate, your honor.

JUDGE RICHEY: Yes, I understand that.[16]

Judge Richey stopped him and asked for a copy of NEPA. He turned to Section 102(2)(C) and asked Cohen: "There is no question but what the ICC has certain authority to act on an emergency basis.... But whether ... [i]t can do that before compliance with this act may perhaps be, more precisely, the question in this instance. Which comes first?"

Cohen shifted his posture slightly and hesitated momentarily before answering. "Well, the real question is this. We are not saying the act does not apply.... But we are saying it does not apply at this stage."[17]

Judge Richey did not hesitate. There was a certainty and evenness in his voice.[18]

> JUDGE RICHEY: [H]ere we have certain long-recognized and established procedures by the oldest independent agency in our entire federal government dealing with the complex matter of rates, which the courts have said over and over again they should have little to do with.... But now we live in the 1970s, as you well know. In 1969, Congress enacted a new law, and I am frankly wondering whether a temporary increase under your suspension procedures might be said to be inconsistent with the requirements of NEPA.... [I]t seems to me you have the cart before the horse, in that the damage may well be done before you can even correct it.
>
> COHEN: Well, your honor, would we not at this stage, then, be substituting our judgment for that of the Commission here?[19]

They seemed to be at a standstill. Cohen had touched the court's nerve: its authority to act at all.

Peter Meyers gathered his papers and walked to the podium. Judge Richey was ready: "Address yourself to the decision of the Supreme Court that the Commission cited to your standing to sue...."[20]

> MEYERS: [T]he Supreme Court denied the Sierra Club standing for the reason that ... in its complaint it did not allege that the injuries which would be caused by the actions complained of would specifically harm ... the members of the [Sierra Club]....
>
> JUDGE RICHEY: That is exactly right. You have five members of SCRAP, do you not?

Peter Harwood Meyers.
Peter Harwood Meyers Collection.

MEYERS: In the complaint, your honor.... And the injury is focused on them in specific ways.... The members of SCRAP live in various areas, your honor....

JUDGE RICHEY: Was that set forth in the complaint?

MEYERS: That is not in the complaint.

JUDGE RICHEY: You see, it says on page [three] of your complaint: 'Plaintiff, Students Challenging Regulatory Agency Procedures ... is an unincorporated association formed by five law students from the National Law Center, the George Washington University, in September 1971. Its primary purpose is to enhance the quality of the human environment for its members and for all citizens....'

MEYERS: Yes.

JUDGE RICHEY: I have serious question about whether or not that is within the gambit of this recent pronouncement by the Supreme Court.[21]

I shifted my position. There was more in the complaint than what Judge Richey had read. Peter made it plain. "But let me point out, your honor, that ... [w]e allege that SCRAP would seek to protect each member of SCRAP's interest in this proceeding. We say specifically on page [three] of their complaint that: 'Each member of SCRAP ... suffered injury' and then list the injuries.... Therefore, we believe that *Sierra Club v. Morton* support[s] the standing of SCRAP...."[22]

It was the right answer. Judge Richey seemed to accept it. I looked at Peter. I realized the obvious. Who knows what the judge is thinking? Peter returned to the facts as we understood them, earnest and deliberate in his tone and manner.

"The Commission in *281*," Peter said, "filed what it has titled a 'draft environmental impact statement.' It is impossible ... to determine whether [it] refers to the selective increase ... which has been suspended, or ... the 2.5 percent surcharge." Peter cited criticism leveled by the Environmental Protection Agency (EPA) and the CEQ. "The draft is relying solely on the parties to the proceeding to provide the Commission with the environmental facts.... The obligation to evaluate independently lies with the federal agency. *Calvert Cliffs* was the talisman." He had introduced it perfectly. He quoted from the decision: "The agency is not simply 'to sit back, like an umpire.'"[23]

Judge Richey stopped him: "I am glad you have raised this.... I have had occasion to read that learned opinion by Judge Wright many times.... The question that I asked the other counsel, I want to ask you, sir: You say this is a significant, distinctive stage of the process.... They say this is only a temporary matter, and that probably is correct, pending a final decision. When is NEPA required to be acted upon?"[24]

MEYERS: It is our position that NEPA has to be —

JUDGE RICHEY: At this stage?

MEYERS: There is authority for that in *Calvert Cliffs*.... And the question comes up: Is there some sort of conflict between the Interstate Commerce Commission procedure which does not allow it to comply to the fullest extent possible? The answer ... is that [NEPA] said to every agency: If you are not ably to comply ... notify us ... and we, Congress, will ... make a determination about what should be done by the agency.... [I]t is very significant that the Interstate Commerce Commission has never done this.

"What section of the NEPA Act is that from?" Judge Richey asked. Peter did not know.[25]

JUDGE RICHEY: Do you want to talk with your associates, sir?

MEYERS: Please, your honor.

We, as his associates, had a role. Clear, distinct, and judge-ordered. Peter walked over to the table. I showed him Section 103 of NEPA. "Good," he said quietly and returned to the podium. "It is Section 103," he told Judge Richey, who started the colloquy immediately in a slightly different direction.

JUDGE RICHEY: It seems to me, gentlemen—and I am not only speaking to you, counsel ...—that, as far as NEPA is concerned, we must determine, first of all, whether or not what the government did here ... was a 'major federal action'.... And if it was ... then it seems to the court that possibly a final impact statement should have been filed and acted upon prior to the action taken....

MEYERS: [T]he Commission ... has informed the court they are treating this *Ex Parte 281* as a major federal action, significantly affecting the quality of the human environment.

JUDGE RICHEY: They do not say that directly.[26]

Judge Richey was not satisfied. Peter relied again on the EPA and CEQ criticisms. They caused only a modest change in the judge's attitude. Peter went right to the nerve: "As your honor knows[,] ... one judge can dismiss the complaint, but only in the most exceptional circumstances.... In other words, your honor, you can only grant this motion to dismiss if you determine this is the most frivolous of suits [and] is totally without merit."[27]

Peter seemed to regain his momentum. He proceeded to evaluate the government's argument that it was in the "suspension stage." What a concept. I wondered if anyone really knew what it meant.

MEYERS: First of all, the provision of the order which we are challenging [i]s not a decision to suspend.... The [2.5 percent] surcharge was due to expire on June 5th. If the Commission did nothing, it would have expired.... The Commission determined to extend the surcharge, exactly the opposite type of decision.... The Commission also argues—and I want to make this point most strongly—the following: Why do we not await the final order in this proceeding? The Interstate Commerce Commission could be referred

to in this regard as the 'tomorrow agency.'... Whenever we come to the
Commission and say: 'Well, NEPA has been in effect for two years now;
why do you not start complying,' they say: 'Later.'[28]

The "tomorrow agency"! George covered his face, head down. "Great
line!" he whispered.

Peter proceeded to *Port of New York Authority*. He was on a roll. "The
government," he said emphatically, "has made a significant mistake in relying on this case.... *Port of New York Authority* is probably in conflict with
the decision of this Circuit in *Calvert Cliffs* ... [a]nd ... in *Port of New
York Authority* you had the application for a single rate change by one single
party...."[29] Excellent. He said everything we wanted. He knew it. It was
obvious from the look on his face. He had performed admirably. I told him
so when he sat down.

Banzhaf rose. He had notes, but only notes. It was classical Banzhaf.
"I think your honor has hit the nail on the head," he began. "The question
before it really is: Did this action have a major environmental impact, and,
perhaps secondary, was it possible for the Commission to conduct itself in
accordance with the NEPA requirements? As to the first, let me give you
three possible answers: a case, a study, and good, old-fashioned common
sense." He had a conversational tone. Determined and confident in manner.
It was Banzhaf's classroom demeanor. The "case" he referred to was *City of
New York v. United States* decided on January 20, 1972, by the United States
District Court in New York. Neither the Commission nor the United States
had cited it.[30]

> BANZHAF: The gist of this case, known as *Bush Terminal*, is that there was
> a railroad which sought to discontinue shipping freight on a line of some-
> thing less than three miles.... The court held that even that small amount
> ... might have enough of a major environmental impact that they sent the
> matter back to the ICC.... Here we are talking about every railroad in the
> country shipping every piece of freight.... As a second point, your honor ...
> the present rates discourage very substantially the recycling of scrap iron and
> steel.... Each year the United States produces more than 413 billion tons of
> solid refuse. [Even if] you assume a thousandth of this, if you take any one of
> these categories ... tires, bottles, cans, any of those, and consider one percent
> of what is here. It would fill this courtroom, probably the entire courthouse.[31]

"Fill this courtroom?" I repeated to myself.

This was quintessential Banzhaf. He now seemed buoyant, confident actually, and in control of the setting. "[NEPA] was passed several years ago by Congress. Since that time the ICC has granted two general rate increases.... [T]here is nothing in ... those two prior proceedings which could possibly, conceivably be compliance with NEPA. It was not until SCRAP went before the Commission and said to them: NEPA applies, and you had better start doing it.... I think at some point we have to draw a halt in this proceeding."[32]

Banzhaf stood silent. The point settled. He grew somber. "There is a verified statement in the record by somebody from the Merichem Company, which treats spent caustic soda ... a by-product of the petroleum process, and its greatest potential use is in making paper. If he does not use it, it is dumped. It is dumped in holes or rivers or streams or the oceans...." And you could see it happening, as Banzhaf gestured and made clear the culprits were seated in the courtroom. There was a slight pause. The effect was dramatic. He was good at it. This was the old Banzhaf, the *Banzhaf v. FCC* Banzhaf.[33]

Banzhaf proceeded to his closing: "Several months ago, your honor ... we obtained an agreement from the general counsel that they would comply fully with the National Environmental Policy Act in return for our promise not to seek at that time a temporary restraining order.... [I]f your honor dismisses this complaint, you are saying, in effect, that no one can ever challenge the ICC's complete and utter failure to comply with [NEPA]." Banzhaf said it as if the burden had shifted to Judge Richey, as if he had only one choice: side with the law, or side with the culprits who have violated it. Banzhaf had delivered. The outcome may be uncertain but he was with us.[34]

Dienelt stood and took his place at the podium. Within a few moments, he was entangled in a complicated argument on top of the complication added by EDF's complaint. George and I looked at each other and shrugged.[35]

DIENELT: As we view this case—and perhaps we view it somewhat differently from both sides—here are really two related issues here. One is the question of the requirement, if there is one, that the Commission file a final impact statement before it implements a surcharge....

"'If there is one?'" George whispered. "What the hell is he talking about?"

DIENELT: [W]e are very much concerned about the Commission's statement, which we believe is made in good faith....

"Good faith?" I whispered to George. His face tightened.

Dienelt proceeded to his *Ex Parte 55* argument. "We have in our complaint," he said, "alleged that the procedures that they finally are establishing in another proceeding, *Ex Parte 55*, the general procedures, are inadequate. And if those procedures are followed here …"[36]

"If?" George whispered, his eyes opened fully, his tone stern. "They didn't follow their procedures, Neil." I reached back and put my hand on his arm but did not move my eyes from Dienelt's every word.

DIENELT: And the one example that I think is clearest … is the strong reliance that they place on outside parties.…

JUDGE RICHEY: Well, I don't think there is anything wrong with that … because any federal agency is allowed to consult other federal agencies.…

DIENELT: I quite agree with your honor that they—

JUDGE RICHEY: (continuing) … I don't think there is much substance to that argument.

DIENELT: I think there is, but I will not pursue it, because I don't think I have conveyed it properly, your honor.[37]

It was now 12:50 p.m. Judge Richey thanked Dienelt and proposed we reconvene at 2:00 p.m., "and then, hopefully, we can get this issue decided promptly." Judge Richey stood. So did we. The hardest part remained: the court's decision.[38]

John Larouche had left just before the argument started. Banzhaf, Peter, George, and I walked downstairs for lunch. Our discussion centered on whether EDF had complicated our position and was unable to articulate its own. "The crucial question," Peter said, "is whether the judge can see that so much is wrong he must transfer it. EDF actually may have helped." George frowned. I raised my finger gently. This was no time for argument.

At 2:00 p.m., the court reconvened. We sat quietly. All the skill and determination and resources in the courtroom—among the nation's Railroads, the Commission, the United States, and EDF, and among the historical forces and the strength of words and actions that we had captured or used to get here—stood impotent in that moment. The power to decide moved inexorably to Judge Richey. I was about to witness my first act of judging in a federal court. My stomach felt empty and uneasy, and the tension in my neck and shoulders was dull and consistent throughout. The journey had been so long and hard to get here. I wanted to say something to George. I was not sure what. So I simply looked up at Judge Richey and waited.

> I want to say to all counsel, first of all, that this case has been very ably argued. As a matter of fact, during the noon hour I had the opportunity to tell three of our active members of the court of appeals and one of the senior judges of that court that this was the best argument I have heard on behalf of the government since coming to the bench on May 19, 1971. I also said that it was equally well argued on the part of the other side, and I mean that very sincerely.[39]

The compliment no doubt reflected Judge Richey's politeness. The only words that mattered were that he had talked to members of the court of appeals.

"I have some difficulty, in the light of the recent Supreme Court decision in the Sierra Case, with respect to the right of the plaintiff to bring this action." George tensed noticeably and looked at me. "Nevertheless, I think that there is enough area for disagreement between the parties that it really should be dealt with more thoroughly ... by the appellate court and perhaps even the Supreme Court." What a smile I must have had. We had done it. "In other words," Judge Richey said, "I think that the question of standing to sue needs further clarification, and I think the claims come in within the standards set forth by the recent Supreme Court decision."

We were in. We really had done it. I knew that it had been close. He said it. But we had done it. What a smile I had— I couldn't help it. Judge Richey, thank you. George was smiling. He tapped and then held my arm. Peter was smiling. Judge Richey said: "I believe the government's motion to dismiss, while it is a close question, should be denied."[40] The remaining question, he continued, was "whether or not we should issue a temporary restraining order, and we have almost had no argument on that, it appears to the court."[41]

Charles Horsky looked uneasy. He had not said anything so far. His clients were in trouble. The Commission could not protect them, not this time, not at least at this moment. If the Commission or the United States were enjoined, it may be embarrassed or angry or in disarray. The Railroads would lose money.

> JUDGE RICHEY: Mr. Horsky is raising his hand. I would be glad to hear from you, sir. You may come forward.[42]

This time Horsky's gait seemed more hurried, his tone less sanguine. "May it please the court," he began, "it seems to me that we have not had argument on the issue raised by the TRO."

"Not quite," Judge Richey replied. "Technically speaking, you could not be more correct. However, as you well know, sitting here listening, as I have, to the argument, as government counsel has very appropriately pointed out, the argument has gone really far beyond the scope of the motion to dismiss."[43]

Horsky seemed nonplussed. Whatever the reason for his silence, he now had to talk fast. I knew George and I were thinking the same thing. The TRO was not that critical to us. We would be in front of the three-judge court very soon. We had survived the exercise of power by the United States. At that moment, I felt like a spectator.

HORSKY: You have not heard the Railroads' side. May I at least say that—

JUDGE RICHEY: You may say anything you wish in my court.

HORSKY: The point I would like to make first … is that a TRO seeks to change the status that now exists…. These 2.5 percent surcharges have been in operation, in effect, since February 5th…. They provide for the Railroads something on the order of … $20 million a month…. The costs of the Railroads have skyrocketed, and this is an attempt to keep them—

JUDGE RICHEY: Alive?

HORSKY (continuing):—alive, literally alive…. The other point … is that … the $20 million a month, if lost to the Railroads, is not recoverable[.]… [A]s citizens, they might have to pay a higher price for something. The air might be polluted[,]… they are certainly intangible…. [T]he balance of equities here seems to me to be unequivocally on the side of the Railroads.[44]

He had made the money argument, strongly and unabashedly, which was used repeatedly to veil mismanagement, deceive the public, and ensure freight rate increases. George looked at me, his lips tight, his face drawn. I knew as I sat there watching and listening that we, SCRAP, now three of us, had challenged this charade. We had changed the rules. It was a transitory moment. At this juncture, a TRO would be too much to grant. There would be feinting in the courtroom. I would be Trotsky. George would be Sacco.

Judge Richey did not have to grant it. His first question suggested he would not. "Let me ask you this, Mr. Horsky, why could we not preserve the status quo by allowing this to continue, this increase, for the period of time necessary for the court to have a hearing by a three judge court...?"[45]

HORSKY: That, in effect—I don't mean to presume, but that seems to be that you are saying you will deny the TRO.... In that event, I will sit down, of course.[46]

But Judge Richey was more contemplative than he first appeared. He sat back and then forward. He did not rule. He wanted to "think the thing through out loud with you."[47] He looked beyond Horsky in a sweeping fashion. He sought to engage all of us in a sort of colloquy. It was an impressive exercise in intelligence and fairness. But Judge Richey had only modest success. He made evident what might have gone unnoticed. He engaged only Horsky and SCRAP. It was SCRAP versus the nation's Railroads. I moved to the edge of my chair and concentrated on Horsky. It was his move.

JUDGE RICHEY: Let me ask ... counsel for [SCRAP]: Would you have any objection to maintaining the status quo, gentlemen, with respect to the current surcharge without the benefit of a restraining order....[48]

Peter was ready. "The crucial fact, your honor," he began, "is it seems that the status quo would not be maintained unless the court issues a temporary restraining order. The order which we are trying to have restrained is the order of April 24th.... The status quo prior to the April 24th order would be [that] the 2.5 percent surcharge would go off as of June 5th...."[49] Okay, Peter! Great argument! Now let them figure out what is the "status quo." We're still in this!

Horsky was standing again. Peter still had the floor. Horsky was not our dancing partner. His partners were sitting passively on the other side of the room. They did not want to dance.

"I see what you mean," Judge Richey said in an even tone. "I think we can probably get the cooperation of the Railroads and the Commission to hold things in abeyance.... Do you not think so, Mr. Horsky?"[50] It had changed; the momentum had changed. Horsky stood motionless. No one came to his defense. Horsky moved to the podium.

HORSKY: We do not want to reduce the rates, your honor. That would cost the railroads $250 million a year.

JUDGE RICHEY: I am not suggesting, as I think out loud, that you do that.... What I am suggesting is this: Is there some way we can do this without the dire consequences the plaintiff suggests?

HORSKY: I think all you have to do is grant the motion to convene the three-judge court, and we will proceed before it.

JUDGE RICHEY: Do you agree?[51]

Judge Richey had directed the question to Fritz Kahn. Now Kahn had to participate. He stood but remained in place. Horsky was still alone. "If I understand the question correctly, …this entails a denial of the application for a temporary restraining order," he said.[52]

Horsky affirmed Kahn's statement with an unadorned enthusiasm. "Yes. Yes," he said, probably gratified he had gotten some support and thankful that Judge Richey had provoked it. Horsky continued, "I should point out, your honor, one thing that perhaps is obvious: Usually a temporary restraining order is conditioned on a bond. We obviously cannot ask for $20 million a month from these people … which I think ought to weigh rather heavily with you, your honor."[53]

Judge Richey agreed that it was an important consideration. He described his concerns with Horsky and "to tell you very frankly," he said, in a conversational tone as if they were in a living room or drinking coffee in the cafeteria downstairs, "it makes a difference to me in this particular type of a case, because it is not as clear cut as some of the others."[54]

At that moment, Banzhaf, now seated to my left, began to rise. Judge Richey turned toward him and asked, "If I delay this matter until I can get in touch with the chief judge and arrange for an early hearing, without signing a temporary restraining order or, in effect, denying it, how would you be harmed, really, for a ten- to fifteen-day period?" Banzhaf did not yield easily. In fact, I had never known him to yield.

BANZHAF: Well, your honor, as we indicated before, there are a wide variety of environmental harms which flow from this…. And I might say parenthetically that they have been claiming this all throughout the proceedings where we have been involved—each time they come in and tell the Commission they are on their last legs[,] and they still seem to be sponsoring prime-time network ads promoting their position.

JUDGE RICHEY: Mr. Horsky?

HORSKY: I don't think I need to answer that last comment.

JUDGE RICHEY: I hope not.[55]

Classic Banzhaf. He got in Wally Schirra. I could not believe it. I had only one thought: George and I would be talking about B's comment for years.

Judge Richey denied the TRO.[56] The financial harm to the Railroads outweighed the environmental harm we had alleged. Judge Richey assured everyone—music more to our ears than theirs—that he would seek expeditious consideration by the three-judge court. It was a victory by any definition. Judge Richey gathered his papers but remained seated. "Are there any questions?"[57] he asked.

Banzhaf rose from his chair and walked to the podium. Everyone was silent. I looked at Horsky. His expression had to reflect what we all were thinking. What was Banzhaf going to say?

> BANZHAF: [T]he court gave recognition before to the argument of the government and the argument of the plaintiff. I would simply like to give recognition and introduce to the court the two gentlemen who are sitting at counsel table with us. They are not counsel yet. Mr. Neil Proto and Mr. George Biondi, who were responsible for about 95 percent of the work that went into this. Mr. Proto and Mr. Biondi.[58]

Banzhaf turned to us and motioned that we stand. We both did. It was a special moment. Judge Richey added to it immeasurably.

> JUDGE RICHEY: How do you do. Nice to see both of you gentlemen. I hope you have enjoyed your experience in the field of environmental law, and I hope that you will continue your interest in it after you graduate. It is a great opportunity for some very substantial contributions in this field. You have performed a great public service in bringing this action, in my opinion, gentlemen. Your professor is also to be admired for his interest and his contribution that he has made in this field other than in this case. You are fortunate to have a man who is not only a teacher, but an activist, somewhat like Mr. Horsky.[59]

We both nodded, as if to thank him. What a present! My parents were coming tomorrow for graduation. What a wonderful story to tell them.

The hearing was over. It was 2:45 in the afternoon. We all stood. George and I grabbed each other's arms. "We did it, fella," he said. "We're still in." Banzhaf shook both our hands. I thanked him for his introduction. Peter had a huge smile. He had been thorough and committed and poised. He and I agreed to meet on Monday at Bacon to discuss strategy. George would be there. John, I reminded everyone, was going to Maine.

"One thing is for certain," Peter said. "We have to amend the complaint." We heard Judge Richey's unease.

"Yeah," George said. "Who are these SCRAP boys?"

GRADUATION

June 4. Moments before graduation. We stood together: my parents on each side of me, and my sister, Diana, and brother, Richard, on each side of them on a small patch of lawn directly across from Crawford. I had on my cap and gown. The graduate—the prodigal son in his singular moment of triumph—tired, taut, drained, and twenty-six years old. Eugene had his new camera. "This is classic," Eugene said to my brother. "My son, the lawyer. Now he's got to get a job."

"These five years have been like a movie, Dee." I took my sister's arm and pulled her closer to me. "Connie Stevens can play you."

"No," Eugene said. "Annette Funicello with blond hair."

"George Maharis can play me. What do you think, Richard?" He looked at me with a studious affectation.

"The way you look," my brother answered, "I'd say Bela Lugosi." I tried to hit him in the arm but missed.

I walked into Lisner and located my assigned seat. I opened the program. Kenny Perlman had done it—Order of the COIF. Ressler received honors. Me too.

The next day, early, my parents, Diana, and Eugene departed for New Haven. Richard already had returned to his home in Laurel, Maryland. I stood at the front stoop of Crawford, waving goodbye, and then just stood, feeling only an apprehension about all that lay before me—SCRAP, the bar, a new job.

I had registered for the bar review course in D.C. with a hundred others. The course was taught by Joe Nacrelli. His approach was expressed simply: Forget everything you learned in law school—everything. His wife, who also looked like a cousin on my mother's side, passed out one-, two-, and three-page mimeographed sheets of rules. Remember only what I tell you, he repeated often. Memorize it. Don't reason it. Big mistake.

The examination was scheduled for July 25 and 26. Each question must be answered by an essay. It would be administered at the new Georgetown Law School. There was no test more important. Every lawyer I knew conveyed the same, unadorned message: "Don't blow it."

18

IN COURT:
THE FORCES COLLIDE,
JUNE 1972

The amendment. June 5. George Biondi, Peter Meyers, and I met at Bacon. John Larouche had returned to Maine for the summer. The briefs already submitted would be transmitted to the three judges now being selected by the chief judge. Two matters needed discussion and drafting. We decided to move to consolidate our complaint in *265/267* with *281*. The longer history was not to be lost by our failure to bring it to the court's attention. We filed our motion to consolidate on June 13.[1]

On June 20, we filed an amended complaint. We added our names and legal residences and the point that each of us "has also repeatedly traveled by automobile from the Washington metropolitan area to his legal residence, and has spent at least a number of weeks at his legal residence in the past two years." The addition would allow us to argue, and offer proof of, definite forms of aesthetic and practical harm. We clarified, as well, that all members of SCRAP were harmed in their individual recreational activities, by increased costs in the marketplace, by air pollution from unnecessary motor carrier usage, and as taxpayers "within the Washington Metropolitan Area and their legal residence."[2]

We also reexamined the briefs filed by EDF, the Railroads, and the Commission. Peter and George noticed separately that the joint memorandum filed by the ICC and the United States made no reference to the decision in *Calvert Cliffs*.[3]

"Suicidal," George said when he told me.

"It's such a crucial decision," Peter added in earnest.

"Sometimes I think—actually most times I think—they're either very cunning or very stupid," I said. "We were right to do this, getting them into court."

George, his finger rising slightly, his smile restrained and mischievous, said evenly, "All we need now is—?"

THE COURT OF APPEALS

June 23. The United States Court of Appeals was housed on the entire fifth floor of the federal courthouse. Its *en banc* courtroom was simple in design and texture: paneled with bleached walnut, cavernous in height and breadth, and without diversion of color. There were no deep reds or blues or mahogany.

I stood inside. Alone. I looked around. I fixed on two bronze castings at the east end of the courtroom: "Justice" and "Authority." I turned slowly and saw the four large statues at the west end: King Alfred, William Blackstone, Justice Joseph Story, and Chief Justice John Marshall. In the simplicity and size of this courtroom, the room's most dramatic feature became plain. The long bench was elevated and capable of seating the entire court of appeals at once, all nine judges. George entered quietly. He put his hand on my shoulder and said in a soft, serious tone, "It's time." I nodded. We walked out into the corridor. Peter was there.

He took us into the counsel's room. On its walls were photographs of the court of appeals' judges; displayed was a history in life and law I did not know but, in that moment, sought to embrace. Atop a table was the court's calendar for the day. Our argument was the only hearing scheduled. The calendar listed the three judges on our panel. I called Peter over. He had just been told, he said. George looked at the calendar and said softly, with a prolonged sigh of amazement and the intonation of a question, "Noooo?"

"It's fate," I said. George looked at it again.

"It's a miracle, Neil. This can only be a miracle," George said.

Inside the courtroom, George and I sat near the counsel table and waited. Scott Lang was to argue for EDF. We all exchanged greetings when he walked into the courtroom. Peter and he discussed how to divide the plaintiffs' 30 minutes of oral argument. William Cohen, representing the United States, and Art Cerra, representing the Commission, already were there. They were huddled together talking. Charles Horsky was there as well. He sat alone.

The clerk told us to rise. In walked Judge J. Skelly Wright of the United States Court of Appeals for the District of Columbia and Judges Thomas Flannery and Charles Richey of the district court. I looked only at Judge Wright. He sat in the center. He was fair in complexion, with blush-red cheeks, thin, graying hair, a stern-looking demeanor, and an erect posture. He exuded no nonsense or unnecessary cordiality. There was no pretense. He got right to business. "Who is going to argue for the plaintiffs?"[4] Peter rose from his chair. Judge Wright motioned him to begin.

"May it please the court," Peter began in the accustomed fashion. He recited the essential facts and then steered right toward the inadequacy of the Commission's compliance with NEPA. I looked at Judge Wright. He seemed to be restraining himself, impatient perhaps, wanting to say something or have Peter say something different. "It seems that the Commission will not comply fully and in good faith until ordered to do so by this court," Peter said.[5]

Judge Wright, patient no longer, interrupted him: "The government and the Commission simply say that, well, well and good; we will get a proper statement when we get around to it in 281; but we do not need a proper statement in connection with these suspension orders, or lack-of-suspension orders."[6] It was the history he wanted—all of it, from the enactment of NEPA forward. Peter was uneasy at first. He talked about the Commission's "only *pro forma* treatment of the NEPA and the CEQ requirements." Then it seemed to click.

> MEYERS: The crucial—the crucial—flaw of the draft impact statement is that this is the fourth time the Commission has granted an increase, and it has never evaluated the impact of, and the alternatives to, the underlying rate structure.[7]

Judge Flannery, it seemed, wanted to bring Peter back to the precise facts of *281* that gave rise to our lawsuit. "You are familiar with … *Port of New York Authority v. United States*, are you not?"[8]

"Yes, your honor."

"How do you distinguish that case from this case?"

Peter was ready. "We believe the *Port of New York Authority* conflicts with this court's decision in *Calvert Cliffs*. *Calvert Cliffs* … said that a draft impact statement … must be done at every important, distinctive stage of the agency process."

Judge Wright stopped him: "That is what the statute says."

Peter looked at him quizzically. "Pardon me, your honor?"

"*Calvert Cliffs* did not have to say that. That is what the statute says."

Peter got it. "Yes," he said, "we think that the *Port of New York Authority* misconstrues the statute."[9]

Judge Wright was moving, homing in on the Commission's vulnerabilities. "In *281*, what rate does that consider? Is this an across-the-board increase?"[10] Peter answered easily. "Well, *281* involves two different, incremental increases. It involves the 2.5 percent surcharge, which is across the board.... And then the railroads have also requested a 4.1 percent selective increase to supplant the surcharge.... The Commission is somewhat ambiguous about even which increase the impact statement applies to.... The only thing we are saying ... is ... do it right.... Don't solely rely on what the parties are willing to submit to you."[11] It was a good answer. I was struck by Judge Wright's ability to solicit it. He also seemed to be engaging in a colloquy with the judges seated to his left and right.

Peter sat down. Scott Lang took over. Judge Wright still seemed noticeably impatient. Lang had barely introduced himself when Judge Wright said, "It seems to me that the attention ought to be directed to this broader picture. The suspension is one thing, but a failure to consider NEPA in connection with the rate structure is unbelievable three years after the act. Now, this is the area to which you ought to address yourself, it seems to me."[12]

Lang was firm in his presentation. He dug deeper and further back. "Since 1962, the question of the rate structure, itself, was first brought to the attention of the Commission by Secretary Udall and by the Bureau of the Mines and ... the Office of Emergency Preparedness.... [E]very time you add to the rate structure in a percentage, across-the-board way, you have the effect of increasing discrimination ... and that ... this is what the ICC should be addressing itself to."[13] Lang seemed more confident than in his first brief appearance before Judge Richey. He also now had stepped onto the right track.

> JUDGE RICHEY: Could the ICC keep on ... approving interim rate increases ad infinitum without ever getting to the stage of making it final?
>
> LANG: Well, conceivably, they could.... [T]he ICC will then say, well, let's put it off until the next case, which is what they did in *265* and *267*, when it was raised.[14]

Judge Flannery—an uncertainty to me—entered the colloquy. "Does not the Commission plan to file an impact statement later?"[15]

> LANG: Your honor ... I have never seen the Commission set a timetable for when it intends to comply with NEPA.[16]

Judge Wright interceded, hard. "That is what hearings are all about. Under NEPA, the public and the parties are supposed to have the draft statement so that they can produce evidence to get the Commission ... to change the statement, to consider alternatives. That is the whole purpose and rationale of the act. You cannot file a statement after everything is finished, particularly a pro forma statement like this one, which looks like it was written by a first-year high school student."[17]

"We're doing well," I whispered to George. It now was plain. Judge Wright understood government. He had been tempered by its good and evil. He was neither intimidated nor deferential to its exercise of power.

Art Cerra walked to the podium. He was dressed neatly: dark business suit, white shirt, and tie. He seemed like a gentle man with an unenviable duty. He had not even begun his argument when Judge Wright asked, "Maybe you will tell me how you can write a [forty-four-]page brief ... without citing *Calvert Cliffs* once. Can you explain that? Are you familiar with that case?"[18]

CERRA: If your honor please, I would like to pass that question.

JUDGE WRIGHT: Are you familiar with that case?

CERRA: Yes, I am very familiar with that case, your honor.

JUDGE WRIGHT: All right.

CERRA: It is an outstanding opinion by the court.[19]

Cerra seemed more like the sacrificial lamb. The structure of the courtroom assured it. The podium's purpose was to make you singularly accountable and with the duty to explain conduct you often did not participate in. Cerra had no such refuge. He sat in the February 3 meeting between us and Fritz Kahn that yielded the MOU. With perseverance, Cerra proceeded to his only argument. He tried to explain that the Commission did prepare a draft EIS based on "supposition" and, by doing so, had provided a public service; somehow, the Commission had extended itself beyond what was required.[20]

JUDGE WRIGHT: What comments did you get from the CEQ?

CERRA: They said they were inadequate. This was not sufficient, and so on and so forth.

JUDGE WRIGHT: What comments did you get from the EPA?

CERRA: Most of the comments were asking the Commission to go into greater depth....

JUDGE WRIGHT: When is the Commission, and how is the Commission, going to get this information?

CERRA: When it puts out its final decision as to whether these rates are adequate, whether the rate structure is adequate, or what have you.

JUDGE RICHEY: Well, the plaintiffs are not so much concerned with whether the rates are adequate. They are concerned with whether or not NEPA has been complied with and whether this will have an adverse effect ... on the environment.[21]

Cerra, we knew, had to defend a six-page draft EIS that had examined none of the significant effects, including the "diversion of traffic." Judge Richey asked, "Now, you say you have not considered that."[22]

"That is what the plaintiffs are saying, your honor...," Cerra responded. "Now, it has been said here this morning by plaintiffs' counsel that the Commission has never looked into the environmental quality of the rate structure. They have an investigation going on right now, *Ex Parte 270*, which was instituted to examine the entire rate structure. Now, that is going to be a massive job, a massive job."

JUDGE WRIGHT: How long will it take?

CERRA: It will take between three to five years.

JUDGE WRIGHT: What do you think will happen to the environment in the meantime?

CERRA: Your honor ... the Commission ... is making every effort possible.

JUDGE WRIGHT: How many final impact statements has the Commission issued to date?

CERRA: In every proceeding that it is undertaking now, your honor, it is making impact statements, but, as to the number, I have no idea.[23]

Judge Wright seemed displeased. He returned to the content of the draft EIS. "Well, counsel says, ... there is no compliance with CEQ regulations, guidelines, and so on, and … [t]he public is operating in the dark…. The blind is leading the blind…."

Cerra did not respond at first. He could say only that the Commission had "serious doubts that there is any merit to that contention."

JUDGE WRIGHT: Well, I have looked at the draft impact statement, and I must say it is a crude document, to say the least.

CERRA: No question about it.

JUDGE WRIGHT: I do not think any more of it than the President's CEQ thought about it, or the President's EPA thinks of it.[24]

Judge Richey, as if moving in tandem with Judge Wright, moved forward, prepared. "It seems to me to be a never-ending process."

Cerra shifted his posture and acknowledged the obvious: "It might very well be."[25]

Cerra tried to move to solid ground, but his posture was still unsteady. "The Commission has … found … that any increase in rates does not affect the transportation of waste materials…. Now, if the hoped-for, ultimate end is to get … a tariff that is going to favor waste products … the Commission … has to make that on the basis of sufficient data submitted to it."[26]

JUDGE WRIGHT: Does it have it now?

CERRA: We hope it has it now, and we hope it can make that determination, your honor.[27]

William Cohen, still counsel for the United States, walked to the podium. He, too, began with the government's best argument. "[T]he issue we have posed is whether a final environmental impact statement is required at the suspension stage in the proceedings."[28]

Judge Wright challenged Cohen's assertion: "Do not your rules, the ICC rules, require a draft impact statement in the middle, so that the … parties can know what to aim at…. Do your rules not provide for that?"[29]

COHEN: I believe they do. There is a draft impact statement—

JUDGE WRIGHT: I understand that, but an agency … must … file … a draft statement that pretends to be a viable document.

COHEN: Well, actually, the Commission's rules do not require a draft environmental impact statement—

JUDGE WRIGHT: You say it does not?

COHEN: It does not.

Judge Wright countered quickly. "Why did you file one?" Cohen was uneasy. Judge Wright had snagged him sharply. The direction he was about to yank was so obvious, I thought, Cohen had to know it was coming.[30]

COHEN: Well, I believe the purpose in the draft here is to—

JUDGE WRIGHT: You have violated your rules by filing one, I guess.

COHEN: Well ... I believe the purpose of a draft statement essentially is to elicit comments....

JUDGE WRIGHT: It is to have an intelligent exchange of ideas so that the environment can be protected by the agency; so that the agency can seek the help of other governmental agencies, of the public[;] ... and so that in the end some reasonable, intelligent document can come out of the agency....[31]

Silence. Judge Wright's displeasure, already acknowledged, was made evident again. "Now, if you are suggesting that this document that was filed in this case serves that purpose, I just happen to disagree with you."[32]

Cohen, however, also would not budge. "But there is nothing to preclude the Commission from preparing another draft and another draft, because the draft is not subject to any judicial review."[33] The United States had made its position plain. The Commission and the Railroads could do what they wanted, when they wanted. Cohen thanked the court and took his seat.

Charles Horsky rose and walked toward the podium. Before he even reached it, Judge Wright began. "Now, Mr. Horsky, we want to talk about the environment. We do not want to talk about the sad plight of the railroads."[34] Horsky grinned slightly, but in that moment, I thought he sensed what we did. He was losing.

HORSKY: I will restrain myself, but I do want to clarify one thing which I think may have been lost in the discussion.... In this case the Commission found—and I quote from its order—"The involved general increase ... will have no significant adverse effect on the movement of traffic by railway or on the quality of the human environment within the meaning of the [National] Environmental Policy Act of 1969."... [I]t seems to me the Commission has done what it is required to do.[35]

Horsky seemed content in his analysis, which was a mainstay of administrative law: An agency finding is entitled to deference by a court. Judge Wright did not acquiesce. "What supporting findings are there for that conclusion?" he asked.[36] Horsky seemed nonplussed.

HORSKY: What supporting findings?

JUDGE WRIGHT: Yes.

HORSKY: That is the finding....

JUDGE WRIGHT: Well, is that not the essence of arbitrariness, just to come up with a fiat like that?

HORSKY: Well, no. They have considered the matter. They have statements before them in the record....

JUDGE WRIGHT: We are supposed to have intermediate findings of fact.... Unless the conclusion that you have just stated is supported by intermediate findings, well, then, the conclusion is not worth the paper it is written on.

HORSKY: It is a finding. It is not a conclusion.

JUDGE WRIGHT: Well, you are talking about labels, now.[37]

Horsky wanted the court to defer to the judgment of the ICC. It was a view of the judicial role that, from everything I knew, was not one Judge Wright shared. Horksy took a different tack. He seemed to grasp, perhaps better than anyone in the room, the legal and social forces at play. "[L]et me come to what I am principally here for, which is this. If I am wrong on all of this, I would like to be heard for a moment on the nature of the relief that might be appropriate or decreed by this court....[I]t is perfectly apparent that the attack here ... is on the ... discrimination, or whatever it is they allege, between recyclable product rates and other rates. Any decree of this court should, therefore, it seems to me, appropriately be confined to a hold-down of those rates, not to the general rate structure of the entire commodity picture."[38]

George looked ashen. "Did he say what I think he said?"

I shrugged and nodded. "George," I whispered, "I think he just acknowledged he lost. But what a move."

Horsky said the Railroads could be helpful in ensuring compliance with NEPA. "If we have been delinquent in the past, we will be delinquent no further."[39]

Judge Wright was having none of it: "Well, let me say this. The responsibility is not on the railroads. The responsibility is on the agency.... And it is our responsibility, of course, to see that the agency complies with the law."[40]

Judge Wright asked Peter if he had anything to add in conclusion. He had one last point to make. Judge Wright allowed it.

> MEYERS: [T]o my knowledge, the Commission has never in any case whatsoever filed a final impact statement by today.[41]

> JUDGE WRIGHT: Well, Mr. Cerra told me there were so many he could not even count them. So there must be some type of misunderstanding between you. We will ask Mr. Cerra that.... Suppose you look it up and let us know tomorrow.

> CERRA: I will, sir.

> JUDGE WRIGHT: Thank you.

THE AFTERWORD

Peter placed papers and notes into his briefcase and received a warm greeting from William Cohen. I sat quietly for a moment. Judge Wright had now seen what we had—here, in a court of law. It was precisely what we had hoped would occur. "Hey, fella," George said. "Let's go." I stood and congratulated Scott Lang and turned to Peter.

"Excellent job," I said. "You were very good." He was beaming. He said something I did not hear. My mind already was elsewhere. Joe Nacrelli. Domestic relations. Contracts. The bar, the bar, the bar, and the bar. I said goodbye.

In response to Judge Wright's inquiry, Art Cerra wrote that only one final EIS had been issued by the Commission since NEPA's enactment. It had been for a railroad abandonment proceeding where the district court in New York had ordered it.[42]

19

VICTORY,
JUNE 1972

The call. July 10. The discipline necessary to prepare for the bar was essential to passing it: to determine precisely what to memorize and understand by which hour of the day. No diversions were permitted except those scrupulously planned and controlled. Even law school seemed irrelevant. Joe Nacrelli told us that every day.

In late afternoon, I walked next door for coffee. No one was on the street or in the Center except a few summer school students and those working with a casualness borne of the heat. I saw Kathleen walking out, engaged in an animated, heated discussion with a man, older than me, neatly dressed, a lawyer if I had to guess. They were familiar, touching. My thoughts abounded about timing and choices in relationships. She looked back and recognized I was there. They left. "Not now," I said aloud. I got my coffee and returned to Crawford, a white foam cup in hand.

I walked by the dorm office toward my apartment. The telephone was ringing inside. I reached for my keys. The coffee, still hot, swished and spilled noticeably as I turned hurriedly to place the key into the door. It was Freda from Banzhaf's office. She was excited. "We won," she said. An AP or UPI reporter had just called. No one else was around. She had given my number to the reporter. "Don't move," she said and hung up. I felt frozen. The light was out, the room dark, the door closed. It was quiet and still. We had won. I could not tell anyone.

I made sure the receiver was flush against the base of the telephone. More silence. I sat down on the swivel chair and put my feet up on the desk. I felt tightness in my calves. I wanted to call home. I could not. I wanted to call George. I could not. I tried to feel satisfied or content or happy. I could not. I could not drink a beer. Joe Nacrelli popped in and out of my thoughts. I was not sure precisely what winning meant. Putting my feet up was all I could think of doing.

The telephone rang. It was a woman. "Margarite" was all I understood. "With UPI," she said. "Well, how do you feel?"

"I feel great," I said. "I don't know exactly what the court said. Who wrote the opinion?"

"Judge Wright."

"Did the court issue an injunction?"

"Yes." It was like the sensation of a 3-D movie. I could see it. Ed Kaier, Fritz Kahn, and Art Cerra. One was stultified in place, the second was falling, and the third was fully prone. None had their feet up.

Margarite and I talked about law school and graduation. She was the recipient of all my excitement and tension. I explained that I was about to take the bar exam and had been studying. She congratulated me on winning and wished me "luck as a lawyer." In the tone of her words, she sounded like an aunt.[1]

I called George. He was ecstatic. He asked me questions I could not answer. I called home and told my mother. "Matty," she called to my dad. "It's Neil. He won. SCRAP! Their case. They won!"

I could not take the night off. I went back to studying. The discipline now seemed more purposeful. We just won a case in the United States District Court against the United States, the nation's Railroads, and Covington & Burling—and a hundred years of corruption and abuse of the public trust. "So, Proto," I said aloud, "how the hell could you not pass the bar exam?"

THE DECISION

It was unanimous. I could envision Judge Wright reading it aloud. George and I sat in the Center savoring every word.[2] "This case is before us on plaintiff's motion for a preliminary injunction and defendant's cross-motion to dismiss." Judge Wright dropped a footnote here. The court, he said, "decided ... to defer action on" our motion to consolidate the complaint in *265/267*.[3]

"It served its purpose," George said. "It was the history we wanted."

"Cerra's letter."

"Yeah."

Judge Wright also concluded that "in light of the fact that [SCRAP] objects to the surcharge only insofar as it increases the shipping costs of recyclable materials, we are restricting our injunction to the movement of these goods."[4]

"Charles Horsky," I said to George.

"It makes sense," he said. "Think about it. It's the precise interest that brought us there. Or are you complaining?"

"No. You're right, George. He was smart about it." He looked at me, eyebrows raised. "George," I repeated. "I'm happy. You're right. We did good."

The court dismissed the Commission's orders that had directed the Railroads to submit a statement regarding the environmental impact. "We need hardly point out," Judge Wright wrote, "that this self-serving statement by one of the parties cannot take the place of an NEPA impact statement which, according to the statute, must be prepared 'by the responsible official.'"[5]

"Verified Statement No. 37?" I asked George, in a mocking tone.

"Dead."

"And the February 3 MOU."

"This worked for us. Old Fritz can't be pleased."

"EDF didn't even want it."

Judge Wright cited the MOU to support the proposition that "[p]artly in response to pressure from SCRAP," the Commission prepared and issued a six-page draft EIS.[6] "[T]he focus of this document is somewhat ambiguous. It could not have been intended to apply to the 2.5 percent interim surcharge, since this had already gone into effect.... The Commission has never adequately explained ... why the ICC finds ... the resources necessary to prepare draft statements based on false hypotheses while it is assertedly without resources to prepare impact statements ... based on real facts[, which] remains one of the enduring mysteries of this case."[7]

"Hey. Well, George. It's good, but it's actually a bad sign—if I got it right."

"Judge Wright believes the 2.5 percent surcharge is still temporary?"

"George? The 'suspension stage.'"

"Please. I know that stage."

In light of the court's "considerable doubt as to whether the Commission will comply with NEPA ... [i]f left to its own devices," the court retained jurisdiction to ensure that any permanent rate increases that "are permitted to take effect are preceded by an impact statement in conformance with NEPA."[8]

"You mean," George said, with an exaggerated sigh of relief, "we can rest now?"

"Rest? What are you, nuts?" I said.

"Neil. I just thought I'd ask."

"George, you think Charles Horsky is resting?"

"Yeah, I do. He's probably in the Bahamas."

"George, if he is, I guarantee you he's on his way back right now."

George smiled. "You mean, you think that J. Skelly Wright deliberately ruined his vacation?"

"George, it happened right in the middle of the piña colada."

We read on. "As a threshold matter," Judge Wright stated, "defendants vigorously contest plaintiff's standing to bring this action." SCRAP, they contended, had "no more than a general interest in seeing that the law is enforced—"[9]

"Music to our ears," George said. "We read Judge Richey and *Sierra Club* correctly."

"In its amended complaint," Judge Wright continued, "plaintiff alleges that its members use the forests, streams, mountains, and other resources in the Washington area for camping, hiking, fishing, and sightseeing, and that this use is disturbed by the adverse environmental impact caused by nonuse of recyclable goods. It is clear that plaintiff organization has standing to raise the rights of its members ... and we think plaintiff has alleged the kind of 'injury in fact' to those members which would give them standing to sue. See *Association of Data Processing* and *Barlow*. Moreover, plaintiff's allegation that its members actually use the environmental resources adversely affected by the Commission action is sufficient to distinguish this case from *Sierra Club v. Morton*."[10]

"We have standing," George declared with a quiet satisfaction.

"But," I added, finger raised sharply.

"But?"

"But he didn't address the other bases we claimed. *Sierra Club* may have yielded only a 'forest, streams[,] and mountains.'"

"It's the easiest," George said. "But I agree. The opinion seems to miss the others."

"Yeah."

"You complaining?"

"Yeah, now I'm complaining. Let's go back and tell him he's wrong."

"Let's vote." George said, bringing our parody to an end.

"Okay. Now, *Arrow Transportation*."

"Hard."

"Two different cultures."

We kept reading. "[A]lthough the *Arrow* doctrine grants the Commission broad discretion at the suspension stage," Judge Wright stated, "we are far from convinced that it is relevant to this case. The thrust of the doctrine seems to be that judicial review is available only when the rates in question are Commission-made rather than carrier-made...."[11]

"What a distinction," I said. "We didn't make it. EDF didn't make it."

"Looks like Judge Wright made it."

Judge Wright continued, "This is not a case where the Commission merely stands silently by and allows carrier-made rates to take effect without suspension. Rather, the Commission issued an order in which it explicitly found that 'the increases here proposed are just and reasonable....'"[12]

"We did say *that*." George raised his head and his eyebrows. It was momentary. We returned to the decision. Judge Wright continued, "This circuit has held that an agency may not use its suspension power in effect to make rates and still avoid judicial review...."[13]

"Wow, George! What reasoning! He's talking to the big guys."

"You mean, 'the Supremes.'"

"Yep."

Judge Wright also found "there is another, more compelling, argument for why this court possesses jurisdiction. In our view, NEPA implicitly confers authority on the federal courts to enjoin any federal action taken in violation of NEPA's procedural requirements...."[14]

"We wanted this," George said.

"Well, we got it."

Judge Wright next addressed the Commission's position that SCRAP could request a review of individual rates and seek a refund. "Our plaintiff ... is not a shipper. It is not concerned with the individual rates paid by individual shippers.... The appropriate time to review this claim is when the overall rate structure is set rather than on a piecemeal basis."[15]

"It was always so peculiar that they couldn't get it," I said.

"They wanted us there forever."

"Well, we didn't go home."

The Commission, Judge Wright wrote, "stands in violation of NEPA unless it can demonstrate either (a) that the April 24 order is not a 'major federal action' or (b) that the April 24 order does not 'significantly [affect] the quality of the human environment.' We conclude that the Commission has failed to prove the truth of either of these propositions."[16]

"Neil, the Commission never pretended it had or wanted to prove either one of these. Well, it was always obvious. He says it here. Quote, '[S]urely this decision—involving as it does almost every railroad in the country and hundreds of millions of dollars in freight charges—requires [an EIS].'"[17]

"George, I'm telling you. He's not talking to the Commission. That's not what this is."

We read on. "The Commission," Judge Wright continued, "seems to take the position that temporary rate increases are not major federal actions because ... [the increase] is ... to be replaced on November 30 by a permanent structure.... This circuit was presented with a similar argument in *Calvert Cliffs* wherein the Atomic Energy Commission argued ... the environmental impact would be fully considered at the licensing stage. The argument was unambiguously rejected."[18]

Also rejected was the Commission's argument that it had already complied with NEPA in an acceptable manner. "The Commission refers us to a provision in its February 1 order wherein it states that 'the involved general increase will have no significant adverse effect.'... On the basis of this single sentence the Commission asks us to believe that ... an impact statement is not required."[19]

"Cerra."

"You feel sorry for him?" George asked.

I exhaled, hesitated a moment, smiled, and said plainly, "No," and then added, with care, "except he was just the messenger. The others—"

"They were hightailing it out of Dodge—I've got to say it—on a rail," George said, laughing.

"Okay. Okay."

"Evidently," Judge Wright wrote, "this stratagem for avoiding the requirements of NEPA is employed by the Commission on a regular basis.... Literally hundreds of Commission orders have now been issued containing the negative statement or finding. It should be obvious," Judge Wright concluded, "that the NEPA requirements cannot be circumvented by so transparent a ruse."[20]

"You want to write a thank-you note to Cerra?" I asked. George seemed to break up in hilarity. "Yeah, on recyclable paper."

"And we'll send it by Railroad."

"It'll never get there. Okay. That's enough."

Finally, Judge Wright undertook a "balancing of the equities"—that is, the relative harm to all the parties and to the public interest if the rate increases on recyclable materials were enjoined. The court rejected the argument that the Railroads had always hidden behind. "While the public has an undoubted interest in the efficient operation of the railroads, the strongest sort of public interest weighs in favor of the preservation of the environment.... [T]he damage done to the environment is likely to be irreparable. Surely it cannot be undone, as the railroads contend, by subsequent rebates to shippers, since once raw materials are unnecessarily extracted from the ground and used, they cannot be returned from whence they came." He characterized "the damage done to the railroads" as "clearly nonfrivolous," but "not overwhelming."[21]

"Okay. Ready? I'm going to read this. Ready?" I asked.

"Ready."

I stood up. "*ORDERED* that the Interstate Commerce Commission be, and it is hereby, enjoined from permitting, and the intervenor railroads be, and they are hereby, enjoined from collecting, the 2.5 percent surcharge referred to in the Commission's order of April 24, 1972[,] insofar as that surcharge relates to goods being transported for purposes of recycling.... This injunction shall apply to shipments originating after July 15, 1972."[22]

"We did it," George said with a comforting satisfaction.

"J. Skelly Wright did it."

"No, the Commission did it."

"You were right the first time. We did it." George leaned over the table and we shook hands.

20

INTO HOSTILE TERRITORY, JULY 1972

To a high Court. July 13. The alarm rang at 6:00 a.m. The coffee was on in moments. My notes were in order. The bar review materials were organized. My memory was sharp and ready for more. I was planning to study most of the day. Peter Meyers wanted to meet in the afternoon at Bacon. He had drafted a letter to the ICC concerning the definition of "recyclable" goods that should be included in the injunction. He had an EPA list. He was certain it was broader than the list relied upon by the Railroads or the Commission.[1]

At 11:00 a.m., I walked down the hall to see if the mail had arrived. There was a letter from my mother. It was postmarked July 9. She had a wonderful approach. One long sentence with commas everywhere as if she were talking to me in the same room, where she could end and begin thoughts and change direction or subject and know, nonetheless, that in the end she would convey all her points and the feelings that underlie her words. She wrote about the family, the city, the nation; about herself and what she was doing; and about me—my schooling, exams, and life. She had always wanted me to have the whole picture. Today, she did it again. After a few pages of prose, she moved into an unusually simple paragraph: "Hope your exams get over soon. How are you making out with the R.R. suit? Just hope it gets to a high court." I closed and locked the office door, then read the letter a second time while walking back to my apartment.

"There's a fight about what constitutes a 'recyclable' material," Peter said when I entered the large room. He was quick to add, "It's the least of our worries." A neatly bundled package of formally typed papers had just arrived. The ICC had applied to the chief justice of the Supreme Court, Warren Burger, to stay the injunction from going into effect. The Commission had been joined by the Railroads. "About forty pages of briefs," Peter said. He was having copies made. "No surprises," he said. He was wrong. We had to respond within the next day or two. This was not a diversion I had planned.[2]

"It's deliberate," I said. "The Railroads know I'm taking the bar in ten days. Why hasn't the United States filed?"

"Tomorrow." Peter pulled out another document from a folder on his desk. "I'm working on a cut-and-paste job." It was a simple response to what all three parties had or were likely to say. The way Peter saw it, if Judge Wright's opinion could not convince Chief Justice Warren Burger to deny the application, SCRAP could not. I said I would wait there until he finished and then review it. I took the briefs prepared by the Railroads and Commission and sat down.

Fritz Kahn used the term "suspension stage" repeatedly. *Arrow Transportation* was in the second paragraph. The Commission was using every device, argument, and cliché possible. My concern increased. Warren Burger was not J. Skelly Wright. "It's new law. It's Wright," Peter said. "And it's the money." Most of the Commission's request was devoted to protecting the Railroads. The injunction, the Commission wrote, "will have an immediate, irreparable, and deleterious effect on the nation's railroads, particularly in the Eastern sector of the country where eight of the railroads carrying a substantial amount of this traffic are in bankruptcy or reorganization."[3]

"Now it's our fault," I said.

"Yeah. I saw it."

"Oh, my. Peter. You see this? In the second sentence. The injunction scheduled for July 16 'would injure the railroads by depriving them of approximately $500,000 per month.'[4] Peanuts."

Peter looked up and reminded me that the Railroads had not yet seen our list of recyclable goods. "It'll get worse," he said.

Peter handed me his cut-and-paste job to review and edit. It was filed the next day. So, too, was the formal notice of appeal by the United States. We were in the Supreme Court: United States of America v. Students Challenging Regulatory Agency Procedures (S.C.R.A.P), et al., No. 72-535.[5]

WITH RELUCTANCE

The chief justice had the authority to undo all that had been done. He could set aside the injunction and refer the case to the entire Supreme Court on an expedited basis. "It would be unusual," Peter said. His words were no comfort. "But there's a history here," he added. Chief Justice Warren Burger had sat on the D.C. Circuit before his elevation to the Supreme Court by President Nixon. His disputes with Judges David Bazelon and J. Skelly Wright were described as "legendary." That knowledge only added to my discomfort.

On July 16, the injunction went into effect. No word from the chief justice. The Commission, with the Railroads' acquiescence if not guidance, defined "recyclable materials" very narrowly. Peter began immediately to draft a second letter protesting the list.[6] The situation made us uneasy. The Railroads would try to show we were unreasonable. I called Peter. He called the Supreme Court; George called me. We waited for the chief justice.

"I can't believe it," I told George when he called early the morning of the eighteenth. "I relieve my tension by reading Joe Nacrelli notes until midnight. Its nuts." I asked what else was going on.

"Do you remember when we went over to the Watergate to deliver our petitions to NAPACA?"

"What the heck is NAPACA?"

"Sandy Weissbard and The National Parks and Conservation Association?"

"Yeah. Okay."

"Well, the Democratic National Committee is there."

"The Watergate? The Democrats are at the Watergate?"

"They got robbed last night, and the guys got caught."

"What were they doing?"

"I'm not sure."

"George. Across the street. Maybe they thought the Howard Johnson's was open for 'all the chicken you can eat for $2.99.'"

"That's where you and Cliff Brown used to go."

"George, we were so bad. We'd just order chicken and water. And then, well, George, we took Fred Spurlock one night. We shut the place down. Maybe the guys who did the break-in thought Howard Johnson's was still open. I'm telling you—they got hungry; they were looking for something to eat, and—"

"You mean the break-in was Fred's fault?"

"George, Cliff and I were not exactly on a diet."

"Neil, if you need a lawyer, let me know. I'd do chicken law."

"Chicken law? George, you took a course?"

George added that the intruders had been or would be arraigned in the United States District Court. "Do they have a judge yet?" I asked. He was not sure. "What were they doing there?"

"Neil, I don't know but, somehow, I don't think chicken law is going to help."

On July 19, the chief justice denied the stay.[7] "[P]rior decisions of this Court confirm the Commission's broad discretion in the exercise of its power of suspension; judicial review of suspension or inaction is most severely limited, if not foreclosed."[8] It was an ominous beginning.

The Railroads also had complained to him about the "unexpectedly broad" interpretation of recyclable materials that we had submitted. "Someone needs to tell him EPA is within the United States government," George said to me.[9]

Chief Justice Burger posed the legal question as a conflict in two statutes: the Interstate Commerce Act and the newly enacted NEPA. He criticized the inexactness of Judge Wright's conclusion that "NEPA implicitly confers authority on the federal courts to enjoin any federal action taken in violation of NEPA's procedural requirements." It was not a judicial role he thought appropriate.[10]

"He's made it clear," I said. "He's prepared to defend the culture."

Chief Justice Burger also believed it "likely that the questions to be presented by this appeal 'are of such significance and difficulty that there is a substantial prospect that they will command four votes for review' when the full Court reconvenes for the October 1972 term." There were two reasons: "The decision below may present a serious question of standing … *Sierra Club v. Morton*, supra[,] and may be read as undermining our *Arrow* decision…."[11]

The injunction would stay in effect. But the chief justice would have evaluated the relative harm to the parties decidedly in favor of the Railroads. "The harm to the railroads," he wrote, "and to the overall public interest in maintaining an efficient transportation network, is immediate and direct. Badly needed revenues will be lost at once…. Unlike the district court, I find it difficult to dismiss this certain loss."[12]

"You can feel his discomfort," George said to me before we turned to the decision's concluding paragraphs.

"It's ideological," I said. "He and Judge Wright are from different worlds."

The chief justice made the difference plain: "Our society … and its govern-mental instrumentalities, having been less than alert to the needs of our envi-ronment for generations, have now taken protective steps. These developments, however praiseworthy, should not lead courts to exercise equitable powers loosely or casually whenever a claim of 'environmental damage' is asserted. The world must go on and new environmental legislation must be carefully meshed with more traditional patterns of federal regulation."[13] Chief Justice Burger also made his unease explicit: "Notwithstanding my doubts … [r]eluctantly, I con-clude that the applications for stay pending appeal should be denied."[14]

"Well, we know where he stands," George said.

"Ironically, George, our fate is going to be determined by the guys in the middle."

"Who's in the middle?" he asked.

"Potter Stewart?"

"That's the middle? Nixon called him a 'strict constructionist.' We're in trouble."

"George, you mean you and Larouche are in trouble. In about three weeks, I'm—"

"I know," he said. "I know."

"Let's celebrate. I'll buy coffee."

"That's it? Neil, come for dinner. We'll drink some wine, tell stories."

"Dinner? George, look at me. I feel worse than I look. The bar. Let's wait till after the bar. Besides, George, there's time. The Railroads are stuck. They're enjoined. Think about this. Ed Kaier and Fritz Kahn and Charles Horsky aren't sitting around tonight celebrating, drinking wine, and telling stories. Well, they might be. But they're not celebrating."

THE BAR EXAMINATION

Georgetown Law School. The first day of the bar exam. The bar was long, challenging, and then flat-out hard. When the proctor told us to break for a few moments, I turned to the woman seated nearby. She returned the look. "The exam was prepared in the Gulag," she said, stretching her arms high and then wide. We both laughed. A new blue book was placed on my desk. At the day's end, finding no comfort from anyone I knew or met, I sat for a moment in the law school's lounge. I hoped I could recall and find comfort in my answers.

"Neil." I looked up. It was one of my classmates, another "P": Charlie Price. He was a solid, hardworking student—always prepared for class, neatly dressed, easily approachable, and confident in his manner. We had some good talks during the year. He was working at the Department of Justice and liked it. I said I was interested in applying but was constrained because of SCRAP. "In the next week or so, once I'm done, I hope to get an interview." He encouraged it.

The second day of the examination began no better than the first. We broke for a luncheon recess during which nobody ate. Nacrelli was right. These questions bore no relation to a law school curriculum. They were malicious, devised only by malcontents, misfits, and designers of torture chambers. "Probably lawyers," I overheard someone say.

We returned for the afternoon session. I took my seat, pencil in hand, and opened the book. There it was. She had done it. This question was written by my mother. The examiners wanted to know the constitutional origins and current status of the law of standing.

21

WASHINGTON, D.C.,
FALL 1972 AND WINTER 1973

Friendship. October 1972. We walked to Morocco's on Pennsylvania Avenue, a few blocks off campus. It was still dusk. The weather was pleasant—a gentle, cool breeze, like the remnant of a summer evening easily felt. The day before I was ready to start work at Justice, Jeff Gocke, David Shisslak, and John Tomsky wanted to take me to dinner.

Eating and talking were great fun. There were questions about my work. I asked about how life in Crawford had changed. Pasta and bread and wine and pizza were everywhere. We discussed the national election. No one seemed engaged by it. The discussion turned to the old days—the demonstrations, mostly, and some episodes, mischievous ones I had forgotten. More wine arrived: red, pungent, and cheap. I wondered aloud what it would have been like to have been the director in a coeducational dorm. "You already were," they reminded me.

The conversation flowed easily among us as we walked up H Street and headed for Crawford. "Neil," someone walking behind me said. "When we get back, come down and see the game room in the basement. It's been painted."

"Sure." To me, the basement was where clothes were washed, storage bins existed, and maintenance security went to fix pipes and wires. Shisslak walked in first. The basement steps had been painted a lighter shade of gray. The narrowness of the concrete stairwell made me think of fire drills, odors that lingered for days, and noise that echoed whenever the doorways slammed open for the fast getaway after a prank. It also was the closing scene of "The Great Flood" of 1971.

The door to the game room was closed. Shisslak knocked. In that moment, the rest of our entourage seemed silent and farther behind me. It was a surprise party. The room was packed. Morton Branzburg, Tomsky, Gary Wigoda, Peter Hollingshead, Tom Bninski, Stu Lesses, Jeff Kaplan, and a dozen more. I could feel my mind quickening, remembering names and episodes with ease. I found myself wading through the twenty or so of them—including some women there now as residents—all crammed tightly, animated, saying hello, and shaking hands. Someone handed me soda in a paper cup. A toast was proposed and then another.

After a few minutes, Hollingshead called everyone to attention. He asked me to come up front. Everyone moved back a few steps. They fell silent. I saw for the first time that a folded white towel was tacked on the wall. Hollingshead was holding a rectangular-shaped object, also covered. He had a special presentation to make, he said, as dorm council president. No one seemed surprised. The council had adopted a resolution he wanted to read. He uncovered the rectangular object. It was a hand-drawn reproduction of the resolution written in black script, with a gold seal in the lower right corner, framed in wood, painted black, and enclosed in glass. He read it aloud:

> A Resolution introduced by Gary J. Wigoda, the 3rd floor Representative, before the William H. Crawford Residence Hall Council and passed by acclamation the 4th day of October, in the year 1972.
>
> WHEREAS, Neil T. Proto was Resident Director of the Welling Hall Residence for men from September 1969, to June 1970; and
>
> WHEREAS, Neil T. Proto was Resident Director of the William H. Crawford Residence Hall from September 1970, to June 1972; and
>
> WHEREAS, during his tenure as Resident Director, Neil T. Proto instilled a spirit of sensitivity and conditions were generally copasetic; and
>
> WHEREAS, in his three years as a Resident Director, Neil T. Proto made many friends who now wish to honor him; and
>
> WHEREAS, while serving as a Resident Director, Neil T. Proto was considered by his residents as a valuable asset to their college experience; and

WHEREAS, in our opinion, Neil T. Proto was a Resident Director whose services and abilities were far and above those of his contemporaries; and

WHEREAS, Neil T. Proto's lectures on the cosmos furthered the knowledge of his residents.

Hollingshead stopped momentarily and looked at me. I stood there, paper cup in hand, my other hand wrapped tightly around my chin, uncertain about what they had done. Assured he had everyone's attention, he concluded:

Therefore be it resolved by the William H. Crawford Residence Hall Council, that we wish to salute and extend our praise to Neil T. Proto and thank him for his contributions to the Residence Halls of George Washington University, and that from here-to-fore, the enlarged basement room established for recreational purposes be called the 'Neil T. Proto Room' in honor of Neil T. Proto, and that he be declared an Honorary Resident of the William H. Crawford Residence Hall and that Neil T. Proto is invited to take part in all functions, services, and facilities of the William H. Crawford Residence Hall as an honored and distinguished member.

Peter D. Hollingshead
President

He handed me the resolution. No one clapped. He said something about the University Board of Trustees. With both hands he carefully removed the white towel on the wall. There it was, engraved in white on black taconite:

THE NEIL T. PROTO ROOM

Named in Honor of

Neil T. Proto

Resident Director

1970–1972

The clapping began. Everyone raised their cups. Photographs were taken.
"Here, here," someone said. "All right, big fellow." It was Morton Branzburg.
John Tomsky came over and shook my hand. "You deserve it," he said. "Congratulations."

Neil Thomas Proto, Crawford Hall, before the plaque of the newly revealed Neil Proto Room. NTProto Collection, and Courtesy of Gelman Library, GWU.

Others followed. We took a group photograph. Some wanted to see the resolution. Others joked about the years on the plaque. "He was only two years old," I heard someone say. Hollingshead wanted a speech. They all did. So did I. The words came with comfort. I was grateful for their friendship.

GEORGE BIONDI

Early November. I agreed to meet George at West Potomac Park. We had not seen each other for months, although we had spoken regularly. He was finding SCRAP difficult. Three new students had been added. Larouche was now chairman.

It was an easy walk. The weather was mild and the sun high. I walked down Constitution Avenue and then cut through the Mall and along the Reflecting Pool. Despite the pool's beauty, the Lincoln Memorial's splendor in front of me, and the trees' retained red and orange flecks of autumn, all I could envision were demonstrations—loud, raucous, and, at times, poignantly necessary.

George looked tired. His face was worn and puffy, his gait slow and methodical. He was wearing a navy pea coat and blue jeans. We greeted each other, walked along the Potomac, and talked about school and Kathy and the Department of Justice and Banzhaf. "I'm ready for graduation and a more normal life," he said.

"Patience," I said. We talked about the election.

"Nixon, easily," he said.

"I agree." I told George I intended to write a book about SCRAP, a "manuscript" I called it. "George, I don't know if it'll ever be a book. I've got all the notes and minutes and documents. I just want to be certain that if I do it, you're willing to read it as I'm writing."

"Of course," he said with the certainty of a friend. "Is B in this book?"

"George, yes, B is in the book. He's got to be in the book."

"Neil, I got stories."

"George, I got stories."

In January 1973, I found out that I had passed the bar exam. My colleagues toasted me the following morning over coffee. My parents were joyous. I called George. Much was troubling him. The date for the oral argument was set for February 28. We arranged to meet at the Supreme Court. He would talk to Larouche to ensure we sat together. "What's wrong?" I asked.

"I've put a lot into this, Neil," he said, "and I had to deal with Banzhaf longer than you did."

"There's only one issue, George. Standing. That's where SCRAP's got to win. And I'll tell you. Here, 'standing' is something the government attacks all the time. If the Supreme Court is not firm about its position, it'll be a mess. The solicitor general will get his way and so will the Commission and a lot of others—these corporate guys, doing whatever the heck they want."

"Neil, you're ready for oral argument."

"George, look. We never understood that freaking 'suspension stage.' At least I never understood it. But I'm telling you, at some point they've got to do an EIS. They can't get around it. This environmental business is changing. The Commission is a freaking anachronism. George, patience."

"Patience? Neil, EDF is still in this. They'll sell us down the river if they can. You know what I mean. They still act as if we're nobody and they're everybody."

"George, I wish I had something good to say. For now, don't worry. If *Sierra Club v. Morton* means what we thought it meant—"

"Yeah. Okay. You're right."

"How's Peter Meyers?"

"Okay."

"Hey, George," I said in closing. "Don't worry. And George."

"Yeah?"

"Be sure to save me a seat."

THE NIGHT BEFORE

Federal and Supreme Court Reporters, filled with judicial decisions, were piled high on the desk and on the floor to my left. I had been writing a brief. My purpose was diverted from an issue on the federal–state relationship into the judicial writings of Justice Louis Brandeis. I honed in on his views, sitting with my legs folded, my body flush against the desk, and my mind still sharp despite the late hour. *Liggett Co. v. Lee* was decided in 1933.[1] Brandeis wrote a dissenting opinion about the formation of corporations and their continued potential for abuse of the public interest. "The prevalence of the corporation in America," he wrote, "has led men of this generation to act, at times, as if the privilege of doing business in corporate form were inherent in the citizen; and has led them to accept the evils attendant upon the free and unrestricted use of the corporate mechanism as if these evils were the inescapable price of civilized life, and, hence, to be borne with resignation."[2] Such a perspective was one, I knew, Brandeis did not share.

"Throughout the greater part of our history[,] a different view prevailed," Brandeis stated. "There was a sense of some insidious menace inherent in large aggregations of capital, particularly when held by corporations. So at first the corporate privilege was granted sparingly[,] and it was believed that under general laws embodying safeguards … the scandals and favoritism … could be avoided." Large corporate interests, however, were too smart for government or government could not tell the difference between its duty and theirs. The effect was clear to Brandeis, but a majority of the Court disagreed.[3]

"Railroads," I said aloud, stopping and rubbing my eyes. I put the book down and sat back in the old, comfortable, severely weathered leather chair that now was mine. My eyes felt heavy. The tension had turned finally to fatigue but the pensiveness remained. The office was silent. So was the hallway outside. It was after eight. I rose slowly, put on my suit jacket, and grabbed my coat—an old, gray wool hand-me-down with a pair of gloves pushed visibly into its pockets—and placed my scarf, the beige one, around my neck. I shut off the lights and walked out. I needed to be up early the next morning. I was going to the Supreme Court of the United States.

22

THE UNITED STATES SUPREME COURT, FEBRUARY 28, 1973

S olicitor General Erwin Griswold is highly respected among his colleagues.[1] He is in appearance a fatherly figure, a sage perhaps, with precisely the capacity for a wisdom borne of experience that is enhanced by his appearance and by his manner of dispensing that wisdom. His hair is grayish, straight, and still full. He was appointed by President Lyndon Johnson in 1967. His morning coat is slightly faded from wear and, because of it and who he is, it projects a demonstrable comfort, not on him but in this setting. He is part of it.

The former dean of Harvard Law School also is cunning, but subtly so. He understands politics and government but not as an academician. He did not become the solicitor general or survive the Nixon transition without both a knowledge and a skill at discerning other people's motives, ideology, and power and then acting and reacting to them. As I watch him, my respect and discomfort increase perceptively. Within his fatherly manner and grayish tone is, I believe, a mystical character who understands the nuances and broad force of ideas and the means of persuasion like few among his peers. He is more like a sorcerer than a counselor, orchestrating in deft strokes, gently moving and nudging those around him and in front of him. His mystical character also derives a power from another, deeper source. He *is* the United States of America.

I cross my arms in front of me, tighten my body and mind, and concentrate on precisely what he is saying. It is his duty, as the appellant, to begin the oral argument before the Supreme Court.

The solicitor general's history of the case is presented in simple terms. As he describes it, SCRAP did not exist until after January 5, 1972, when "protests were filed by shippers and other interested parties, and environmental groups, including the appellee here S.C.R.A.P., oppos[ing] the [2.5 percent] surcharge on the ground that the prevailing rate structure discourages the movement of recyclable goods and that an across-the-board surcharge would further discourage recycling." We have become mere protestors, one group in a long line emerging during the opening moment of the solicitor's argument, like malcontents and self-interested shippers who remained passive until the 30 days within which the Commission must decide whether the "proposed surcharge should [or should] not be suspended."[2] There it is, clear, simple, and devastating: the suspension stage. He has placed SCRAP right in the middle of it.

Solicitor General Griswold then describes the Commission's compliance with NEPA. As if describing the actions of a different, responsible, and thoughtful agency of government, he says the "Commission also specifically found that the temporary surcharge would appear to have no significant adverse effects on the environment within the meaning of the [National] Environmental Policy Act. And there was evidence before the commission to support that finding."[3] In fact, the Commission "finding" was the *pro forma* "boilerplate" contained in the February 1, 1972, order. The only "evidence" was a mystery to the district court. He is good at this, I thought. He has not misspoken. He has, however, gilded the facts with gold or honey, and I dislike him for doing it.

It is approaching noon. The solicitor general brings his opening statement to a close: "I have stated the basic facts without bringing in the legal issues. These are numerous and somewhat intertwined. Questions relating to the Interstate Commerce Act and the procedures of the Commission will be presented by Mr. Cox. I would like to repeat, though, that there is no difference between our positions, either in substance or approach, and I want to claim the benefit of any argument that he will make."[4]

The chief justice demurs gently. "We will resume after lunch."[5] My stomach churns. I do not like the beginning. The context is set. It is not the one we understood to exist in the winter of 1971 through the spring of 1972. I am not alone in my disquiet. I can see the discomfort on George's face and John's too. SCRAP has met its match. In these opening minutes of the fray, the United States has radically taken command of the rules.

We all stand. I look around as I wait for John and George to say hello to friends seated nearby. In the front of the courtroom, I can see Peter Meyers and Professor Banzhaf huddled together trying, I suspect, to understand what had occurred so far and how it relates to their own strategy. John Dienelt is there too. He is standing alone. The solicitor general and his entourage also are huddled together. On their side, I see a different formation. The solicitor general is in the center and the others—Kahn, Cox, Kaier, and Christian—are looking at him, reaching without touching, his power emanating outward, mixing and blending with theirs. They are, as usual, moving in unison. As I turn away and look toward the back of the courtroom and its doorway, I see a familiar face—gentle, fair complexion, and partially hidden by others moving in and around her as she disappears. It is Kathleen.

"Let's go, Proto," John says. When the three of us get outside, we see that the weather has turned damp. A mist has fallen and covered the steps, ground, and trees with a slight layer of wetness. The texture of the day remains gray and chilled. We walk gingerly across the street to the Capitol and find a cafeteria in the basement. I order soup and a glass of milk. We are in a hurry.

"Well, what do you think?" George asks. I am not sure what to think. None of us are.

"No questions have been asked yet," I say.

"We don't know what the Court's thinking. We know there are basically two issues. Standing and whether NEPA applies," John says, with clarity.

"The Court is changing," I say. "As I read more and more of its opinions, I can see it. The last few years have made a difference."

"It would have been great if Hugo Black were still on the Court," George muses.

"Yeah," I add. "I don't know how he would have voted—well, there's his dissent in *Arrow*—but it would have been great. Can you imagine? Him and Douglas together."

"He would have been for us," George says with a warm smile. "The SCRAP boys."

"Powell is not sitting. I don't know why," I say, looking at the both of them.

"He's a Railroad lawyer," John says.

"It's good for us. He's old guard," George adds.

"Old guard? He just got appointed," I say.

"You know what I mean," George responds, eyebrows raised slightly.

"Yeah. I do," I say, with knowing agreement.

"Standing is the most important issue," I say with certainty. "If we win on standing, then eventually the Commission will have to prepare an EIS." We all agree. I tell them both, as I had described to George alone, that in the few months I had been at Justice, I could see the standing issue was important. "It's raised in almost all environmental cases," I say. "I don't know about the solicitor's office, particularly in nonenvironmental cases, except, well, except he's here and they're arguing, at least in the brief, for a broad principle."

"Yeah," George says. "And he's here every day."

We finish lunch quickly, put our coats on, and head outside. It seems for a moment like old times. The three of us walking and laughing and worrying and joking and learning together, caught up in the commitment we have made and knowing the seriousness of what we have started and want to finish. Now, being in the Supreme Court, listening to the words that would affect the fate of our singular effort, the feeling reemerges about defining a principle of law that would ensure access to the courts.

We get back with a few minutes to spare. I look for Kathleen but don't see her. Her only connection to SCRAP is me. "I saw her too," George says, taking my arm. The courtroom is filling up. We take our seats.

"Mr. Solicitor General," the chief justice says, "you may proceed."[6]

"The first issue in the case to which I will turn," the solicitor general begins, "is the familiar question of standing. We have a remarkable situation here. Five law school students—though I am told they are a changing group, some of them have graduated and others have taken their places—but I understand there [are] still five, proceeding not as lawyers but as plaintiffs, though not as taxpayers, have tied up all the railroads in the country and with the aid of the District Court have prevented the railroads from collecting $500,000 to a million dollars a month for the past [eight] months on shipments of recyclable materials."[7]

He is talking about me. I am the only graduate. I am not sure what point he is making, except it is not an idle one nor is it helpful to us. He also puts the responsibility for the allegations of standing and for the outcome of the issue squarely on SCRAP, not EDF. I like it. The solicitor general refers the justices to that portion of the appendix that is attached to the government's brief and that contains our amended complaint. He reads from it. The words are intimately familiar to me. He makes it unequivocally certain. We are responsible, no one else.[8] "Now, it will be seen that these allegations are entirely general. It is not said which forests, rivers, streams, or mountains. We don't even have a particular valley as we did in the Mineral King case last year.... It's obvious that these allegations could be made by any member of the public who wishes to make them."[9]

There is nothing he says that I agree with. He draws the line sharply. I also think that he is not representing the state of the law. The thought only confirms my sense of his cunning. Then comes the first question from Justice Rehnquist: "Did the District Court take testimony on this—?"

> GRISWOLD: No, Mr. Justice, the District Court not only didn't take testimony, but there is no evidence to support the standing, and the position of S.C.R.A.P. The District Court didn't require any proof even of these allegations.[10]

What a question. The answer is simple. No. There is no testimony in the record. Justice Rehnquist must know that. And the solicitor general—well, we are entitled to have our allegations accepted as true. No one challenged their truthfulness, although we would have been ready if they had done so. Rehnquist knows that.

"Who in your opinion would have standing?" Justice Stewart asks.

The solicitor general answers, "I'm not sure that anyone would have standing to obtain an injunction in this case."[11] It is an answer filled with legal nuances. The question he actually answers is "Who in your opinion would have standing in the suspension stage to obtain an injunction?"[12] But at that moment, I think, Solicitor General Griswold reveals more than he needs to. It is the historical imperative. We are the Commission, the Interstate Commerce Commission. No one challenges the Commission.

Then, with only slight hesitation, the solicitor general transforms this absolutist answer into an affirmative argument. He chides those who "feel that standing is no longer a relevant argument, though I wonder if our predecessors were always that wrong."[13] In doing so, he seeks to place himself alongside the Supreme Court and, perhaps, to remind those sitting before him that precedent is on his side. His is an extreme articulation of what the Court, in fact, has not done. Standing always is a relevant argument, including in *Sierra Club v. Morton*.

The solicitor general continues, "The implications ... should be carefully explored and considered. Before going further, I may observe that if there is standing in this case, it would be helpful, I think, and a contribution to candor if this Court would indicate that standing is no longer required or to say that standing is required and that there is standing in this case."[14] It is a slick correlation. If SCRAP has standing, then "standing is no longer required." He knows that this, too, is an extreme position. The Court will have to wholly ignore the Article Three requirement of case or controversy to reach such a conclusion. The Court has never done that. It could not. In *Sierra Club*, it had reaffirmed the importance of standing. He is painting us as an extreme, beyond the purview of precedent or common sense. The justices react:

JUSTICE WHITE: Would the United States have standing? ...

GRISWOLD: Yes, I think so, Mr. Justice[,] ... to enforce the laws of the United States....[15]

JUSTICE BRENNAN: A person in the business of recycling, as some companies are, would they have standing?

GRISWOLD: A person who had a business interest would have standing, yes.

JUSTICE BRENNAN: It comes down to the dollar business.

GRISWOLD: No, I don't think it would be limited to a dollar amount as in *Sierra Club v. Morton* in the opinion by Mr. Justice Stewart.... [F]or example, a person who owns a piece of land and [is] in violation of an environmental statute[,] his view is going to be obstructed[.] ... It isn't something that deals with the public in general.[16]

The solicitor general pauses for a moment, as if he has answered the question and, in doing so, has touched finally our greatest source of discomfort: Who can challenge a nationwide rate increase? He muses for a moment further, and with the simple gesture of raising his forefinger as if emerging from discerning, deep contemplation, he draws attention to himself—like the teacher, like the mentor, or, to me, like the wizard. "Standing is not a fiction and never has been and should not be," the solicitor general begins. "If anyone has standing to bring a suit like this, it will mark a substantial shift in the balance under our traditional and constitutional separation of powers[.] If everyone is a private Attorney General free to raise any public question at his whim or because of his academic or abstract interest, more and more questions will be thrown into the courts[.] In my view that would not be good for the courts[;] it would not be good for the country."[17]

No one on the bench disrupts the flow of his thought. No one interrupts or questions him. With the exception of Justice Douglas, who is writing, the justices remain silent and attentive. The solicitor general continues, "Perhaps more pertinent, it's not the sort of division of function which was intended by the framers as I see it when they established the Constitution."[18] I feel my eyes tense sharply, sensing a change in his tone—subtle, more sleek. "For the courts today are progressive and forward-looking and innovative. But it has not always been so."[19] His is a cautionary thought, and he passes through it quickly. "Of course, the courts should do their duty. They should exercise their judicial power without fear or favor. But the judicial power does not authorize a general overriding sort of oversight of all legal questions arising in the government, a sort of ombudsman to whom all may resort when they feel so impelled. It was for this reason that the judicial power was extended to cases or controversies, and that should mean bona fide disputes by a party who has a real stake and who can show how he has been hurt. That is not this case with respect to any of the appellees."[20]

His point is a profound constitutional argument: the judicial role and its place among the three branches. The solicitor general is not, I think, arguing our case alone except to place it into a broader context he thinks he could win. He is using his power as solicitor general of the United States, not merely his skill as a reasoner or learned practitioner. It is precisely because he has moved into "theory" that, I hope, he has undermined his own case. Here, I count on the practical experience of Justices Marshall and Douglas, and on Justice Stewart's confidence in his reasoning in *Sierra Club v. Morton*.

The solicitor general next turns to NEPA "and its application to the action of the ICC which has been enjoined here."[21] He begins by describing NEPA, which is "obviously a statute of great importance establishing a clearly stated public policy, and it is obviously to be taken seriously by all agencies of the government." From this seemingly fair recitation, he then moves hard to undercut it: "There is nothing in the statute which limits these phrases to any particular agencies or types of agencies. For example, literally the statute applies to decisions of this Court and, after all, this Court is a Federal agency and if this Court takes an action[,] it can well be a major Federal action. For example, this Court's decision in this case or[,] in the last term, the *Sierra Club* case or in a case involving school busing at least arguably may have a significant environmental effect."[22]

I lean closer to George. "I never heard such an argument." George just shakes his head.

The solicitor general next turns to the heart of the government's NEPA argument: It does not apply at the "suspension stage."

GRISWOLD: "Our submission is that as a matter of statutory construction, the National Environmental Policy Act was not intended to displace the Interstate Commerce Act when the application of NEPA is not feasible in the light of the scheme for prompt action established by the [Interstate] Commerce Act....[23]

JUSTICE WHITE: Is this the Commission's current position on the applicability of NEPA?

GRISWOLD: As to suspension orders, yes, sir, Justice.

JUSTICE WHITE: I see. But not as —

GRISWOLD: Not as to their final action.[24]

I hope this is an inquiry that will lead to our position, namely that the 2.5 percent surcharge is not in the "suspension stage." I move to the edge of my seat. Solicitor General Griswold continues: "[T]hey will develop the materials which as a part of their final action will include an appropriate environmental protection statement. The Commission does not take the position that NEPA is never applicable...."

JUSTICE REHNQUIST: Well, here, literally speaking, the determination of the Commission was to do nothing, wasn't it? It was to not suspend.

GRISWOLD: Almost, Mr. Justice ... the Commission was obviously confronted with the task of determining its duty in the light of the two statutes taken together.... [I]n this case the Commission made a specific finding that the proposed across-the-board temporary surcharge "will have no significant adverse effect on the quality of the human environment." The court below said that this finding appears to be no more than glorified boilerplate. Perhaps this [conclusion by the court] did not adequately recognize the Commission's experience in the field....[25]

He is starting to confuse his own position. If they have no obligation under NEPA at the "suspension stage," why did they make any "finding" at all, and what did they base it on? George moves his hand gently onto my forearm. We know what this means.

JUSTICE STEWART: Do you say, Mr. Solicitor General, that the Commission was obligated under NEPA to do even as much as it did in a statement that you have just quoted ...?

GRISWOLD: Yes, Mr. Justice, I think that they were required to—

JUSTICE STEWART: Do that much.[26]

Justice Potter Stewart.
Library of Congress

The solicitor general seems uneasy. He has been caught, at least for the few of us who believe the Commission has no idea—because it does not care—what it has been doing. "Well, perhaps not," General Griswold responds. "I think that was helpful. That's one way that they can make NEPA not applicable. The other way is by saying that NEPA should not be construed in any event...."[27] He is making rational a process that, in our view, was intended not to include compliance with NEPA at any stage. In their own way, the justices are able to make the most confident solicitor general uneasy. Perhaps it is their way of saying that, in the end, "we decide the meaning of the law."

A red light signals that the solicitor general's time has expired.

Hugh Cox is tall and lean. He rises to the podium with what, to me, seems both confidence and comfort. His morning coat fits him perfectly. He is at that moment more than the nation's Railroads. He is Covington & Burling—powerful in its own right, savvy, connected, and thorough in its knowledge of the law at an expense I cannot fathom. He is not just the supple litigator of a Charles Horsky. He also is Dean Acheson. He is corporate America: the Rockefellers, Morgans, and Harrimans. His presence, his merely being here, has meaning. The thought passes. Another one enters. We forced him here.

"Mr. Chief Justice, and may it please the Court," he begins in the accustomed manner. He turns immediately to his argument. The district court does not have authority to enjoin the Commission from permitting the "interim rate increase and the railroads from collecting it." It is the *Arrow Trans-*

portation argument, and Cox puts it plainly and unequivocally: "[I]t is my submission that even if it is assumed that the plaintiffs have standing, that NEPA applies, that the Commission did not comply with NEPA, even on those assumptions, that injunctive relief was erroneous."[28]

Cox places the full strength of his clients and his power beneath his argument. He moves tightly against the podium: "Now, this is a point of great practical importance to the rail transportation system of this country. This injunction, as it has been said, has caused and will continue to cause substantial revenue loss to the railroads and particularly to the railroads in the northeastern part of the United States who are least able to stand it.... [O]ne of the most difficult and constant problems that the railroads of this country have had for 25 years is the lag, the time lag that exists between the time when they must pay increased costs and the time when they can partially offset those costs by increasing the rates.... The railroads have to endure it.... But the railroads are gravely disturbed by any judicial alterations ... of the Interstate Commerce Act which increases that ... time lag."[29] It is the classic argument once again. This time, here in the Supreme Court and described by Hugh Cox, it has resonance because as I think about it, Louis Brandeis is not sitting as the appellee, preparing at this moment to challenge all that Cox has said about the nation's Railroads. On this subject, at this time, in this place, Cox is authoritative.

He then propounds his final argument. He seeks to transform the Railroads into something they neither have been nor want to be: environmentally thoughtful. "[T]he Court can understand why this situation concerned the railroads and has concerned the rail transportation system of this country because the railroads need this revenue, they need it to ... prevent diversion of traffic to trucks which are, as the appellees say themselves, an environmental consequence. They need it, as a matter of fact, for their own environmental projects on which they spend a great deal of money."[30]

"What gall," George whispers to me.

The justices then force Cox to define his position. He seems to welcome the questions, which begin with Justice Brennan, the author of *Arrow Transportation*: "I take it you are arguing that the fact that NEPA is involved here shouldn't make any difference in the applicability of *Arrow*."

COX: That's right. That's precisely the point. Precisely the point.

JUSTICE BRENNAN: [B]ecause it is an imposition of the courts before the Commission has even purported to take final action.

COX: That's right, and before it has ever considered the lawfulness of the rates.[31]

Justice White asks if there "is any possible argument that NEPA injects factors which the Commission should consider separately and apart from justness and reasonableness? Or would it be a part of that concept?" SCRAP's argument, supported by the district court, is that NEPA had such an effect.[32]

> COX: Well, I would say that if you give those terms their broadest meaning, Mr. Justice White, that NEPA would require ... the Commission in considering and determining justness and reasonableness to take into account environmental factors.... But my submission is that this assertion of power ... is in fact inconsistent with the Interstate Commerce Act and with this Court's decision in *Arrow*.

> CHIEF JUSTICE BURGER: Is there any indication, Mr. Cox, in the legislative history of NEPA that would suggest that [Congress] intended to modify the *Arrow* doctrine?

> COX: There is absolutely no indication....[33]

Cox is interrupted but is seemingly unperturbed by it. Chief Justice Burger states, "Perhaps that's because no one thought freight rates could affect the environment at the time."

Cox acknowledges that that would be "reasonable speculation," and then adds that "[SCRAP's] ultimate reliance in this case is on the NEPA argument.... So that the ultimate reliance on this extraordinary injunctive relief is simply that NEPA changed the law."[34] Hugh Cox's time has expired. The chief justice thanks him, and turns his head only slightly to the right: "Mr. Meyers."[35]

Peter Meyers rises purposefully. He arranges his papers with care on the podium's surface. With deliberateness, he also places some papers on the shelf beneath the surface and scans the podium to be certain he understands its dimension and feel. I hope at that moment that Peter's appearance, radically incongruous when compared to the solicitor general and Hugh Cox, is understood by the justices, at least some of them. For most of the nineteenth century, long hair was commonplace. Only recently, I had read Justice Joseph Story's description of Daniel Webster's argument before the Supreme Court in the *Dartmouth College* case in 1819. Webster had brought the "whole audience ... to the highest excitement."[36] I now look at Chief Justice Burger. It is not likely that he shares my thoughts.

We know that Peter has a heavy burden. He has to change the rules of engagement. George turns to me. "He has worked hard," he says. I nod, place both hands firmly on the edge of the seat beneath me, and move my body slightly forward. I scan the bench to see if everyone is paying attention. Justice Douglas is still writing. He looks frail, his face gaunt and sullen. Justice White has summoned a page and is talking to her. Justices Rehnquist and Stewart seem intensely focused on Peter.

"Mr. Chief Justice, and may it please the Court. Every year this nation produces more than 4 billion tons of solid refuse. Only a very small fraction of this scrap is recycled, even though most of it is capable of being recycled and reused. Railroad freight rates which are authorized by the Interstate Commerce Commission are a major factor discouraging recycling. This is what this case is all about."[37]

It is a perfect beginning. He is trying to change the rules. "Congress," Peter says, "specifically focused on the recycling problem and declared that it was the responsibility of all Federal agencies to, and I quote, 'enhance the quality of renewable resources and approach the maximum attainable recycling of depletable resources.'" He places this duty, and the Commission's conduct as it has affected us, into historical perspective:

> In the three years that NEPA has been in effect, the Commission has failed totally to fulfill this duty ... and has refused to implement the procedural obligations of [NEPA] requiring the preparation of environmental impact statements. The Commission has granted three general rate increases on recyclable materials since 1970. This case is the third, without ever making a detailed assessment of their environmental impact, [and] without attempting to accommodate its procedures to the requirements of NEPA[.] It is hard to imagine a case where both the Council on Environmental Quality and the Environmental Protection Agency have more strongly protested an agency's implementation of NEPA.[38]

Peter next relates this history to the ICC's April 24 order that "suspended" the 4.1 percent selective rate increase but made "permanent" the 2.5 percent surcharge. He is interrupted. The justices are not going to help him make his argument.

JUSTICE REHNQUIST: Mr. Meyers, what if the Commission had simply declined to suspend the rates, in effect done nothing? What would be your position then as to the requirement of an environmental impact statement?

MEYERS: It's S.C.R.A.P.'s position, your Honor, it does not matter what action the Commission takes, whether it suspends or not suspends. The important factor in this case is that when the Commission is ... considering whether or not to allow increased rates on recyclable commodities to go into effect, it is required to know what effect those rate increases will have.[39]

I look at George, somewhat perplexed. This argument is less refined than our position, which was expressed in the lower court, that we were not in the "suspension stage."

"It makes no difference," George whispers, knowing precisely what I am thinking. "It's a cleaner argument. Be patient."

"Complicated," I whisper to George.

Perhaps, as George says, it really makes no difference, not in the short run—*Arrow Transportation* is too strong a precedent—and not in the long run, where I suspect *Arrow Transportation* would be irrelevant to protecting the Commission. In that moment, I lose track of Peter's explanation. He is bogged down within the minutiae of facts necessary to describe the precise location in the Commission's proceeding that probably never will be agreed upon. Then he catches me, deeply, as he returns to the strength of our argument: the history of the Commission's action. Peter tries to draw the Court into this bigger picture as he says,

More important, is the fact that the Commission should have begun its environmental assessment when NEPA went into effect three years ago. It should not have waited until the railroads came to them with their proposed increase. It will always be, in the Commission's language, impossible for the Commission to comply if it does nothing. It will have its first 30-day suspension period ... then it will issue its final order and it will be impossible to comply in that proceeding. And then the second time the railroads come ... it will be impossible to comply at the suspension stage and by the final order. And this can go on forever.[40]

Peter has aimed at the main problem; the Commission's greatest vulnerability. Under its interpretation, NEPA will never apply.

"Are you arguing," Justice White asks, "that if the Commission can't get its job done with respect to the environmental impact, that it must suspend until it does?"[41]

Without hesitation, Peter says, "In this case we do. There has to come an end to the time where the Commission can continue to grant these incremental increases."[42] Peter is solidly in place. The more he finds refuge in the perverse manner in which the Commission operated, the more arbitrary and indefensible its actions seem.

> MEYERS: The Commission didn't say it wasn't possible to comply with NEPA. The Commission has in effect left it to its counsel to make this argument to this Court now more than 3 years after NEPA has been in effect.... The Commission ... has not gone to the President to propose changes.... [T]he Commission says [that] because they have done nothing previously, 'We can't comply now[.]'[43]

Peter is using the "moral imperative" argument. The "who the heck are these guys to say the law does not apply to them?" argument. I like it a lot. Justice Marshall joins the fray: "You said the ICC should have had this done long before this. Is that correct?"

> MEYERS: That's correct, your Honor.

> JUSTICE MARSHALL: Why?

> MEYERS: NEPA, when it went into effect in 1970[,] placed upon the Commission ... a specific duty to encourage recycling.

> JUSTICE MARSHALL: On the Commission?

> MEYERS: On all Federal agencies.... Now, the Commission knows, there should not be any doubt that the railroads, for example, will be requesting another rate increase in the next year or two. This is no secret.[44]

It is a good argument. Peter is poised in his demeanor and skilled in his advocacy. The morning coat would have been a distraction, a charade, a shield. He is candid in a manner that the Court probably will never realize. He has served SCRAP and himself well from beginning to end. When the red light goes on signaling the end of his argument, I want to get up and shake his hand.

John Dienelt stands and walks to the podium. His task, as I understand it from George, is to argue standing. Instead, and in a not uncustomary manner, he begins his argument by attempting to answer questions that various justices have raised during the oral argument thus far.

Justice Thurgood Marshall.
Library of Congress

He first seeks to distinguish this case from the facts that existed in *Arrow Transportation*. He is articulate in doing so, but I know that even Judge Wright had difficulty doing it.[45] I am not sure it could be done now. Dienelt thinks differently. He dwells on the "suspension stage" and its relationship to the Commission's duty to comply with NEPA. Justices White and Brennan engage him in hypotheticals about when NEPA might apply and the arcane notions of tariff filings and variations on general rate increases and seven-month investigations.[46] Chief Justice Burger joins them. Dienelt's answers only raise more questions. Some are put clumsily with concepts and law and hypotheticals mixed inappropriately, and it makes matters worse. Quagmire. Dienelt's time is moving quickly. Peter's clarity is being diffused. Dienelt is finally reduced, no doubt out of frustration, to simply pleading, "Even if they didn't suspend, your Honor, they could do something."[47]

Dienelt turns to standing. He had wanted, he says, "to leave the standing question principally to the brief."[48] He addresses the issue with confidence at first, asserting plainly that the plaintiffs are prepared to prove their harm but, in a moment, he gets into precisely the argument that brings back all the old feelings of distrust. "I believe that there really is no serious issue here," Dienelt begins. "The plaintiffs in this case are injured. They allege injury, in fact. The case doesn't simply involve five law students, and it's not an academic exercise to them. The conservation groups whom I represent [include] 130,000 citizens. These people use and enjoy the environment. There can't be any dispute about that."[49] He has separated "the conservation groups whom I represent" from SCRAP. My lips tighten.

Justice Rehnquist asks, "How was that membership figure established in the record in this case?"[50]

DIENELT: We allege the membership of each of the organizations in our complaint, your Honor.

CHIEF JUSTICE BURGER: Beyond the allegation?

DIENELT: I was going to address Mr. Justice Rehnquist's question. There was no proof put on with respect—no testimony taken.... We would be shocked if anyone would challenge the fact that we represent this large number of members or that those people enjoy the environment....

CHIEF JUSTICE BURGER: They could.... [T]o see if your allegation is correct?

DIENELT: If they wish to challenge such a basic thing as the veracity of our membership.

CHIEF JUSTICE BURGER: Well, isn't that a form, to borrow a phrase that you have used, isn't that a form of boilerplate allegation in a complaint for standing?

DIENELT: Well, it's accepted boilerplate, and it's also something that we can prove if we are put to it[.][51]

Justice Stewart, the author of *Sierra Club*, seems displeased, impatient. It is visible. He leans forward in his chair and looks straight at Dienelt. His hand juts forward as he speaks, finger pointed: "What has the size of your membership got to do with the question? What on earth has it got to do with the question? The size? The number of your members?"[52]

DIENELT: Nothing. One person is—

JUSTICE STEWART: If anything, if [*Sierra*] holds anything, it holds that.

DIENELT: That's correct, your Honor. I agree. I was responding to the point about the five law students. One law student, one person—

JUSTICE STEWART: One law student or a hundred million. It doesn't have anything to do with the problem of standing.

DIENELT: That's correct, your Honor.[53]

Justice Stewart has caught him—Stewart, the Eisenhower appointee, the conservative coming to our defense and the defense of a principle he believes in. I place both hands together tightly, fingers stretching and touching, and then I push hard on my chin. I look at Justices Douglas and Marshall and wonder what they are thinking and why. Dienelt keeps talking, but I do not hear precisely what he says until the argument returns to standing.

JUSTICE WHITE: Could any citizen who pays higher prices challenge the consequence of a price board's order authorizing an increase in meat prices?

DIENELT: I would submit he had standing. He might not prevail on the merits, your Honor, but—

JUSTICE WHITE: You would think he does have standing?

This is our "increased cost in the marketplace" claim. It is written in the complaint. I always liked it and the "urban harm" claim. The Court has displayed little interest in either. Justice White, almost mischievous, his purpose unclear, declares with certainty: "So the Sierra Club or the membership is irrelevant. Any citizen."[54]

DIENELT: Any citizen, your Honor, that's correct.

JUSTICE WHITE: And if it isn't right about any citizen, if that isn't correct about any citizen, it isn't correct about your plaintiffs.

DIENELT: That's correct, your Honor.[55]

It is an effective answer and needs to be said but, I think, Justice White has something different in mind: If the individual members of SCRAP do not have standing, neither does EDF.

"Thank you, gentlemen," Chief Justice Burger says. "The case is submitted."[56] It is 2:30 p.m.

I raise the collar of my overcoat as I step from beneath the Supreme Court's colonnade among dozens of others: a few who are opening umbrellas, a young couple who share a map while pointing toward the Capitol across the street, and a small cadre of students who are dressed casually in jackets and sweaters and who are neat enough to get into the Court but defiant of the wetness and chill outside. Whatever lingering relationship I have to SCRAP is now at an end except perhaps for that singular telephone call that would follow what we all hope is a successful decision. John and George, I knew, have much more to do, including more legal actions that SCRAP has filed against the Commission. I, too, have other responsibilities.

John, George, and I had agreed to meet at the bottom of the steps at street level. I look with futility at those still leaving the courthouse. Kathleen isn't there. When they arrive, John and I shake hands. I wish him luck and express the hope that our paths will cross again. Someone calls John's name, one of the students who had been in the courtroom. I watch John walk away, buoyant, grin intact, probably feeling relieved and satisfied. I am not sure we will ever see each other again.

"What do you think, George?" I ask.

"I'm not sure. Peter was excellent. There was one part I liked a lot. Justice Stewart—"

"Yeah. I know," I say.

"What about you? What do you think?"

I pull my beige scarf higher around my neck. George looks at me with an unmistakable seriousness, borne of almost two years of commitment and hard work and the molding of a special bond in our friendship. "I think, George, that we changed the rules. That in our own way, we changed the rules. I don't know about *this* case, but I think over time."

I check my scarf again to be certain it fits tightly. I hear the pop of more umbrellas opening. At the top of the stairs, one pop causes me to look up. It is Kathleen, her smile deliberate and directed.

"Take care of yourself," I say to George, almost as an aside as I back away a few steps from him. "Give my regards to Kathy. And George—" I say evenly, stopping in place, my right arm extended slightly, my hand and forefinger raised partially. He walks closer to me. I place my arm through his, and we both turn toward the Court. I lean close to him. "We did good," I say softly. "Your parents would be proud of this."

He smiles. His eyes are tired and strained. Inside, I know he feels what I do. "So would yours, Neil," he says. "So would yours."

I turn and walk deliberately up the stairs as Kathleen waits, watching and, it seems, welcoming and weighing my intention. I got under her umbrella. "Can we get out of the 'suspension stage'?" she asks.

"What a great line." I take her arm. "You think I have standing?"

"We'll see. My car," she says "is parked nearby."

EPILOGUE

I nside the Supreme Court. On June 18, 1973, the United States Supreme Court concluded that SCRAP had standing to sue the United States and the Interstate Commerce Commission.[1] The Court's opinion was written by Justice Stewart. He was joined by Justices Douglas, Brennan, Marshall, and Blackmun. Justices White and Rehnquist and Chief Justice Burger dissented; they concluded SCRAP did not have standing.

The Court also concluded that NEPA did not confer upon the three-judge district court the authority to preliminarily enjoin the 2.5 percent freight rate increase during the suspension stage of the Commission's review. Justice Stewart relied on *Arrow Transportation* to reach his conclusion. He was joined by Justices Brennan, White, Blackmun, and Rehnquist and by Chief Justice Burger. Justices Douglas and Marshall wrote separate dissenting opinions; they each concluded that the three-judge district court had the authority to preliminarily enjoin the rate increase from going into effect until the Commission complied with NEPA. Justice Powell did not participate in the case.

As set out below, based on notes from the Justices' papers, Justice Blackmun—who had cited *Sierra Club v. Morton* in finding standing to sue for Jane Roe in *Roe v. Wade*, decided in the same term as *SCRAP*—expressed a special view of standing to sue in environmental matters, but with apparent

Justice William O. Douglas.   Justice Harry Blackmun.   Justice William Brennan.
Library of Congress   Library of Congress   Library of Congress

reluctance sided with the majority decision that the ICC had no obligation to
prepare an Impact Statement here. Justice Brennan appears to have reversed
his initial position that NEPA did require the ICC to prepare an Impact
Statement. If he, and Justice Blackmun, had retained that position, the vote
would have been 4 to 4. The tie vote would have affirmed the correctness of
Judge Wright's decision on the ICC's obligation to comply with NEPA in the
manner SCRAP sought from long before the lawsuit was filed.

*   *   *

The now public papers of various Supreme Court justices who decided
United States of America v. SCRAP include the comments and thoughts noted
by each; how each sought to understand the controversy in the form it reached
them; and how they described each other's attitude about the Constitution,
the corporate and governmental obligations, the Congress's intention, and
the meaning of past decisions. The papers reveal tension and disagreement. A
recitation of the raw notations and some related observations based on what
is in the papers of Justices Douglas, Marshall, and Blackmun makes that fact
plain.[2]

During the conference, Justice Blackmun noted Chief Justice Burger's view:
"no standing," and "Arrow[.] ICC could not get up an impact statement[.]"

Justice Douglas described Burger's view as he "can't relate railroad rate
to environment—if this is standing any one can stop US for anything—
arrow point is tied in with NEPA—NEPA could not get up impact state-

ment reviews." In another note, apparently also reflecting what Burger said in conference, Douglas wrote: "Chief—mad—thinks RR don't involve environment[.]" Justice Marshall's file on the SCRAP case did not contain his conference notes.

According to Justice Blackmun, Justice Douglas supported standing: "standing—people other than recycling factory ... we are all buried in rubbish[.]"

With respect to whether the district court could preliminarily enjoin the ICC under NEPA, Douglas stated that the "AEC [Atomic Energy Commission] got exemption[.] Act is all inclusive—a great jolt to all industry. 42 vol[ume] IS [Impact Statement] in Alaska Pipeline case[.] This rate on the periphery but within legis[lative] hist[ory]: tried to cover everything[.] Let Cong. disagree ... by exemption[.] A Special Master might be concerned ...[.]"[3] Justice Douglas's own notes also identified his position: "affirms."

Justice Brennan, according to Blackmun, stated: "Only a prelim[inary] injunct[ion] aspect here[.] standing—affirms[.] OK & suff[icient.]"

With respect to the meaning of *Arrow*, Justice Brennan stated, "Arrow would govern <u>but</u> <u>for</u> NEPA[.] Is the rate proceeding under NEPA? Face of this st[atute] seems to say so[.]"

Justice Douglas noted Brennan's comments as follows: "There is standing under <u>Sierra</u> <u>Club</u> case—but for NEPA this would be Arrow case on the preliminary injunction order—NEPA has broad language—agencies do not include courts (... said they might include Special Masters in our original cases) affirms[.]"

Justice Stewart, who was assigned the duty to write the opinion of the Court, stated, according to Blackmun: "Standing? Sierra did not go too far, although my language w[oul]d seem to include?... We deal in allegations here. H[ave] to concede th[e]y h[ave] standing u[nder] S[ierra] Club[.] Arrow precludes the injunction. The ICA is specific and NEPA is general, and former takes precedence. Wo[uld] h[ave] to file answer[.]"

Justice Douglas wrote the following about Stewart: on standing, "every living inhabitant has standing in air pollution—in theory he accepts they have standing under <u>Sierra</u>—and that no power to issue an injunction because of Arrow[.] ICC need not file impact statement in that 30 day period—[.]"

Justice White stated, according to Blackmun: "No standing in sense of no c/c, ie no JD" and "No power for injunction[.]"

Justice Douglas noted that "<u>BW</u> reverses—no standing even if there was, there is no power to issue injunction—no case or controversy—no jurisdiction[.]"[4]

Justice Marshall, as noted by Blackmun, stated "S[ierra] Club is read as written[.] h[ave] standing[.] NEPA very broad. Cong[ress] will straighten NEPA out[.]"

Douglas notes that Marshall, "on standing <u>Sierra</u> Club covers it—on merits, NEPA is so broad there is <u>no</u> way out—NEPA should be straightened out + perhaps railroads would do it[.]"

Justice Blackmun noted Justice Rehnquist's comment as: "Do BRW[.]"

"Reversed[.] agree with BW" is Justice Douglas's note on Rehnquist's comments. Presumably, both are referring to Justice Byron R. White.

Justice Douglas noted that Justice Blackmun stated that "agencies are dragging their feet—There is standing here—reverses on the merits[.]" In his own personal notes (two handwritten pages), Justice Blackmun posed questions as well as comments. Among those, he stated that

> "It seems to me this one has a profound policy … here—<u>a new stat[ute] & a new & recognized prob[lem.] G[overnmen]t agencies … are dragging their feet[.] Now is a good time to narrow it down[.] But Close[.] Standing[.] My dissent in Sierra Club impels me to find standing here—easy[.] These people and all of us are users of the environment</u>[.] In any event, the motion of NASMI to intervene should save it.[5] <u>The policy-value of service-theory is a natl policy</u>[.] (Harm to Env[ironment] is not reflected in the cost of products[.] Issue of exceeding JD[.] NEPA w[oul]d seem to require Dis[trict] Ct protection ability[.] <u>Arrow</u> is a bar—this is procedural, and substantive— merely the failure to file an impact statement or an adequate one … —no refund aspect[.] The genl rule is that the statement is reqd—the exception is when it is not[.] On balance … the RR's prevail on the 30-day suspension[.] The 30[-]day provision argument is appealing but not entirely persuasive— ICC can extend or order withholding—this is too far out of line with the more leisurely time requirement in NEPA[.][6] To <u>assume</u> no impact is not enough. (The temporary vs permanent aspect is somewhat troublesome but I suspect impact statement is now to be a way of life + routine— … into basic decision anyway). Preserve the ICC JD[.]

According to Justice Blackmun's conference notes and a subsequently written letter by Justice Stewart to "The Conference," the vote was 5–3 in support of SCRAP's standing and 5–3 that the district court had no jurisdiction to issue a preliminary injunction. Justices Douglas, Brennan, Stewart, Marshall, and Blackmun voted to affirm SCRAP's standing. Chief Justice Burger and Justices White and Rehnquist voted to reverse the district court decision on SCRAP's standing. Chief Justice Burger and Justices Stewart, White, Rehnquist, and

Blackmun voted to reverse on the district court's jurisdiction to issue a preliminary injunction. Justices Brennan, Douglas, and Marshall would have affirmed.

Justice Douglas's file on SCRAP also contains various newspaper and magazine articles, and government studies. They concern controversies involving the following:

- NEPA and highway construction in San Antonio
- EPA's link between air pollution and respiratory ailments
- Natural resources and long-range forecasts on their depletion
- Economics of recycling of metals and minerals from urban refuse
- Energy conservation and recycling in urban areas
- Specific recycling projects in Lowell, Massachusetts; San Diego County, California; and Edmonston, Maryland
- Attitude and regulations of the Securities and Exchange Commission involving corporate disclosures required by NEPA
- Views on environmental matters of Senators Edmund Muskie and Henry Jackson and Congressman John Dingell, especially in support of NEPA's purpose and the importance of the public's role in its implementation

Many of the facts and analyses contained in these documents were reflected in Justice Douglas's handwritten notes for inclusion in his dissenting opinion.

Justice Marshall's file contains a draft concurring opinion written by Justice Blackmun that, with a significant modification, became his concurring opinion on standing (Blackmun also joined Justice Stewart's opinion of the Court on standing, Part II). It appears that Justice Stewart's original draft opinion—not with respect to SCRAP's standing (Part II) but with respect to why a preliminary injunction should not have been issued (Part III)—included the following sentence: "In view of the attenuated nature of the alleged harm and the consequent difficulty the plaintiffs would have in ultimately showing *they* were in fact injured, we have the gravest doubts whether, as a matter of equity, a preliminary injunction was justified upon the complaint in this case."

Justice Blackmun objected to this sentence in his draft concurring opinion. He appears to have been joined in this objection by Justice Brennan (who also joined Blackmun's concurring opinion before and after the sentence's removal). Justice Stewart removed the sentence, as he noted in a recirculated opinion. Justice Blackmun's concurring opinion was published, as modified.[7]

Justice Brennan apparently changed positions from his original vote to affirm with respect to the district court's jurisdiction to issue a preliminary injunction. From the documents, although not explicitly expressed, his change may be related to the narrow nature of the holding in Justice Stewart's majority opinion: namely, that *Arrow* precluded the issuance of a preliminary injunction while a rate request was in "suspension" (being collected by the Railroads but still under investigation by the ICC) but not the issuance of an injunction following a declaratory judgment that the ICC's final approval of the rate increase was illegal.[8]

Such speculation warrants another one: Justice Blackmun's personal notes suggest his unease about whether *Arrow* should preclude compliance with NEPA. Perhaps he came close to deciding that a preliminary injunction could be issued. If Justice Brennan had retained the view he expressed during conference, a four to four vote would have affirmed the district court decision.

In the end, these conference notes and my observations from the papers add to the richness of the story but not its finality. Precedent, by its nature, lingers. It, and what underlaid and formed it, often have an unsuspected intellectual, cultural, and practical life.

ACKNOWLEDGMENTS
AND REFLECTIONS

I n 1973 and 1974, with the benefit of contemporaneous notes and documents, and with events and discussions still vivid in mind, I drafted a
manuscript about Students Challenging Regulatory Agency Procedures
(SCRAP). My primary intent at that time was to capture what I suspected
would be the least-known part of the story: the tumult of the era, roughly
1967 to 1973, especially in Washington, D.C.; the setting we lived in, just
blocks from the White House; and the events, personalities, and choices—
some ethical and moral and others related to family, grades, relationships,
and personal lives—that we daily confronted as students. And I wanted to
describe how those factors tempered and defined our formation and our
decisions about how to proceed, foremost against the Interstate Commerce
Commission (ICC) and the nation's Railroads, when we were carving out a
strategy and tactics without precedent and into an unwelcoming environment of comfortable, arranged relationships. Especially important was what
we were learning and how we learned it during the almost eight months of
controversy that occurred in front of the ICC, with members of Congress,
and with environmental groups before we decided to sue the United States in
the U.S. District Court for the District of Columbia. Throughout the original drafting, I had the full benefit of the recollections and critiques of George
Vincent Biondi, my friend and a member of SCRAP.

Once it was completed, I put the unedited draft aside in order to embrace fully my duty as an appellate lawyer in the U.S. Department of Justice. I returned to the draft only intermittently, aware of how the experience with SCRAP had tempered how I thought about, practiced, and wrote about the law in public and private settings, and how I fashioned my expectations of my students and myself as a teacher.

In 1995, when, in private practice in Washington, D.C., I was representing, *pro bono*, Protect Historic America—a group that included historians David McCullough, James McPherson, John Hope Franklin, C. Vann Woodward, Shelby Foote, Doris Kearns Goodwin, and Richard Moe—in its effort to stop the development of Disney's theme park in Northern Virginia. At the time, I had the extraordinary benefit of having the group's central organizer, Nick Kotz (a dedicated journalist, writer, historian, and Pulitzer Prize recipient, who had been taken by my written advocacy) critique portions of my manuscript. He especially forced me to think deeper about why I was writing, what form editing might take, and how to ensure that *To a High Court* was accessible to an informed readership. Accessibility had been central to my thinking from the outset, in large part because of the interest my parents; my brother, Richard; and my sister, Diana, took in what I was doing and because I had needed them to help me think about the values underpinning the choices my colleagues and I were making.

My editors and sometime literary guides, Barbara Hart, Linda Stringer, Marcy Gessel, and Ashley Young of Publications Professionals LLC, were expectedly thoughtful throughout their review of the 2006, and now this new edition of *To a High Court*. Working closely with them and the skilled craftmanship of Friesen Press was the insightful and practical guidance of Jane Reilly of Smith Publicity. And I'll always be grateful for the typing and research support from Karen Buterbaugh, Nancy Sheliga, Ron Brower, Michelle Rose, and Marilyn Johnson and for the consistent encouragement of my former colleague Suzanne Cartwright with respect to the 2006 edition.

My deepest and most valued gratitude rests with my parents, Celeste and Matthew Proto, whose special place in my life is partially reflected in the story. There was a moment in the late spring of 1981, while I was working in Washington, D.C., when a violent rainstorm began to flood the basement of their home in New Haven. Undaunted, they removed boxes of SCRAP documents from harm's way to safety and preservation. It is not exaggeration to say, this book would not have been possible without their intercession.

I am especially grateful for the endorsements provided by two pioneers in the teaching and formation of environmental and natural resource law: Professor William Rodgers Jr. of the University of Washington (ret.) and Professor John Bonine of the University of Oregon. John Bonine, who was among the bold cadre of lawyers at the newly formed U.S. Environmental Protection Agency at the same time as I was at the Department of Justice, understood the practical meaning of encouraging students to learn the reality of law as I did in SCRAP. The approach wasn't popular, except to students. I'm also grateful for the thoughtful comments provided by constitutional scholar Erwin Chemerinsky, dean of the University of California, Berkeley, School of Law; and the late former congressman and Georgetown law professor, the Reverend Robert Drinan, S.J., who gracefully endorsed a story he'd once taught only through court decisions.

Insightful comments and encouragement were provided by Congresswoman Rosa DeLauro (D-Conn.), the longest-serving House member in Connecticut's history, whose career has been devoted to ensuring public rights and justice, including before the judiciary; the late Leon Billings, who guided the United States Senate in the formative period of the nation's response, in environmental law and policy, to deter corporate abuse and to prescribe responsible government conduct; and Dan Lauria, whose acting and directorial experience ensured that he'd see the human imperatives that broadened the story's appeal and added a thematic reflection of the story's meaning in cinema.

In 2009, Fred Lawrence, who was then dean of the George Washington University (GWU) Law School, and Professor and Assistant Dean Susan Karamanian invited the members of SCRAP to return to the school to make a presentation to students and faculty about our recollections and experience and about the ways SCRAP influenced how we thought about law. It was fun and very special for the four of us who were able to return—including the opportunity to meet alone, our first time in decades. Remarks by GWU Law Professor Joshua Schwartz, a former colleague at the Justice Department, placed the case into its historical and personal context, and those of Professor Richard Lazarus, then of Georgetown and now of Harvard, added a broader legal and cultural framework as well as his own research on standing to sue.

In 2011, I donated two sets of papers to GWU. The first set was to the Gelman Library, which houses GWU's archives. That collection "dates from 1968 to 2006, with the bulk of the material dating between 1968 and 1972. It includes correspondence, memoranda, minutes, reports, notes, photographs, newspapers, memorabilia, posters [from the political campaigns of 1968 and 1972 and the anti-war demonstrations], articles, and the original metal sign from Welling Hall. Most of the material pertains to the political unrest among students at GWU, and throughout the country, during the late 1960s and early 1970s."[1]

The second set was to the GWU Law School Library and includes all the research materials for *To a High Court*; the original documents filed with the ICC; and the various notes, reports, and correspondence with the public, various conservation and environmental groups, and members of Congress. The collection also includes the original "cut and paste" of the complaint that provided the basis for SCRAP's "standing to sue," the papers filed in the litigation, transcripts of the lower court hearings, the transcript and recording of the United States Supreme Court oral argument, and the notes of the various justices in reaching their decision.[2]

The four students who joined me to form SCRAP—George Biondi, John Larouche, Kenneth Perlman, and Peter Ressler—each set and attained a standard of excellence, as well as a commitment to work collegially and thoughtfully, in order to establish and responsibly fulfill our purpose. In seeking to capture the special quality of that effort and the hard questions and decisions we confronted, I sought from the outset to reconstruct fairly and accurately the content and tone of our discussions. I also sought to give full and proper recognition to the consistent encouragement—displayed best at difficult moments—provided by Professor John Banzhaf, as well as the dedicated effort of Peter Harwood Meyers, Banzhaf's special assistant. With respect to a few individuals whose privacy I sought to preserve, I combined their traits with others and changed their names while still capturing the purpose they served in the story. In the end, however, the content of *To a High Court* is wholly my responsibility.

Neil Thomas Proto
Washington, D.C., and New Haven, Connecticut
February 2023

APPENDIX

The following pages contain a copy of the amended complaint in *Students Challenging Regulatory Agency Procedures (S.C.R.A.P.), Plaintiff and Council on Environmental Quality, Involuntary Plaintiff, v. The United States of America and the Interstate Commerce Commission, Defendants*, No. 971-72 (filed June 20, 1972, in the United States District Court for the District of Columbia). It was the allegations of interest and harm contained in this amended complaint that the Supreme Court relied upon to conclude SCRAP had "standing to sue."

IN THE UNITED STATES DISTRICT COURT

FOR THE DISTRICT OF COLUMBIA

STUDENTS CHALLENGING REGULATORY
AGENCY PROCEDURES (S.C.R.A.P.),
    2000 H Street, N. W.
    Washington, D. C. 20006

                    Plaintiff,

and

COUNCIL ON ENVIRONMENTAL QUALITY,
    722 Jackson Place, N. W.
    Washington, D. C.

        Involuntary Plaintiff,

                V.

THE UNITED STATES OF AMERICA,

and

THE INTERSTATE COMMERCE COMMISSION,

            Defendants.

CIVIL ACTION NO. 971-72

AMENDED COMPLAINT TO SET ASIDE AND ENJOIN ORDERS
OF THE INTERSTATE COMMERCE COMMISSION
REGARDING RAILROAD FREIGHT RATES

I.

DESCRIPTION OF THE ACTION

1. This is an action to enjoin, set aside, annul or suspend
Decisions and Orders of the Interstate Commerce Commission, for failure to
comply with the requirements of the National Environmental Policy Act of
1969 (NEPA), P.L. 91-190, 83 Stat. 852, 42 U.S.C. Sec. 4321 et seq., in a
general railroad freight rate increase proceeding, presently being conducted by the Interstate Commerce Commission, and entitled Ex Parte 281,
Increased Freight Rates and Charges, 1972. By order of February 1, 1972
in this proceeding, the Commission granted the nation's railroads a 2.5
per cent surcharge on freight rates and charges until June 5, 1972. By
order of April 24, 1972 in this proceeding, the Commission is seeking to
extend the effective period of such surcharge beyond June 5, to November 30,
1972. The 2.5 per cent surcharge on rail freight charges presently in effect
and the proposed extension of this surcharge until November 30, 1972 are

2.

national in scope and cover the transportation of vast quantities of environmentally significant (recyclable) materials such as scrap iron and steel,
and glass, paper, textile, and petroleum wastes, as well as virtually all
other materials transported by rail in the United States. Plaintiffs seek
an order that the present 2.5 per cent national freight rate surcharge and
its proposed extension are major Federal actions significantly affecting
the quality of the human environment, with respect to which defendants must,
accordingly, comply with the requirements of NEPA at each distinctive
stage of the agency review processes concerning such actions. Plaintiffs
also seek an order preliminarily and permanently enjoining defendants from
further allowing the nation's railroads to collect increased freight charges
authorized by the Commission order of February 1, 1972, until defendants have
fully performed their non-delegable duty to prepare, circulate for comment,
and make available to the public an adequate and detailed statement of
environmental impact and alternatives in Ex Parte 281, as required by
Sec. 102(2)(C) of NEPA, 42 U.S.C. Sec. 4332(2)(C). Plaintiffs also seek
an order preliminarily and permanently enjoining defendants from implementing their order of April 24, 1972, purporting to extend the present
surcharge beyond June 5, 1972, to November 30, 1972, until the environmental effects of such an action can be adequately considered. And finally,
plaintiffs seek an order permanently enjoining defendants from allowing
any additional and separate rail freight increases from becoming effective,
in whole or in part, until defendants have fully complied with all substantive and procedural provisions of NEPA in this proceeding.

2. Plaintiffs hereby incorporate by reference all of the
allegations made in their Complaint to Review and Set Aside Decisions and
Orders Of The Interstate Commerce Commission Regarding Railroad Freight Rates
(in Ex Parte 265/67) and all arguments and assertions set forth in their earlier
official protests to the Commission in Ex Parte 281. Certain portions, however
are repeated herein for the convenience of the Court.

3.

II. JURISDICTION AND VENUE

3. This Court has jurisdiction, and venue is proper, under
28 U.S.C. Sec. 1331(a)(Federal Question); 28 U.S.C. Sec. 1336(a) and 2321 -
2324 (I.C.C. Orders, Enforcement and Review); 28 U.S.C. Sec. 2284 (Three-
Judge Court); 28 U.S.C. Sec. 1398(a)(Venue); 28 U.S.C. Sec. 2201 - 2202
(Declaratory Judgments); 28 U.S.C. Sec. 2325 (Preliminary Injunctions); and
5 U.S.C. Sec. 701 - 706 (Administrative Procedure Act). The amount in
controversy, exclusive of interest and costs, exceeds $10,000.

III. PARTIES

A. Plaintiffs

4. Plaintiff, Students Challenging Regulatory Agency Procedures
("S.C.R.A.P.") is an unincorporated association formed by five law students
from the National Law Center, the George Washington University, in September
1971. Its primary purpose is to enhance the quality of the human environment
for its members, and for all citizens, by (i) investigating the transportation
freight rate structure of the railroads of the United States and its impact
upon the nation's environment; and (ii) by demonstrating, through the submission of formal documents to the Interstate Commerce Commission and other
actions, that said Commission is obligated to take cognizance of environmental
factors in prescribing the national railroad freight rate structure.

Neil T. Proto, a member of S.C.R.A.P., maintains his legal residence in New Haven, Connecticut. George V. Biondi, a member of S.C.R.A.P.,
maintains his legal residence in Atlanta, Georgia. John E. Larouch, a member
of S.C.R.A.P., maintains his legal residence in Milo, Maine. Each of these
members of S.C.R.A.P. has spent most of the last two years living in the
Washington metropolitan area. Each of these members of S.C.R.A.P. has also
repeatedly travelled by automobile from the Washington metropolitan area to
his legal residence, and has spent at least a number of weeks at his legal
residence in the past two years.

4.

The procedure employed by the Commission in Ex Parte 281 caused injury to the organizational interests of S.C.R.A.P. and to each member because S.C.R.A.P. was denied the opportunity to participate in a meaningful manner with respect to the environmental issues.

In addition, each member of SCRAP suffered economic, recreational and aesthetic harm directly as a result of the adverse environmental impact of the railroad freight structure, as modified by the Commission's actions to date in Ex Parte 281. Specifically, each member of SCRAP:

(i) has been caused to pay more for finished products purchased in the marketplace, made more expensive by both the non-use of recycled materials in their manufacture, and the need to use comparatively more energy in the reduction of a raw material to finished products;

(ii) uses the forests, rivers, streams, mountains, and other natural resources surrounding the Washington Metropolitan area and at his legal residence, for camping, hiking, fishing, sightseeing, and other recreational aesthetic purposes. These uses have been, and will continue to be, adversely affected to the extent the freight rate structure, as modified thus far in Ex Parte 281, encourages the destruction of virgin timber, the unnecessary extraction of raw minerals, and the discharge and accumulation of large quantities of otherwise recyclable solid and liquid waste materials such as scrap iron and oil wastes;

(iii) has been, and continue to be, exposed to the quality of the air within the Washington Metropolitan Area and their legal residences. The railroad freight rate structure, as modified thus far in Ex Parte 281, encourages the greater discharge of large quantities of air pollutants such as flyash in these areas to the detriment of plaintiff's health and opportunities for recreation. Rate increases also foster the diversion of freight traffic from rail to motor carrier, increasing the likelihood of an unnecessary threat to human health from increased air pollution and other sources.

5.

(iv) Each of these municipalities is forced to expend additional sums of tax money to store, burn, dump, or otherwise dispose of the otherwise reusable waste materials -- thus increasing the tax burden on plaintiffs.

5. Plaintiff, The Council on Environmental Quality (CEQ), established by Act of Congress, 42 U.S.C. 4342, et seq., is the governmental entity principally charged with implemementation of the National Environmental Policy Act. Pursuant to statute, and Presidential Order No. 11514, 35 Fed. Reg. 4247 (March 7, 1970), it has issued guidelines setting forth how Federal agencies must comply with the Act in the drafting and circulation of environmental impact statements, 36 Fed. Reg. 7725 (April 23, 1971). The Council on Environmental Quality has expressed an official interest relating to the subject of this action, and its absence as a party herein may, as a practical matter, impair or impede its ability to protect that interest.

B. Defendants

6. Defendant Interstate Commerce Commission, whose headquarters are in the District of Columbia, is the Federal agency charged with regulating substantially all surface transportation in the United States, under the Interstate Commerce Act, 49 U.S.C. 1 et seq. As part of its official duties under the Interstate Commerce Act, the Commission approves national freight rates and tariffs and establishes transportation policy for the railroads of the United States.

7. The United States of America is also being made a party to this action, as is required by 28 U.S.C. Sec. 2322.

IV. Specific Allegations

8. On December 13, 1971, the nation's railroads filed before the Interstate Commerce Commission a document entitled "Petition for 2-1/2 per cent Surcharge on Freight Rates and Charges" subsequently docketed at the Commission as Ex Parte 281, Increased Freight Rates and Charges,

6.

1972. In this petition, the railroads requested the Commission to "authorize, on an interim basis, effective January 1, 1972, the application of a
2-1/2 per cent surcharge on all bills for freight services," subject to
a refund provision.

9. The Commission, in an order served December 21, 1971,
340 ICC 358, delayed the 2.5 per cent increase from going into effect until
February 5, 1972, ordered the railroads to update their present tariffs,
and ordered the railroads to submit "a statement regarding the environmental
impact of the proposal," before any actual rate increases were allowed to
go into effect.

10. On January 3, 1972 the railroads filed Verified Statement
No. 37 in Ex Parte 281 alleging that there was no environmental impact what-
soever of the proposed 2-1/2 per cent surcharge. This position was vigor-
ously protested by the Council on Environmental Quality, The Environmental
Defense Fund, and S.C.R.A.P. (See plaintiff's formal protest in Ex Parte
281, dated January 20, 1972; and letter from Timothy Atkeson, General
Counsel, C.E.Q., to Robert L. Oswald, Secretary of the Interstate Commerce
Commission, dated January 17, 1972).

11. On February 1, 1972, the Commission entered an order in
Ex Parte 281, granting the railroads a temporary 2-1/2 per cent surcharge,
not effective before February 5, 1972, and expiring not later than June 5,
1972, _____ I.C.C. _____.

12. Shortly after entering its February 1 order approving the
2.5 per cent surcharge, defendant Interstate Commerce Commission became
aware of plaintiff S.C.R.A.P.'s intention to enjoin the operation of the
proposed surcharge before it went into effect on February 5, 1972, on the
grounds that defendant had not complied, to that date, in Ex Parte 281, with
the requirements of the National Environmental Policy Act.

13. Negotiations were begun between plaintiff S.C.R.A.P. and
representatives of the General Counsel to the Commission. On February 3,
1972, defendant Interstate Commerce Commission issued its findings in
Ex Parte No. 55 (Sub-No. 4), establishing formal agency procedures and

7.

rules for the implementation of NEPA generally in all Commission proceedings significantly affecting the environment, stating that "an agency's
responsibility pursuant to NEPA is not simply 'to sit back, like an
umpire, and resolve adversary contentions at the hearing stage. Rather it
must itself take the initiative of considering environmental values at
every distinctive and comprehensive stage of that process.'" 340 I.C.C.
431, at 440.*

14. Later on the afternoon of February 3, 1972, Mr. Fritz Kahn,
General Counsel to the Commission, entered into a "Memorandum of Understanding" with plaintiff S.C.R.A.P. and the Environmental Defense Fund, whereby
the Commission, through its General Counsel, agreed that it would "shortly
issue a draft environmental impact statement in accordance with the requirements of NEPA, and will otherwise comply with the requirements of that Act,
in Ex Parte 281." In return for what they believed to be a firm commitment
of the Commission to comply in good faith to the fullest extent possible
with the procedural and substantive requirements of NEPA, plaintiff S.C.R.A.P.
and the Environmental Defense Fund agreed not to enjoin the implementation of
the 2.5 per cent surcharge before February 5, 1972, and under such an understanding the surcharge was allowed to go temporarily into effect on February 5.

15. Since February, defendant Interstate Commerce Commission
has apparently decided not to comply fully with the procedural provisions of
NEPA; has disavowed its earlier manifest intentions to plaintiffs to make
NEPA applicable at each distinctive and comprehensive state of its agency
review processes; and has largely ignored its own Rule #250 concerning full
agency compliance with NEPA.

16. On March 6, 1972, more than one month after the last rate
increase was approved, the Commission filed with CEQ a document entitled
"Draft Environmental Impact Statement, Ex Parte 281, Increased Freight Rates

---

* Plaintiffs' allegations that the ICC has failed to follow even its own
rules with respect to the implementation of NEPA should not be construed as
an admission that these rules are adequate to meet the requirements of NEPA
or the Final Guidelines of CEQ.

8.

and Charges, 1972." This document purportedly was filed pursuant to the
requirements of Sec. 102(2)(C) of NEPA and Sec. 10 of the Council on Environmental Quality's "Final Guidelines" for preparing statements on proposed
federal actions significantly affecting the environment, 36 Fed. Reg. 7724,
April 23, 1971.

17. The Commission's March 6 document does not meet the requirements for the comprehensive environmental analysis required of a draft environmental impact statement under NEPA and the CEQ "Guidelines" generally because
it fails to discuss adequately the environmental impact of and alternatives
to the 2.5 per cent surcharge on freight rates authorized on February 1, 1972;
it fails to discuss the environmental impact of and alternatives to the present
rate structure which discriminates against recyclable materials and in favor
of the primary materials with which they compete, which discrimination will
be aggravated by any extension of the present surcharge; and finally, it
relies solely on the parties to the proceeding, rather than on the Commission,
to take the initiative in making the required comprehensive environmental
analysis. In relying on parties to the proceeding to furnish it with even the
most basic environmental information, rather than looking primarily to its own
staff resources for such information as is required by NEPA, defendant Interstate Commerce Commission in its March 6 "environmental impact statement"
fails conspicuously to:

> (a) attempt, in good faith, any reasonable discussion concerning
> the probable environmental effects of the Ex Parte 281 surcharge,
> other than the grossly inadequate apology offered to the public
> and the Council on Environmental Quality that "[t]he imposition
> of, or failure to impose, a surcharge of 2.5 per cent as a perma-
> nent part of the railroad rates applicable on freight services
> might have some impact on the environment; however, based on
> the varying predictions of the parties to date, it is unclear what
> the effect would be." Draft Environmental Impact Statement, Ex
> Parte 281, Increased Freight Rates and Charges, 1972, p.2. Such
> a feeble attempt at discussion of environmental probabilities
> Sec. 102(2)(C)(i) of NEPA, 42 U.S.C. 4332(2)(C)(i), and Secs.
> 6(a)(i) and 6(a)(ii) of the Final Guidelines of the Council on
> Environmental Quality, 36 Fed. Reg. 7724 (April 23, 1971);
>
> (b) expose, in any manner whatsoever, the substantial knowledge
> and expertise of the Commission staff concerning the exact effects
> of rail freight rate increases on the movement, or lack of move-
> ment, of particular categories of rail traffic, including the
> effects of percentage surcharges on such categories of traffic,

9.

which effects may indirectly prove unavoidably adverse to the
environment. Defendant Interstate Commerce Commission is the
largest repository of such information in the nation, and thus
its two-paragraph discussion of these issues in its March 6
environmental impact statement can only be termed inadequate
for an agency of its kind, under Sec. 102(2)(C)(ii) of NEPA,
42 U.S.C. 4332(2)(C)(ii), and Sec. 6(a)(iii) of the CEQ Guidelines, 36 Fed. Reg. 7724 (April 23, 1971);

(c) do more than itemize, rather than discuss in detail, the
statutory alternatives to the present structure of the 2.5 per
cent surcharge open to the Commission, once again calling on
private parties to fulfill the Commission's function of gathering and presenting the economic and scientific facts necessary
to make an intelligent environmental decision, thus failing to
attain the standard of good faith effort in rigorously exploring
viable alternatives to proposed agency action required by
Sec. 102(2)(C)(iii) of NEPA, 42 U.S.C. 4332(2)(C)(iii), and
Sec. 6(a)(iv) of the CEQ Guidelines, 36 Fed. Reg. 7724 (April 23,
1971);

(d) relate, in any fashion, to the present proceeding in
Ex Parte 281, its conclusion that "long-term productivity of
our land and other resources would be clearly enhanced by
recycling and reusing such waste materials," thus violating
the substantive purpose of Sec. 102(2)(C)(iv) of NEPA,
42 U.S.C. 4332(2)(C)(iv), and Sec. 6(a)(v) of the CEQ Guidelines, 36 Fed. Reg. 7724 (April 23, 1971);

(e) discuss adequately the relationship of the 2.5 per cent
surcharge on scrap iron and steel to irretrievable commitment of depletable natural resources such as iron ore and
coal to large manufacturing processes which are crucially
important in terms of the overall environmental profile of
the nation. In devoting a total of 15 words to this discussion, the Commission inadequately fulfilled the purposes of
Sec. 102(2)(C)(v) of NEPA, 42 U.S.C. 4332(2)(C)(v), and
Sec. 6(a)(vi) of the CEQ Guidelines, and completely ignored
the policy provision of Sec. 101(b)(6) of the same statute,
which section states that a central theme of the entire
Act is to "enhance the quality of renewable resources and
approach the maximum attainable recycling of depletable
resources," 42 U.S.C. 4331(b)(6).

18. On March 30, 1972, plaintiff filed a protest to the Commission
requesting the Commission to prepare an adequate draft environmental impact
statement at this stage of the proceedings in conformity with the CEQ Guidelines considering the impact of and alternatives to all rate increases con-
templated in Ex Parte 281 and the impact and alternatives to the present under-
lying rate structure.

19. On April 6, 1972, plaintiff filed their comments on the Commission's March 6th document, reiterating plaintiff's request for an adequate
draft environmental impact statement and suggesting a methodology for the
Commission to follow in conducting the comprehensive environmental analysis

10.

required by NEPA and the CEQ Guidelines.

20. On April 24, 1972, the defendant Interstate Commerce Commission extended the operation of the 2.5 per cent surcharge authorized on February 1, 1972, beyond June 5, 1972 to November 30, 1972, without having first determined, pursuant to NEPA and the Final Guidelines of the Council on Environmental Quality, what environmental impact, if any, will result from such an extension of the surcharge on recyclable materials, and without having first considered, in any manner, alternatives available to avoid possible adverse aspects of this environmental impact.

21. Upon information and belief, because the present rail freight rate structure appears to impose lower overall costs for shipment of primary materials than for competing secondary (recyclable) materials, the 2.5 per cent surcharge has thus far exacerbated economic disincentives to recycling in the present rate structure, and has (a) adversely affected the aggregate amount of recycling of waste materials, (b) imposed additional costs to society for disposing of waste materials which are not recycled because of increased transportation costs, and (c) encouraged more rapid and irreversible depletion of non-renewable resources.

22. Upon information and belief, any extension of an indiscriminate across-the-board freight surcharge on recyclable materials will have an immediate and significant effect on the quality of the human environment because it will (a) adversely affect the aggregate amount of recycling of waste materials, (b) impose additional costs to society for disposing of waste materials which are not recycled because of transportation costs, and (c) encourage more rapid and irreversible depletion of non-renewable resources.

IV. RELIEF REQUESTED

WHEREFORE, Plaintiffs pray:

A. That upon final hearing and determination this Court set aside, annul, and suspend the aforesaid orders of the Interstate Commerce Commission, regarding the imposition of a 2.5 per cent surcharge applicable to freight services, in Ex Parte 281, Increased Freight Rates and Charges, 1972;

11.

B. That this Court issue a declaratory judgment that the present
2.5 per cent national freight rate surcharge and its proposed extension are
major Federal actions significantly affecting the quality of the human environment, with respect to which defendants must, accordingly, comply with the
requirements of the National Environmental Policy Act at each distinctive
stage of the agency review processes concerning such actions;

C. That defendant Interstate Commerce Commission be permanently
enjoined from further allowing the railroads of the United States to collect
increased freight charges authorized by the Commission order of February 1,
1972, until defendant Interstate Commerce Commission has fully performed its
non-delegable duty to prepare, circulate for comment, and make available to
the public an adequate and detailed statement of environmental impact and
alternatives in Ex Parte 281 in the manner provided for by the Final Guidelines
of the Council on Environmental Quality, and Sec. 102(2)(C) of the National
Environmental Policy Act referred to herein;

D. That defendant Interstate Commerce Commission be preliminarily
and permanently enjoined from implementing its order of April 24, 1972, allowing an extension of the present 2.5 per cent surcharge beyond June 5, 1972,
to November 30, 1972, until the environmental effects of such an action can
be adequately considered;

E. That defendant Interstate Commerce Commission be permanently
enjoined from allowing any additional and separate rail freight increases
from becoming effective, in whole or in part, until defendants have fully
complied with all substantive and procedural provisions of the National
Environmental Policy Act in Ex Parte 281;

F. That this Court retain jurisdiction over this action until the
adequacy of all environmental impact statements issued in Ex Parte 281 can be
determined; and

12.

G. That this Court grant such other and further relief as may be
necessary and appropriate.

Respectfully Submitted,

John F. Banzhaf III

Peter H. Meyers
2000 H Street, N. W. (Room 301)
Washington, D. C. 20006
(202) 659-4310

Attorneys for Plaintiff Students
Challenging Regulatory Agency Procedures
(S.C.R.A.P.)

Neil Thomas Proto
George Vincent Biondi
John Eric Larouche

Of Counsel

June 20 1972

CERTIFICATE OF SERVICE

I hereby certify that I have this 20th day of June, 1972, personally served copies of the foregoing AMENDED COMPLAINT TO SET ASIDE AND ENJOIN
ORDERS OF THE INTERSTATE COMMERCE COMMISSION REGARDING RAILROAD FREIGHT RATES,
to the following:

William Cohen, Esq.
Department of Justice
Washington, D. C. 20530

Fritz R. Kahn, Esq.
James P. Tao, Esq.
Interstate Commerce Commission
Washington, D. C. 20423

Timothy Atkenson, Esq.
Philip Soper, Esq.
Council on Environmental Quality
722 Jackson Place, N. W.
Washington, D. C. 20006

John F. Dienelt, Esq.
Scott H. Lang, Esq.
Environmental Defense Fund
1712 N Street, N. W.
Washington, D. C. 20036

Charles A. Horsky, Esq.
Michael Boudin, Esq.
888 Sixteenth Street, N. W.
Washington, D. C. 20006

Peter H. Meyers

IN THE UNITED STATES DISTRICT COURT
FOR THE DISTRICT OF COLUMBIA

STUDENTS CHALLENGING REGULATORY
AGENCY PROCEDURES (S.C.R.A.P.),

                 Plaintiff,

and

COUNCIL ON ENVIRONMENTAL QUALITY,

       Involuntary Plaintiff,

          v.

THE UNITED STATES OF AMERICA and
THE INTERSTATE COMMERCE COMMISSION,

          Defendants.

FILED

JUN 20 1972

JAMES F. DAVEY, Clerk

Civil Action
No. 971-72

MEMORANDUM OF POINTS AND AUTHORITIES
IN SUPPORT OF AMENDED COMPLAINT

Plaintiff S.C.R.A.P. has filed this day an Amended Complaint as a
matter of course under Rule 15(a), Federal Rules of Civil Procedure, which
provides: "A party may amend his pleading once as a matter of course at any
time before a responsive pleading is served."

The defendants have previously filed a motion seeking dismissal of
the complaint by Judge Richy prior to the convening of the three-judge court.
This motion was denied. The defendants have not yet filed their answer in this
suit.

It is clear that a motion to dismiss is not a "responsive pleading"
within the meaning of Rule 15(a), and that a complaint may be amended as a
matter of course after such motions are made. See cases cited in Wright &
Miller, Federal Practice and Procedure: Civil § 1483, at p. 412 fn 94 (1971);
Moore's Federal Practice π 15.07[2], at p. 852 fn 6 (1968).

The only changes in the amended complaint are contained in paragraph two (2) and in paragraph four (4).

Peter H. Meyers
Room 301, 2000 H Street, N. W.
Washington, D. C. 20006
(202) 659-4310
Attorney for Students Challenging Regula-
tory Agency Procedures (S.C.R.A.P.)

June 20, 197

IN THE UNITED STATES DISTRICT COURT
FOR THE DISTRICT OF COLUMBIA

STUDENTS CHALLENGING REGULATORY
AGENCY PROCEDURES (S.C.R.A.P.),

              Plaintiff,

and

COUNCIL ON ENVIRONMENTAL QUALITY,

      Involuntary Plaintiff,

         v.

THE UNITED STATES OF AMERICA and
THE INTERSTATE COMMERCE COMMISSION,

         Defendants.

FILED

JUN 2 0 1972

JAMES F. DAVEY, Clerk

Civil Action
No. 971-72

NOTICE OF AMENDED COMPLAINT

      Please take notice, that the Amended Complaint attached hereto has been filed in this action as a matter of course pursuant to Rule 15(a), Federal Rules of Civil Procedure, by S.C.R.A.P. on this 20th day of June, 1972. A Memorandum of Points and Authorities is also attached.

      The only changes made in this Amended Complaint are made in paragraphs two (2) and four (4).

Peter H. Meyers
Room 301, 2000 H Street, N. W.
Washington, D. C. 20006
(202) 659-4310

Attorney for Students Challenging
Regulatory Agency Procedures (S.C.R.A.P.)

ENDNOTES

NOTES TO PROLOGUE

1. Robert Woodward & Scott Armstrong, *The Brethren: Inside the Supreme Court* (Justice Stewart) (New York: Simon and Schuster, 1979), 18; *Sierra Club v. Morton*, 405 U.S. 727 (1972).
2. *Atchison, Topeka & Santa Fe Railroad Co. v. Wichita Board of Trade*, 412 U.S. 800 (1973).
3. Frank Norris, *The Octopus* (New York: Bantam Books, 1971), 32–33.
4. *United States & Interstate Commerce Commission v. Students Challenging Regulatory Agency Procedures* (hereinafter SCRAP) and *Aberdeen & Rockfish Railroad Co. v. SCRAP*, RG267, Records of the Supreme Court of the United States, 267-15, Case Nos. 72-535 and 72-562 (argued February 28, 1973; 2 reels).
5. National Environmental Policy Act, 42 USC 4321 et seq.
6. Robert Fellmeth (Project Director)—Ralph Nader Study Group on Interstate Commerce Commission and Transportation, *The Interstate Commerce Ommission* (New York: Grossman Publications, 1970), 13–14.
7. *SCRAP v. United States*, 346 F. Supp. 189 (DDC 1972) (J. Skelly Wright, J).
8. United States, Memorandum of Points and Authorities in Support of Motion to Dismiss, in *SCRAP v. United States*, 346 F. Supp. 189 (1972) (copy in author's possession).
9. *United States & ICC v. SCRAP*, Case Nos. 72-535 and 72-562 (argued February 28, 1973; written transcript), 7.

NOTES TO CHAPTER 1—NO SANCTUARY

1. See Elmer L. Kayser, *Bricks Without Straw: The Evolution of George Washington University* (New York: Appleton-Century-Crofts, 1970) for a general history of the university. Today, the university substantially exceeds these boundaries.
2. D. Colen & Henry Ziegler, "SDS—Police Confrontation Leads to Over 20 Arrests," *The Hatchet—George Washington University*, November 8, 1968.
3. Ibid.
4. "Students 'Sit-In' at Rice Hall," *The Hatchet—George Washington University*, November 8, 1968. Similar forms of demonstration occurred the following term (personal observation by author).
5. "145 Arrested in March on Watergate," *Washington Post*, February 20, 1970.
6. Richard Harwood & Haynes Johnson, "Ohio Guardsmen Kill 4 Students," *Washington Post*, May 5, 1970; "D.C. Students Urge Strikes," *Washington Post*, May 5, 1970; Sanford Ungar & Paul Valentine, "Area War Protest Escalates, Rally Boundaries Set Up," *Washington Post*, May 7, 1970; B. D. Colen, "Memorial Service Held for Kent Four," *Washington Post*, May 9, 1970; Leonard Downie Jr. & William Claborne, "GWU Eruption Most Serious," *Washington Post*, May 10, 1970; Richard Harwood, "Some Eruptions Occur at Nightfall," *Washington Post*, May 10, 1970. See also Leonard Downie Jr. & Joseph D. Whitaker, "Tear Gas Routs Rock-Throwing Students at AU," *Washington Post*, March 12, 1970; and Paul Valentine, "20,000 Rally for Victory; Envoy Reads Mild Ky Text," *Washington Post*, October 4, 1970.

NOTES TO CHAPTER 2— BANZHAF AND THE PLACID EGGSHELL

1. Jerome H. Skolnick, Director, *The Politics of Protest: Black Militants, Student Riots, Anti-War Demonstrations* (*Skolnick Report to the National Commission on the Causes and Prevention of Violence*) (New York: Ballantine Books, 1969); Governor Richard J. Hughes (NJ) & Chairman and former Governor William W. Scranton (PA), *Report of the National Advisory Commission on Civil Disorders* (New York: Bantam Books, 1968); Hugh Davis Graham & Ted Robert Gurr, *The History of Violence in America: A Report to the National Commission on the Causes and Prevention of Violence* (New York: Bantam Books, 1969); Daniel Walker, Director, *Rights in Conflict: The Violent Confrontation of Demonstrators and Police in the Parks and Streets of Chicago During the Week of the Democratic National Convention* (*The Walker Report to the National Commission on the Causes and Prevention of Violence*) (New York: Bantam Books, 1968).
2. Bob Dylan, "The Lonesome Death of Hattie Carroll" and "Only a Pawn in Their Game" in *The Times They Are A-Changin'* (New York: Columbia Records, 1964).

3. Abe Fortas (Associate Justice, United States Supreme Court), *Concerning Dissent and Civil Disobedience* (New York: Meridian Books, World Publishing, 1969); William O. Douglas (Associate Justice, United States Supreme Court), *Points of Rebellion* (New York: Vintage Book, 1970).

4. Douglas, *Points of Rebellion*, 79–80.

5. *Banzhaf v. Federal Communications Commission* [hereinafter *FCC*], 405 F.2d at 1082, 1086 (D.C. Cir. 1968).

6. *Banzhaf v. FCC*, 405 F.2d at 1087; Joseph C. Goulden, *The Superlawyers: The Small Powerful World of the Great Washington Law Firms* (New York: Weybright and Talley, 1972), 363–64.

7. *Banzhaf*, at 1082.

8. *Id.* at 1084–85.

9. Goulden, *The Superlawyers*, 362 (and personal knowledge). Banzhaf used the term "Sue the Bastards" regularly in various settings with me and others.

10. See, for example, Edward F. Cox, Robert C. Fellmeth, & John E. Schulz, *The Nader Report on the Federal Trade Commission* (New York: Grove Press, 1969).

11. *Marbury v. Madison*, 5 U.S. 137 (1803), (Marshall, CJ).

12. Goulden, *The Superlawyers*, 366–67.

13. Personal observations by author.

NOTES TO CHAPTER 3—THE CONVERSATION

1. Harry Caudill, *Night Comes to the Cumberlands: A Biography of a Depressed Area* (Boston: Atlantic Monthly Press Book, 1963).

2. Ibid., 75, 93–96.

3. Ibid., 394.

4. National Committee for Defense of Political Prisoners, *Harlan Miners Speak: Report on Terrorism in the Kentucky Coal Fields* (1932; repr., New York: De Capo Press, 1970), v–vi.

5. See, for example, Editorial, "Control of the Mine Workers," *Washington Post*, December 3, 1970; William Chapman, "Bitter Contest for Control of UMW Laced by Insults, Promises, Charges," *Washington Post*, December 13, 1970. Also see film footage of United Mine Workers election in *Harlan County, USA* (Cabin Creek Films, RCA/Columbia Pictures, 1976).

6. "Yablonski, 2 in Family Are Slain," *Washington Post*, January 6, 1970.

7. National Committee for Defense of Political Prisoners, *Harlan Miners Speak*, v–vi. (The excerpt is from "Aunt Molly Jackson's Kentucky Miners' Wives Ragged Hungry Blues.")

NOTES TO CHAPTER 4—
STUDENTS CHALLENGING REGULATORY
AGENCY PROCEDURES (SCRAP)

1. S. Chesterfield Oppenheim, *Unfair Trade Practices*, 2d ed. (St. Paul, MN: West Publishing Co., 1965).
2. National Environmental Policy Act of 1969 (NEPA), 42 U.S.C. § 4321.
3. NEPA, 42 U.S.C. § 4331(b)(6), Sec. 101(b)(6).
4. NEPA, 42 U.S.C. § 4332(2)(c), Sec. 102(2)(C).
5. NEPA, 42 U.S.C. § 4333, Sec. 103; see also Exec. Order No. 11514, (Sec. 2(b)), 35 Fed. Reg. 4247 (March 7, 1970).
6. NEPA, 42 U.S.C. § 4342, Sec. 202; see also Council on Environmental Quality (CEQ) Guidelines, 36 Fed. Reg. 7724 (April 23, 1971).
7. CEQ Interim Guidelines, Section 10(b), 35 Fed. Reg. 7391 (May 12, 1970); CEQ Guidelines, 36 Fed. Reg. 7724 (April 23, 1971).
8. *Calvert Cliffs' Coordinating Committee, Inc. v. United States Atomic Energy Commission*, 449 F.2d 1109 (D.C. Cir. 1971). Judge Wright also makes particular reference to the special and decisive role that Senator Henry Jackson (D-Wash.) played with respect to NEPA's Section 102(2)(C) impact statement requirement and his advocacy for its enactment. See also Dorothy Fosdick, ed., *Henry M. Jackson and World Affairs: Selected Speeches, 1953–1963* (Seattle: University of Washington Press, 1990); Dorothy Fosdick, ed., *Staying the Course: Henry Jackson and National Security* (Seattle: University of Washington Press, 1987). The special role of Senator Edmund Muskie (D-Maine) also is referenced similarly by Judge Wright, *Calvert Cliffs*, at 1125, n. 35. Muskie's history and contribution to environmental law are discussed in "Notes to Chapter 9—Managing the Deluge, Fall 1971," and in "Epilogue" in this volume.
9. Arthur S. Miller, *Capacity for Outrage: The Judicial Odyssey of J. Skelly Wright* (Westport, CT: Greenwood Publishing Group, 1984); *United States v. Washington Post Co.*, 446 F.2d 1322 (D.C. Cir. 1971) (Wright, J., dissenting); *rev'd* 446 F.2d 1327 (1971) en banc; *aff'd New York Times Co. v. United States*, 403 U.S. 713 (1971).
10. *Calvert Cliffs* at 1111. The Coordinating Committee's standing to sue was not challenged.
11. *Id.*
12. *Id.* at 1119.
13. *Id.* at 1119, n. 21.
14. The history of *Ex Parte No. 265* and *Ex Parte No. 267* is documented from Interstate Commerce Commission (ICC), *Ex Parte No. 265*, Increased Freight Rates, 1970, and *Ex Parte No. 267*, Increased Freight Rates, 1971, 339 ICC 125

(decided March 4, 1971, served March 23, 1971), 130 [hereinafter *Ex Parte No. 265/267*].

15. *Ex Parte No. 265/267*, 339 ICC at 131.
16. *Id.* and personal observation by author.
17. *Ex Parte No. 265/267*, 339 ICC at 132.
18. *Id.* at 205, 205–19.
19. Letter from Russell Train, Chairman, Council on Environmental Quality, Executive Office of the President, to George Stafford on October 9, 1970, in Docket File *Ex Parte No. 265/267* (copy in author's possession).
20. ICC, *Ex Parte No. 55* (Sub-No. 4), Implementation of P.L. 91-190, National Environmental Policy Act of 1969 and Related Requirements, 340 I.C.C. 431 (decided January 14, 1972, served February 3, 1972) [hereinafter *Ex Parte No. 55*]. At this juncture, *Ex Parte 55* was in draft form.

NOTES TO CHAPTER 5—THE PARTICIPANTS

1. *Ex Parte No. 265/267*, 339 ICC at 201–19.
2. *Id.* at 203.
3. *Id.*
4. *Id.*
5. *Id.* at 203–4.
6. *Id.* at 204–5.
7. *Id.* at 204.
8. *Id.* at 205–8.
9. *Id.* at 207.
10. *Id.* at 208.
11. *Id.* at 209.
12. T. M. Barnes, "The Impact of Railroad Freight Rates on the Recycling of Ferrous Scrap to the Institute of Scrap Iron and Steel, Inc." (Columbus, OH: Battelle Columbus Laboratories, January 14, 1972). See specifically the Introduction and Summary, 1 (final in author's possession).
13. Ibid., 17–19.
14. *Ex Parte No. 265/267* at 213.
15. National Association of Secondary Material Industries (NASMI), *Ex Parte No. 267*, Verified Statement and Arguments, Before ICC (October 14, 1970); letter from Varcarro to Garson (Office of the Secretary, ICC) re: *Ex Parte No. 265* (July 17, 1970) (in author's possession); NASMI, *Ex Parte No. 267*, Final Brief, Protestants (January 22, 1971).
16. John F. Stover, *American Railroads: The Chicago History of American Civilization* (Chicago: University of Chicago Press: 1961), 123; see also Richard Hofstadler, *The Age of Reform* (New York: Vintage Books, 1955), 58; Richard Hofstadler,

The American Political Tradition and the Men Who Made It (New York: Vintage Books, 1948), 178–79.

17. Stover, *American Railroads*, 118.

18. *Wabash, St. Louis & Pacific Railway Co. v. Illinois*, 118 U.S. 557 (1886); Stover, *American Railroads*, 131.

19. Stover, *American Railroads*, 137–40; Hofstadler, *American Political Tradition*, 193.

20. Stover, *American Railroads*, 118.

21. Ibid., 131–33.

22. Ibid., 134.

23. Ibid., 136.

24. See, generally, Alpheus T. Mason, *Brandeis: A Free Man's Life* (New York: Viking Press, 1946), 199–200. Senator LaFollete and Brandeis developed a close, substantive relationship; see ibid., 367–68.

25. Ibid., 212.

26. Senate Committee on Commerce, *Failing Railroads: Hearings on S. 4011, S. 4014, and S. 4016*, 91st Cong., 2d sess. (Part 3), 1970, 625–982. [hereinafter *Failing Railroads*]; see also Surface Transportation Subcommittee of the Senate Committee on Commerce, *Northeastern & Midwestern Railroad Transportation Crisis: Hearings on S. 2188 and H.R. 9142*, 93rd Cong.,1st sess., 1973.

27. Stover, *American Railroads*, 140 (Mann-Elkins Act, Pub. L. No. 61-218, 36 Stat. 552 [1910]).

28. *Arrow Transportation Co. v. Southern Railway Co.*, 372 U.S. 658 (1963).

29. *Id.* at 660, n. 2.

30. *Id.* at 661, n. 3.

31. *Id.* at 661, n. 3; at 662, n. 4.

32. *Id.* at 663.

33. *Id.* at 673–74.

34. *Id.* at 659.

35. Robert Fellmeth, Project Director, Ralph Nader Study Group on Interstate Commerce Commission and Transportation, *The Interstate Commerce Ommission* (New York: Grossman Publications, 1970), 16.

36. Subcommittee on Surface Transportation of the Senate Committee on Commerce, *Surface Transportation Act: Hearings on S. 2362*, 92nd Cong, 1st sess. (1971 & 1972), 160–67 (statement of Stephen Ailes, President, Association of American Railroads [AAR])[hereinafter *Surface Transportation Legislation*].

37. Senate Subcommittee, *Surface Transportation Legislation* at 168.

38. *Id.* at 161.

39. Fellmeth, *The Interstate Commerce Ommission*, 409.

40. "'Sophisticated Lobbying,' Special Report," *Newsday, Long Island Newspaper*, October 12, 1971.

41. Ibid.; see also *Surface Transportation Legislation*, supra note 36 at 148 (statement of George Smathers, General Counsel, ASTRO).

42. Ibid., *Newsday*.
43. Frank Norris, *The Octopus* (New York: Bantam Books by arrangement with Doubleday & Company, 1971); Frank Norris, *The Epic of the Wheat: The Pit, A Story of Chicago*, Vol. 2 (New York: Grove Press, 1956). This edition contains a note from Norris describing his original intention to publish three books in *The Epic of the Wheat*. The third (unwritten) was to be *The Wolf*, "its pivotal episode the relieving of a famine in an Old World community."
44. Norris, *The Octopus*, 437.

NOTES TO CHAPTER 6—STANDING

1. U.S. Constitution, art. III, § 2.
2. *Flast v. Cohen*, 392 U.S. 83, 106 (1968). Meyers's lecture is based on my class notes and personal recollection. He is now a professor of clinical law at the George Washington University Law School.
3. *Association of Data Processing Service Organizations, Inc.* [hereinafter *ADAPSO*] *v. Camp*, Comptroller of the Currency, 397 U.S. 150 (1970).
4. *ADAPSO v. Camp*, 397 U.S. at 152.
5. *Id.* at 153–54.
6. *Barlow v. Collins*, 397 U.S. 159 (1970).
7. *Id.* at 167–74. Justices Brennan and White concurred in the result but dissented on the question of standing. Their dissenting opinion also applied to *ADAPSO v. Camp*.
8. *ADAPSO*, 397 U.S. at 154; *Barlow*, 397 U.S. at 172, n. 5.
9. *Sierra Club v. Hickel*, 433 F.2d 24 (9th Cir. 1970).
10. *Id.* at 26–28.
11. *Id.* at 29–30.
12. *Id.* at 30.
13. This poem, in its original, is in the author's possession. The name of the unintended perpetrator of "The Great Flood" was removed from the poem to preserve his privacy. "The Sponges" were three residents, each of whom aided in the cleanup and added to the literary lore of the episode.

NOTES TO CHAPTER 8—
THE MIDNIGHT SURPRISE

1. "Roads to Ask ICC for 2.5% Surcharge on Freight Rates," *Wall Street Journal*, December 2, 1971.
2. Ibid.; see also Stephen M. Aug, "Rails Seek 2.5% Surcharge," *Washington Evening Star*, December 2, 1971; "Rails Ask 2% Cargo Rate Hike," *Chicago Tribune*, December 2, 1971.

3. Copy of original in author's possession.
4. Petition Under Rule 72 to Intervene for the Purpose of Petitioning for Reconsideration Pursuant to Rule 101, and for Extraordinary Relief Pursuant to Rule 102. Filed by SCRAP (December 12, 1971) in *Ex Parte No. 265/267* (copy in author's possession).
5. *Id.* at 1.
6. *Id.* at 2.
7. *Id.* at 2–3.
8. *Id.* at 4–6.
9. Petition for Reconsideration Pursuant to Rule 101. Filed by SCRAP (December 12, 1971) in *Ex Parte No. 265/267* (copy in author's possession).
10. *Id.* at 2, 5–6, 11–13.
11. *Id.* at 14.
12. *Id.* at 15–17.
13. Petition for Extraordinary Relief Pursuant to Rule 102. Filed by SCRAP (December 12, 1971) in *Ex Parte No. 265/267* (copy in author's possession).
14. *Id.* at 1–2, 6.
15. Juan M. Vasquez, "Law Students See Ecology Peril in I.C.C. Rail Freight Increases," *New York Times*, December 12, 1971; see also "Students Say Rail Rates Discourage Recycling," *Washington Evening Star*, December 14, 1971.

NOTES TO CHAPTER 9—
MANAGING THE DELUGE

1. Petition for 2½ Percent Surcharge on Freight Rates and Charges. Filed by the Association of American Railroads (December 13, 1971) in ICC, *Ex Parte No. 281*, Increased Freight Rates and Charges, 1972 (copy in author's possession).
2. National Parks and Conservation Association, *Ex Parte No. 265/267*, Notice of Joinder December, 1971 (draft in author's possession).
3. *Id.* at 4.
4. Senator Magnuson (D-Wash.) had emerged as an advocate of consumer interests, especially through his staff on the Commerce Committee; see, for example, Warren G. Magnuson & Joan Carper, *The Dark Side of the Marketplace: The Plight of the American Consumer* (Englewood Cliffs, NJ: Prentice-Hall, 1968); Warren G. Magnuson & Elliot A. Segal, *How Much for Health?* (Washington: RB Luce, 1974); Shelby Scates, *Warren G. Magnuson and the Shaping of Twentieth-Century America* (Seattle: University of Washington Press, 1997).
5. Edmund S. Muskie had a distinguished career as a public servant in the Maine legislature and as governor, United States senator, and secretary of state. He was, during this period especially, as the nation recognized the need to confront the harm of air and water pollution, the Senate's leader in crafting and advocating legislation, including NEPA. He is buried in Arlington National Cemetery. His

archival collection is at Bates College, Lewiston, ME; at the Edmund S. Muskie School of Public Service at the University of Southern Maine, Lewiston, ME; and at the Edmund S. Muskie Foundation in Bethesda, MD. See also Katherine Whittemore, "Farewell to a Tailor's Son," *Yankee Magazine*, 1997. See http://www.muskiefoundation.org (accessed December 3, 2004); Edmund Muskie, *Journeys* (Garden City, NY: Doubleday, 1972); and United State Senate, *Memorial Tributes in the Congress of the United States*, 104th Cong., 2nd Sess., 1996.

6. On Senator Mike Mansfield (D-Mont.), see, for example, Louis Baldwin, *Honorable Politician: Mike Mansfield of Montana* (Missoula, MT: Mountain Press Publishing, 1979); Don Oberdorfer, *Senator Mansfield: The Extraordinary Life of a Great American Statesman and Diplomat* (Washington, DC: Smithsonian Books, 2003). Senator Mansfield is interred at Arlington National Cemetery.

7. Vic Reinemer served as Senator's Metcalf's executive assistant and director of his Senate Subcommittee on Banking, Management, and Expenditures. He co-authored, with Senator Metcalf, *Overcharge* (New York: C. McKay, 1967).

8. *Failing Railroads*, supra, Chapter Five, note 26.

9. *Id.* at 715.

10. James Branscome, "Appalachia—Like the Flayed Back of a Man," *New York Times Magazine*, December 12, 1971, sec. 6.

11. *Failing Railroads*, supra, Chapter Five, note 26 at 625.

12. See, for example, David Broder & Haynes Johnson, "Nixon: New Respect, New Doubts," *Washington Post*, December 13, 1971.

13. Letter from Banzhaf to ICC Chairman George M. Stafford of December 17, 1971 (copy in author's possession).

14. Letter from the director of corporate transportation at ADM to Banzhaf of December 15, 1971, cc to R. L. Oswald, secretary, ICC (copy in author's possession).

NOTES TO CHAPTER 10—FINDING CLARITY

1. ICC, Press Release, "Quick Publication and Institution of 2.5% Surcharge by Nation's Railroads Denied by ICC Today" (December 22, 1971) (in author's possession). See also ICC, *Ex Parte No. 281*, Increased Freight Rates and Charges, Report and Orders (December 21, 1971), 340 I.C.C. 358.

2. Press release at 2–3.

3. Ibid., 3.

4. SCRAP, *Ex Parte No. 281*, Formal Protest in Reply to the Commission's Initial Order (December 29, 1971), 6–7 (copy in author's possession).

5. Letter from Banzhaf to Oswald of December 28, 1971; see also letter from Banzhaf to Oswald of December 29, 1971 (both copies in author's possession).

6. 28 U.S.C. § 1253 (1971).

NOTES TO CHAPTER 11—THINKING AHEAD

1. Robert J. Samuelson, "Pennsylvania Directors Ignored Warning of Ruin, Hill Study Says," *Washington Post*, January 2, 1971.
2. *Failing Railroads*, supra, Chapter Five, note 26 at 778.
3. Ibid., 778.
4. House of Representatives Committee on Banking and Currency Staff Report (Committee Print), *The Penn Central Failure and the Role of Financial Institutions*, 92nd Cong, 1st sess., 1972, 779 [hereinafter *Penn Central Failure*].
5. House Committee, *Penn Central Failure*, at CHART 1 (facing 2).
6. Ibid., Chart 3 (facing 190).
7. Ibid., Chart 4 (facing 312).
8. Theodore Dreiser, *The Financier* (New York: New American Library, 1967), 140, 441.
9. House Committee, *Penn Central Failure*, 313.
10. Ibid., 313–75, including Chart 5 (facing 368).
11. Ibid., 345–65.
12. Associated Press, "3 Charged in Pennsy Bankruptcy," *Washington Post*, January 5, 1972.
13. Charles L. Smith, *Ex Parte No. 281*, Verified Statement No. 37—Traffic Executive Association, Eastern Railroads (January 4, 1972) (in author's possession).
14. *Ex Parte No. 281*, Memorandum of Railroad Respondents, 38 (January 28, 1972) (quotes the conclusion stated in Verified Statement No. 37; in author's possession).
15. Verified Statement No. 37 (in *Ex Parte No. 281*), 3.
16. Ibid., 2.
17. Ibid., 9.
18. *Ex Parte No. 265/267*, Reply of Railroads to Petitions of Students Challenging Regulatory Agency Procedures (S.C.R.A.P.), National Parks and Conservation Association, Institute of Scrap Iron and Steel, Inc. (January 17, 1972), 1–2 (in author's possession).
19. *Id.* at 5.
20. *Green County Planning Board v. Federal Power Commission*, 455 F.2d 412 (2nd Cir. 1972).
21. *Id.* at 420.
22. *Id.*
23. EDF, Izaak Walton League, and National Parks and Conservation Association, *Ex Parte No. 281*, Joinder, January 1972.
24. SCRAP, EDF, Izaak Walton League, and National Parks and Conservation Association, *Ex Parte No. 281*, Formal Protest and Request for Suspension of the Operation of the Tariff of Emergency Change, X-281 (filed January 20, 1972) (in author's possession).

NOTES TO CHAPTER 12—IN PREPARATION

1. Memorandum of Understanding. Submitted to Proto and others by EDF (January 24, 1972) (in author's possession).
2. Ibid.
3. Ibid., ¶1.
4. Ibid., ¶2.
5. Ibid.
6. Ibid., ¶3.
7. Ibid.
8. Ibid.
9. Ibid.
10. ICC, Press Release, "Emergency Surcharge on Rail Freight Shipments Authorized to Go Into Effect," *Ex Parte No. 281*, February 1, 1972 (in author's possession).
11. See, for example, "Students Say Rail Rates Discourage Recycling," *Washington Evening Star*, December 14, 1971, infra; Cong. Record, S1280 (Senate) (February 1, 1972), Statement by Mr. Taft (Ohio) describing SCRAP's action before the ICC; "SCRAP Unit Hits Rail Industry," *Journal of Commerce* (January 4, 1972); "Students Charge ICC Violated NEPA by Authorizing Freight Rate Increases," *Environmental Reporter* (Washington: The Bureau of National Affairs, 1972), 1123 (see particularly, "Among the Congressmen supporting the students' position was Charles A. Vanik (D-Ohio) …").
12. ICC, *Ex Parte No. 265/267*, Order (service date, February 2, 1972).
13. *Id.* at 1.
14. *Id.* at 3.
15. Memorandum of Understanding (signed February 3, 1972) (referenced in *S.C.R.A.P. v. United States*, 346 F. Supp. 189, n. 5 (USDC, 1972) (original MOU in author's possession).
16. "Implementation of Public Law 91-190, National Environmental Policy Act of 1969 and Related Requirements," *Ex Parte No. 55*, 340 I.C.C. 431 (decided January 14, 1972; service date, February 3, 1972)(in author's possession)[hereinafter *Ex Parte No. 55*].
17. *Ex Parte No. 55* at 436.
18. *Id.* at 444.
19. *Id.*

NOTES TO CHAPTER 13—THE SOCIAL FORCES

1. Stanley Karnow, "Nixon Off to China Amid Bipartisan Cheers," *Washington Post*, February 17, 1972.
2. John P. MacKenzie, "High Court Upholds State Loyalty Oath," *Washington Post*, April 18, 1972.

3. Stephen Isaacs, "Anti-Semitism in Florida May Help Lindsay Drive," *Washington Post*, February 17, 1972.
4. "90 Feared Dead in W. Va. Flooding," *Washington Post*, February 27, 1972.
5. Colman McCarthy, "Destroy a Mountain and It's Destroyed Forever," *Washington Post*, March 24, 1971; see also, for example, "Appalachia: Putting a Big Stake on Small Business," *Washington Post*, March 9, 1972; "Harry Caudill and His Land," *Washington Post*, July 7, 1972; "The Strip Mine Debate: This Land Is Whose Land?" *Washington Post*, July 27, 1972; "The Scars from Strip Mining: Can the Land Be Reclaimed?" *Washington Post*, May 6, 1973; "Is Appalachia Visible from Washington?" *Washington Post*, December 30, 1975.
6. *Flast v. Cohen*, 392 U.S. at 111; *Barlow v. Collins*, 397 U.S. at 178.

NOTES TO CHAPTER 14— THE LINES ARE DRAWN

1. ICC, *Ex Parte No. 281*, Draft Environmental Impact Statement, Order (decided March 1, 1972, served March 6, 1972) (in author's possession).
2. *Id.* at Summary, 1.
3. *Id.* at 2–3.
4. *Id.* at 5–6.
5. ICC, *Ex Parte No. 281*, Order accompanying draft EIS (service date, March 6, 1972) (in author's possession).
6. *Id.* at 2, 5.
7. *Id.* at 2.
8. Proto–Biondi Analysis of Verified Statements (in author's possession); March 23, 1972, Hearing Witness Schedule and Dienelt Correspondence with ICC (Dienelt to Wallace [Hearing Examiner] and Kaier, concerning witness examination) (in author's possession).
9. Letter from Caudill to Proto of March 22, 1972 (in author's possession).
10. Dee Brown, *Bury My Heart at Wounded Knee: A History of the American West* (New York: Holt, Rinehart, & Winston, 1970), xv.

NOTES TO CHAPTER 15— SEARCHING FOR COMFORT

1. *Sierra Club*, 405 U.S. 727 (1972) (Douglas, J., dissenting); see also John P. MacKenzie, "Ecologists Lose Suit but Win," *Washington Post*, April 20, 1972.
2. *Sierra Club* at 733–34.
3. *Id.* at 734.
4. *Id.* at 735.

5. *Id.* at 736.
6. *Id.* at 741–60.
7. *Id.* at 726–27
8. *Id.* at 745.
9. Peter Osnos, "B-52s Again Strike Deep Inside North," *Washington Post*, April 22, 1972.
10. Draft Complaint at 2, *SCRAP v. United States* (Docket No. 806-72; challenging *Ex Parte No. 265/267*) (in author's possession).
11. ICC, *Ex Parte No. 281*, Order (service date, April 24, 1971) (in author's possession).
12. *Id.* at 2.
13. Complaint to Review and Set Aside Decisions and Orders of the Interstate Commerce Commission Regarding Railroad Freight Rates, *SCRAP v. United States* (filed April 25, 1972) (Docket No. 806-72) (in author's possession).

NOTES TO CHAPTER 16— FINDING OUR OWN RULES

1. *Port of New York Authority v. United States*, 451 F.2d 783 (2d Cir. 1971).
2. *Id.* at 789.
3. *Id.* at 788, 790, n. 30.
4. Draft Complaint at 10–11, *SCRAP v. United States* (Docket No. 971-72).
5. Memorandum of Points and Authorities in Support of Motion for Preliminary Injunction at 5, *SCRAP v. United States* (filed May 12, 1972) (Docket No. 971-72) (in author's possession).
6. *Id.* at 6–7.
7. Complaint to Set Aside and Enjoin Orders of the Interstate Commerce Commission Regarding Railroad Freight Rates, *SCRAP v. United States* (filed May 12, 1972) (Docket No. 971-72) (in author's possession).

NOTES TO CHAPTER 17— IN COURT: A COLLOQUY IN LAW AND MONEY

1. Following a thoughtful, highly praised professional and personal life, Judge Richey died in 1997. See, for example, Tribute to Judge Charles Richey (U.S. Senate, March 20, 1997), S2723 (Senator Ernest Hollings). Although Richey was not a graduate of George Washington's National Law Center, an award in his name was inaugurated in 2003 for his commitment to civil rights and equal justice.
2. Motion for Temporary Restraining Order, *SCRAP v. United States* (filed June 1, 1972) (Docket No. 971-72); Motion for Preliminary Injunction, *SCRAP v. United States* (filed May 24, 1972) (Docket No. 971-72) (in author's possession).

3. Motion of EDF, Izaak Walton League of America, NPCA to Intervene as a Party, *SCRAP v. United States* (filed June 2, 1972) (Docket No. 971-72) and Complaint for Injunctive and Declaratory Relief, *SCRAP v. United States* (filed May 31, 1972) (Docket No. 971-72), both hand-delivered on June 2, 1972 (in author's possession).

4. Motion of Aberdeen & Rockfish Railroad Co., et al. for Leave to Intervene (Railroads); Motion to Dismiss, ICC and United States, Joint Memorandum of Points and Authorities in Opposition to Motion for Preliminary Injunction and in Support of Motion to Dismiss, *SCRAP v. United States* (all hand-delivered June 2, 1972) (Docket No. 971-72) (in author's possession).

5. Official Transcript at 2, *SCRAP v. United States* (filed June 2, 1972) (Docket No. 971-72; Judge Charles Richey) (in author's possession).

6. *Id.* at 3–6.

7. *Id.* at 7–8.

8. *Id.* at 8.

9. *Id.* at 9–11.

10. *Id.* at 11–12.

11. *Id.* at 14–15.

12. *Id.* at 19–21.

13. *Id.* at 22–23.

14. *Id.* at 23–24.

15. *Id.* at 25.

16. *Id.* at 30–31.

17. *Id.* at 33.

18. *Id.* at 34–35.

19. *Id.* at 35.

20. *Id.* at 37–41.

21. *Id.* at 40.

22. *Id* at 41–44.

23. *Id.* at 44.

24. *Id.* at 45–46.

25. *Id.* at 46.

26. *Id.*

27. *Id.* at 52, 55–56.

28. *Id.* at 59.

29. *Id.* at 59–62.

30. *Id.* at 62–63.

31. *Id.* at 64–65.

32. *Id.* at 67.

33. *Id.* at 71–72.

34. *Id.* at 72, 73–74.

35. *Id.* at 75.

36. *Id.* at 76.

37. *Id.* at 77–78.
38. *Id.* at 79.
39. *Id.* at 91.
40. *Id.* at 92.
41. *Id.* at 92–93.
42. *Id.* at 93.
43. *Id.*
44. *Id.* at 93–95.
45. *Id.* at 96.
46. *Id.*
47. *Id.*
48. *Id.* at 98.
49. *Id.*
50. *Id.* at 99.
51. *Id.* at 99–100.
52. *Id.* at 100.
53. *Id.* at 100–1.
54. *Id.* at 101.
55. *Id.* at 106.
56. *Id.* at 106–7.
57. *Id.* at 107.
58. *Id.*
59. *Id.* at 107–8.

NOTES TO CHAPTER 18—
IN COURT: THE FORCES COLLIDE

1. Motion by Plaintiff SCRAP for Consolidation of Actions, *SCRAP v. United States*, 346 F. Supp. 189 (filed June 13, 1972) (Docket Nos. 806-72 and 971-72) (in author's possession).
2. Amended Complaint to Set Aside and Enjoin Orders of the Interstate Commerce Commission Regarding Railroad Freight Rates, at ¶4, *SCRAP v. United States* (filed June 20, 1972) (Docket No. 971-72). See Appendix.
3. Joint Memorandum of Points and Authorities in Opposition to Motion for Preliminary Injunction and in Support of Motion to Dismiss, *SCRAP v. United States* (Docket No. 971-72) (in author's possession).
4. Official Transcript at 2, *SCRAP* (Three-Judge Court) (June 23, 1972) (Docket No. 971-72).
5. *Id.* at 4.
6. *Id.* at 6.
7. *Id.*
8. *Id.* at 9.

    9. *Id.*
  10. *Id.* at 11.
  11. *Id.* at 11–12.
  12. *Id.* at 14.
  13. *Id.* at 14–15.
  14. *Id.* at 15.
  15. *Id.* at 18.
  16. *Id.* at 19–20.
  17. *Id.* at 21.
  18. *Id.* at 22.
  19. *Id.* at 22–23.
  20. *Id.* at 24–26.
  21. *Id.* at 25.
  22. *Id.* at 28–29.
  23. *Id.* at 30.
  24. *Id.* at 32.
  25. *Id.* at 32–33.
  26. *Id.*
  27. *Id.* at 36.
  28. *Id.* at 37.
  29. *Id.* at 38–39.
  30. *Id.* at 39-40.
  31. *Id.* at 40.
  32. *Id.*
  33. *Id.* at 44.
  34. *Id.* at 44–45.
  35. *Id.* at 45.
  36. *Id.* at 45–46.
  37. *Id.* at 46–47.
  38. *Id.* at 49.
  39. *Id.*
  40. *Id.* at 58.
  41. *Id.*
  42. Letter from Cerra to Judge Wright of June 27, 1972, at 2 (in author's possession).

NOTES TO CHAPTER 19—VICTORY

  1. "Rail Rate on Freight Cut Back," *Washington Post*, Business & Finance, July 11, 1972; "Recyclable Goods Excluded From Rail Rate Surcharge," *Wall Street Journal*, July 11, 1972; "Railroad Surcharge Overruled," *New York Times*, July 12, 1972; Stephen M. Aug, "Court Alters ICC Decision on Rail Freight Rate Rise,"

Washington Evening Star, Business Finance, July 11, 1972; "'SCRAP' Wins Transport Case on Recyclables," *Environmental Action Bulletin 7*, July 22, 1972.

2. *Students Challenging Regulatory Agency Procedures (SCRAP) v. United States*, 346 F. Supp. 189 (D.D.C. 1972). We are reading from the Slip Opinion, reported in *SCRAP*. The subsequent page citations are to the reported decision.

3. *SCRAP v. Unites States*, 346 F. Supp. at 191, n. 1.

4. *Id.* at 192.

5. *Id.* at 193, n. 4.

6. *Id.* at 193, n. 5.

7. *Id.* at 194.

8. *Id.* at 194–95.

9. *Id.* at 195–96.

10. *Id.* at 195.

11. *Id.* at 196.

12. *Id.*

13. *Id.* at 197.

14. *Id.*

15. *Id.* at 198.

16. *Id.* at 199.

17. *Id.* at 200.

18. *Id.* at 199.

19. *Id.* at 200.

20. *Id.* at 200, n. 16.

21. *Id.* at 201.

22. Order, *SCRAP* (Docket No. 971-72), which accompanied the Slip Opinion.

NOTES TO CHAPTER 20—
INTO HOSTILE TERRITORY

1. Letter from Meyers to Arthur Cerra, ICC, of July 12, 1972. The attached list was provided by the Solid Waste Management Office, EPA, in response to Peter's request. See also Informal Complaint of SCRAP Concerning Tariff Supplement 18, *SCRAP v. United States* (August 8, 1972) (Docket No. 971-72) (in author's possession).

2. Application for Stay, *Aberdeen & Rockfish Railroad Co. v. Students Challenging Regulatory Agency Procedures* (hereinafter *Aberdeen & Rockfish R.R. Co.*), 409 U.S. 1207 (1972) (Docket Nos. A-72 and A-73) (in author's possession). The Three-Judge District Court had denied a stay earlier the same day.

3. Application of the Interstate Commerce Commission for Stay Pending Appeal of the Judgment of the United States District Court at 2, *Aberdeen & Rockfish R.R. Co.* (July 13, 1972) (Docket Nos. A-72 and A-73) (in author's possession).

4. Application, *Aberdeen & Rockfish R.R. Co.*, at 1.
5. Notice of Appeal, *United States v. SCRAP* (in author's possession).
6. See note 1.
7. *Aberdeen & Rockfish R.R. Co.*, 409 U.S. 1207 (1972); see also Elise Carper, "Rail Rate Rollback Let Stand," *Washington Post*, July 21, 1972.
8. *Aberdeen & Rockfish R.R. Co.*, 409 U.S. at 1208.
9. *Id.* at 1209, n. 2.
10. *Id.* at 1214.
11. *Id.* at 1215.
12. *Id.* at 1216.
13. *Id.* at 1217–18.
14. *Id.* at 1218. On December 18, 1972, the Supreme Court noted "Probable Jurisdiction" in the appeal by the United States and the ICC in No. 72-535, and by the Aberdeen & Rockfish Railroad Company et al. in No. 72-562; see 409 U.S. at 1073–74 (December 18, 1972).

NOTES TO CHAPTER 21—WASHINGTON, D.C.

1. *Liggett Co. v. Lee*, 288 U.S. 517 (1933) (Brandeis, J., dissenting in part).
2. *Id.* 238 U.S. at 548.
3. *Id.*

NOTES TO CHAPTER 22— THE UNITED STATES SUPREME COURT

1. See Griswold autobiography, *Ould Fields, New Corne: The Personal Memoirs of a Twentieth Century Lawyer* (St. Paul, MN: West Publishing, 1992).
2. Written Transcript & Oral Argument at 5, *United States v. SCRAP*, Supreme Court of the United States (filed February 28,1973) (Docket Nos. 72-535 and 72-562). The author also relied upon the official audio disk of the argument to identify individual justices, whose names do not otherwise appear in the written transcript. Any conflict in words used or omitted between the written transcript and audio disk were resolved by relying on the audio disk.
3. Written Transcript, *SCRAP*, at 6.
4. *Id.* at 7.
5. *Id.*
6. *Id.* at 8.
7. *Id.*
8. *Id.* at 9–10.
9. *Id.* at 10. The reference to the "Mineral King case" is actually to *Sierra Club v. Morton*.
10. *Id.*

11. *Id.*
12. *Id.*
13. *Id.* at 11.
14. *Id.*
15. *Id.* at 11–12.
16. *Id.* at 13.
17. *Id.* at 14.
18. *Id.*
19. *Id.*
20. *Id.*
21. *Id.*
22. *Id.* at 16–17.
23. *Id.* at 17.
24. *Id.* at 17–18.
25. *Id.* at 21.
26. *Id.* at 21–22.
27. *Id.* at 22.
28. *Id.* at 22–23.
29. *Id.* at 23–24.
30. *Id.* at 26.
31. *Id.* at 27.
32. *Id.* at 28.
33. *Id.* at 29.
34. *Id.* at 30.
35. *Id.* at 33.
36. Maurice G. Baxter, *Daniel Webster and the Supreme Court* (Amherst, MA: University of Massachusetts Press, 1966), 31; *Trustees of Dartmouth College v. Woodward*, 4 Wheat 518, 17 U.S. 518 (1819).
37. Written Transcript, *SCRAP*, at 33.
38. *Id.* at 34.
39. *Id.* at 34–36.
40. *Id.* at 40.
41. *Id.*
42. *Id.* at 41.
43. *Id.* at 42.
44. *Id.* at 43.
45. *Id.* at 46–52.
46. *Id.* at 52–58.
47. *Id.* at 52.
48. *Id.* at 58.
49. *Id.*
50. *Id.* at 58–59.
51. *Id.* at 59.

52. *Id.* at 60.
53. *Id.*
54. *Id.* at 61.
55. *Id.*
56. *Id.* at 63.

NOTES TO EPILOGUE

1. *United States of America v. Students Challenging Regulatory Agency Procedures (SCRAP)*, 412 U.S. 669 (1973).
2. William O. Douglas Papers, Manuscript Division, Library of Congress, Washington, D.C.; Thurgood Marshall Papers, Manuscript Division, Library of Congress, Washington, D.C.; and Harry A. Blackmun Papers, Manuscript Division, Library of Congress, Washington, D.C. This inquiry, recently undertaken, is deliberately cautionary and preliminary in nature: The handwritten notations are not always easily or even decipherable, and the files designated with the SCRAP case numbers do not appear to be complete. The papers of Chief Justice Burger are in St. Paul, Minnesota; Justice Stewart's papers are at Yale University.
3. Indecipherable words are identified with ellipsis. To provide clarity for the reader, I have added a period [.] where it appears a thought ended. In a limited way, I bracketed the full name of an abbreviated reference to a well-known agency or term. I did not seek to correct the grammar or add (sic), for what is obviously shorthand or deliberately cryptic notes. When a comment is underlined, it is because it was underlined in the original.
4. Justice Douglas's notes appear to explain Justice Blackmun's use of "c/c" (presumably "case of controversy") and "JD" (presumably "jurisdiction").
5. NASMI did not participate in the district court in any manner. Before the Supreme Court, it filed an *amicus curiae* brief in support of SCRAP (in author's possession). Justice Blackmun may have been referring to the fact that NASMI and three individual shippers had intervened in the second SCRAP suit filed in the district court that challenged what had become, indisputably, a permanent rate increase.
6. Adjacent to this note, beginning with "The 30[-]day provision" and ending with "requirement in NEPA," is a question mark.
7. Justice Blackmun's draft concurring opinion quoting this sentence is included in Justice Marshall's *SCRAP* file, although the stamp on it suggests it was circulated to all the Justices. Justice Brennan's agreement with Blackmun's objection is noted in a hand-written exchange with Justice Blackmun ("I agree and fully approve your change—Bill"), written in response to an explanation by Blackmun to Brennan as to why he was modifying his draft concurring opinion in response to Justice Stewart's omission of the sentence. Justice Stewart's recirculated

opinion, which precedes Brennan's handwritten exchange with Blackmun, also contains a handwritten note ("omission") at the outset of Part III of his opinion as ultimately published.

8. In 1963, Justice Brennan wrote the Court's opinion in *Arrow Transportation*.

NOTES TO ACKNOWLEDGMENTS AND REFLECTIONS

1. The papers are described online at https://searcharchives.library.gwu.edu /repositories/2/resources/424.

2. The papers are described online at https://www.law.gwu.edu/neil-thomas-proto scrap-papers.

INDEX

Note: Illustrations are indicated by page numbers in *italics*.

AAR. *See* Association of American Railroads (AAR)
Abernathy, Ralph, 128
Acheson, Dean, 58–59, 111
Action for Smoking and Health (ASH), 94–96
AEC. *See* Atomic Energy Commission (AEC)
Anderson, Sherwood, 18
Appalachia, 31, 96, 105, 165
Archer-Daniels-Midland Company, 125–26
Arrow Transportation Co. v. Southern Railway Co., 66, 111, 133, 174–75, 183, 198, 229, 247, 257, 259, 263, 268, 309n8
in complaint, 188–89
before Judge Richey, 200
significance of, 57–59

at Supreme Court, 253–55
ash, 38, 47–48, 104
ASH. *See* Action for Smoking and Health (ASH)
Association of American Railroads (AAR), 37–38, 59–60, 95, 109
Association of Data Processing Service Organizations v. Camp, Comptroller of the Currency, 69, 71, 179–80, 183, 192, 228
Atchison, Topeka and Santa Fe Railroad Company v. Wichita Board of Trade, xvi–xvii
Atkeson, Timothy, 145, 185
Atomic Energy Commission (AEC), 33–34

Bacon Hall, 9–10, 98, 117, 139, 187
Baltimore Gas and Electric (BG&E), 33
Bamford, Robert C., 137
banks, 143

Banzhaf, John III, 11–15, *12,* 34,
    67–68, 71, 93–96, 98, 101, 107,
    112–14, 117, 121–22, 125,
    129–30, 137–38, 185, 195,
    197–99, 206–7, 212–13
    Interstate Commerce Commission
    and, 149–53
    in origin of idea, 26–28
    SCRAP and, 41–44
Barlow v. Collins, 69–70, 165, 179–80,
    183, 192, 228
Barron, Jerry, 26
Baylor, Warner L., 109
Bazelon, David, 13, 196, 235
Bentley, Caroline, 54, 73, 85, 115, 170
Bevan, David, 141–43
BG&E. *See* Baltimore Gas and Electric
    (BG&E)
Biondi, George, x, xvi, xvii, *23,* 23–26,
    28–31, 34–57, 60–62, 65–67,
    71–85, 91–101, 103, 105–7,
    109–33, 136–37, 139–40, 144–
    48, 150–51, 154–57, 167–72,
    175, 177–85, 187–93, 195–97,
    199, 206–10, 213–16, 223–24,
    226–31, 235–37, 242–43,
    247–48, 251–52, 262
Biondi, Kathy, 53–54, 80
Black, Hugo, 58, 69
Blackmun, Harry, 179–80, 263–64,
    264, 265–67, 308n7
Black Panthers, 10
Bninski, Tom, 240
botulism, 29–30
Boyle, Tony, 19
Brandeis, Louis, xvi, 56–57, 141, 181,
    244
Brandeis: A Free Man's Life (Mason), 57
Branzburg, Morton, 87–88, 90, 240,
    241
Brennan, William J., xvi, 58, 69–70,
    179–80, 250, 254–55, 259,

    263–64, *264,* 265, 267–68,
    309n7–309n8
Brown, Cliff, 6, 87–89
Bryan, William Jennings, xvi–xvii, 56
Burger, Warren, xvii, *xvii,* 69, 179,
    234–36, 255, 260, 263–64,
    266–67, 308n2

Calhoun Hall, 5–6
*Calvert Cliffs Coordinating Committee
    v. Atomic Energy Commission,*
    33–35, 39–40, 57, 145, 204,
    206, 215, 217, 219, 292n8,
    292n10
Cambodia, 5
Campbell Soup Company, 13–14
Carmichael, Stokely, 128
Caudill, Harry, 17–18, 20, 123, 162,
    174–75
CDU. *See* Civil Disturbance Unit
    (CDU)
CEQ. *See* Council on Environmental
    Quality (CEQ)
Cerra, Art, 152–53, 155, 216, 219–21,
    224, 226–27
Chase Manhattan, 143
Chiang Kai-shek, 159
China, 159
Chou En-lai, 159
Christian, Betty Jo, 152–53, 155
cigarettes, 12–13
Circle Theatre, 2–3, 159
City of New York v. United States, 206–7
Civil Disturbance Unit (CDU), *3,* 3–4,
    6, 20–21
Clark, Thomas, 58
climate change, xi
Cohen, William, 201–2, 216, 221–22,
    224
*Concerning Dissent and Civil Disobedi-
    ence* (Fortas), 11
Continental Illinois National Bank, 143

Council on Environmental Quality (CEQ), 38–39, 47, 65, 102, 104, 145–46, 185, 191, 204, 217

Covington & Burling, xviii, 34, 58, 111, 151, 179, 197, 226, 253

Cox, Hugh B., xviii, 253–55

Cumberlands, 17–18

Cutler, Herschel, 49–51, 60, 62, 82

Davey, James F., 193

Democratic National Convention (1968), 10

Department of Justice (DOJ), x, 179, 238, 242, 271

Department of Transportation (DOT), 47, 120, 122

Dienelt, John, 111, 113, 129, 148, 151–54, 171–72, 197, 207–8, 258–59, 261

Dingell, John D., 117

DOJ. See Department of Justice (DOJ)

Dos Passos, John, 18

DOT. See Department of Transportation (DOT)

Douglas, William O., xv–xvi, 11, 34, 69–70, 165, 179–80, 250–51, 263–67, 264

Dreiser, Theodore, xvi–xvii, 18, 20, 142, 162

Duluth, Missabe, and Iron Range Railway, 51, 60

Dylan, Bob, 10

Eastern and Western Railroads, 36

EDF. See Environmental Defense Fund (EDF)

EIS. See environmental impact statement (EIS)

Eisenhower, Dwight D., x

Environmental Defense Fund (EDF), 116, 119, 123, 138–39, 147, 180

bombshell with, 129–30

confrontation, 170–72

Ex Parte 55 and, 197

Ex Parte 281 and, 146

joins with SCRAP, 111–12

National Parks and Conservation Association and, 115

SCRAP and, 148–49

environmental impact statement (EIS), 32, 39, 60, 65–66, 104, 114, 145, 151, 156, 167–70, 184, 220, 227, 248

Environmental Protection Agency (EPA), xi, 204–5, 220–21, 233, 236

EPA. See Environmental Protection Agency (EPA)

Epic of the Wheat, The (Norris), 63

Ex Parte 55, 39, 46, 155, 197, 208, 293n20

Ex Parte 265/267, 36–37, 39–40, 46, 48, 50, 65–66, 74, 91, 104–5, 113–14, 125, 133–34, 136–37, 144–45, 148, 150, 181–83, 185, 192, 226, 292n14

Ex Parte 270, 220

Ex Parte 281, 113–14, 125, 148, 153–54, 181, 184–85, 187, 192, 199–200, 204–5, 218

Fairness Doctrine, 12–13

FCC. See Federal Communications Commission (FCC)

Federal Communications Commission (FCC), 12–13, 29, 149, 207

Federal Power Commission (FPC), 145

Federal Trade Commission (FTC), 13–14, 29

Flannery, Thomas, 217, 218

Flast v. Cohen, 165

fly ash, 38, 47–48, 104

Food and Agriculture Act of 1965, 70

Ford, Gerald, xv–xvi

Fortas, Abe, 11
Fourteenth Amendment, 104
FPC. *See* Federal Power Commission
   (FPC)
Freedman, Monroe, 15
freight rates, 34–37, 45–47, 50, 58, 66,
   91, 99–102, 149, 191, 230–31
FTC. *See* Federal Trade Commission
   (FTC)

George Washington University (GWU),
   v, vi, 1–4, *3,* 7, *21,* 301n1
global warming, xi
Gocke, Jeff, 54, 60, 63, 73, 123–24,
   163, 176, 239
Gould, George J., 56
Goulden, Joseph, 14
*Green County Planning Board v. Federal
   Power Commission,* 145–46,
   298n20
Greenhouse, Linda, xi
Griswold, Erwin, xviii, *xviii,* 181,
   245–46, 249–50, 252–53
Guthrie, Woody, 10

Hanson, John, 6, 79
Harlan, John, 69
Harriman, Averell, 5
Harriman, E. H., 56
Harris, Louis A., 137
Harris, Patricia, 115
Hartke, Vance, 120, 124
Hatfield, Mark, 5
Hechler, Ken, 175
Hodge, Charles, 142–43
Hollingshead, Peter, 240–41
Horsky, Charles, 197, *197,* 199,
   209–12, 216, 222–23, 227–28
Humphrey, Hubert H., 124

ICC. *See* Interstate Commerce Commission (ICC)
inequity, 10

Institute of Scrap Iron and Steel, 38, 47,
   136–37
Interstate Commerce Act of 1887, x,
   97, 265
Interstate Commerce Commission
   (ICC), ix, xi, xviii, xix, 46–47,
   51–52, 82, 122
   Council on Environmental Quality
      and, 145–46
   defies National Environmental Pol-
      icy Act, 167–78
   initial focus on, 30
   joinder document and, 116
   makes move, 149–51
   Mansfield and, 119
   National Environmental Policy Act
      and, 32, 133
   in petition, 102, 104–5
   power and significance of, 34–42
   rates and, 55–57
   recyclables and, 231, 234
   as violating National Environmental
      Policy Act, 229–30
Izaak Walton League, 115–17, 119,
   146, 180

Jackson, Henry, 292n8
Jackson, Robert, xvi
Johnson, Lyndon, 245
Josephson, Matthew, 180–81

Kahn, Fritz, 152–55, 191, 197–201,
   212, 226, 237
Kaier, Edward A., 59, 173–74, 237
Kaplan, Jeff, 240
Kennedy, Ethel, 5
Kennedy, John F., 33
Kennedy, Robert, xvi, 5, 10, 128
Kennedy, Ted, 121
Kent State, 5
Khrushchev, Nikita, 159
King, Coretta Scott, 5
King, Martin Luther Jr., 10, 86

Kluszewski, Ted, 11
Kramer, Robert, 15

Lang, Scott, 197, 199, 218, 224
Larouche, John, x, xvi, 29–33, 40–42,
    44, 47–48, 51, 53, 65–66, 68,
    74–78, 82, 91–101, 105–6,
    111–17, 120–23, 129–30, 133,
    139–40, 151, 167–71, 174, 179,
    182, 184, 187–89, 208, 247,
    262
Lassiter, Olbert F., 143
Lauria, Dan, xi
Lenin, Vladimir, 159
Lesses, Stu, 240
Leventhal, Harold, 196
Liggett Co. v. Lee, 244
Lindsay, John, 124, 161
Liptak, Adam, x–xi

Magnuson, Warren G., 117, 296n4
Mansfield, Mike, 119
Marbury v. Madison, 14
Marshall, John, 14, 69
Marshall, Thurgood, xvi, 179, 251,
    258, 259, 263, 266–67, 308n7
Marvin Center, 21
Marx, Karl, 159
Marxism, 162
Mason, Alpheus Thomas, 57
Massachusetts v. EPA, xi, xiv
McCarthy, Joseph, 3
McGovern, George S., 124
McKeeley, Kathleen, 21, 56, 82–83,
    137–38, 171, 225, 247, 262
memorandum of understanding
    (MOU), 138, 146, 148–49, 151,
    153–56, 168, 219, 227, 299n15
Merichem Company, 46, 207
Metcalf, Lee, 117–19, 180
Meyers, Peter Harwood, xviii, xviii–xix,
    27–29, 41–49, 52, 66–78, 84,
    92–94, 96–97, 100–103, 106,

    112–13, 125, 129, 151, 175,
    178, 182–83, 187–92, 195–98,
    202–6, 203, 215–18, 224, 231,
    234–35, 243, 247, 255–58, 262,
    295n2
Mitchell, John, 19
Mitchell Hall, 2
Moore, William H., 56
Morgan, J. P. Sr., 56–57
Morgan Guaranty Trust, 143
MOU. *See* memorandum of under-
    standing (MOU)
Muskie, Edmund S., 117, 124, 296n5

Nacrelli, Joe, 214, 225–26, 238
Nader, Ralph, xix, 14, 34, 36, 55, 59,
    81, 162, 165, 180–81
NASMI. *See* National Association of
    Secondary Material Industries
    (NASMI)
National Association of Secondary Ma-
    terial Industries (NASMI), 38,
    46, 51, 55, 60–62, 156, 308n5
National Commission on the Causes
    and Prevention of Violence, 10
National Environmental Policy Act
    (NEPA), xix, 46, 62, 97, 145,
    153, 156, 292n8, 296n5
  Burger on, 236
  case under, 188
  compliance with, 39, 45, 47–48,
    191, 223
  Council on Environmental Quality
    and, 185
  environmental impact statement
    and, 42, 60, 114, 144
  government argument on, 251–55
  ICC in violation of, 229–30
  initial focus on, 31
  Interstate Commerce Commission
    and, 32, 133
  Interstate Commerce Commission
    defies, 35, 167–78

Judge Wright on, 34
Meyers on, 257–58
in petition, 104
standing and, 65–66
National Parks and Conservation
     Association (NPCA), 114–17,
     119, 235
National Socialist White People's Party,
     3
National Student Association, 5
NEPA. *See* National Environmental
     Policy Act (NEPA)
New York, New Haven, and Hartford
     Railroad, 56
New York Times, x, xi, 99, 102, 108–9,
     123, 136
Night Comes to the Cumberlands (Cau-
     dill), 17–18
Ninth Amendment, 104
Nixon, Richard, *3,* 5, 62, 71, 123–24,
     159, 195, 235, 242
Norris, Frank, xvi–xvii, 63–64, *64*
NPCA. *See* National Parks and Conser-
     vation Association (NPCA)

O'Neal, Dan, 119
Oswald, Robert, 137

Pankowski, Ted, 116
PASNY. *See* Public Authority of the
     State of New York (PASNY)
Patman, Wright, 143
Penn Central, 123–24, 141–43, 189–90
Pentagon Papers case, 33
Perlman, Kenneth, x, 27–29, 37–38,
     41–43, 45–53, 66, 72, 74,
     76–80, 84, 93–98, 100, 103,
     105, 107, 112–13, 125, 139
Pertschuk, Mike, 119
Points of Rebellion (Douglas), 11, 34
police, *3*
Politicos, The (Josephson), 180
Populist Party, 56

*Port of New York Authority v. United
     States,* 188–90, 198, 200, 206,
     217
Powell, Lewis, x, 71, 179
Price, Charlie, 237–38
protests, 3–6, 10, 20–22, *21,* 130
Proto, Celeste, xiv, 85–87, *86,* 107,
     134–36, 163–64, 214, 226, 233
Proto, Diana, 107, 134–36, 163–64,
     196, 214
Proto, Matthew, 22, 85–89, *86, 89,*
     107, 134–36, 163–64, 214
Proto, Neil, *xii, 4, 242*
     Atlanta visit with Biondi family,
          177–78
     bar exam, 237–38
     basketball game, 87–90
     Christmas Eve, 1971, 134–36
     elected chairman of SCRAP, 42
     graduation, 214
     Miami trip, 175–77
     surprise party, 240–42
Proto, Richard, 63, 86, 87, 153, 173, 214
Public Authority of the State of New
     York (PASNY), 145

Quakers, xv, 106, 117, 130

Railroads, xvi–xvii, xix, 18, 30, 37–38,
     41, 59–64, 101, 119–20, 123,
     173. *See also* Association of
     American Railroads (AAR);
     freight rates; *specific railroads*
Randall, Faith, 96
rates. *See* freight rates
Rauh, Joseph, 19
rebates, 56
Rebozo, Bebe, 62
recyclables, 38, 231, 234–35
Rehnquist, William, 71, 179, 249, 252,
     256–57, 263, 266–67
Reinemer, Vic, 117–18, 120, 123
Reitze, Arnold, 28

Report of the National Advisory Commission on Civil Disorders, 10
Republican National Convention (1968), 10
Ressler, Peter, x, 27–28, 30–31, 37, 78, 96, 99–101, 214
restraining order. *See* temporary restraining order (TRO)
Resurrection City, 10
Rice Hall, 1–2, 25, 49, 228
Richey, Charles, 195, 198, *198,* 199–213, 217–18, 221, 301n1
riots, 10
Roberts, John G. Jr., x, x–xi, xi, xiv
Rockefeller, David, 143
Rockefeller, John D., 56, 143
Roe v. Wade, 263–64
Roosevelt, Theodore, 56

Saunders, Stuart, 141
Scalia, Antonin, x
Schirra, Wally, 59, 61
SCRAP. *See* Students Challenging Regulatory Agency Procedures (SCRAP)
Seeger, Pete, 10
Shisslak, David, 239–40
Short, Gail, 127
Shriver, Sargent, 115
Sierra Club v. Hickel, 70–71, 78, 112, 116, 149, 174
Sierra Club v. Morton, xvi, xx, 162, 175, 178–80, 183, 192, 198, 201, 204, 209, 228, 236, 243, 249, 251, 260, 265
Sinclair, Upton, 14
Sino-Soviet Institute, 3–4
Smathers, George A., 55, 61–62, 83–84, 111, 119, 126, 156
Smith, Charles L., 144
smoking, 12–13
soup, 13–14

SOUP. *See* Students Opposing Unfair Practices (SOUP)
Southern Railway, 58
Spurlock, Fred, 6, 21–22, 235
Stafford, George M., 38, 125, 145–46
Stalin, Joseph, 159, 162
standing, 70–71, 76–77, 103, 149, 199, 201, 243, 259–60, 263, 265
steel companies, 51
Steenland, Pete, 6, 17–19, 79
Steffens, Lincoln, 14
Stewart, Potter, x, xvi, 69, 179–80, 252, *253,* 260–61, 263, 265–67, 308n2
Stillman, James, 56
Stinking Creek, Tennessee, 165
stock market, 143
Stockton Hall, 9
Students Challenging Regulatory Agency Procedures (SCRAP), x, xviii, xix–xx, 25–44, 60, 103, 108, 126, 129
Environmental Defense Fund and, 138–39
Students Challenging Regulatory Agency Procedures (SCRAP) v. United States, xix, 185–86, 192–93, 289n8, 299n15, 301n2, 301n4, 301n10, 301n13, 302n3–302n4, 303n1–303n3, 305n1–305n2. *See also United States v. Students Challenging Regulatory Agency Procedures (SCRAP)*
Students for a Democratic Society, 3–4
Students Opposing Unfair Practices (SOUP), 13–14, 67–68
Superlawyers, The (Goulden), 14
Susman, Tom, 121

Taft, Robert A., 117
Tao, James, 39
Tarbell, Ida, 14, 162

temporary restraining order (TRO),
    187, 190–92, 195, 210, 213
tobacco, 12–13
Tomsky, John, 87, 129, 176–77,
    239–41
Train, Russell E., 39
TRO. *See* temporary restraining order
    (TRO)
Truman, Harry S., 58, 159
*Trustees of Dartmouth College v. Wood-
    ward,* 255–56
Twenty-sixth Amendment, 124

Udall, Tom, 218
United Mine Workers, 19
*United States v. Students Challenging
    Regulatory Agency Procedures
    (SCRAP),* ix, x, xi, xiv, 234–37,
    245–68, 306n2, 306n5, 308n2.
    *See also United States v. Students
    Challenging Regulatory Agency
    Procedures (SCRAP)*

Vaccaro, John, 55
Vanik, Charles A., 117
Vietnam War, 10, 124, 130, 182

Vole, John, 120

*Wabash, St. Louis & Pacific Railway Co.
    v. Illinois,* 56
Wallace, George C., 124
Walrath, Laurence, 137
Warren, Earl, 5, 58
Washington Post, 19, 59, 101–2, 124,
    141, 143, 165
Weathermen, 10
Webster, Daniel, xvi, 255–56
Weissbard, Sandy, 115, 117, 235
Welling Hall, 2, 5, 128
wheat, 63
White, Byron, xvi, 69–70, 179, 250,
    252, 255, 257, 259, 261, 263,
    266
Wigoda, Gary, 240
Wilson, Jerry, 21
Winnings, Freda, 96, 98, 100, 102
Wirtz, Willard, 124
Wright, J. Skelly, xix, 25, *26,* 33–34,
    196, 204, 217–24, 226–27,
    229–31, 235–36, 264, 292n8

Yablonski, Jock, 19

ABOUT THE AUTHOR

The author, on the Bainbridge Ferry, circa today.
NTProto Collection.

The author, 1972.
NTProto Collection.

Neil Thomas Proto's public service and private practice in law includes environmental, Native Hawaiian, urban, nuclear power, Native American, and constitutional litigation in the U.S. Supreme Court and courts of appeals. He served as an appellate lawyer in the U.S. Department of Justice (1972–1977), as general counsel to the President's Nuclear Safety Oversight Committee (1979–1981), and as a partner in Washington, D.C. law firms.

Neil has taught at Yale University and at Georgetown University's McCourt School of Public Policy. He has written two other books: *The Rights of My People: Liliuokalani's Enduring Battle with the United States, 1890–1917*

(2009) and *Fearless: A. Bartlett Giamatti and the Battle for Fairness in America* (2019), which was a finalist in Biography for the Next Generation Indie Book Awards and received the Bronze Award in Biography by Foreword Reviews. He has also authored numerous articles on baseball, space exploration, basketball, and the lives of Sacco and Vanzetti, T. E. Lawrence, and Ernest Shackleton. His play, *The Reckoning: Pecora for the Public*, on the causes of the 1929 stock market crash, premiered in Seattle (2016). His podcast, *Downfall*, a series on Giamatti, Pete Rose, and the fate of Baseball, premiered in 2021. He chaired New Haven's yearlong commemoration of the seventy-fifth anniversary of the execution of Sacco and Vanzetti (2002) and co-wrote the book, with director Tony Giordano, for the adapted musical, *The American Dream*, which was performed at the Shubert Theatre in 2002. Neil is a member of the Dramatist Guild and also served on two New Haven theater boards, Long Wharf and the Shubert. He served on the board of the Franklin and Eleanor Roosevelt Institute, represented Protect Historic America *pro bono* in its successful effort to stop a Disney theme park in Northern Virginia, and is a Fellow in the Royal Geographical Society.

Neil graduated from Southern Connecticut State University and received his master's degree from the Elliott School of International Relations at the George Washington University (GWU). He went on to receive his law degree at GWU. As a law student, he chaired Students Challenging Regulatory Agency Procedures (SCRAP), which successfully sued the United States in a case that reached the Supreme Court. Aspects of his life's work and experience are held in collections at GWU, the University of Hawaii Law School, and Southern Connecticut State University. Neil, born in New Haven, Connecticut, resides in Washington, D.C.

REVIEWS FROM THE 2006 EDITION OF
TO A HIGH COURT

"A large part of the story's appeal is its setting in the personal lives of SCRAP's members...[anti-war demonstrations]...law school and the bar exam,...romantic interests and... deeply held philosophical beliefs.... [R]eal people.... the power of resourcefulness, determination, and audacity [with] recollections of our idealism...."

—Antoinette R. Stone, Esq. "Making Law By Making Trouble,"
The Philadelphia Lawyer

"Riveting....[I]ts lesson for holding government accountable could not be more current."

—Rosa DeLauro, *Member of Congress, Connecticut*

"[T]he imagination and persistence of students can sometimes achieve more than professionals...."

—John Bonine, *Professor of Law,*
University of Oregon School of Law

"I wish every student of the law shared [such] moments."

—William H. Rodgers, Jr., *Ret. Professor of Law,*
University of Washington Law School

"Scholars, students, and those interested in law all would benefit from reading this outstanding book."

—Erwin Chemerinsky, *Dean, University of California,*
Berkeley School of Law (formerly of UC Davis School of Law)

" [E]nvironmental protection was born, midwifed by a bunch of law students..."

—Leon G. Billings, *President,*
The Edmund S. Muskie Foundation

"Students fighting Goliaths....I can't wait for the movie."

—Dan Lauria, *actor, writer, and director*